Andrew Tobias'

MANAGING YOUR MONEY

THE OFFICIAL REFERENCE

Version 7

Compiled by Mary O'Neil

Brady

New York   London   Toronto   Sydney   Tokyo   Singapore

BRADY

Simon & Schuster, Inc.
15 Columbus Circle
New York, NY 10023

Manufactured in the United States of America

10 9 8 7 6 5 4 3 2 1

Library of Congress Cataloging-in-Publication Data

Tobias, Andrew P.
    [Managing your money]
    Andrew Tobias' Managing Your Money : the official reference,
version 7. — 2nd ed.
        p.   cm.
    Includes index.
    1. Tobias, Andrew P. Managing your money. 2. Finance, Personal-
-Computer programs. I. Title. II. Title: Managing your money.
HG179.T52   1990
332.024'002855369—dc20   90-25727
ISBN 0-13-355116-4   CIP

The Managing Your Money General Disclaimer

Managing Your Money is designed to help you do all your financial planning and record-keeping. It may save you time and should definitely help you organize your affairs and sharpen your financial focus. But you should know that we can't and won't take responsibility for the results (good or bad) you achieve using it. Before you make a decision or take an action that involves what for you is a significant amount of money or a significant risk, we strongly advise you to seek a second opinion from someone you trust, such as a good accountant or tax lawyer, to be sure you and this program or book are working right together.

The Ever-Changing Tax Code

Comments and screens in this book regarding the tax laws are believed (but not warranted) to be accurate as of mid-1990. We've also provided simple ways to update the program in the event of changes. Where possible, MECA will advise newsletter subscribers of changes they should be making. However, the ultimate responsibility for ascertaining and interpreting current tax law rest with you, not us.

Trademarks:

CONTENTS

CHAPTER 2 DESK

CHAPTER 3   MONEY

CHAPTER 4   TAX

CHAPTER 5   INSURE

CHAPTER 6   ANALYZE

CHAPTER 7   PORTFOLIO

CHAPTER 8 NET WORTH

CHAPTER 9 CONNECTIONS

APPENDIX   381

INDEX   399

Introduction

INTRODUCTION

Welcome to Managing Your Money Version 7 — *the book*. It's meant to offer a little extra perspective. When you're using the program itself, you're down at street level. We like to think we provide good street signs, but this book lets you rise above the city in a helicopter and whip around at will.

HOW WE'RE ORGANIZED

This book is a "hard copy" of all the Managing Your Money screens and HELP to be read at your leisure or to be used as a quick reference. To accommodate the transition from screen to script, we've arranged our contents to follow Managing Your Money's Menu Bar:

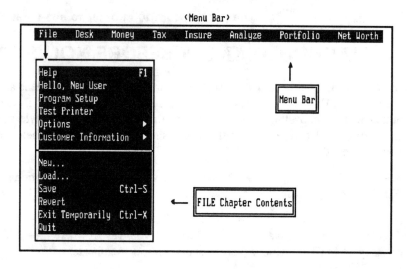

This way, we take you screen-by-screen through the entire program. Below each screen you'll find its HELP, just as if you had pressed F1. Above each screen we show the keys you would press to reach it. In the screen photo itself, where appropriate, we've put the page to turn to in this book to see the screen that pressing a function key evokes.

How to get to this screen

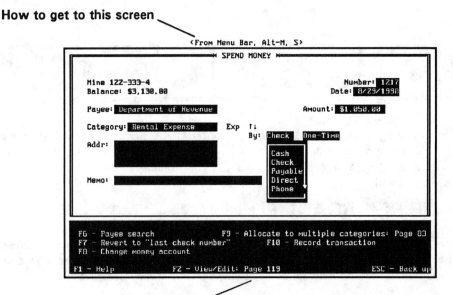

The page to turn to in order to see what F2 does

WHAT YOU SHOULD KNOW BEFORE YOU START

A Note on Style: Because these pages are essentially print-outs of MYM's screens and HELP messages, they follow MYM's style, which in some cases departs from that of Brady Books. Worse, captured in hard copy this way, it's easier to notice that MYM's style sometimes departs from itself! It's a lot easier to spot the inconsistencies from up in the helicopter than from down on the ground.

Optional Features: For the purposes of this book, we've activated all the Optional features under the FILE menu to include the additional capabilities in MONEY, DESK, TAX, and PORTFOLIO.

Text vs. Screen Shots: To save wear and tear on your eyes where possible, we've incorporated many of MYM's *text only* screen shots into our regular text. You'll notice this mainly in Hello, New User.

The Appendix: The Installation and Assistance-Backing-Up screens are located in the Appendix, along with the HELP Index and Close Out Previous Year screen.

Chapter 9: We've included screens from our sister programs, *Managing the Market* and *TaxCut*, because of MYM's connections to these programs — as mentioned in Chapter 4 and 7. (The 1990 tax law wasn't final when these screen shots were taken, but you should get a pretty good idea of how *TaxCut* works.)

Discrepancies: Once again this year, because of different publishing deadlines (thank you Burt Gabriel, Geraldine Albert, and Tom Dillon at Brady for your patience), there is a possibility that what you see on your screen and what you see in our screen shots may differ slightly.

ACKNOWLEDGEMENT

This book was assembled and adapted from Managing Your Money entirely by Mary O'Neil, and on a very tight schedule. The words are from Managing Your Money and thus are mine. The work was all hers. Thanks, Mary!

1

File

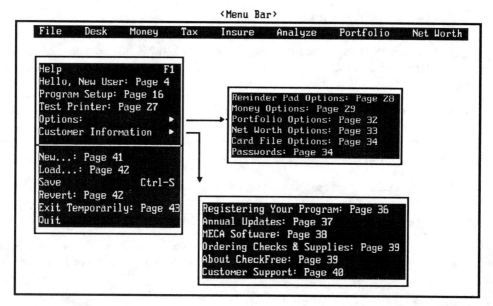

<Menu Bar>

| File | Desk | Money | Tax | Insure | Analyze | Portfolio | Net Worth |

Help   F1
Hello, New User: Page 4
Program Setup: Page 16
Test Printer: Page 27
Options: ▶
Customer Information   ▶

New...: Page 41
Load...: Page 42
Save   Ctrl-S
Revert: Page 42
Exit Temporarily: Page 43
Quit

Reminder Pad Options: Page 28
Money Options: Page 29
Portfolio Options: Page 32
Net Worth Options: Page 33
Card File Options: Page 34
Passwords: Page 34

Registering Your Program: Page 36
Annual Updates: Page 37
MECA Software: Page 38
Ordering Checks & Supplies: Page 39
About CheckFree: Page 39
Customer Support: Page 40

THE MENU BAR

To switch among Menu Bar options use the arrow keys or, holding down the Alt key, press the letter of your choice: Alt-F for FILE, Alt-M for MONEY, Alt-P for PORTFOLIO — and so on. (For veteran MYM-ers, the old F1 through F9 options are also active: e.g., F2 for Reminders, F3 for MONEY, F4 for Tax, and so on.)

To select an item from one of the pulldowns, highlight it and press Enter or just press its "hot key" — usually its first letter. If you can't see the highlighting, press Alt-F, P, S to adjust screen colors.

Think of the Menu Bar as the trap door through which you can enter any part of the program and out through which you should exit. No matter how deep you're buried in the program, just press ESCape repeatedly to pop up toward the surface, then Alt-F, Q to exit.

Press Ctrl-K at any time (except in HELP or the word processor) for a list of Quick Key shortcuts. Ctrl-X lets you exit temporarily to DOS, but only if you've "turned it on." To do so, select Program Setup on the FILE menu, and then Preferences.

HELLO, NEW USER!

Welcome to MANAGING YOUR MONEY. This brief tutorial will tell you what the program does and show you how it works. The first thing you need to know is that there is practically no way you can gum things up. The next thing you need to know is that no matter where you are in the program, with few exceptions, just press the F1 key to get HELP. Even now. (Try it!)

[If anything even remotely confusing were happening, there would be a few tips and clarifying remarks within HELP. Sometimes, as now, there will be just a short note; sometimes several "pages" to leaf through. But whenever you've had enough, just press ESCape to get back to work.]

Press ESCape and HELP vanishes. Even if you're an old hand with computers, PLEASE visit all the HELP screens each time you venture into a new chapter. Some won't tell you anything you wouldn't expect, but here and there you'll find a valuable suggestion or clarification.

Please note: When a HELP message is on the screen, the screen is "frozen." You can't enter any data or issue commands. But as soon as you press ESCape, you'll get rid of HELP and be back in action.

■ THE ALT AND CTRL KEYS

Whenever we ask you to press Alt-something or Ctrl-something, hold down the Alt or Ctrl key and then, while holding it down, press the other key. For example, pressing Ctrl-N from anywhere in the program (except the wordprocessor and HELP) summons our pop-up calculator.

■ TYPE-AHEAD

Your keyboard has a memory. The good news is that you can "Type-Ahead" and we'll catch up. For example, from the Menu Bar you could type − all in rapid succession − Alt-M (for MONEY), S (for Spend) and the name of the person you want to pay. By the time you finished, we'd have caught up to you. Or press Alt-P, M, F6, F7, F6, go out for a jog, and return to find we've called Dow Jones (if you have Managing the Market) and updated all your PORTFOLIO prices. (The bad news is that if you hold a key down too long, we'll think you typed it twice. Careful! Your keyboard is sensitive!)

After just a little practice you'll find Type-Ahead and some of our keyboard shortcuts quite handy. You'll also find we've done our best to respect the value of your time. When you first buy shares of a stock, for example, you'll be asked questions about it − its dividend, who recommended it (so you can track the performance of different sources of ideas) and more. You needn't answer them all if you don't want to, but once you have, you'll never have to again. Any subsequent purchases of the same stock, for your own portfolio or your children's, or for the three hypothetical ones you manage as a hobby, will all reflect your answers.

When you write a $50 check to Dr. Bob in MONEY, you won't have to tell TAX that you have another $50 medical deduction — it will know. And you won't have to tell NET WORTH that you're fifty bucks poorer. It will know, too. MANAGING YOUR MONEY is integrated.

A QUICK TOUR

MANAGING YOUR MONEY has eight major functional areas (and a lot of handy minor ones). Two of the eight are "pop-ups," available from almost anywhere in the program at the drop of a Ctrl key: Ctrl-R for the Reminder Pad and Ctrl-C for the Card File. The other six — MONEY, TAX, INSURE, ANALYZE, PORTFOLIO, and NET WORTH — reside like shot glasses on the Menu Bar. (You can reach the Reminder Pad and Card File from the Menu Bar as well, under DESK.)

■ THE REMINDER PAD — CTRL-R

Enter your birthday list and for the next 500 years it will faithfully jog your memory. You can enter weekly, biweekly, half-monthly, monthly, quarterly, semi-annual, and annual reminders. You can maintain your daily schedule. You can make and prioritize To-Do lists. (Separately, in PORTFOLIO, we automatically remind you when bonds are about to mature, options are expiring, and that sort of thing.) There are a few other nice features that make the Reminder Pad helpful and easy to use, as you'll see.

■ MONEY

A place to pay your bills and keep multiple checking accounts, credit card accounts, and savings accounts, MONEY is for many the heart of the program. It helps you to make personal budgets and cash-flow projections — something most of us always mean to do but never get around to. It prints checks and invoices, if you want it to. And at the same time, it will keep track of each expenditure by category, compare what you spend with your budget (if you can bear to look), and print a list of all your charitable contributions, or whatever else you want, at tax time. It can even pay bills electronically, through CheckFree, if you have a modem.

You don't have to use this section of the program to get your money's worth — just as, if you own no stocks or bonds, you don't have to use the portfolio section. But when you see how well it works, and can tie in with the rest of the program, I think you'll want to.

■ TAX

TAX takes what it knows about you from elsewhere in the program and estimates your tax. This helps you to keep track of where you stand vis-a-vis the IRS. And, by allowing you to enter hypothetical information, it helps you see how to stand somewhere else. What's more, if the tax law changes, you should be able to change right along with it.

The TAX ESTIMATOR won't print your actual tax forms. But it does include Schedules A, B, C, D, E, F, SE, 2106, and the Alternative Minimum Tax, as well as the tax brackets and rules for 1990 and 1991. (If you do want to print a precise, IRS-acceptable return, *Andrew Tobias' TaxCut* works well with MANAGING YOUR MONEY and is available to registered MYM users at a reduced price.)

■ INSURE

INSURE lets you calculate how long you're likely to live, given your background and habits (we claim no special accuracy here), helps you calculate how much life insurance you need, and tells you what it should cost. It's also a place to record and organize all your insurance policies (not just life), and all your Vital Records, from your blood type to your spouse's passport number. It prints a comprehensive report that will assure your affairs are always in order.

■ ANALYZE

ANALYZE does anything a good pocket calculator would — but in English. There are also powerful subsections to help you plan for retirement and your kids' education, project rates of return on prospective rental properties and business deals, analyze possible mortgage refinancings, see the effects of inflation, produce customized amortization schedules, decide whether to buy, rent, or lease — and more.

■ PORTFOLIO

PORTFOLIO is my favorite. Even if you don't own any stocks or bonds, you can learn a lot about investing by giving yourself 50,000 hypothetical dollars — hey, make it $100,000! — and trying your hand at making it grow.

If you do own securities, and particularly if you are at all an active investor, I think you'll find this section of the program invaluable. It won't tell you which stocks to buy. But it will let you analyze your portfolio(s) — in seconds — in ways you might not even have considered before, let alone found time to do on a regular basis. And it can handle stamps and coins and wines or anything else you happen to collect; print a Schedule D; even provide some perspective on how good a day this is to be buying or selling.

■ NET WORTH

NET WORTH draws your assets and liabilities from elsewhere in the program, pumps you for others you might not have listed, and tallies your net worth. I don't agree with the T-shirt (it says: WHOEVER HAS THE MOST THINGS WHEN HE DIES, WINS), but I do like to figure my net worth from time to time — and to see it grow. Whenever you have to submit a personal balance sheet, a quick print-out from this chapter can save an hour's work.

■ THE CARD FILE

Press CTRL-C from almost anywhere in the program — it can store data on everyone you know, dial phone numbers, print mailing labels, phone directories, envelopes, Rolodex cards — even generate personalized mailings. (Now you, too, can send junk mail.)

As you can see from this very quick tour, there's a lot here! You surely won't need all of it right away, and shouldn't try to tackle it all at once. But it will be there when you need it. Thinking of refinancing your mortgage? Just select Mortgage Refinancing from the ANALYZE menu. Wonder what you'd save using a discount broker? Select Portfolios from PORTFOLIO and then F7.

The advantage over buying a dozen separate programs (apart from its being cheaper) is that ours all work the same way. Learn one and you've learned them all. The Navigational Shortcuts you'll find in Chapter 1 of the manual apply across the entire program. The Command Line you see at the bottom of the screen (right now, F1 and ESCape are the only commands active) you'll see EVERYWHERE: F1 for help; F2 to view or edit what you're pointing at; F3 to delete it; F4 to print; F5 to add something new; Escape to back up to what you were previously doing.

A QUICK HOW-TO

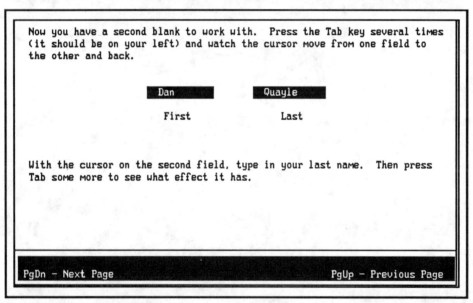

But what if you change your name? Use the Tab, DELete, INSert and Backspace keys and all the arrow keys to move through your answers and change them (maybe to your boss's name). If you make a mistake, just type over it. (Holding down the Ctrl key when you press the left or right arrow speeds you to the beginning or end of what you've typed; holding it down when you press Home or End deletes from wherever you are to the beginning or end.)

Keep playing! When you're comfortable, press PgDn to continue. (To use the arrow keys for typing numbers instead of navigation, note that the NumLock key turns the numeric keypad on and off. Try it.)

```
╔══════════════════════════ PAGE 15 ══════════════════════════╗
║ ┌────────────────────────────────────────────────────────┐ ║
║ │ Now it's time to type a number. We've added a field for │ ║
║ │ your age. Use the Tab key or arrow keys to move the     │ ║
║ │ cursor to the age field -- but wait! We want you to     │ ║
║ │ make a mistake.                                         │ ║
║ │                                                         │ ║
║ │ Type abc in the age field.                              │ ║
║ │                                                         │ ║
║ │           First name: Dan                               │ ║
║ │           Last name: Quayle                             │ ║
║ │           Your age: 444                                 │ ║
║ │                                                         │ ║
║ │ See the error message at the bottom of the screen?      │ ║
║ │ Whenever you enter impossible data of some sort, an     │ ║
║ │ error message will appear. You'll have as much time     │ ║
║ │ as you need to make amends. (But we won't budge until   │ ║
║ │ you do.) Now, please fix it. Enter your age and press   │ ║
║ │ PgDn when you're ready.                                 │ ║
║ └────────────────────────────────────────────────────────┘ ║
║                                                             ║
║ PgDn - Next Page                        PgUp - Previous Page║
╚═════════════════════════════════════════════════════════════╝
Sorry, computers are for youngsters only.  Try again.  ◄──  Error message
```

```
╔═════════════════════════════════════════════════════════════╗
║ ┌────────────────────────────────────────────────────────┐ ║
║ │ Occasionally you'll have to enter a date. The correct   │ ║
║ │ format is MM/DD/YY (for example, 12/5/85 for December   │ ║
║ │ 5, 1985), but we'll accept 12.5.85, 12-05-85, 12x5w85   │ ║
║ │ or just about anything else you come up with.           │ ║
║ │                                                         │ ║
║ │ Type in your birth date.                                │ ║
║ │           First name: Dan                               │ ║
║ │           Last name: Quayle                             │ ║
║ │           Your age: 43                                  │ ║
║ │           Your birth date: 2/4/47                       │ ║
║ │                                                         │ ║
║ │ You can change anything just by typing over it. So      │ ║
║ │ while you're here, type in several more dates (including│ ║
║ │ February 43rd, etc., to see what you can and can't get  │ ║
║ │ away with). And try typing just the month and day (we   │ ║
║ │ supply the current year) or even just the day. If you   │ ║
║ │ type "3" and press Tab or Enter, we supply the current  │ ║
║ │ month and year. Press PgDn when you're ready.           │ ║
║ └────────────────────────────────────────────────────────┘ ║
║                                                             ║
║ PgDn - Next Page                        PgUp - Previous Page║
╚═════════════════════════════════════════════════════════════╝
```

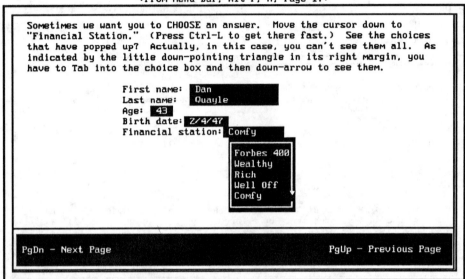

<From Menu Bar, Alt-F, H, Page 17>

Indicate your choice by typing its first letter. (Sometimes you'll have to type a second or third letter to distinguish "Squeezed" from "Squirming.") Try it. Try it again. (And now, for fun, move up to your Birth Date and press Alt-D to see what day of the week it fell on.) Press PgDn when you're ready.

Type YOUR SALARY and press Tab or Enter. When entering money amounts, you never have to bother with dollar signs or commas (though we'll accept them). If you lost money this year, enter a negative number, like -2000. "Negative" money is always displayed with surrounding parentheses.

Scroll Lists Now. Suppose we have a list of US presidents and their causes of death. (Thanks to the Lincoln Library of Essential Information, we do.) It won't all fit on the screen, so we show you only a portion of the data and let you scroll up and down to see the rest. Press PgDn to see what we mean.

<From Menu Bar, Alt-F, H, Page 19, F9>

```
        President           Cause of Death
        George Washington   Acute laryngitis
        John Adams          Natural causes
        Thomas Jefferson    Chronic diarrhea
        James Madison       Natural causes
        James Monroe        Natural causes
        John Quincy Adams   Paralysis
        Andrew Jackson      Dropsy
        Martin Van Buren    Asthma
```

The cursor is pointing to George Washington, but there is no blinking
underline. That's because the cursor is acting only as a pointer. You
can't type anything here. (No harm in trying.) Use the Up and Down
arrows to move through this list (or Tab and Shift-Tab). Press them once
or hold them down. We beep if you try to go too far. To take giant
steps, you can use PgDn and PgUp -- which is why on this and the next few
screens we ask you to press F9 to proceed.

F9 — Next Page   F10 — Previous Page

<From Menu Bar, Alt-F, H, Page 19, F9>

```
        President           Cause of Death
        George Washington   Acute laryngitis
        John Adams          Natural causes
        Thomas Jefferson    Chronic diarrhea
        James Madison       Natural causes
        James Monroe        Natural causes
        John Quincy Adams   Paralysis
        Andrew Jackson      Dropsy
        Martin Van Buren    Asthma
```

Another way to move through a list is with the Home and Endkeys. Try them.

F9 — Next Page   F10 — Previous Page

<From Menu Bar, Alt-F, H, Page 21>

```
          President            Cause of Death
          Andrew Johnson       Paralysis
          Ulysses S. Grant     Cancer of the tongue
          Rutherford B. Hayes  Neuralgia of the heart
          James A. Garfield    Assassinated
          Chester A. Arthur    Bright's disease
          Grover Cleveland     Reelected; see below
          Benjamin Harrison    Pneumonia
          Grover Cleveland     Heart failure

     Speed scroll -
Or try something even better.  Do you see the phrase speed scroll below
and to the left of the scroll box?  Whenever you see that, just press the
first letter or two of the item you're looking for and we'll take you
right to it.  Type GR.  Bang:  Grover Cleveland.  But now type G and then
wait a few seconds before typing R.  See the difference?
```

F9 - Next Page   F10 - Previous Page

<From Menu Bar, Alt-F, H, Page 19, F9>

```
          President             Cause of Death
          George Washington     Acute laryngitis
          John Adams            Natural causes
          Thomas Jefferson      Chronic diarrhea
          James Madison         Natural causes
          James Monroe          Natural causes
          John Quincy Adams     Paralysis
          Andrew Jackson        Dropsy
          Martin Van Buren      Asthma

     Speed scroll -
Speed scroll has about a two-second attention span.  After that, it clears
its slate and is ready to start a new search.  Just remember that your
cursor must be positioned on one of the scrollable items -- not on a field
you can type into -- for this to work.  Not every scrollable screen is
equipped with speed scroll, but most are.  It's a big convenience.
```

F9 - Next Page   F10 - Previous Page

<From Menu Bar, Alt-F, H, Page 19, F9>

```
           President          Cause of Death
           George Washington  Acute laryngitis
           John Adams         Natural causes
           Thomas Jefferson   Chronic diarrhea
           James Madison      Natural causes
           James Monroe       Natural causes
           John Quincy Adams  Paralysis
           Andrew Jackson     Dropsy
           Martin Van Buren   Asthma

      Here's that date again:  3/18/57 .

      Try to get there with the Up or Down arrows.  You can't.  Your keyboard's
      "Scroll Lock" function is on.  Press Scroll Lock to shut off or reinstate
      this function -- or, simpler, just use the Tab or Enter or right arrow key
      to do what the down arrow can't.  (Or jump to the Last field with Ctrl-L.)
```

```
   F9 - Next Page                              F10 - Previous Page
```

■ THE CALCULATOR – CTRL-N

Ctrl-N pops you into the calculator from anywhere in the program (except within the word processor or HELP). Press it now. (Hold down the Ctrl key while pressing the letter N.) See the display at the foot of the screen? Press ESCape. It's gone!

Now summon the calculator again — Ctrl-N — and enter a formula. For example, to calculate fifty-six and one eighth, type: 56 + 1/8 and press Enter. The formula goes away, and the result — 56.125 — appears in the result memory labeled "r" on your right. Press Enter a second time and you pop out of the calculator. Jump back into the calculator (Ctrl-N) and see what it can do:

> \+ ADDITION
> \- SUBTRACTION
> x or * MULTIPLICATION (the "x" or "*")
> / DIVISION (the "/" below "?")
> ^ EXPONENTIATION (the "^" above "6")

You can save an answer in one of the five memories at the bottom of the screen by storing it with the equals key (=). To store "The Number of Seconds in a Day" in memory a, type: a = 60*60*24 and press Enter.

Try out memories b, c, d, and e also. Multiply "a*c." Try typing "a=r." When you're ready, leave the calculator by pressing ESCape or the Enter key. (You must always exit before you can proceed. When the calculator's on, the screen is "frozen.")

Once again, jump into the calculator. Notice how the memories retain their contents? The calculator only forgets when you leave the program.

You may use parentheses in a formula for grouping, as in this conversion of 72 Fahrenheit to Celsius: (72-32) * 5/9. Type in this formula and press Enter. Now press it again. You pop out of the calculator, and your result is pulled into this field. Leaving with the Enter key drops your answer into the field your cursor was on. To leave without pulling up your answer, use ESC instead.

I've gone on too long already about this — nothing in MANAGING YOUR MONEY will require use of the calculator, it's here for your convenience only. But one last feature is so nifty I can't resist...

With your birth date here, summon the calculator. Now, press F6. F6 pulls the number on the screen down to the calculator. In the case of dates, like this one, the number we pull down is actually the number of days since Jan. 1, 1900. Now type +10000 and press Enter twice. Now you know when you were (or will be) 10000 days old. Date arithmetic can be useful in determining such things as the exact fraction of years you've held an asset.

MATHEMATICIANS:

SPECIAL CALCULATOR FUNCTIONS

In addition to the standard stuff, the calculator has three mathematical functions: trunc, abs, and log.

- ■ TRUNC (3.6) truncates 3.6 to 3.
- ■ ABS (-4) takes the absolute value of -4 and makes it 4.
- ■ LOG (2) returns the natural logarithm of 2 — .693147.

The formula for the 7.5% sales tax on a 35-cent candy bar is thus:

$$trunc(35x.075 + .5).$$

Using trunc avoids fraction pennies. Adding the half cent keeps the formula from always rounding DOWN. The formula for figuring out how much money you'd have if you had a nickel for every $1,000 of Donald Trump's net worth, if worse comes to worst and he turns out to be as deeply in the red as some people think, would be:

$$abs(-400000000x.05).$$

The formula for the natural log of 76 trombones would be: log (76) — but don't think for a minute I have any notion what that means.

■ THE WORD PROCESSOR — CTRL-W

Just as it has a pop-up calculator, so MYM includes MYM-Write, our ever-ready word processor. Hold down the Ctrl key and press the letter W any time at all to summon it. Even now. (To return, just press ESCape.) HELP behind MYM-Write provides a summary of its commands. For full instructions, please see Chapter 10 of your manual.

Use MYM-Write to print a fast memo or jot notes for a speech without having to quit what you were doing in MYM. But its greatest value lies in the way it can attach notes of any length to specific records.

Throughout the program you'll find places to type a single line of text — a check memo, for example. But you'll also find that we offer the chance to add as much detail beneath that line as you like (by pressing F2).

Don't worry if the word processor looks a little intimidating at first. As long as you can type with two fingers, you're more than halfway there. With a quick read through Chapter 10 and a little practice, you'll be setting margins and mail-merging with the best of them. Whenever you leave the word processor, you'll be back where you were when inspiration struck.

GOOD-BYE, NEW USER!

Okay. We're almost done. My hope is that MANAGING YOUR MONEY will be a time-saving tool that becomes part of your life — and that your life may be a little better organized and prosperous because of it.

One way to use it is to set aside an hour a week for your finances. Keep a folder of all the bills you have to pay and other financial transactions you wish to record (checks you wrote by hand during the week, bank deposits you made, credit card receipts). Every Saturday morning turn me on and clean out the folder. It takes a little time and discipline to get organized. But in the long run it will save you time. And, very likely, money as well.

Final thought: There's a lot here. You've really purchased a whole family of powerful programs for the price of one. So don't feel you have to use everything right away; and don't be surprised if it takes you a few hours just to explore, let alone master, the program's capabilities.

Now, if it's your first time into the program, we're going to ask you some setup questions. Thereafter, play around all you want. But before you enter any data for real, please finish reading Chapter 1 of the manual.

Remember: Check HELP each time you encounter a new screen. Okay. Off you go. Good-bye, new user!

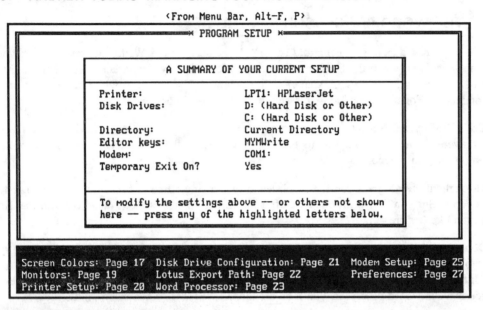

<From Menu Bar, Alt-F, P>

PROGRAM SETUP

Here, in computerese, is a summary of your current setup. To change these settings or anything else, just press the highlighted letter of your choice. If you can't see the highlighted letter, begin by pressing S for screen colors and read HELP.

Don't miss Preferences, which includes:

- a Sound On/Off choice for our annoying beep;
- a chance to switch to Canadian/European date format;
- a place to activate Save-Minder and adjust its frequency;
- a place to change the name and address we use for your reports and invoice headings.

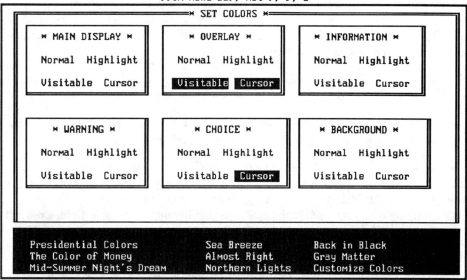

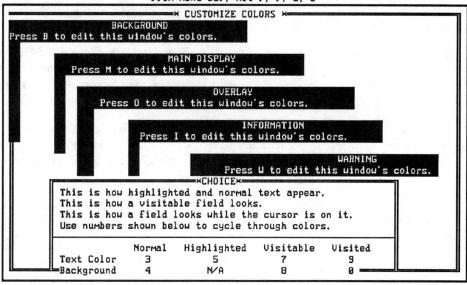

SCREEN COLORS

We offer eight color schemes and the chance to customize your own. The first thing to do, before you consider customizing, is to press the first letter of each of our eight choices. If you have a color monitor, it really makes no difference which you choose. Try one; when life gets boring, come here and switch to another.

But if you have a monochrome monitor, as I do on my not-at-all-cheap laptop, it's important to get enough "shades of gray" to let you see the different elements of the program properly.

MYM has 6 different kinds of "tiles." On each, can you see a difference between normal and highlighted text? (How else will you know when we're shouting at you?)

Can you make out a "visitable" field, or does it not have a distinguishable background? (It needs to look different so you know it's a field to which you can maneuver your cursor. Otherwise, you might think it's just unchangeable text when, in fact, what's displayed is just one of several choices.) And when the cursor is highlighting a visitable field, does it look different from when it's not? (This, too, is important, or else you won't know which field you're "pointing at.")

It's NOT terribly important that all the background colors be different. (In fact, to a conservative soul, it can be just a little too colorful that way.) But if you can't make out the difference between normal and highlighted text and spot visitable and "visited" fields on all 6 tiles, then you need to choose a different color scheme or customize one of your own.

Press C on the main color screen to customize colors. Then, for each of the 6 tiles in turn, press its first letter to bring it to the foreground — press M, for example, to work with the colors on the tile we call "Main Display" — and then press the numbers shown to rotate through various text and background shades. (It's numbers, not F-keys, that you press.)

At first it's confusing — and a little alarming when one of the colors you choose causes our numbers themselves to disappear, because they're suddenly the same color as the background — but with a little patience and experimentation, you'll be able to arrange things so that you can distinguish each different element on each of the 6 tiles.

- **HINT:** To clean the slate, just ESCape back to the main color screen, choose *Back to Black* or *Gray Matter* as your color scheme, and then press C again to do add dabs of color (or gray shades) as needed.

MONITORS

<From Menu Bar, Alt-F, P, M>

```
═══════════════════════════ ✳ MONITORS ✳═══════════════════════════

   SCREEN FLICKER:
   On some computers with monochrome monitors we experience an annoying,
   pulsating screen flicker.  Press the Space Bar several times.  If your
   screen does flicker, tell us in the field below, and when you leave Program
   Setup, the flickering will stop.


     Does the screen flicker? No
```

```

═══════════════════════════════════════════════════════════════════
```

<From Menu Bar, Alt-F, P, P>

```
═══════════════════════ ✳ PRINTER SETUP ✳═══════════════════════

   Below are some common printers.  If your printer is one of these or if it
   emulates one of these, select it, press F7, and we'll automatically set
   up our program to run with your printer.

   If your printer does not match one of those listed below, or if you find
   a problem with printing, press F6 and we'll let you customize or edit the
   existing printer control codes.



   For ALL Printers                    Printer Port: 1st
   Paper length in inches: 10.5        Printer width in columns: 80

   ─────────────────────────────────────────────────────────────────
   For SERIAL Printers Only:          Baud rate:          Parity:

   ─────────────────────────────────────────────────────────────────

   F6 - Customize or edit printer setup: Page 20
   F7 - Load control codes for a  HPLaserJet
```

<From Menu Bar, Alt-F, P, P, F6>

```
════════════════ ⋈ CUSTOMIZED PRINTER SETUP ⋈ ════════════════

Below, enter the control codes for your printer which you'll find listed in
your printer manual.  Be certain to use decimal and not hexadecimal codes.

Normal Printing . . . . . . . .
                    (continued)
Near Letter Quality . . . . on:
                           off:
Bold  . . . . . . . . . . . on:  27  40  115 51  66
                           off:  27  40  115 48  66
Compressed Characters . . . on:     27   40  115 49  54   72
                           off:     27   40  115 49  48   72
Compressed Line Spacing . . on:  27  38  108 56  68
                           off:  27  38  108 54  68
Double-width  . . . . . . . on:
                           off:
Underline . . . . . . . . . on:  27  38  100 68
                           off:  27  38  100 64
Top of form string (form feed):  12
In Normal printing the printer prints 10 characters per inch
In Compressed printing the printer prints 17 characters per inch
```

PRINTER SETUP

Press Ctrl-L to pop-up your choice of printers. TAB into the choice box and scroll up and down to find your printer. Select it and press F7.

If you don't see your printer on our list, choose the one we call BLANK OUT. This is the "lowest common denominator" and, chances are, your printer will work with it for plain vanilla printing. Later, when you've found in your printer manual the setup strings required for "compressed printing" and the other special styles it may be capable of, just come back here and press F6 to enter them. Or else try each of the printer setups we do offer — select Test Printer on the FILE menu to test it — until you find one that works.

If nothing prints at all, but your printer is on and properly cabled to your computer, try switching "Printer Port" from 1st to 2nd. If it still doesn't print, you may have a "serial" printer. If so, check your printer manual for the proper "baud rate" and "parity," call your computer dealer — or just keep trying different parity and baud rate combinations (there are only 10 in all).

■   Be sure to leave the baud rate and parity boxes blank if you have a parallel printer (blank them out with the space bar)!

We ordinarily format for pages that are 11 inches — 66 lines — long. But to print on legal size paper, enter 14. We'll automatically multiply by 6 lines per inch in Normal mode or by 8 lines per inch in Compressed mode to get the number of lines per page. (If you use a laser printer, you may find a 10.5-inch page length generally works best.)

Be sure to let us know if you have a wide printer (132 columns versus the typical 80 columns) so we can take advantage of it.

For the F6-customizable settings, you'll need your printer manual — but only if our settings fail you or you want to do something fancy. If you've lost your computer manual or, like most, it's in Chinese, please don't call us for help; call your retailer or printer manufacturer.

But if this is your first time into the program, don't let any of this slow you down. There will be plenty of time to get your printer working as you gradually build up the data you'll want to print.

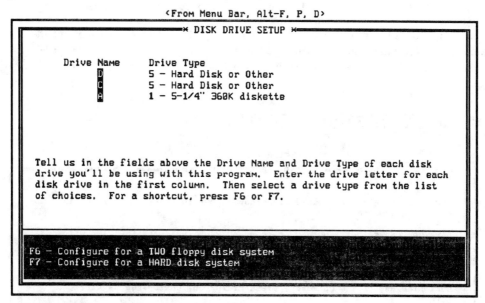

```
                          <From Menu Bar, Alt-F, P, D>
╔════════════════════════════ ✳ DISK DRIVE SETUP ✳══════════════════════════╗

            Drive Name    Drive Type
                   D       5 - Hard Disk or Other
                   C       5 - Hard Disk or Other
                   A       1 - 5-1/4" 360K diskette




        Tell us in the fields above the Drive Name and Drive Type of each disk
        drive you'll be using with this program.  Enter the drive letter for each
        disk drive in the first column.  Then select a drive type from the list
        of choices.  For a shortcut, press F6 or F7.


      ┌──────────────────────────────────────────────────────────────────────┐
      │ F6 - Configure for a TWO floppy disk system                           │
      │ F7 - Configure for a HARD disk system                                 │
      └──────────────────────────────────────────────────────────────────────┘
╚═══════════════════════════════════════════════════════════════════════════╝
```

DISK DRIVE SETUP

Most people will just press F7 to tell us they run MYM on a hard drive called C, with a floppy drive called A. If we've guessed wrong about the size of your floppy drive, just TAB over and change it. (TAB into the choice box that pops up and press the number that corresponds to the kind of floppy drive you do have.) To blank out a drive you entered by mistake, just TAB to it and press the Space Bar.

RAM DRIVES

If you know what a RAM drive is, and you use one, be sure to specify it here — we'll put it to good use in speeding up the program.

EXTENDED AND EXPANDED MEMORY

Managing Your Money automatically detects expanded memory and puts it to use speeding the program. It does NOT utilize extended memory.

LOTUS 1-2-3 EXPORT SETUP

Most of our numeric reports can be printed to disk in a format that's easily imported into programs compatible with Lotus 1-2-3.

Tell us here where you keep your 1-2-3 data files, and we'll automatically send all such reports directly there, without your having to type in the path and the ".prn" extension each time. For example, if you keep your Lotus data files in a subdirectory of your Lotus directory called "files," your data path would would be: C:\LOTUS\FILES.

1-2-3 data directory: C:

When you choose to print a report to disk with the "123" format, we'll append the ".prn" extension to your file name and send the report to join your other 1-2-3 data files. Later, when you run 1-2-3, use the "/FIN" (File-Import-Numbers) command to import it.

WORD PROCESSOR SETUP

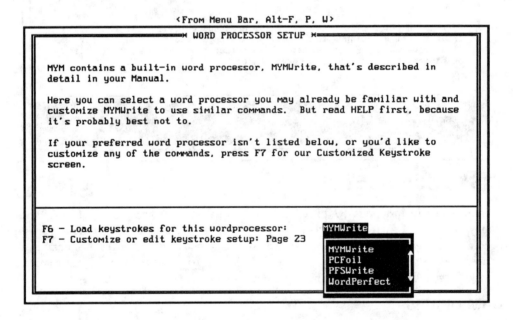

```
<From Menu Bar, Alt-F, P, W>

* WORD PROCESSOR SETUP *

MYM contains a built-in word processor, MYMWrite, that's described in
detail in your Manual.

Here you can select a word processor you may already be familiar with and
customize MYMWrite to use similar commands.  But read HELP first, because
it's probably best not to.

If your preferred word processor isn't listed below, or you'd like to
customize any of the commands, press F7 for our Customized Keystroke
screen.

F6 - Load keystrokes for this wordprocessor:     MYMWrite
F7 - Customize or edit keystroke setup: Page 23
                                                  MYMWrite
                                                  PCFoil
                                                  PFSWrite
                                                  WordPerfect
```

```
                              <From Menu Bar, Alt-F, P, W, F6>
╔══════════════════════════════════════════════════════════════════╗
║ ╔═══════════════════════════ CUSTOMIZE KEYSTROKES ═══════════════╗ ║
║ ║                        CURSOR MOVEMENT                          ║ ║
║ ║   Ctrl-PgUp                │ Beginning of document              ║ ║
║ ║   Ctrl-PgDn                │ End of document                    ║ ║
║ ║   Home                     │ Beginning of line                  ║ ║
║ ║   End                      │ End of line                        ║ ║
║ ║   Up arrow                 │ Up                                 ║ ║
║ ║   Down arrow               │ Down                               ║ ║
║ ║   <--                      │ Left                               ║ ║
║ ║   -->                      │ Right                              ║ ║
║ ║   PgUp                     │ Previous Page                      ║ ║
║ ║   PgDn                     │ Next Page                          ║ ║
║ ║   Tab                      │ Tab                                ║ ║
║ ║   Enter                    │ Next line                          ║ ║
║ ║                                                                ║ ║
║ ║    To customize any command: (1) position the cursor; (2) press F6; (3) ║
║ ║    with WAIT flashing, press the two keystrokes you prefer to use for   ║
║ ║    this command (or just one, plus the Space Bar).                      ║
║ ╚════════════════════════════════════════════════════════════════╝ ║
║ ┌──────────────────────────────────────────────────────────────┐ ║
║ │                                    PgDn - Next page             │ ║
║ │  F6 - Begin recording keystroke    Space - End recording keystroke │ ║
║ └──────────────────────────────────────────────────────────────┘ ║
╚══════════════════════════════════════════════════════════════════╝
```

WORD PROCESSOR KEYSTROKE SETUP

If I were you, I wouldn't do anything here: I'd give MYM-Write's own keystroke setup a try. It's designed specifically to work with MYM. It would be different if we could actually emulate your own word processor. Instead, we only approximate the word processors listed, because we have fewer commands and because our commands, in some cases, work differently.

But play around as much as you like. And, whichever set of commands you choose, feel free to use F7 to fine-tune it (see below). Then use F4 to print your keystroke list, if you like, though HELP will adapt itself to whichever commands you've chosen. (When actually typing in MYM-Write, just summon HELP to refresh your memory.)

Please read Chapter 2 of the manual to learn what MYM's word processor does and how to use it. You'll find instructions on imbedding "dot commands" to invoke underlined or compressed printing, centered lines, automatic page headings and such; and "substitution codes" to create form letters with your address list — and lots more.

CUSTOMIZING

The 3-step instructions are at the bottom of the screen. Basically, you just point to the command you want to change, press F6, and tell us the new keystroke you want to use. But note these points:

- You may use two keystrokes for a command, but it's probably better to use just one. (Why use two when one will do?)

- If you use the Ctrl or Alt key in combination with some other key — Ctrl-right-arrow, say — that still counts as just one keystroke.

- Use the Space Bar after you enter the first keystroke to tell us you're done — that this command will REQUIRE just one keystroke.

- There are a lot of keys we won't let you use, to keep you from getting into trouble. For example, no command can start out with a letter or number. If it did, you could never type words that included that letter, or amounts that included that digit.

- To switch existing commands you'll have to be a little creative. Say you wanted to switch the meaning of PgUp and PgDn. Well, you couldn't just tell us that the new command for "Next Page" is PgUp, because that keystroke is already in use. So first you'd change it to, say Ctrl-F10, then change PgUp to mean PgDn, then change Ctrl-F10, which was really just sort of a holding pen, to mean PgUp.

PRINT KEYSTROKE CHART

Fill in the blanks and press F4 or back out with ESCape. However you customize your keystrokes (though we recommend sticking mostly with the MYM-Write default), we'll print out your list here. (You'll also find it on the screen whenever you press F1 for HELP while actually writing or editing a document.)

‹From Menu Bar, Alt-F, P, 0›

```
━━━━━━━━━━━━━━━━━━━━━━━━━×┤ MODEM SETUP ├×━━━━━━━━━━━━━━━━━━━━━━━━━

   If you have a Hayes-compatible modem, MYM can auto-dial phone numbers in
   the Card File.  Please press F1 if you need HELP telling us:



      Modem port  1st              Modem dial prefix  ATDT


   If you use a long distance service that requires calling a local number
   and entering an account number, please tell us:



      The local phone number to call   ███████████
      Your account number    ███████████
      Send the account number  after  dialing the long-distance number
```

MODEM SETUP

AUTO-DIALING IN THE CARD FILE

Chances are, there's nothing you have to do here. But if auto-dialing doesn't work, here's the place to fix it. To see if it works, visit the Card File (Ctrl-C). Press Ctrl-F and then D if F6 is not already set to Dial, then point to a card with a phone number and press F6.

If you get "can't access the modem," check first to be sure the phone line is plugged in to your modem. (Is the modem working with any of your other programs?) If so, you may have misspecified your "port" on this screen. There are only four possibilities (with 1 and 2 by far the most common), so try them all. But remember: YOU HAVE TO LEAVE PROGRAM SETUP AND SAVE YOUR CHANGES before they take effect. Don't try a new setting until you've done that.

The "Modem dial prefix" we suggest — ATDT — is standard for most modems. If you need to "dial 9 to get an outgoing line," then it would be "ATDT9," (the comma tells the modem to pause briefly while it waits for the second dial tone). But check your modem manual to see if it's different.

Should auto-dialing still not work — though it probably will (flipping switch #6 of your modem sometimes does the trick) — I'd strongly recommend your not spending time trying to fix it. Of the hundreds of features in the program, this one, although we could not resist including it, is possibly the least useful.

- **CHECKFREE Users:** Please note that this modem setup information is NOT used by the optional CheckFree interface. Instead, we go by the information you supply when you activate that option in MONEY.

- **MANAGING THE MARKET Users:** MTM has its own Setup screen.

- **MCI/SPRINT Users:** If you need us to dial a local phone number and then enter your account number before placing a call, enter those numbers here. Then, in the Card File, precede long distance numbers with an "M" — e.g., M202-456-1212 for the White House. The M tells us to check these modem instructions and dial the extra numbers first.

PREFERENCES

<From Menu Bar, Alt-F, P, R>

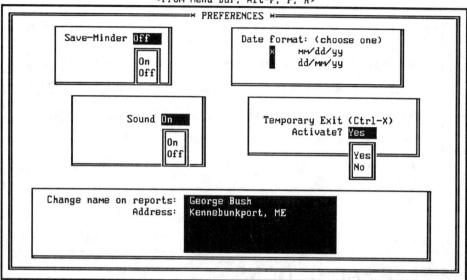

PRINTER TEST

<From Menu Bar, Alt-F, T>

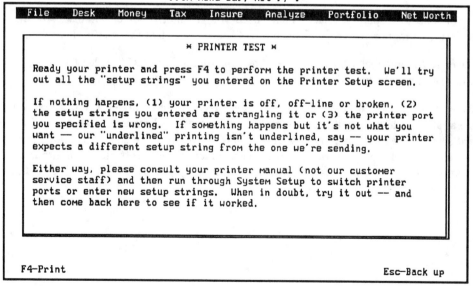

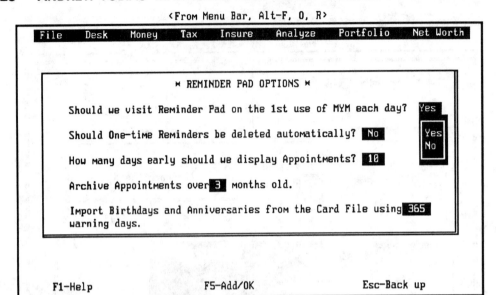

<From Menu Bar, Alt-F, O, R>

```
 File    Desk    Money    Tax    Insure    Analyze    Portfolio    Net Worth
```

```
            ╳ REMINDER PAD OPTIONS ╳

   Should we visit Reminder Pad on the 1st use of MYM each day?   Yes

   Should One-time Reminders be deleted automatically?  No      Yes
                                                                No
   How many days early should we display Appointments?  10

   Archive Appointments over 3 months old.

   Import Birthdays and Anniversaries from the Card File using 365
   warning days.
```

```
   F1-Help              F5-Add/OK              Esc-Back up
```

REMINDER PAD OPTIONS

You have a lot of choices on this screen but it's hard to do any lasting harm, and you can make changes whenever you want.

Answer YES to display your reminders, once you've entered some, automatically the first time into the program each day. If this begins to annoy you, just change it to NO.

Answer NO to automatically deleting expired one-time reminders — at least at first, so you see how we remind you of things past-due.

I set Appointments to begin showing up 1 day early. You may prefer a longer lead time or none at all. I archive appointments over 0 (zero) months old because I have no need to keep April's appointments at my fingertips in May. We'll tell you more about this option (and give you a chance to change your mind) when we encounter appointments old enough to archive. I import Birthdays and Anniversaries with 10 warning days, to have time to select and mail a card or gift.

Keep Pace with Today's Micro-computer Technology with:

Brady Books
and
Software

Brady Books and software are always up-to-the-minute and geared to meet your needs:

- Using major applications
- Beginning, intermediate, and advanced programming
- Covering MS-DOS and Macintosh systems
- Business applications software
- Star Trek™ games
- Typing Tutor

Available at your local book or computer store or order by telephone: (800) 624-0023

////BradyLine

You rely on Brady's bestselling computer books for up-to-date information about high technology. Now turn to *BradyLine* for the details behind the titles.

Find out what new trends in technology spark Brady's authors and editors. Read about what they're working on, and predicting, for the future. Get to know the authors through interviews and profiles, and get to know each other through your questions and comments.

BradyLine keeps you ahead of the trends with the stories behind the latest computer developments. Informative previews of forthcoming books and excerpts from new titles keep you apprised of what's going on in the fields that interest you most.

- Peter Norton on operating systems
- Winn Rosch on hardware
- Jerry Daniels, Mary Jane Mara, Robert Eckhardt, and Cynthia Harriman on Macintosh development, productivity, and connectivity

Get the Spark. Get *BradyLine*.
Published quarterly, beginning with the Summer 1990 issue. Free exclusively to our customers. Just fill out and mail this card to begin your subscription.

Name _____

Address _____

City _____ State _____ Zip _____

Name of Book Purchased _____

Date of Purchase _____

Where was this book purchased? *(circle one)*

   Retail Store   Computer Store   Mail Order

Mail this card for your free subscription to BradyLine

F
R
E
E

67-35511

Brady Books
15 Columbus Circle
New York, NY 10023

ATT: J. Padlad

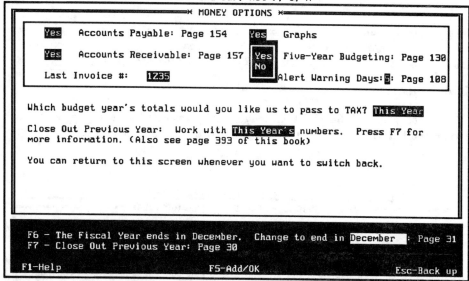

‹From Menu Bar, Alt-F, O, M›

MONEY OPTIONS

PAYABLES & RECEIVABLES

Unless you run a small business, you'll probably want to leave ACCOUNTS PAYABLE and ACCOUNTS RECEIVABLE set to NO, to avoid cluttering the screen with things you don't need. (If you do activate Receivables, we then ask for your "Last Invoice #" so we can number new ones accordingly. If you don't number the invoices you send, just leave it blank.)

FIVE YEAR BUDETING

This may also be more than you want, but we can prepare this budget *for* you when you make up your regular budget, so it's probably best to say YES. You can always switch off later.

CHECKALERT WARNING DAYS

If you set CHECKALERT WARNING DAYS to 0, we'll wait until a future transaction is due before asking you to confirm its execution. But if you don't use MYM every day, and/or want your payments actually to *arrive* on their due dates, then you'd probably want to allow for perhaps 5 or 10 Warning Days. You can always postpone a payment, so it can't hurt to err on the side of prudence and use plenty of warning days.

NOTE, HOWEVER, THAT WARNING DAYS DO NOT APPLY TO CHECKFREE TRANSACTIONS.

These will show up on the CheckAlert screen and be executed by CheckFree on the date you specified.

BUDGET TOTALS TO PASS TO TAX

Ordinarily, you'll want to use TAX to estimate your current year's taxes. But if you want to take a look at what your taxes might be next year, based on your budget for next year, TAB to this field and select "1 Year," meaning one year beyond the current one.

FISCAL YEAR

Press F6 to change your FISCAL YEAR only if you're absolutely sure this applies to you. Be sure to make a full backup first, just in case you should want to switch back.

```
                    <From Menu Bar, Alt-F, O, M, F7>
┌─────────────────────────────────────────────────────────────────┐
│┌─────────────────────────────────────────────────────────────────┐│
││═══════════════ MONEY OPTIONS -- CLOSE OUT PREVIOUS YEAR ═════════││
││                                                                   ││
││                                                                   ││
││   Close Out Previous Year:                                        ││
││                                                                   ││
││   Now that the new year has begun, and until you run through COPY ││
││   (Close Out Previous Year, on the FILE menu), you have TWO years ││
││   open at once.                                                   ││
││                                                                   ││
││   That's fine, but we need to know which year you want us to use  ││
││   when we can't use both -- for example, in displaying the        ││
││   "annual totals" on the Budget Categories screen (which we also  ││
││   pass through to TAX).   WHICH annual totals?  And in analyzing  ││
││   your capital gains position in PORTFOLIO -- yes, but for which   ││
││   year?                                                           ││
││                                                                   ││
│└─────────────────────────────────────────────────────────────────┘│
└─────────────────────────────────────────────────────────────────┘
```

<From Menu Bar, Alt-F, O, M, F6>

```
══════════════════════════╗ CHANGE FISCAL YEAR ╠══════════════════════════

     WARNING!  If you're not sure what a fiscal year is or whether you
     should be on one, you almost certainly should not be.

     You are changing this data set's active dates, which currently run
     between 1 January 1990 and 31 December 1991.

     After the change, this data set will be active for dates between 1
     December 1989 and 30 November 1991.



     In any case, be sure to press F1 and read the Help before switching.



     Alt-F6 - The Fiscal Year currently ends in December.
              Change it to end in November.
```

CHANGE FISCAL YEAR

If you haven't yet begun entering budgets and transactions, changing your fiscal year is a snap. Just do it. Otherwise, what we do depends on what month you're in. MYM keeps 24 months "active" at any one time. When you change the fiscal year, we slide those 24 months forward or backward to accommodate you. In no event will you ever lose any transactions; and you can use MONEY's Report Generator to produce reports on short years, long years, or any other kind of odd years generated by your switch.

Say it's now May 13, 1991. You've been on a normal calendar year but now want to switch to a November fiscal year. The active 24 months up to now were January, 1991 through December, 1992. To accommodate your switch, we'll slide them back a month. Now, instead of 1/91-12/92, they cover 12/90-11/91. Come December 1, 1991, we'll welcome you to the new year (a month earlier than most people celebrate it) and you'll have up to 12 months to Close out the Prior (11-month) Year. In years to come, you'll have 12 months' data covering each December 1 through November 30.

But what if you're already into the 17th month, not the 5th, of this 24-month period. You've already entered your 1991 transactions, it's May, 1992 and you've never accepted our offer to Close Out Prior Year (1991)?

To avoid the possibility of losing some budget numbers (though not transactions), the first thing to do in that situation is to go through COPY for 1991, so you have all your records for that period, with a backup copy on disk should you ever need to generate new reports.

By going through COPY and lopping off the previous 12 months, May now again becomes the 5th, not the 17th, month of your active 24.

All this is more complicated than it sounds. It won't be once the transition has been made. I never thought Congress should have allowed fiscal years in the first place.

Just follow these steps:

1. Backup your budget.dbs and little7.dbs files onto floppies labeled "Before Changed Fiscal Year."

2. Proceed with the change.

3. If you're not happy, copy the old ones back.

PORTFOLIO OPTIONS

<From Menu Bar, Alt-F, O, P>

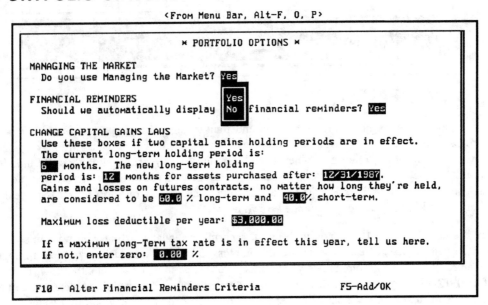

```
                    × PORTFOLIO OPTIONS ×

MANAGING THE MARKET
   Do you use Managing the Market? Yes

FINANCIAL REMINDERS
                               Yes
   Should we automatically display No  financial reminders? Yes

CHANGE CAPITAL GAINS LAWS
   Use these boxes if two capital gains holding periods are in effect.
   The current long-term holding period is:
   6   months.  The new long-term holding
   period is: 12  months for assets purchased after: 12/31/1987.
   Gains and losses on futures contracts, no matter how long they're held,
   are considered to be 60.0 % long-term and  40.0% short-term.

   Maximum loss deductible per year: $3,000.00

   If a maximum Long-Term tax rate is in effect this year, tell us here.
   If not, enter zero: 0.00 %


   F10 - Alter Financial Reminders Criteria          F5-Add/OK
```

<From Menu Bar, Alt-F, O, P, F10>

```
* PORTFOLIO OPTIONS *

        * ALTER FINANCIAL REMINDER CRITERIA *
PORTFOLIO's Financial Reminders will automatically remind you when a
position is within 45 days of going long-term.  We won't bother
reminding you if the gain or loss is less than $250.00 .  Also, we will
Omit  assets in your hypothetical portfolios and Omit  assets in your
IRA/Keogh portfolios.  (Type over any of these parameters to change them;
enter "0" days if there is no capital gains holding period or you don't
care to be reminded of it.)

If you've specified price objectives for any of your stocks, we'll remind
you when they've been met.  (Will you sell?  Or raise your objective,
only to see the stock fall back to where you bought it?) If you've
entered mental stop losses, we'll remind you when they've been reached.

If you've used the proper option symbols, we can deduce their expiration
(see "Commonly Asked Questions" at the end of Chapter 7 in your manual).
We assume options expire the 3rd Friday of each month (as all currently
do), and begin reminding you 20 days in advance, as we do for bond
maturities, also.


F10 - Alter Financial Reminders Criteria          F5-Add/OK
```

NET WORTH OPTIONS

<From Menu Bar, Alt-F, O, N>

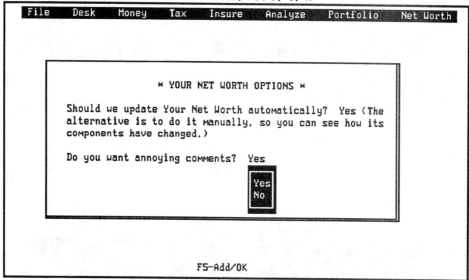

```
File   Desk   Money   Tax   Insure   Analyze   Portfolio   Net Worth



            * YOUR NET WORTH OPTIONS *

    Should we update Your Net Worth automatically?  Yes (The
    alternative is to do it manually, so you can see how its
    components have changed.)

    Do you want annoying comments?   Yes
                                     Yes
                                     No



                       F5-Add/OK
```

CARD FILE OPTIONS

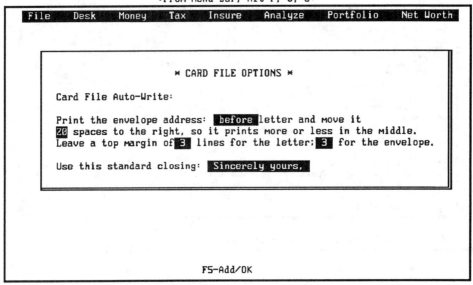

<From Menu Bar, Alt-F, O, C>

```
 File   Desk   Money   Tax   Insure   Analyze   Portfolio   Net Worth


              ✻ CARD FILE OPTIONS ✻

    Card File Auto-Write:

    Print the envelope address:  before letter and move it
    20 spaces to the right, so it prints more or less in the middle.
    Leave a top margin of 3 lines for the letter; 3 for the envelope.

    Use this standard closing: Sincerely yours,




                        F5-Add/OK
```

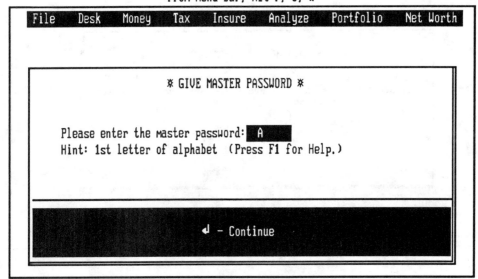

<From Menu Bar, Alt-F, O, W>

```
 File   Desk   Money   Tax   Insure   Analyze   Portfolio   Net Worth


               ✻ GIVE MASTER PASSWORD ✻


    Please enter the master password: A
    Hint: 1st letter of alphabet  (Press F1 for Help.)


                  ↵ - Continue
```

```
                    <From Menu Bar, Alt-F, O, W>
          ════════════════* SET PASSWORDS *════════════
  ┌──────────────────────────────────────────────────────────┐
  │ Managing Your Money allows three levels of access:         │
  │                                                            │
  │       Level ONE:  complete access                          │
  │                                                            │
  │       Level TWO:  cannot change or add transactions        │
  │                                                            │
  │       Level THREE:  access to nonfinancial sections only   │
  │ You may set passwords for each level, or have none at all.  We do require │
  │ a MASTER password, which will be your safety should you forget or wish to  │
  │ change the others.  The master password should be something unique to      │
  │ you, such as your mother's maiden name or maybe your first automobile.      │
  │ Enter this in the "Hint" field — "The name of my first dog" — so when       │
  │ we ask for the Master Password along with that hint, you'll be sure to      │
  │ remember.                                                   │
  │          Enter your passwords:                              │
  │          Level 1: Opensezame                                │
  │          Level 2:                                           │
  │          Level 3:                                           │
  │          Master Password: a                                 │
  │          Reminder: 1st letter of alphabet                   │
  └──────────────────────────────────────────────────────────┘
  ▓ F10 - Save passwords and continue ▓
```

PASSWORDS

Most people don't need MYM's optional password protection. Nor is it so secure that it would foil a truly determined snoop. But for everyday situations, like wanting your secretary to be able to update your Card File and Reminders without ogling your Portfolio or Bank Balances or Loans or Net Worth, our password scheme could be quite handy.

The MASTER Password serves only one function: it lets you into the room where you can see, set or change your Everyday Passwords. It's easy to remember your MASTER Password because you get to assign it a hint that we'll always display when we ask for it.

The MASTER Password we start you off with is, simply, "the first letter of the alphabet" — A. You should change this to something only you will know, like "the name of my first-grade teacher" or "that special hotel in France."

If you should ever fail three times to supply your Everyday Password correctly, we'll simply ask for the MASTER and supply the hint, so you can refresh your memory.

The Everyday Password you yourself use should naturally be the Level ONE password that allows complete access. Again, it should be something only you will know ... but don't worry about forgetting it. If you do, we'll ask for the MASTER Password and supply that hint. If you'd like your accountant to be able to see any of your records but not change or add any financial transactions, assign him or her a Level TWO password.

To your children, meanwhile, you might assign a Level THREE password, so they could always check your Reminders and Card File or play with the modules of ANALYZE or estimate their life expectancies in INSURE or use the word processor ... but never see what you own or owe. To remove password protection altogether, just blank out all but the MASTER.

CUSTOMER INFORMATION

REGISTERING YOUR PROGRAM

Sending in registration cards on toasters is silly. With software, it's silly not to. Here are just a few of the important reasons why:

- As a registered owner of Managing Your Money, you'll immediately qualify for free Technical Support.

- Your 90 day damaged disk replacement "insurance" will be activated...just in case your dog acquires a taste for plastic.

- We'll keep you informed about important changes to the tax laws and improvements and enhancements to the program.

When you register, you'll also have the option of becoming a member of Managing Your Money PLUS.

As a PLUS member, you'll receive a complete copy of our annual update to Managing Your Money released each fall and four quarterly issues of our newsletter, Managing Your Money BETTER.

Each annual update incorporates new features, powerful enhancements to existing ones and important changes to the federal tax laws. Our quarterly newsletter, Managing Your Money BETTER, provides in-depth discussion of important program features, commentary from users such as yourself, and other relevant observations from the world of personal finance. Together, they're the best way to get the most out of the investment you've made.

How do you register? Just fill out and send us the registration card that accompanied your program, or press F4 and we'll print a new one for you. Our standard warranty is free; but we like to think the Plus PLAN, at $49.95, is an even better bargain!

MANAGING YOUR MONEY PLUS

Managing Your Money PLUS is a membership program available exclusively to owners of Managing Your Money. It's a great way to stay current and get the most out of your investment. As a PLUS member, here's what you'll get:

- ## A COMPLETE COPY OF OUR ANNUAL UPDATE TO MANAGING YOUR MONEY

Good as Managing Your Money is, we have every intention of continually improving it each year — by adding new features we think are terrific, as well as staying on top of important changes in the tax laws. We'll send you one complete program update during the year of your membership with easy instructions for making the switch.

- ## FREE TECHNICAL SUPPORT

As a PLUS MEMBER, you'll continue to receive free technical support from our staff of trained professionals — available Monday through Friday, 9:00 AM — 5:00 PM Eastern time.

- ## OUR QUARTERLY NEWSLETTER, "MANAGING YOUR MONEY, BETTER"

To give you the best advice on how to get the most out of Managing Your Money and to provide you with comments on relevant and timely subjects from the world of personal finance.

- ## 12 MONTH DAMAGED DISK "INSURANCE"

In case you spill coffee or the family dog acquires a taste for plastic, send us your damaged disk, we'll replace it free of charge.

How do you join Managing Your Money PLUS? It's simple. Just turn on your printer, and we'll print a PLUS membership offer. Simpler still, pick up the phone and call 203-222-9150 to place your order. We'll immediately schedule you to receive the next copy of our newsletter and the annual update to Managing Your Money when it's released in the fall.

OTHER MECA SOFTWARE

There's a whole family of personal and small business financial software from MECA available to registered users at substantial savings:

- ## ANDREW TOBIAS' MANAGING YOUR MONEY...APPLE II AND MACINTOSH VERSIONS

MYM for the Apple is now in its fourth version and operates very much like the program you're now using. Our best-selling Macintosh version takes full advantage of the Macintosh interface, and was called "the Mercedes of personal finance" by MacWeek Magazine.

- ## ANDREW TOBIAS' CHECKWRITE PLUS

A powerful, single-entry accounting program, it is a stand-alone version of Managing Your Money's MONEY section — and perfect for managing many small businesses.

- ## ANDREW TOBIAS' TAXCUT

A professional level federal income tax preparation program, TaxCut helps you prepare your 1040 form and up to 38 additional forms and schedules. Forms print from your printer in IRS-approved format, ready to sign and send. TaxCut imports much of your data from Managing Your Money or Checkwrite Plus so you don't have to reenter it.

- ## ANDREW TOBIAS' MANAGING THE MARKET

Accessible right from the PORTFOLIO menu, this optional package calls Dow Jones, updates all your stock, bond, mutual fund and option prices, and signs off fast. Or use it to call Dow Jones for any other purpose, from news and research to airline reservations, sophisticated financial reports, or the weather in Madrid. Regularly $149.95, it's available to registered users at $79.95.

ORDERING CHECKS AND SUPPLIES

Printing your checks right from your printer is one of the best time-saving features of Managing Your Money. It's fast, easy ... and surprisingly inexpensive.

Deluxe Computer Forms offers personalized, continuous-form, and sheet-fed (laser) checks. They're a snap to load into your printer, guaranteed 100% compatible with your software, and require no special permission from your bank. You can choose from standard personal or business sized checks — or customize them with a logo or background design of your choice. Deluxe can produce standard checks in only three days and customized checks in as few as five.

To order, turn on your printer, and we'll print an order form. Better still, call Deluxe toll free at 800-328-0304 (in MN call 612-631-8500). When you call, please be certain to reference the Deluxe-Managing Your Money compatibility number: C0-5400.

Deluxe also produces many other top-quality forms and supplies. If you're using Managing Your Money to run a business, continuous-form invoices may be of particular interest. They, too, are guaranteed compatible with Managing Your Money.

Deluxe also offers a complete range of home office supplies: diskettes, continuous-form printer paper or customized stationery, binders, Rolodex cards, crack n' peel labels, or any number of computer accessories.

The comparison is better still because, as a registered MECA customer, you are entitled to a 10% discount on the entire line of supplies and accessories. Everything except pre-printed forms. For prices, call Deluxe toll free at 800-328-0304, and be certain to reference the Deluxe-Managing Your Money compatibility number, C0-5400, to receive the discount.

ABOUT CHECKFREE

CheckFree Corporation is the nation's leading provider of electronic payment services. With CheckFree, instead of printing your checks on your printer, you pay your bills electronically right through the Federal Reserve — but with your existing checking account.

Electronic bill paying through CheckFree is available to you as an optional feature on the MONEY menu. All you need are a Hayes-compatible modem and a CheckFree Customer ID Number. To sign up and obtain an ID number, send CheckFree the order form that accompanied Managing Your Money, or call CheckFree directly at 800-882-5280.

CUSTOMER SUPPORT

Two types of support are available Monday — Friday, 9:00am — 5:00pm Eastern time (during peak periods, extended hours are in effect):

■ CUSTOMER SALES & SERVICE

If you're interested in registering your program, purchasing the annual update to Managing Your Money or any other MECA program, or if you need any other form of non-technical support, these are the folks to call. Please be prepared to tell us your computer type (IBM/Mac/Apple) and disk size (3.5" or 5.25") and have your credit card handy. Call 203-222-9150.

■ TECHNICAL SUPPORT

If your problem is technical, our trained staff is prepared to assist you. But before you call, we'd like to ask that you do a few things first.

1. Read the HELP screen! More often than not, it'll tell you exactly what you need to know.

2. Check the User's Manual. We've tried to anticipate a lot of your questions.

3. Save your work up to that point and then employ a little old-fashioned trial and error. If you make a mistake, you can always leave without saving (or select Revert from the FILE menu).

4. If all else fails, do call us at: 203-222-9087.

Please remember to have ready the type of computer you're using and a brief description of your problem.

■ IMPORTANT NOTE:

If your question concerns CheckFree you should direct your call to their Technical Support Hotline at 614-899-7500.

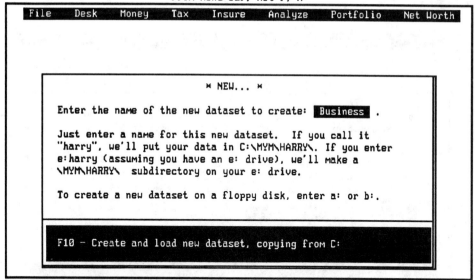

‹From Menu Bar, Alt-F, N›

NEW — CREATING A NEW SET OF DATA

FOR HARD-DISK USERS ONLY!

Here's what happens on this screen:

First you tell us the name of the new data set you want to create. It could be GRANDMA or BUSINESS or MY-1992 or anything else.

Then you tell us which existing data set you want us to clone. Usually, the data set to choose (especially if it's the only one!) is the one called "ORIGINAL." We will copy it into a new subdirectory we'll create — c:\mym\grandma or c:\mym\business or whatever you've named this dataset — to form the basis of your new records.

LOAD

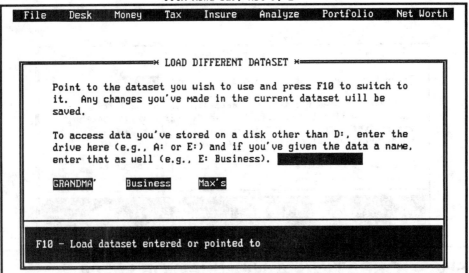

<From Menu Bar, Alt-F, L>

```
  File    Desk    Money    Tax    Insure    Analyze    Portfolio    Net Worth
```

══════════════ ✻ LOAD DIFFERENT DATASET ✻ ══════════════

Point to the dataset you wish to use and press F10 to switch to
it. Any changes you've made in the current dataset will be
saved.

To access data you've stored on a disk other than D:, enter the
drive here (e.g., A: or E:) and if you've given the data a name,
enter that as well (e.g., E: Business).

GRANDMA'   Business   Max's

F10 - Load dataset entered or pointed to

REVERT

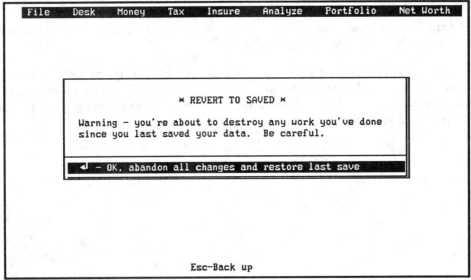

<From Menu Bar, Alt-F, R>

```
  File    Desk    Money    Tax    Insure    Analyze    Portfolio    Net Worth
```

✻ REVERT TO SAVED ✻

Warning - you're about to destroy any work you've done
since you last saved your data. Be careful.

⏎ - OK, abandon all changes and restore last save

Esc-Back up

EXIT TEMPORARILY TO DOS
(HARD-DISK USERS ONLY)

1. Press Ctrl-X from anywhere within MYM.

2. If nothing happens, this feature is not turned on. Just press P from the FILE menu and then R.

    When you ARE out in DOS, remember:

1. Don't load any "memory resident" software — programs that will continue to reside in working memory even after you return to MYM.

2. Type "Exit" to return to MYM.

2

Desk

```
                         <From Menu Bar, Alt-D, R>
    ┌══════════════════* REMINDERS FOR Sunday 9/2/1990 *══════════════════┐
    ║                                                                      ║
    │   Date                  Message                                      │
    │   ──────────────────────────────── REMINDERS ──────────────────     │
    │   12/25/1990 114 days  Christmas is coming!                          │
    │   7/1/1991   302 days  Send in your registration card!            ×  │
    │   ─────────────────────────────────── TO-DOs ──────────────────     │
    │   7/1/1991   C HIM     Reorganize the closets                       │
    │   7/1/1991   A HER     Write a will                                ×  │
    │   7/1/1991   A YOU     NEW USERS: highlight this line and PRESS F2! ×  │
    │                                                                      │
    │                                                                      │
    │                                                                      │
    │                   An × means the item has detail                    │
    │                                                                      │
    └──────────────────────────────────────────────────────────────────────┘
   ┌──────────────────────────────────────────────────────────────────────┐
   │  F6 - Different Day - 9/30/90        F9 - TO-DO List: Page 57          │
   │  F7 - Appointments: Page 53         F10 - Import dates from Card File  │
   │  F8 - Reminder Pad: Page 49                                            │
   │                                                                        │
   │      F2-View/Edit: Page 50      F3-Delete      F4-Print: Page 51       │
   └──────────────────────────────────────────────────────────────────────┘
```

THE REMINDER PAD: TODAY'S REMINDERS

Here we display Today's Reminders (or any other day's — F6). We list your Appointments (if any) first, followed by your Reminders, your To-Do items, and any upcoming birthdays/anniversaries you've imported (F10) from the Card File. Page down to see them all or use F4 to print a list.

Appointments are minute-by-minute sorts of things. Press F7 to add new ones. Press F8 to add Reminders, which may be one-time (the date your C.D. matures or your daughter graduates), monthly (pay the rent, collect the rent) or just about anything else. Press F9 to set up a prioritized To-Do list. Please read HELP behind the screens for adding new Reminders, Appointments, and To-Do's.

To attach a note to an item — or to see or change the note on any existing item — point to it and press F2. On this level, you'll see: "Bernie — drinks." But an asterisk to the right of the line will remind you there's detail below: the four key questions you want to ask him.

Press Alt-D while highlighting a date anywhere in MYM to see the day of the week on which it fell or falls. Or press Ctrl-D to summon our graphic Date Display.

Notice that we remind you (naturally enough) only of UPCOMING dates. If you want to remember someone's birthday each year, start by entering his NEXT birthday (NOT the day he was born in 1951, or his birthday just past). Thereafter, we'll take care of updating it each year.

(Speaking of birthdays, you won't see a separate list of those imported from the Card File, only those that are current. To see them all, select Options from the FILE menu and set "warning days" on Reminder Pad Options to 365. You could then print a list, if you wanted, and set the warning days back to something more sensible, like 10.)

There's just one way to gum things up. DON'T MONKEY AROUND WITH THE DATE WHEN YOU FIRST TURN THE PROGRAM ON. If you skip six months ahead, for example, you are liable to LOSE all the one-time reminders you've entered for the next six months — because the program will, not unreasonably, figure their time has passed and it's okay to erase them. If that happens to you, because you type in "5/8/97" just for fun, we will feel rotten — but it won't be our fault. (Quit the program WITHOUT SAVING and re-enter with the correct date.)

Press F7, F8, or F9, respectively, to change or delete Appointments, Reminders, or To-Do items. But don't miss this handy feature: F3 deletes a one-time Reminder or sends a periodic Reminder into hibernation until next time. We can do that for you automatically once your Reminder expires, if that's how you've set Reminder Pad Options (I don't recommend it). But even so, F3 is handy if you take care of the reminder early and don't want to keep seeing it. It saves having to go to the Reminder maintenance screen to tidy things up.

You may delete expired Appointments manually on the Appointments screen, but it's easier to let us take care of it. Each new month we'll offer to delete the prior month's Appointments — or to archive them (why throw out your old datebook?).

Press F4 for reports or, for specific reports on Reminders or Appointments or To-Dos, visit one of those screens (F7, F8, or F9) and press F4 there.

<From Menu Bar, Alt-D, R, F8>

```
╔══════════════════════════════════════════════════════════════════╗
║                        ══* REMINDER PAD *══                        ║
║                                                                    ║
║                                                                    ║
║ Date       Reminder                              Warning Days  Type║
║ 12/25/1990 Christmas is coming!                          365    A  ║
║ 4/15/1991  File Form 4868 for Federal Income Tax Extension  15  A  ║
║ 7/1/1991   Send in your registration card!             * 999    0  ║
║                                                                    ║
║                                                                    ║
║                                                                    ║
║                                                                    ║
║                                                                    ║
║ Speed scroll —                                                     ║
║                  An * means the Reminder has detail                ║
╚════════════════════════════════════════════════════════════════════╝
```

```
 F7 — Appointments: Page 53                    F10 — Copy Reminder
 F9 — TO-DO List: Page 57

 F2-View/Edit: Page 50    F3-Delete    F4-Print: Page 51    F5-Add/OK: Page 50
```

REMINDER PAD: YOUR ENTIRE LIST

To jot down a new Reminder, press F5 and press F1 for HELP there. To edit an existing Reminder, point to it and press F2. To delete one entirely, place the cursor anywhere on it and press F3. To print this list, in whole or in part, press F4. To attach a note to a Reminder, press F2 twice.

On this level, you'll see: "Library Books Due." But an asterisk to the right of the line will remind you there's detail below: the titles of the books you've borrowed.

If you don't want a Reminder to vanish when its date has passed — in case, though reminded, you forget to take care of it — set the Reminder Pad Option on the FILE menu accordingly, or else give this one a future date. The books are due May 1; but instead of using May 1 as the date with 5 warning days, use June 1 and 35 warning days. The Reminder itself could read: "May 1 — Library Books Due." We'll begin reminding you April 25, but keep reminding you until June. Or perhaps you should set this up not as a Reminder but as a To-Do item. Press F9 to add a new chore.

Hint: You can often save a few keystrokes. If it's a One-Time reminder, you can leave that field blank. We'll automatically tag it One-Time. And if it needs no warning days, skip that field too. We'll automatically enter zero.

```
                        <From Menu Bar, Alt-D, R, F8, F5>
┌────────────────────────────────────────────────────────────────────────┐
│  ═══════════════════════════*═ REMINDER PAD ═*════════════════════════   │
│                                                                          │
│   Date       Reminder                              Warning Days  Type     │
│   12/25/1990 Christmas is coming!                          365    A       │
│   4/15/1991  File Form 4868 for Federal Income Tax Extension 15   A       │
│   7/1/1991   Send in your registration card!            * 999     O       │
│                                                                          │
│  ┌────────────────────────────────────────────────────────────────────┐ │
│  │                        * ADD REMINDER *                             │ │
│  │                                                                    │ │
│  │                                                                    │ │
│  │ Date      Reminder                              Warning Days Type   │ │
│  │                                                                    │ │
│  │                                                                    │ │
│  └────────────────────────────────────────────────────────────────────┘ │
│   Speed scroll -                                                          │
│                   An * means the Reminder has detail                      │
│                                                                          │
├──────────────────────────────────────────────────────────────────────────┤
│  F1-Help        F2-View/Edit            F5-Add/OK           Esc-Back up    │
└──────────────────────────────────────────────────────────────────────────┘
```

ADDING OR EDITING A REMINDER

The format for the date is 4/15/91, but you can type 04-15-91, 4?15?91, 4p15k91, 4/15 (we'll supply the year), 15 (we'll supply the current month and year) or anything else that gets the idea across. Or use Ctrl-D to choose the date graphically. If you don't like something you've typed, just back up and type over it.

As you see, we allow you to tag your Reminders "One-time" (we'll delete them for good when their time has passed — and even do it automatically if you choose that Reminder Pad Option on the FILE Menu), "Annual" (we'll merely put them to sleep until next year), and lots of choices in between — for your quarterly tax payments, semi-annual bond payments, and so on.

But how far in advance do you want us to begin nagging you? That's what we mean by Warning Days. If you type in a June 20 Reminder with 5 warning days, it will show up on June 15 and continue to appear through June 20.

After that it will disappear forever (if it's a "one-time" Reminder) or go into hibernation until next week, next month, etc., depending on its type. Or, if you set FILE's Reminder Pad Options not to delete reminders automatically, it will hang around, increasingly overdue, until you delete or deactivate it manually.

A Reminder you want displayed at all times — "Floss After Every Meal" — you can tag "Annual" with 365 warning days. To add a note to this reminder or edit an existing one, press F2 and type to your heart's content.

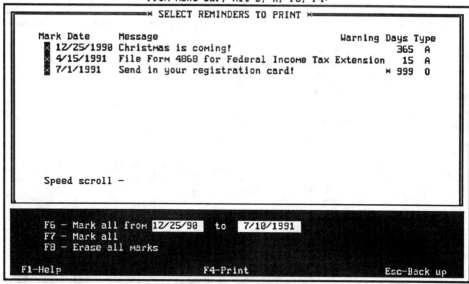

<From Menu Bar, Alt-D, R, F8, F4>

```
═════════════════════× SELECT REMINDERS TO PRINT ×═════════════════════
   Mark Date    Message                               Warning Days Type
   ▓ 12/25/1990 Christmas is coming!                          365  A
   ▓ 4/15/1991  File Form 4868 for Federal Income Tax Extension 15  A
   ▓ 7/1/1991   Send in your registration card!             × 999  0




      Speed scroll -



    F6 - Mark all from 12/25/90   to   7/10/1991
    F7 - Mark all
    F8 - Erase all marks

 F1-Help                      F4-Print                      Esc-Back up
```

SELECTING REMINDERS TO PRINT

1. Mark the items you want to print. To mark them all, just press F7. To mark all that fall due between two dates, enter those dates and press F6.
2. Press F4.

If you're trying to print all your current reminders — the ones that apply today — forget this print-out and, instead, back up to Today's Reminders and choose one of the two reports we offer there.

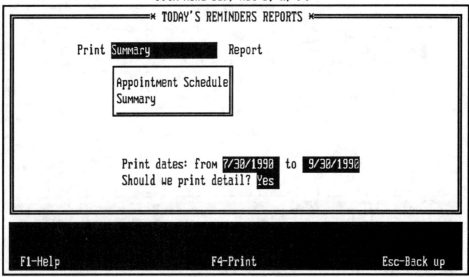

<From Menu Bar, Alt-D, R, F4>

```
╔══════════════* TODAY'S REMINDERS REPORTS *══════════════╗
║                                                         ║
║        Print ▐Summary          ▌      Report            ║
║              ┌─────────────────────┐                    ║
║              │Appointment Schedule │                    ║
║              │Summary              │                    ║
║              └─────────────────────┘                    ║
║                                                         ║
║                                                         ║
║         Print dates: from ▐7/30/1990▌ to ▐9/30/1990▌    ║
║         Should we print detail? ▐Yes▌                   ║
║                                                         ║
╚═════════════════════════════════════════════════════════╝

   F1-Help                  F4-Print              Esc-Back up
```

PRINTING YOUR REMINDER PAD

Fill in the blanks and press F4. Or press ESCape to chicken out. If printing or condensed printing doesn't work, select Program Setup from the FILE menu to better match your printer (please see ITS manual) and MYM.

Printing to the screen is fast and, except for reports over 80 columns, shows how your report will look on paper.

To send a report to the disk in drive a:, say, give it a filename like a:this.rpt. If you run the program on floppies, it's best to then replace the disk in drive a: with another, before you press F4 again to proceed, so as not to clutter your working disks. (And it's best to print to the drive not being used by the file called 2.chp that runs the Reminder Pad.) When the disk drive stops, switch back to your original data disk and resume your work.

Once you've printed the report to disk, you may wish to summon our word processor (Ctrl-W) and load "a:this.rpt" back in for a touch up. Then save it again and/or print out a copy for your boss. With printing, a little trial and error is worth twice its weight in HELP.

<From Menu Bar, Alt-D, R, F7>

```
=================* APPOINTMENTS *=================

 Date       Times        Message
 6/11/1991  11:00a- 2:30p Janie's Graduation -- please God
 6/15/1991   8:00a- 3:00p Chaperone Janie's Dance
 8/1/1991    9:00a-       Meet with Travel Agent - OOO! Bahamas!




 Speed scroll -
               An * means the Appointment has detail
```

```
 F8 - Reminder Pad: Page 49                F10 - Copy Appointment
 F9 - TO-DO List: Page 57

 F2-View/Edit: Page 54    F3-Delete    F4-Print: Page 55    F5-Add/OK: Page 54
```

APPOINTMENTS: YOUR ENTIRE LIST

To enter a new Appointment, press F5 and read HELP there. To edit an existing one, point and press F2. To delete one, including the little sample appointment we've started you off with, press F3. But it's easier to let us delete or archive it automatically the first time you visit the chapter next month. Read HELP behind Reminder Pad Options on the FILE menu to see how this works.

To enter a series of similar Appointments (follow-up dental visits, for example), enter the first, then press F10 to copy it. Enter the time and date of your next Appointment, press F5, and then do this once more if it's a crown, twice more if it's (no! no!) a root canal.

```
                      <From Menu Bar, Alt-D, R, F7, F5>
┌──────────────────────────────────────────────────────────────────┐
│┌═══════════════════════════ APPOINTMENTS ═══════════════════════┐│
││                                                                  ││
││ Date       Times        Message                                  ││
││ 6/11/1991  11:00a- 2:30p Janie's Graduation -- please God        ││
││                                                                  ││
││                                                                  ││
││┌══════════════════════ ✳ ADD APPOINTMENT ✳ ══════════════════┐││
│││                                                              │││
│││ Date       Times        Message                              │││
│││ ▐    ▌    ▐  :  ▌▐-  : ▌▐                                  ▌ │││
│││                                                              │││
│││                                                              │││
││└══════════════════════════════════════════════════════════════┘││
││                                                                  ││
││ Speed scroll -                                                   ││
││        An ✳ means the Appointment has detail                     ││
│└────────────────────────────────────────────────────────────────┘│
│                                                                    │
│                                                                    │
│  F1-Help  F2-View/Edit                F5-Add/OK        Esc-Back up  │
└────────────────────────────────────────────────────────────────────┘
```

ADDING OR EDITING AN APPOINTMENT

The format for the date is 4/15/91, but you can enter 4/15 (we'll supply the year), 15 (we'll supply the current month and year), or anything else that gets the idea across. Or use Ctrl-D to choose the date graphically.

Tell us when the Appointment begins. Its end-time is optional. If it starts or ends on the hour, you can leave that blank — we'll append the ":00" automatically. Likewise, if it's PM you needn't tell us — if you leave that blank, we'll append the P. In fact, if you just wanted to note that Janie was coming in on the 13th at 3, you could type: "13 TAB 3 Ctrl-L Janie" and press F5 and let us do the rest. If you don't like something you've typed, just back up and type over it.

To add detail, press F2 and type as much as you want. An asterisk at right will remind you there's more below.

‹From Menu Bar, Alt-D, R, F7, F4›

```
╔════════════════════════⊧× SELECT APPOINTMENTS TO PRINT ×╪════════════════════╗
║                                                                              ║
║     Mark Date      Time    Message                                           ║
║     ▓ 6/11/1991   11:00a   Janie's Graduation -- please God                  ║
║     ▓ 6/12/1991    8:00p   Chaperone Janie's Dance                           ║
║                                                                              ║
║                                                                              ║
║                                                                              ║
║                                                                              ║
║                                                                              ║
║                                                                              ║
║                                                                              ║
║       Speed scroll -                                                         ║
║                                                                              ║
╠══════════════════════════════════════════════════════════════════════════════╣
║       F6 - Mark all from  6/11/1991   to   6/12/1991                         ║
║       F7 - Mark all                                                          ║
║       F8 - Erase all marks                                                   ║
║   F1-Help                        F4-Print                    Esc-Back up     ║
╚══════════════════════════════════════════════════════════════════════════════╝
```

SELECTING APPOINTMENTS TO PRINT

1.   Mark the items you want (use F6 or F7 to automate the process).

2.   Press F4.

If you're trying to get a report of all your current appointments — the ones that apply today — forget this print-out and, instead, back up to Today's Reminders and choose one of the two reports we offer there.

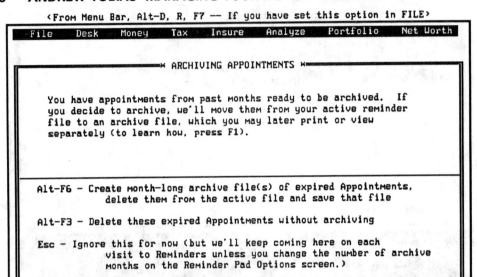

<From Menu Bar, Alt-D, R, F7 — If you have set this option in FILE>

```
 File    Desk    Money    Tax    Insure    Analyze    Portfolio    Net Worth

                        ═══ ARCHIVING APPOINTMENTS ═══

      You have appointments from past months ready to be archived.  If
      you decide to archive, we'll move them from your active reminder
      file to an archive file, which you may later print or view
      separately (to learn how, press F1).


    Alt-F6 — Create month-long archive file(s) of expired Appointments,
             delete them from the active file and save that file

    Alt-F3 — Delete these expired Appointments without archiving

    Esc — Ignore this for now (but we'll keep coming here on each
          visit to Reminders unless you change the number of archive
          months on the Reminder Pad Options screen.)
```

ARCHIVING APPOINTMENTS

The first time you visit the Reminder Pad each month we check to see if you have any old appointments on file. If any go back more months than the number you specified in Reminder Pad Options on the FILE menu, we need to know what to do with them. Do you normally throw out your datebooks or save them? That's the decision you make here. It's just that it's an electronic datebook, not leatherette.

Alt-F6 dumps a past calendar month's appointments into an archive file it creates — called MAY91.ARK, if they're for May, 1991 — and then automatically saves your newly-thinned-out current reminder data file.

Alt-F3 just deletes the expired appointments. ESCape lets you put off the decision.

I set the number of months in Reminder Pad Options to 0, so January's appointments can be archived (or deleted) the first time I visit in February. But you may prefer to have them hang around awhile. You can always change it.

We put each month's appointments into a separate archive file — never half a month's, and never reminders or projects, just appointments.

To view archived appointments press Ctrl-W, change "*.doc" to "*.ark" and press F8. This will put the list of all your archived files into MYM-Write. Point to the one you want and press F2 to view or edit or print a report for your boss or the IRS.

<From Menu Bar, Alt-D, R, F9>

```
=* TO-DO LIST *=

Date        Project                         Warning Days Who Impt Completed
7/1/1991    Reorganize the closets                 999  HIM  C
7/1/1991    Write a will                       *   999  HER  A
7/1/1991    NEW USERS: highlight this line and PRESS* 999 YOU A




Speed scroll -
                    An * means the TO-DO has detail

F7 - Appointments: Page 53          F9 - Sort by:  3: Date-Who-Impt
F8 - Reminder Pad: Page 49          F10 - Copy TO-DO

F2-View/Edit: Page 58  F3-Delete    F4-Print: Page 59   F5-Add/OK: Page 58
```

TO-DO LIST

Do you keep a "To-Do" list? Do you keep track of several ongoing projects? You can organize all that here. Just press F5 to add your new items. (And F3 to delete the few samples we started you off with.) If you're not sure how to fill in our "Add To-Do" pop-up, just press F1 for HELP. When you're happy with your new item, press F5 to add it to the list.

As you'll see if you press Ctrl-F, that list may be sorted — and then printed (F4) — six ways. (In sorting by "who," we go by the last initial — the K in JFK — on the assumption you'd want to sort by last name.) You can print a report that shows just the items Sally is responsible for, ordered by date due or importance; or a list of just the most important items; or just the projects that have been completed — and so on. Not bad if you want some ammunition ready before you go in to see your boss or before one of your employees comes in to see you!

We don't delete your To-Dos once the completion date passes (even MYM-ers occasionally miss a deadline), but we do stop displaying them on Today's Reminders screen, so you may want to come back here as the date approaches and extend it. That's one way to meet a deadline. Or, if you're shooting for May 1, enter a June 1 due date (so it keeps popping up), but as part of the Project description type: "Promised May 1st!"

To copy an item (if, say, two people are responsible for a project), point to it and press F10. Make any changes you want and then press F5 to add it to the list.

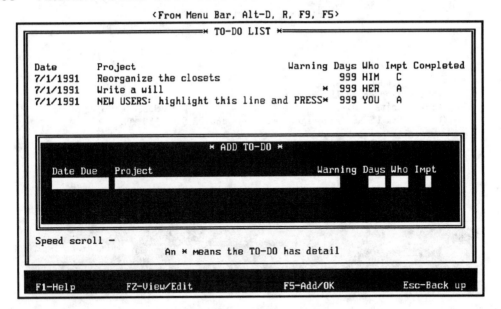

<From Menu Bar, Alt-D, R, F9, F5>

```
═══════════════════════════════╡ TO-DO LIST ╞═══════════════════════════════

Date        Project                            Warning Days  Who  Impt Completed
7/1/1991    Reorganize the closets                    999   HIM   C
7/1/1991    Write a will                         ╳    999   HER   A
7/1/1991    NEW USERS: highlight this line and PRESS╳ 999   YOU   A


          ┌────────────────────────╳ ADD TO-DO ╳────────────────────────┐

            Date Due   Project                        Warning Days Who Impt
            ▓▓▓▓▓▓▓▓▓   ▓▓▓▓▓▓▓▓▓▓▓▓▓▓▓▓▓▓▓▓▓▓▓▓▓▓▓▓▓▓   ▓▓▓  ▓▓  ▓



          Speed scroll -
                        An ╳ means the TO-DO has detail


  F1-Help          F2-View/Edit              F5-Add/OK          Esc-Back up
```

ADDING A TO-DO ITEM

Enter the hoped-for completion date, a description of the project, the number of days in advance you want us to begin reminding you of it (Warning Days), the initials of the person who's responsible, and its importance. Then (or later) press F2 to attach notes or subprojects. When you're happy with what you've done, press F5 to add it to your list. (You can always come back and make changes.)

NOTE: When we sort by "who," we look first to the THIRD initial — the **K** in JFK, not the J. If you leave the third initial blank, it will come first in the sort order (a blank comes before any other letter of the alphabet). So if you don't know the middle initial, just leave it blank — J_K — or leave the first space blank — _JK — but don't leave the third space blank (JK_).

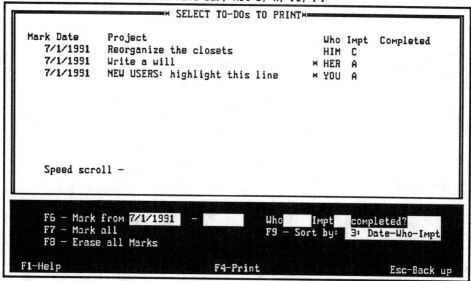

<From Menu Bar, Alt-D, R, F9, F4>

SELECTING TO-DO'S TO PRINT

1. Mark the items you want. If you like, you can use F6 to automate this:

    Press Ctrl-F and then tell us the date range you want us to include. If you specify a "Who," we'll mark only his or her projects. (But you can then use F6 to mark a second person's projects as well — the marks are cumulative.) Similarly, you can limit our marks to just one level of importance. (Or use F6 to auto-mark the A's and then come back to mark the B's, also.) And you can limit the marks to completed or uncompleted projects.

2. Press Ctrl-L and then TAB and F9 to select a sort order for your report.

3. Press F4 when you're ready. We'll ask whether you want to print detail (any notes you may have appended) and whether you want us to skip to a new page for each new person or date or level of importance (depending on how you asked us to sort the report).

```
                              <From Menu Bar, Alt-D, C>
┌─────────────────────────────────────────────────────────────────────┐
│ ┌══════════════════════════ ⋈ CARD FILE ⋈ ═══════════════════════════┐ │
│ │                                                                     │ │
│ │ Last Name        First Name    Who              Home Phone          │ │
│ │ Orwell           George         Futurist         305-555-2934        │ │
│ │ Pacific Gas & Elect  .          Gas Leaks                            │ │
│ │ Reagan           Ronald         Top Dog          202-456-1414        │ │
│ │ Telenet          .              1200-baud                            │ │
│ │                                                                     │ │
│ │                                                                     │ │
│ │                                                                     │ │
│ │                                                                     │ │
│ │                                                                     │ │
│ │ Speed scroll —                                                      │ │
│ └─────────────────────────────────────────────────────────────────┘ │
│ ███████████████████████████████████████████████████████████████████ │
│  F6 - Auto-Write this card: Page 66        F9 - Sort by Last Name    │
│  F7 - QuickEdit Special Codes: Page 62     F10 - Copy this record    │
│  F8 - Display  Work  phone                                           │
│                                                                      │
│  F2-View/Edit: Page 63   F3-Delete    F4-Print: Page 66   F5-Add/OK: Page 63 │
└─────────────────────────────────────────────────────────────────────┘
```

YOUR CARD FILE

Here's the main Card File screen, complete with a few cards we've started you off with as samples. To see the kinds of data you can keep on friends, clients, customers, patients, employees, club members and the like, press F2 to view a sample — and please read THAT help screen, also. Point and press F3 to delete the samples when they begin to annoy you.

Press F4 to open up a wealth of printing options: labels, envelopes, phone lists to carry in your briefcase, rolodex cards, personalized junk mail, and more. Press F5 to add records of your own. As your list grows, you'll find Speed Scroll invaluable. You can jump straight to any record just by typing its first letter or two. In fact, with Type-Ahead, you can be typing those letters even before you get to this screen — press Ctrl-C to summon your Card File but then, without waiting, type the first letters of the card you're after. By the time you look up (if you type the way I do, with your eyes on the keyboard), the card will be ready and waiting.

F6 will auto-dial the phone number you're pointing to (if it's set to "Dial" and you have a modem) or auto-write a letter. To switch between "Dial" and "Auto-Write, just press Ctrl-F and make your choice.

■   If you have trouble dialing, select Program Setup from the FILE menu and then Modem Setup, and read HELP there.

■   To set Auto-Write options, visit Card File Options on the FILE menu.

F7 is your key to Special Codes, which can be very powerful here. The choice box to its right offers either "Quick Edit," which is a fast way to assign or reassigning codes to your cards, or "View/Edit," which is where you decide what each code means and come to refresh your memory. F8 toggles the righthand column from Home Phone to Work Phone to Other Phone.

Note that Auto-Write decides which of your three addresses to use — Home, Work, or Other — depending on which of phone column is displayed.

F9 sorts the list. Ordinarily, you'll want to sort by last name, but press Ctrl-L and TAB to see your other choices. Sort by "Who," and you can Speed Scroll straight to your Plumber, even if you've forgotten his name. Sort by phone number, and you almost instantly can see everyone you know in the 214 area code (Dallas). Sort by first name if you find yourself stuck with something on the tip of your tongue. (Fred Br..., Ber... Bru... — AGH! This is so frustrating! PRUITT! Yes! Of course!)

F10 copies an existing record. This is handy if you've just come back from lunch with three guys from Mitsubishi for whom much — but not all — of the information is the same. You want a card for each, and F10 saves a lot of grunt work.

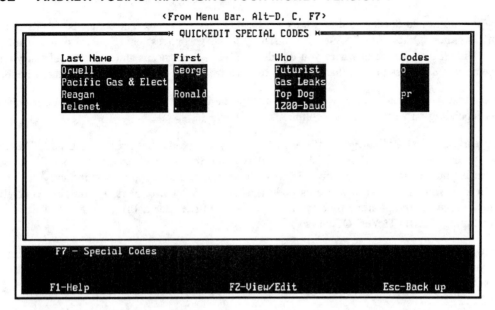

```
                        <From Menu Bar, Alt-D, C, F7>
╔══════════════════════════════════════════════════════════════════════╗
║            ══════════════■ QUICKEDIT SPECIAL CODES ■══════════════     ║
║                                                                        ║
║      Last Name          First        Who                Codes          ║
║      Orwell             George       Futurist           o              ║
║      Pacific Gas & Elect .           Gas Leaks                         ║
║      Reagan             Ronald       Top Dog            pr             ║
║      Telenet            .            1200-baud                         ║
║                                                                        ║
║                                                                        ║
║                                                                        ║
║                                                                        ║
║                                                                        ║
║                                                                        ║
║                                                                        ║
║   ────────────────────────────────────────────────────────────────   ║
║      F7 - Special Codes                                                ║
║                                                                        ║
║      F1-Help                  F2-View/Edit              Esc-Back up    ║
╚══════════════════════════════════════════════════════════════════════╝
```

QUICKEDIT SPECIAL CODES

Quickly run down the right hand column typing C's next to everyone on your Christmas card list. Run down again typing 0 for people who didn't respond to the Fund Drive, 1 for those who gave up to $25, 2 for $25-$100, 3 for ... you get the idea. Then you can print phone lists or mailing labels of all donors, all non-donors, just big donors — whatever. Assign tennis partners a T, bridge players a B, males and females M's and F's — you name it.

It may take a little while to go through your list this way, but having done it once you'll have a lot of power at your command when you go to print lists or labels. If you can't remember what code stands for what, just press F7 to see.

Hint: F7 toggles in and out of your Special Codes list. ESCape will also take you back out, of course, but it's easier just to flip in and out with two touches of the same key.

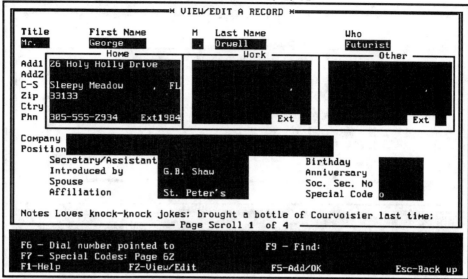

ADD OR EDIT A CARD

Here you build your Card File. I have hundreds of cards in mine. Take a look at the Sample records to see how they've used the screen. To move quickly around the screen, hold down the Alt key and press any number across the top of your keyboard. We jump ahead that many fields. This MYM shortcut is particularly handy here. And if you've come to view or edit an existing card, note our other shortcut: Page Scroll. Use the PgUp, PgDn, Home, and End keys to move from card to card, automatically saving your work as you go.

You may assign each card up to 6 Special Codes. Code clients with a C, friends with an F, classmates with lower-case c, people crazed for lobster with a semicolon. Anything can be a code; press F7 to maintain a list of what each means. Later, you'll be able to print a list of JUST your clients, JUST classmates, or JUST people crazed for lobster — or even a list of only those clients who are also classmates.

If you use a long distance carrier that requires dialing a local number first, enter an M in front of any phone number you'd like us to call that way. Your local access number and account number go in the Modem Setup section of Program Setup on the FILE menu.

Press F2 to append notes or to see or change notes you've already begun. You can keep running diaries of all your contacts with customers; keep track of the gifts you've exchanged over the years; children's and pets' names — anything.

<From Menu Bar, Alt-D, C, F4, F4>

```
╔═══════════════════════════════════════════════════════════════════╗
║═══════════════════════════*═ CARD FILE ═*═════════════════════════║
║                                                                    ║
║        ┌─────────────────────────────────────────────────┐        ║
║        │              *═ CARD FILE REPORTS ═*             │        ║
║        │                                                  │        ║
║   Print│ Labels    Report with heading: Fundraising       │        ║
║        │ ┌─────────┐                                      │        ║
║        │ │Phone List│                                     │        ║
║        │ │Addresses │ If Mailmerge, full document name: class.doc │ ║
║        │ │Full Card │                                      │        ║
║        │ │Labels    │                                      │        ║
║        │ │Rolodex   │ If Full Card, print blank fields Yes, │       ║
║        │ └─────────┘          formfeed after each card? Yes │      ║
║        └─────────────────────────────────────────────────┘        ║
║                                                                    ║
║   ┌───────────────────────────────────────────────────────────┐   ║
║   │ F6 - Setup formats for labels, Rolodex cards and envelopes: Page 68 │ ║
║   └───────────────────────────────────────────────────────────┘   ║
║                                                                    ║
║  F1-Help              F4-Print: Page 66            Esc-Back up      ║
╚═══════════════════════════════════════════════════════════════════╝
```

CARD FILE REPORTS

1. In the first field, tell us what you want to print: PHONE LIST, ADDRESSES, FULL CARD, LABELS, ROLODEX, or MAIL MERGE.

2. In the second field, give your report a heading — ALUMNI FUND LIST — or just leave this blank.

3. (a) If you'll be doing mail merge, blending the contents of a letter you've written with the cards you've selected, say, tell us where to find that letter — c:\mym\ltl-leag.ltr. For more on Mail Merge, see below.

    (b) If you've chosen the full-card report and you don't want us to print fields for which you've entered no data, choose NO. If you want us to start a new page after each card, choose YES.

    (c) If you'll be printing labels, Rolodex Cards or envelopes, F6 will let you customize the printing to fit your situation.

4. When everything is as you want it, press F4 again to print. If your printer fails to respond, select Program Setup from the FILE menu and then Printer Setup and read HELP.

MAIL MERGE

For this to work, you must first have created a document in MYM-Write that contains "substitution codes." This is explained in detail in the manual, but here's a summary: You can embed substitution codes anywhere in a MYM-Write document. Wherever it sees one, the Mail Merge print-out will substitute whatever it stands for. Want to start each sentence with your correspondent's first name? Or mention the name of his company? Just embed those codes. Where no such information exists (someone with no "position," say), we'll just ignore it rather than leave an unsightly gap where "Sales Manager" might otherwise might have appeared.

SUBSTITUTION CODES

Here are the substitution codes you can use in your document:

[da] = Today's date (in English)   [ln] = Last name
[a1] = 1st address line*   [zi] = Zip*
[ti] = Title (Mr., Ms.)   [po] = Position**
[a2] = 2nd address line*   [cy] = Country*
[fn] = First name   [co] = Company**
[ci] = City*   [ph] = Phone number*
[mi] = Middle initial   [wh] = Who?
[st] = State*

*Prints for marked addresses
** Prints for work addresses only

Thus a letter might begin this way (square brackets and all):

[da]
[ti] [fn] [ln]
[po]
[a1]
[a2]
[ci], [st] [zi]
[cy]

Dear [ti] [ln]:

I am writing to you, [ti] [ln], because I can think of no one better suited to participate in Guadeloupe Petroleum 1992-D. Believe me, [ti] [ln], this is no form letter. You and you alone have been selected to have first crack at this truly extraordinary opportunity.

Sincerely,
Thadeus Petropolemides

You'd save that letter as "GUAD-1992.LTR" and moments or months later you could enter the Card File — Ctrl-C — mark the prospects to whom you want to send it, choose Mail Merge as your report style, and then print it. Each page of your "report" would be another of these letters, addressed to another person on your list.

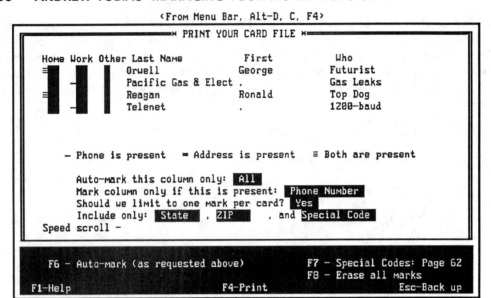

PRINT CARD FILE

THE BASIC IDEA

First tell us which cards you want to include; then press F4 again and we'll ask what you want to print — a phone list, labels, whatever.

MARKING CARDS ...

You've got lots of flexibility in choosing whom to include and whether to print all their addresses or just one. You can mark cards manually, one by one, or use F6 to automate the process.

... MANUALLY

To mark specific cards manually, Speed Scroll down to them and type X's beside each. Or, to print MULTIPLE envelopes or labels, mark each address with the NUMBER of copies you want us to print (up to 9) instead of an X.

Note that a single horizontal bar to the left of a card means it's got a phone number; a double bar means it's got an address; and three horizontal bars mean you've entered both.

... WITH AUTO-MARK (F6)

To auto-mark cards, answer our questions in the middle of the screen before you press F6.

■ **AUTO-MARK THIS COLUMN ONLY: [ALL, HOME, WORK, OTHER]**

Well, do you want us to limit the marks to one of the three columns? Or do you want us to mark them all, if the rest of your criteria are met? Usually you'd choose ALL, but it's up to you.

■ **MARK COLUMN ONLY IF THIS IS PRESENT: [PHONE, ADDRESS, BOTH, DON'T CARE]**

It's fine to choose "Don't Care," but if you're here to print a phone list, you might want to mark only columns with a phone number. If you're here to print mailing labels, you might want to skip the cards that have no address.

■ **SHOULD WE LIMIT TO ONE MARK PER CARD?**

Ordinarily, no. But if you're sending out a mailing, you may well not want to send copies to someone's Home, Office, and Work addresses. If you choose YES, we mark the first column that meets your criteria — Home, if that one does, or Work, if Home doesn't, or Other, if neither Home nor Work does.

■ **INCLUDE ONLY: STATE, ZIP, SPECIAL CODE**

The simplest thing to do is leave these blank. But if you'd like to include only cards from Florida, just enter FL in the STATE field, and we'll exclude from your list any without an FL address.

To narrow things even further, you could, instead or in addition, enter something in the ZIP field. Entering 02138 would lead us to mark only cards that have that precise zip code. Entering 0213 or 021 or even just 02 or 0 is also acceptable, however, and broadens the criterion to include not just Cambridge, Massachusetts (in the case of 02138), but ALL of Massachusetts (in the case of 02).

■ **SPECIAL CODES**

The real power comes with SPECIAL CODES. We will mark any cards that contain the codes you enter here (so long as they meet whatever other criteria you've specified). So if you entered A$r, we'd mark any cards you'd coded with an A or a $ or an r.

It gets better. A minus sign in front of a code means no card with that code will be included. Say you'd coded all foreign addresses with an "f" and were now doing a domestic mailing. This would be an easy way to exclude all foreign addresses. Just include -f in the Special Codes field. Linking two or more codes with a plus sign means both (or all) must be present for the card to qualify. You want tennis players (T), but only those who are also single (S) because you're going to put together a little party. And, again, you don't want to invite anyone from out of the country (it's not going to be THAT big a party). So you'd enter: T+S-f. We'd mark any card that included both T and S among the codes you'd assigned it, but not f. (Admittedly, this is kind of abstruse. If you simply want a complete phone list, say, choose "ALL" columns but "only if PHONE NUMBER is present," answer "NO" where we offer to mark just one column per card and leave everything else blank. It's that simple.

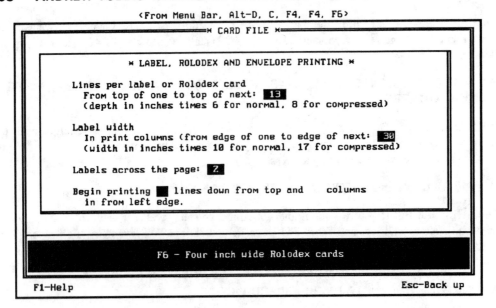

<From Menu Bar, Alt-D, C, F4, F4, F6>

```
═══════════════════════ ✳ CARD FILE ✳═══════════════════════

            ✳ LABEL, ROLODEX AND ENVELOPE PRINTING ✳

   Lines per label or Rolodex card
      From top of one to top of next:  13
      (depth in inches times 6 for normal, 8 for compressed)

   Label width
      In print columns (from edge of one to edge of next:  30
      (width in inches times 10 for normal, 17 for compressed)

   Labels across the page:  2

   Begin printing ▇ lines down from top and    columns
      in from left edge.


              F6 - Four inch wide Rolodex cards


   F1-Help                                       Esc-Back up
```

LABEL, ROLODEX, AND ENVELOPE PRINTING

This is actually easier than it looks — if you have a ruler. It lets you print almost any kind of label, Rolodex card, or envelope. (For more on printing envelopes, especially with a laser printer, see those sections of Chapter 2 in the manual.) Rather than try to figure this all out on the first attempt in a heroic attempt not to waste 40 cents worth of labels, just try a few and then make adjustments.

For Rolodex cards, choose the width of card you have and press F6. If you are using a non-standard Rolodex card or index card instead, simply enter the correct lines per card on the first line.

We'll remember your settings so you won't have to do this again. (To remember a second set, press Ctrl-W and jot notes to yourself in a file you save as "label.fmt", "envelope.fmt" or "rolodex.fmt" or some such.) When you're happy with the settings, press ESCape to back up.

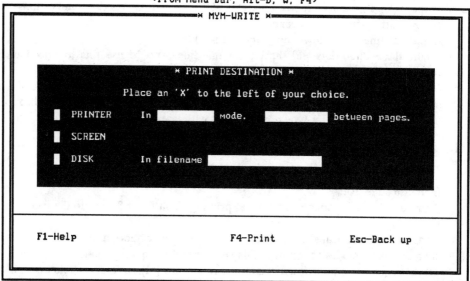

<From Menu Bar, Alt-D, W, F4>

PRINTING

Fill in the blanks and press F4 again, or chicken out with ESCape. If normal printing doesn't work, select Program Setup on the FILE menu and then Printer Setup. Read *its* HELP.

DOT COMMANDS AND SQUIGGLY BRACKET COMMANDS

If you used dot commands and/or squiggly bracket commands in your document, and if your printer is capable of obeying them, the result should be reflected when you print. For details, see your manual, but here are the available commands and what they instruct your printer to do.

Squiggly bracket commands may be imbedded anywhere in your text: {ul} and {ep} toggle on and off underlined and emphasized printing. Here's how you'd emphasize {ep}this{ep} word. In printing, the "{ep}" would disappear and "this" would print bold.

Here are the dot commands you can use in MYM-Write to achieve certain modes of printing, if your printer can handle them and you've configured Printer Setup properly:

.ds   Double space everything below the next line.

.ss   Single space everything below the next line.

.pa   Start a new page, even if there's still room on this one.

.cpnn   Start a new page if fewer than "nn" lines (some 1-or 2-digit number) remain on this page.

.prnn   Eject this page and start numbering those that follow from "nn" (any one- or two-digit number).

.pann   If [pa] is in a header or footer line, this will eject the page and renumber those that follow starting from "nn" (as above).

.ce   Center the line that follows (but only that line).

...   Ignore these three dots and the rest of this line. (You'd use this to imbed in the document something you didn't want printed out.)

.ht   Stop printing temporarily and allow "hot type" — typing something in on the fly straight from your keyboard. (Careful! Never print-to-disk if you've embedded a hot-type command.) Hot-type doesn't work with laser printers.

TOGGLES

.ch   Turns on (and off) compressed horizontal printing. You'll get 17 characters to the inch instead of 10.

.cv   Turns on (and off) compressed vertical printing. You'll get 8 lines to the inch instead of 6.

.qp   Turns on (and off) quality printing. If your printer offers "draft" and slower-but-sharper "final" modes of printing, this will turn on the quality mode.

.ul   Turns on (and off) underlined printing. (Or use the {ul} squiggly bracket command. It's probably easier.)

.ep   Turns on (and off) emphasized, or "bold" printing. (Or use the {ep} squiggly bracket command.)

.dp   Turns on (and off) double-width printing.

NOTE:

■ All dot commands affect printing to the printer, but only those like "go to new page" or "begin double-spacing" will affect printing to the screen or to a disk file.

■ All dot commands MUST be alone on a line to themselves, flush left.

■ To "turn off" a dot command, insert a new one with the opposite meaning or, in the case of those that "toggle," just insert the same one again.

■ None of these fancy things works in "iceberg mode" (where you're just attaching a note to an entry). They work only in "document mode" (where you've pressed Ctrl-W to compose a whole separate document.)

■ Commands can cancel each other out. Every time you send an emphasized printing command (or any of the others), it turns that mode on or off. Thus, if you begin your whole document with an ".ep" (emphasized printing) dot command flush left, the document will print all in bold face. But if when you do go to print it you tell us on the print screen to print "in emphasized mode," we'll send a second emphasized printing signal — that will cancel out the first.

HEADERS AND FOOTERS

These commands allow you to set up one or two header lines and one footer line. These lines will appear at the top and bottom, respectively, of all subsequent pages. If you use them, header lines will be followed by one blank line before your actual text starts.

In each case, follow the dot command immediately — without pressing the Space Bar or Enter key — with what it is you'd like us to print.

.h1   Print whatever's on this line as the first header line
.h2   Print whatever's on this line as the second
.fo   Print whatever's on this line as the footer line

If you wanted every page of your document to have the heading, "Jack Rabbit Report," you'd enter this dot command at the beginning of your document: .h1   Jack Rabbit Report.

To have us insert page numbers and/or the date, just type [da] for today's date and [pa] for page number — brackets and all. In the following example, this would cause the date to print at the top of every page (at the left margin): .h1[da].

And this would print the word "Page" followed by a space and then the page number at the bottom of every page (in the center, because we inserted some spaces): .fo Page [pa].

WHEN IN DOUBT, TRY IT OUT.

MYM-WRITE

<From Menu Bar, Alt-D, W>

```
╔═════════════════════════════ MYM-WRITE ═════════════════════════════╗
║                                                                      ║
║      Letters.doc                                                     ║
║      Book.doc                                                        ║
║      Chap.doc                                                        ║
║      Fundraise.doc                                                   ║
║      Merge.doc                                                       ║
║                                                                      ║
║                                                                      ║
║                                                                      ║
║                                                                      ║
║──────────────────────────────────────────────────────────────────── ║
║   F6 - Start a NEW document: Page 72                                 ║
║                                                                      ║
║   F8 - Display the directory of: [ d:\v7\1990\*.doc ] : Page 74      ║
║                                                                      ║
║   F1-Help                                               Esc-Back up  ║
║                                                                      ║
╚══════════════════════════════════════════════════════════════════════╝
```

THE DOCUMENT MANAGEMENT SCREEN

Here you select the document you want to work with and, once you finish, decide whether and how to save it. The choices we show on this screen vary depending on what you're doing. It's important to *read* them!

When you first get here, you'll have two choices:

F6 to start a new document;
F8 to work with one you've created before.

START A NEW DOCUMENT — F6

Press F6 and you get a blank slate (titled NO NAME because we don't know yet what you're going to want to call it), ready to type. Type as much or as little as you like, pressing F1 at any time for HELP remembering MYM-Write's commands.

When you're finished typing, press ESCape to quit. You're back at this document-management screen and we're asking you: "With respect to the work you've just done: do you want to toss it in the trash (F6)? Or save it (F10)?"

At this point, even before you make that choice, you may also press F4 to print the document or F2 to view/edit it again.

SAVE A DOCUMENT — F10

If you opt to save it, we will put it into its own file, with whatever name you choose. Just enter a name of up to 8 characters (no spaces or punctuation); we'll append ".DOC" to it and stick it in the data directory with the rest of your MYM data.

Your file name might be ARCHIE or 8-12-91L or AUTO-INS or ENVELOPE — anything DOS will accept. We'll save it as ARCHIE.DOC or 8-12-91L.DOC or AUTO-INS.DOC or ENVELOPE.DOC.

If you give it a different extension — .LTR, say — we'll accept it; but you'll find it easier to let us just put ".DOC" extensions on your file names, because they'll also be easier to retrieve.

Similarly, you may supply path names — A:ARCHIE — would cause us to save it as ARCHIE.DOC on the floppy in your A: drive. D:\LETTERS\1991\ARCHIE.LTR would cause us to save it as ARCHIE.LTR on the 1991 subdirectory of the LETTERS directory of your D: drive. But ordinarily, you'll want to ignore this needless complication.

When you press F10, we'll save your document — unless we find there's one by the identical name already in existence. In that case, we'll give you a chance to change your mind. (But ordinarily, you *won't* change your mind, because this is just what you intended. You had a document called ARCHIE.DOC; you've come here now to work with it some more and have no need to save the old draft; so you just write the new version over the old one.)

```
                          <From Menu Bar, Alt-D, W, F6>
┌─────────────────────────────────────────────────────────────────┐
│ Editor                        NEW DOCUMENT                        │
│ L       T      T      T      T      T      T      T      T    T R  │
│ September 30, 1990                                                 │
│                                                                   │
│                                                                   │
│ Resolution Trust Company                                          │
│ Washington, DC                                                    │
│                                                                   │
│ Dear Sirs:                                                        │
│                                                                   │
│ I am interested in a nice little bank, nothing too big, maybe a nice │
│ southeast exposure...                                             │
│                                                                   │
│                                                                   │
│                                                                   │
│                                                                   │
│ Esc - Back up            F1 - Help                                │
│                                              Line 1,Col 1    INS  │
└─────────────────────────────────────────────────────────────────┘
```

‹From Menu Bar, Alt-D, Ctrl-W, F2›

```
╔══════════════════════════════════════════════════════════════╗
║                        ═╪ MYM-WRITE ╪═                         ║
║                                                                ║
║                                                                ║
║                                                                ║
║                                                                ║
║                                                                ║
║                                                                ║
║                                                                ║
║                                                                ║
║                                                                ║
║          With respect to the document you just worked on:      ║
║                                                                ║
║   F6 - Abandon this version without saving it: Page 74         ║
║   F10 - Save it as ████████████████████ in Document mode: Page 73║
║                                                                ║
║                                                                ║
║   F1-Help      F2-View/Edit           F4-Print      Esc-Back up║
║                                                                ║
╚══════════════════════════════════════════════════════════════╝
```

DOCUMENT MODE

To the far right of F10 is a choice pop-up. Ordinarily, you will want to select DOCUMENT mode. Save in ASCII mode only if you want us to strip out all our own peculiar codes (like the rulers and other things you can't see) for use with some other word processor.

To have your cake and Edith, too, just save it first in document mode as ARCHIE.DOC; then, a second later, as ARCHIE.ASC in ASCII mode.

ABANDON THIS VERSION — F6

If this is a new document and you choose to abandon rather than save it, it's gone. But if you had already saved it once and now had just come back to look at it and perhaps make a few changes, "abandoning" it does *not* delete it ... it just ignores whatever changes you may have made on this visit.

SELECT AN EXISTING DOCUMENT TO WORK WITH OR PRINT — F8

To work with a document you created earlier — including reports you "printed to disk" — press F8. We'll display all the ".DOC" files you've previously created in this directory (or on this floppy).

Do you see the name of the document you want? If so, highlight it with the cursor and press F2 to summon it to the screen. Then, when you're done looking and/or tinkering, press ESCape and you're back here, faced with the same choices: F4 to print it, F6 to throw your tinkerings in the trash, F10 to save, F2 to work with it again.

If after pressing F8 you don't see the document you want to work with, it must have a different extension (.LTR perhaps or .RPT?) or be located on a different directory or disk. Just press F8 again and tell it where to look. For example, enter A:\REPORTS\1991-BUD.RPT and F8 will search the \reports subdirectory of the floppy in drive a: looking for a file called 1991-BUD-.RPT.

- For a summary of MYM-Write commands, just summon HELP while typing.

- For a summary of squiggly bracket and dot commands you can imbed to effect underlined printing, double-spacing, headers and such, press F4 to print a document and then F1 for HELP.

- For the substitution codes to use with mail merge documents, visit the Card File, press F4 to print and F1 for HELP. Or just see your manual.

<From Menu Bar, Alt-D, N>

```
  File    Desk    Money    Tax    Insure    Finance    Portfolio    Net Worth



                        ═══× NUMERIC CALCULATOR ×═══

   Enter:                                              r=0

   a=0         b=0         c=0         d=0         e=555

   F6 - Import current number            F7 - Edit last formula
                        ↵ to calculate



   F1-Help                                        Esc-Back up
```

NUMERIC CALCULATOR — CTRL-N

This is the calculator HELP screen. For a little practice, reread pages 22-25 of HELLO, NEW USER. But in brief:

+ Adds   **- Subtracts**   **x or * Multiplies**   **/ Divides**   **^ Exponentiates**

CTRL-N   Exits the calculator so that you can get back to work.

ENTER   Calculates the formula in the Enter field ... or ... if the Enter field is blank, returns you to the screen, pulling whatever's in the "r" up with you.

F1   Pulls the value from the screen down into the formula in the Enter field.

3

Money

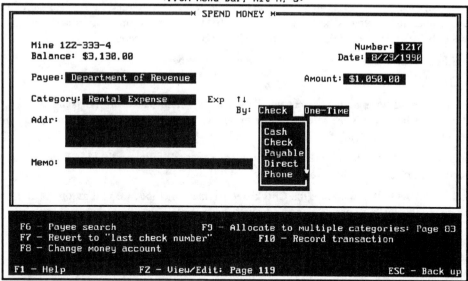

SPEND MONEY

First check the top left corner of the screen to see which account we're working with. If it's not the one you want, press F8 (visible only if you more than one account) to change it. Then TAB from field to field and fill in the blanks. Press F10 to record your work when you're done (or F9 if you want to allocate this expenditure to more than one budget category.)

■ CHECK NUMBER

Press Ctrl-F to jump here if we've guessed wrong. Type in the correct number or, if we're not too far off, hold down the Alt key and tap either the plus or the minus key at the top of your keyboard to adjust it. Try it. Charge card items and such obviously don't need check numbers. (If you're getting them anyway, back up to the Menu Bar and select Money Accounts. Point to this account, press F2, and blank out "Last Check Number" with the Space Bar.)

We start you off with a number one higher than the "Last Check Number." If you skip to an even higher number, the "Last Check Number" will jump to that higher number, and we'll increment from there. (To get it back down, if you goofed, visit the Money Account as just described and type over it.)

If you enter a LOWER check number (because, say, you and your spouse share a checking account, but carry around separate books of checks), we'll increment from that lower level until you leave the screen (or type in some new number). When you next return here, we'll be back to numbering from the highest check in your account. To get us to do that WITHOUT having to leave the screen or type in that number by hand, just press F7 — Revert to Last Check Number. This option appears only when you've begun numbering from a lower number.

If you post date your check, we will delete any check number entered here when we add this future transaction to your CheckAlert Register. Later, when its time comes and you execute it, we will assign it what is then the next check number for this account.

CheckFree Users: CheckFree does not allow check numbers.

■ DATE

If we've guessed wrong, just correct us. To get to this field fast from the "starting" position on the Payee field, press the left arrow (or up arrow or Shift-TAB). The Alt-plus, Alt-minus shortcut works in this field, too. Try it.

We start you off with today's date. If you change it, we'll stick with THAT date until you change it again (or leave the screen).

CheckFree Users: If you choose the CheckFree payment method, we will automatically bump the date ahead four business days. (And leave it there, unless you then change it back.)

■ PAYEE

Enter the name of whomever you're paying, using abbreviations as needed. (Believe me, they'll still take the check.)

■ PAYEE SEARCH

But wait! Is this someone you've paid before? If so, enter just enough to make a "unique" match and then press F6. We'll search back through the previous expenditures in this account (but only this account) and, if we find a payee that begins with these letters (whether upper- or lower-case), we'll display the most recent transaction. Change anything you like and then press F10.

- If it's a payment you allocated to a single budget category last time — GROCERIES — that's where we'll allocate it this time, too (unless you change it).

- If it's one you split among two or more categories last time and the amount is the same this time, we'll allocate it exactly as before (again, unless you change it).

- If it was split among two or more categories last time and you've changed the amount, a choice will pop up when you press F10: We'll offer to split the allocation in exactly the same PROPORTIONS as last time; or, if you prefer, you can do a new allocation manually.

■ CATEGORY

If you would like to allocate this expenditure to a budget category — whether for budgeting or simply for use later in organizing your tax records -- you can do it three ways:

1. TAB to this field and enter the first letter or two of the category name, if you know it.

2. TAB to this field and use the down and up arrows to select it.

3. Press F9 and select it there — or press F5 on that screen to add a new category and THEN select it.

If you want to split the expenditure over two or more categories, as you frequently may, press F9.

■ PAYMENT METHOD ("BY")

Are you paying or did you pay this by CHECK? That's the most frequent method for most people. But perhaps you paid CASH (remember cash?) or perhaps this money was snatched DIRECTly from your account by the electric company, or paid with a bank-by-PHONE arrangement, where you call and tell the bank whom to pay, or through an ATM (automated teller machine). Two other options may appear here as well:

- CheckFree (CFree) will show up if you've activated it and this is, in fact, your CheckFree account.

- Payables will show up if you've switched on that MONEY option on the FILE menu. When you "pay" a bill by the Payable method, you're not really paying it at all — and your bank balance will not go down. Rather, you're instructing us to put this payment on your Payables List (a "to-be-paid" list, really), ready to be executed there.

To select one of these payment methods, just press its first letter (or first two letters, if Check and CFree are vying for the honor), or TAB into the choice box and select it that way.

NOTE: for credit card accounts, "Direct" is probably as good a designation as any. But I just ignore it and leave it at "Check." It doesn't make any practical difference.

■ PAYMENT FREQUENCY

You'd normally leave this set to One-Time. But if you'd like to set it up as a regular payment that we'll then add to the CheckAlert screen, tell us the frequency. Type its first letter or TAB into the choice box and select it that way. If you DO choose a recurring frequency, a field appears asking you how many times it should recur. Enter the actual number or, if it's to recur indefinitely, a large number.

- Except in the case of payments by CheckFree — CheckAlert will not execute any of these future payments without your confirmation first. And you can change or delete any of them on the CheckAlert Register.

- If this is a payment that does not recur regularly or that does, but with a different amount each time, you should probably choose "One-Time" here and, instead, add it to your Quick List. (To do that, just point to it on the Check Register screen and press F6.)

■ ADDRESS

It's fine to skip the address if you don't need it printed on the check or, with a credit card receipt, as part of the record you keep for the IRS.

■ MEMO

Feel free to skip the memo, also — or expand it by pressing F2. (Only the first memo line prints on your check. Additional lines are for your own records.)

- F2 jumps to the Memo from anywhere on the screen.

- Remember that with a CheckFree transaction, the memo is for your use only and does NOT get transmitted.

MEMO POWER!

Don't miss the additional power memos can provide! It comes from the fact that MONEY's Report Generator can search your memos from particular "strings" of characters, including in its report only those that "match." Say you allocate gifts to a budget category called gifts. Fine. But what if you wanted to see only gifts to Billy or Babs? Or say you have five rental properties, with a single budget category for each, but wanted a way to see what you spent on plumbing repairs across all five of them? Just enter unique words or codes anywhere on your memos (on the second line if you don't want them to print out on your checks) and you'll later be able to use them in generating reports.

If you are a consultant, you could put the name of each client (or some briefer code) in the memo area. Your expenditures would fall into categories like PHOTOCOPYING, ENTERTAINMENT, CAB FARE, etc.; but to see a report of all your expenditures on a given client, or for with regard to a given job, you'd just tell the Report Generator to retrieve any expenditures with that code in the memo.

NONCASH EXPENDITURES

To record noncash "expenditures" — like the coat you gave the Salvation Army or the $3,325 in depreciation on the Dreamy Treat Ice Cream truck you drive or the $12,391 loss generated by that great limited partnership you're in — set up a Non-Cash account called (say) "Gifts in Kind." Then "spend" the money this way:

Payee: Salvation Army — FUR COAT!

Amount: $1,885.

Budget allocation: CHARITABLE CONTRIBUTIONS.

Highlighting the nature of the item in the payee line — FUR COAT! — will remind you that this is a special, noncash, transaction. As such, it doesn't affect your cash flow projection or net worth (don't forget to delete the chinchilla from your household inventory in NET WORTH), but will show up when you print reports of transactions for tax purposes if you include this account in your report.

CHECKFREE LIMITS

A single CF merchant can have no more than 12 one-time payments pending. We won't let you enter another while 12 are on the CheckAlert Register waiting to be paid. Nor can a single CF merchant with a recurring payment pending — such as your monthly mortgage — be assigned a second recurring payment or any one-time payments.

- The easy way around this is to set up a second CF merchant with a slightly different name. Use Bank of America for your recurring mortgage payment, but BankAmerica Car Loan Dept, say, to pay your car loan.

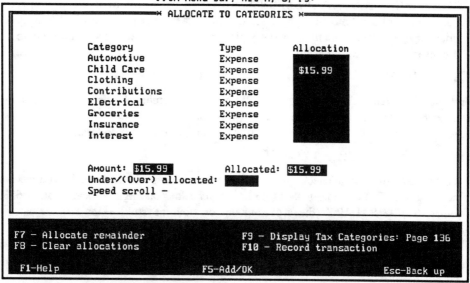

<From Menu Bar, Alt-M, S, F9>

```
════════════════════════ × ALLOCATE TO CATEGORIES ×════════════════════════

              Category              Type          Allocation
              Automotive            Expense
              Child Care            Expense        $15.99
              Clothing              Expense
              Contributions         Expense
              Electrical            Expense
              Groceries             Expense
              Insurance             Expense
              Interest              Expense


              Amount: $15.99          Allocated: $15.99
              Under/(Over) allocated:
              Speed scroll -


   F7 - Allocate remainder          F9 - Display Tax Categories: Page 136
   F8 - Clear allocations           F10 - Record transaction

   F1-Help                    F5-Add/OK                     Esc-Back up
```

ALLOCATE TO BUDGET CATEGORIES

ALLOCATING TO JUST ONE CATEGORY

If you're allocating to just one category, just Speed Scroll to it and press F7. The entire amount will be allocated there. (Ordinarily, though, it's faster to do the allocation on the previous screen, without even coming here.)

F10 TO PROCEED

When you're ready, press **F10** (not F5) to record what you've done.

ADDING A NEW CATEGORY

Press F5 here if you'd like to add a new category to your list.

SEEING THE TAX TREATMENT

Before you allocate a transaction you may want to be sure it's going into the right tax barrel. To check the tax barrel you assigned this budget bucket to, just press F9. And then press it again to get back to work.

SPLITTING A TRANSACTION OVER MORE THAN ONE CATEGORY

Normally, though, you'll only need to come here when you want to split your allocations, part to one category, the rest to another (up to 14 in all). Speed Scroll from one to the next making your allocations and then, to be sure you've allocated everything (and to spare yourself a little typing), make the last one with F7.

We don't force you to allocate exactly 100% to categories (you can allocate less or even more), but you really should. Two very useful categories in that regard are UNALLOCATED

INCOME and UNALLOCATED EXPENSE. If you allocate more or less than you actually spent or received, keep things tidy by visiting one of these and pressing F7. We'll dump in the under- or over-allocation and keep everything in balance. In fact, it's best always to make your final (or only) allocation using F7.

SPLITTING QUICK LIST TRANSACTIONS

Even Quick List transactions may be split. MYM will remember the proportions of the split and allocate future amounts in the same proportions. But note that for this to work intelligently, you MUST allocate the entire transaction, no more and no less.

ALLOCATING YOUR PAYCHECK

Ordinarily, you will allocate checks you write to expense categories and checks you receive to income categories. But consider your $1,633.68 paycheck. You might allocate that $1,633.68 as follows: $2,722 SALARY (the gross amount on your paystub) — an income category; $661.55 FEDERAL WITHHOLDING (an expense); $101.33 FICA; $72.14 HEALTH INSURANCE — and so on.

ALLOCATING INCOME TO AN EXPENSE CATEGORY, AND VICE VERSA

Don't use a minus sign here to indicate an expense — we know they're negative. But should you have occasion to allocate income to an expense category, or vice versa, a minus sign IS needed, because income is a negative expense. A $200 check from Blue Cross could be entered in an income category ("REIMBURSEMENTS"). But if you highlighted an expense category ("MEDICAL EXPENSES") and pressed F7, we'd enter minus $200, because, happily, your medical expenses for the year just declined by $200.

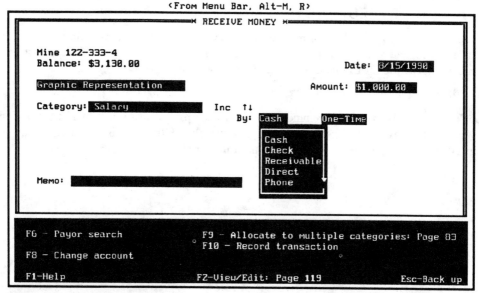

<From Menu Bar, Alt-M, R>

RECEIVE MONEY

First check the top left corner of the screen to be sure we're working with the right account — and press F8 (visible only if you have more than one) if we're not. Then tell us who paid you what, when, and how.

■ PAYOR

The first field is for the payor, but you need only enter the first letter or two if they've ever paid you before. Press F6 and we'll search back through the receipts in this account (but only this account) and display the first one we find that matches. Make any changes you like and then press F10.

■ CATEGORY

Select one or press F9 just as you would on the Spend Money screen. (Read HELP there if you need a refresher.)

■ PAYMENT METHOD ("BY")

Chances are, they paid you by CHECK, but maybe you got a suitcase full of CASH or the money was deposited DIRECT to your account by the Social Security administration or someone wired the funds into your account by PHONE. Or, if this is your "Petty Cash" account, perhaps this was money you received from an ATM (in which case you might actually prefer to record this in one step on the Transfer Money screen). Or maybe you didn't actually get paid at all — you're just owed the money. If you've switched on our Accounts Receivable option on FILE's Options menu, then RECEIVABLE will be one of the methods here. Choose it and we won't increase your bank account; we'll just add this prospective payment to your Receivables list. Visit that screen to print an invoice or execute the receipt when the money actually comes in the door.

■ PAYMENT FREQUENCY

If you get a quarterly dividend or monthly rent check — or any other recurring payment you want us to remind you of on the CheckAlert screen — you can use this feature just as on Spend Money. Read HELP there if you need a refresher.

■ MEMO

The "memo" can be helpful in reminding you what the payment was for ("a gift from Mom" ... "reimbursed expenses for Chicago trip"), especially if the IRS is wondering why you didn't declare it as income. Press F2 if you need more room.

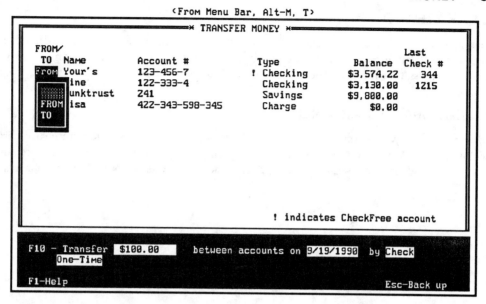

<From Menu Bar, Alt-M, T>

TRANSFER MONEY

If you moved $200 from your checking account to your savings account — or wish to do so now — here's the easiest way to tell us.

First type an F to tell us FROM which account the transfer's being made and a T to tell us the one it's going TO.

Then move down to the F10 line and tell us the amount and date of the transfer and the method. Did you make (or are you making) the transfer by check? By phone? By using an Automated Teller Machine (ATM)? Or was it one of those "direct" transfers that happens automatically, by pre-arrangement? If you choose Check, we'll supply the next check number unless you override it with one of your own.

To have CheckFree send the money, if it's coming FROM your CheckFree account, enter "CF" in the "payment by" field.

WHAT WE DO AFTER YOU PRESS F10

After we make the transfer, you'll find the payment in the Check Register of the FROM account. Edit it if you like and/or allocate it to budget categories. (We don't do that on the Transfer screen, because transferring money between accounts really isn't "spending" it in the ordinary way. You're no poorer.)

You'll find a receipt in the same amount in the Check Register of the TO account, along with a nice memo telling you exactly where it came from. Again, edit and/or allocate it if you like, although normally you wouldn't need to.

SEPARATED AT BIRTH

Note that once the transfer is made, its two halves become independent of each other. Changing or deleting one will not affect the other ... so if you DO have occasion to make a change to one side of the transaction, you will probably want to make it to the other side, as well.

PAYING CREDIT CARD BILLS

If you pay VISA, you are transferring money from your checking account to your charge card account and can do it here. (Or else pay it like any other bill and then call your VISA account to the screen and "receive" what you paid.) See "Handling Charge Accounts" in your manual.

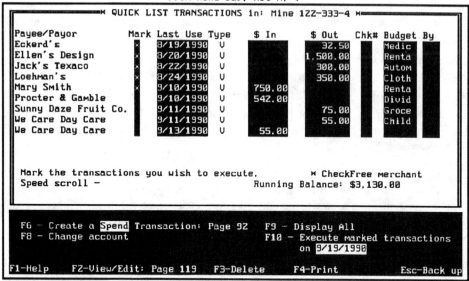

〈From Menu Bar, Alt-M, Q〉

```
═════════════════ ✕ QUICK LIST TRANSACTIONS in: Mine 1ZZ-333-4 ✕ ═════════

 Payee/Payor         Mark Last Use Type    $ In      $ Out  Chk# Budget By
 Eckerd's             ×  8/19/1990  U                32.50       Medic
 Ellen's Design       ×  8/20/1990  U             1,500.00       Renta
 Jack's Texaco        ×  8/22/1990  U               300.00       Autom
 Loehman's            ×  8/24/1990  U               350.00       Cloth
 Mary Smith           ×  9/10/1990  U     750.00                 Renta
 Procter & Gamble        9/10/1990  U     542.00                 Divid
 Sunny Daze Fruit Co.    9/11/1990  U                75.00       Groce
 We Care Day Care        9/11/1990  U                55.00       Child
 We Care Day Care        9/13/1990  U      55.00                 Child



 Mark the transactions you wish to execute.        ✕ CheckFree merchant
 Speed scroll —                          Running Balance: $3,130.00



 F6 - Create a Spend Transaction: Page 9Z   F9 - Display All
 F8 - Change account                        F10 - Execute marked transactions
                                                  on 9/19/1990

 F1-Help      FZ-View/Edit: Page 119   F3-Delete    F4-Print       Esc-Back up
```

QUICK LIST

YOUR QUICK LIST

Here is your Quick List. It's a powerful way to record transactions. You may use it extensively, as I do; or you may ignore it and do most of your work on the Spend and Receive Money screens. It's purely a matter of personal preference.

SELECT THE PROPER ACCOUNT

The account we're working with is displayed at the top of the screen. If it's not the one you want, press F8.

ADDING NEW TRANSACTIONS

To add new transactions — except any involving loans (which we create for you when we create the loan itself) — press F6 (having first set it to the kind of transaction you want to create: Spend, Receive, or Transfer). Or visit your Check Register and point to any existing transactions you'd like to add, pressing F6 for each as you go. They'll be waiting for you here when you return.

ADDING A CHECKFREE TRANSACTION

If it's a CheckFree transaction you add here, enter "CFree" as the payment method. The first time you go to execute it, we'll burp and take you to the CheckFree Merchant screen, where we'll say "No Matching Merchant Found." Just press F5 there to add this one, and the extra information CheckFree needs.

ALL, NO GLOBALS, WITH GLOBALS

Once you do have some Quick List transactions, use F9 to specify just how broad a list you want to see. The simplest thing is just to select ALL, as I do, and leave it at that. But if the folks you pay with your personal checking account are different from the ones you pay with, say, the checking account you maintain for your rental property or for the bridge club of which you're treasurer, you may prefer to look at just those.

For the narrowest possible list — namely, only those transactions attached to this account — select "No Globals" before you press F9. For a slightly less narrow list — namely, those attached to this account plus any tagged "Global" — select "With Globals."

To run through all your transactions to see how they're currently tagged — and to tag some global — highlight the first one on your list, press F2 to view/edit it, and then use Page Scroll to view/edit the rest.

USING THE QUICK LIST

To execute a bunch of transactions once you've set them up, just mark the ones you want. The instant you mark one, we adjust the Running Balance at the lower right side of the screen, so you can see the effect executing it would have. (If you then TAB over and change the amount, the Running Balance changes accordingly.)

Mark the desired transactions with X's and we'll execute them in alphabetical order.

Or mark them from a thru z as you Speed Scroll from one to the next, in whatever order your bills happen to be, and we'll follow THAT order instead. That way, the stack of checks you wind up with will match your stack of invoices and reply envelopes.

LAST USE/DATE

The Last Use column is helpful if you're wondering, "Didn't I already pay that? Did my check and their current bill, showing a past due amount, cross in the mail?"

Ordinarily, you can skip right over this column because we automatically update it as of the date you specify at the bottom right corner of the screen. But what if you don't want to use that date for all your transactions? For the exceptions, just enter the date you DO want to use in the Last Use column and we'll use that date instead.

For payments by CheckFree, we automatically adjust the date four business days ahead (unless you've already entered an even later date).

TYPE

For your information, we remind you of the "type" of Quick List transaction this is. V means VARIABLE (a holdover from the days when MYM distinguished between "fixed" and "variable" transactions). T stands for TRANSFER. The letters M, S, I, and B denote loan transactions: MORTGAGE, SPECIAL, INTEREST-ONLY, and BIWEEKLY.

CHECK NUMBER

If you enter one, we'll use it. Otherwise, if you're making this payment by check, we'll supply it for you. Say you're here both to record a check you wrote out of your wallet but also to pay some new bills. You'd enter the actual check number of the one you already paid, but let us supply check numbers for the ones you're about to print.

PAYMENT METHOD ("BY")

The first time you execute a transaction here you'll have to tell us how you want to do it — by check, CheckFree, "direct," etc. Thereafter, we'll do it the same way unless you change it.

EDITING A TRANSACTION

Press F2 to check (or change) the address and memo you may have attached to this transaction.

ALLOCATING A TRANSACTION

Press F2 and then F9 to check or change the budget allocation. Otherwise, we'll allocate it in exactly the same proportions as before. But note: we base our proportions only on what you allocated, not on what you failed to allocate or overallocated. If you allocated only $90 of a $100 payment to PHONE-BIZ, and failed to allocate the rest to PHONE-PERS, or even just to UNALLOCATED EXPENSE, we'll see that 100% of the amount you DID allocate went to PHONE-BIZ (not 90%), and so allocate 100% of future transactions there, too. (To fix this, just allocate 90% of today's expenditure to PHONE-BIZ and 10% to UNALLOCATED EXPENSE, if that's what you want. We'll split future allocations the same way.)

MORTGAGE PAYMENTS

If you're making an extra payment to principal on a mortgage, just type in the new, higher-than-usual amount. We'll recognize the excess as a principal prepayment and automatically recalculate your future monthly principal-and-interest budget splits. If you're paying a late fee, use a separate check. Otherwise, we'll mistake it for principal prepayment.

To change the escrow amount of a mortgage payment, or something else about it, select Loan Records from the MONEY menu and edit it there. Your changes will then be reflected here.

F10 — EXECUTE

When you press F10, we'll execute all your transactions as of the date shown (which you're free to change) ... except those for which you entered your own date in the Last Use column. But first we check to see if you've done anything you can't, and advise you accordingly if you have.

- At first, this could be frustrating if you've marked 20 or 30 transactions. You'll have trouble spotting the offending one(s). So until you get the hang of it, you might want to execute just a few at a time.

CHECKFREE LIMITS

A single CF merchant can have no more than 12 one-time payments pending. We won't let you enter another while 12 are on the CheckAlert Register waiting to be paid. Nor can you make a payment here by CheckFree to a merchant that already has a recurring transaction pending on the CheckAlert Register.

- The easy way around this is to set up a second CF merchant with a slightly different name. Use Bank of America for your mortgage payment, but BankAmerica Car Loan Dept, say, to pay your car loan.

```
                        <From Menu Bar, Alt-M, Q, F6>
╔════════════════════════════════════════════════════════════════╗
║          ══════ * QUICK LIST TRANSACTIONS in: Mine 122-333-4 * ══════      ║
║   ┌──────────────────────────────────────────────────────┐   ║
║   │              * CREATE QUICK SPEND TRANSACTION *          │   ║
║   │                                                          │   ║
║   │                                                          │   ║
║   │     Payee: │Center for the Fine Arts│  Amount: │$50.00│  │   ║
║   │     Addr:  ┌──────────────────────┐                     │   ║
║   │            │                      │                     │   ║
║   │            │                      │                     │   ║
║   │     Memo:  │monthly donation│                           │   ║
║   │                                                          │   ║
║   └──────────────────────────────────────────────────────┘   ║
║                                                                ║
╠════════════════════════════════════════════════════════════════╣
║   F9 - Allocate to budget categories: Page 83                  ║
║                                                                ║
║   F1-Help          F2-View/Edit          F5-Add/OK     Esc-Back up ║
╚════════════════════════════════════════════════════════════════╝
```

CREATE A QUICK SPEND TRANSACTION

FILL IN THE BLANKS

Fill in the check (don't waste memory on addresses for payees who include reply envelopes, and don't worry about the amount — you'll be able to change it with each use); then press F9 to allocate it among your budget categories.

SPLIT ALLOCATIONS

If you split the allocation over several categories, we'll remember the proportions and allocate future payments the same way.

But we WON'T remember under- or over-allocations, so be sure to allocate it entirely, even if that means dumping leftovers (or leftunders) into your UNALLOCATED EXPENSE category.

THE MEMO

The memo is a good place for your 31-digit account number (say) — but not for things that change each time. You MAY come and edit the memo each time you prepare to execute this Quick List transaction ... but that sort of defeats the quickness. Note that with CheckFree, the memo is for your use only. It is NOT transmitted to CheckFree.

GLOBALIZATION

To make this transaction GLOBAL, go ahead and add it here; then press F2 to view/edit it — a new field will appear allowing you to change the account it's attached to.

CHECKFREE

To set it up for use with CHECKFREE, finish here and specify "CFree" as the payment method on the Quick List screen. The first time you try to execute it, we'll take you to the CheckFree Merchant list screen, where you can press F5 to add this one (and supply the additional information CheckFree needs).

HINT: TWO FOR ONE

You can set up two (or more) transactions for the same payee — "Hertz" for personal rentals and "Hertz (D)" for deductible ones, each with the proper budget allocation. In paying bills, you can then mark whichever one applies. Or, better: use upper case letters for all your business transactions — HERTZ — and lower case for personal ones — Hertz.

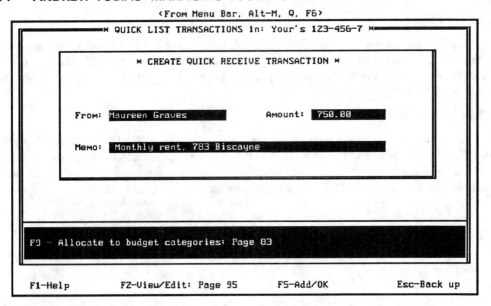

```
<From Menu Bar, Alt-M, Q, F6>
═ QUICK LIST TRANSACTIONS in: Your's 123-456-7 ═

        ═ CREATE QUICK RECEIVE TRANSACTION ═


  From: Maureen Graves          Amount: 750.00

  Memo: Monthly rent, 783 Biscayne


F9 — Allocate to budget categories: Page 83

F1-Help        F2-View/Edit: Page 95      F5-Add/OK        Esc-Back up
```

CREATE A QUICK RECEIVE TRANSACTION

Just fill in the blanks. The amount can be changed each time you use this transaction, so enter anything if you're not sure what it will be. Press F9 to choose the budget category(ies) you'd like income from this source allocated to. If it's your paycheck, remember that the amount here should be the actual amount of the check ($683.97, say) ... but that when you allocate, the GROSS amount ($1,100) should go into an income category called SALARY, and the deductions listed on your paystub should go into EXPENSE categories like FICA, FEDERAL WITHHOLDING, STATE WITHHOLDING, and HEALTH INSURANCE.

When you press F5, we'll add this transaction to your Quick List — attached to the account listed at the top of the Quick List screen. (To make it GLOBAL, for use with any account, point to it on the Quick List screen, press F2, and make the change. But I don't bother with that, because when I summon the Quick List, I just set it to "ALL," to include ALL my Quick transactions.)

```
╔══════════════ ✳ VIEW OR EDIT QUICK RECEIVE TRANSACTION ✳ ═══════════════╗
║                                                                          ║
║                                                                          ║
║        From: ▌Mary Smith      ▌        Amount: ▌$750.00▌                  ║
║                                                                          ║
║        Memo: ▌                                    ▌                      ║
║                                                                          ║
║                                                                          ║
║        This transaction is assigned to Your's 123-456-7.  To reassign    ║
║        it, display your choice here before leaving this screen:          ║
║                   ▌Your's        123-456-7          ▌↑↓                   ║
║                                                                          ║
║                                                                          ║
║  ─────────────────────── Page Scroll 6 of 11 ───────────────────────     ║
║ ┌──────────────────────────────────────────────────────────────────────┐║
║ │ F9 – View/Edit budget allocations: Page 132                           │║
║ └──────────────────────────────────────────────────────────────────────┘║
╚══════════════════════════════════════════════════════════════════════════╝

    F1-Help        F2-View/Edit              F5-Add/OK        Esc-Back up
```

VIEW OR EDIT A QUICK RECEIVE TRANSACTION

Get a boost in your paycheck? Switch employers? Grandpa amend the name of your trust fund? Make any changes you want; check to be sure your budget allocations are still correct (F9); and press F5.

If you deposit this check in a variety of accounts — sometimes your checking account, sometimes your savings account, sometimes your CMA — make this transaction available to all. Press the up arrow until "Global" is displayed.

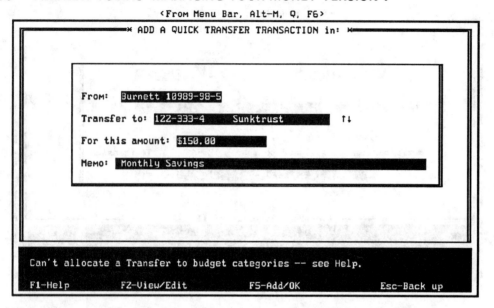

CREATE A QUICK TRANSFER TRANSACTION

FILL IN THE BLANKS

If you frequently transfer money to one of your accounts, just select that account with the up or down arrow and enter the amount of today's transfer (or any amount — you can always change it).

WHY NO BUDGET ALLOCATIONS — AND A WAY AROUND THAT

These are just money transfers, so we don't allocate them to budget categories. (When you move money from one account to another, you haven't "spent" it. It's still yours. See "How to Budget for Savings" and "How to Handle Credit Cards" in Chapter 3 of the manual.) If you do want to allocate this transaction to budget categories, set it up, instead, as two: a Quick Spend in one account and a Quick Receive in the other.

IF YOUR PAY GETS DEPOSITED TWO PLACES

This screen is handy if, say, $50 of your pay goes directly to a savings account each week. Set up a Quick Receive transaction for your paycheck as if it all went into a single account, but then set up a Quick Transfer for that $50, as well. If the name you give the transfer comes right after the Receive transaction alphabetically (call one "Procter&Gamble: Paycheck" and the other "Procter&Gamble: Savings," say), then when your paycheck comes you'll just mark off the Receive and the Transfer — bing, bing — one after another, and all will be right.

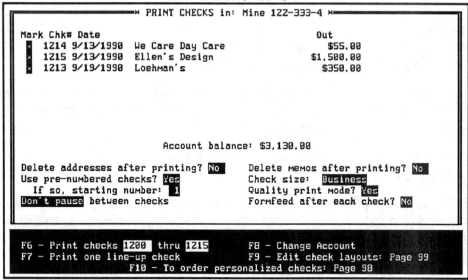

〈From Menu Bar, Alt-M, P〉

PRINT CHECKS

Printing checks is like printing any other "report," only on more expensive paper. It doesn't affect your underlying data. Print the same checks ten times until they look right, if you like; we'll show just one expenditure. (If they still don't look right, press F9 to adjust our format!) First check the title at the top of the screen to be sure this is the account you want (if you have more than one), and press F8 if it's not.

LINE-UP CHECKS

Then print as many line-up checks as necessary (F7). NONE should be necessary with a sheet-fed, laser printer — or with any other kind of printer, for that matter, once you get the hang of how far forward to advance the paper. Then fill in the blanks and press F6.

■ STARTING NUMBER

If you use pre-numbered checks — as almost everyone does and should — be sure to tell us the number of the first real one you'll be printing, in case we haven't guessed right. This would be the case if, say, you were up to check #1043 but gummed it up in the printer or used it as a line-up check. If you tell us the first actual check number will be #1044 instead, we'll renumber all the checks in MYM to match. I.e., we'll print #1043 on your real check #1044 — and then change the number to #1043 in MYM, too.

■ DELETE AFTER PRINTING? (NO!)

If you choose to "delete addresses after printing," they won't take up space or your disk but will still remain safely in your Quick List for use the next time, if that's where they came from. Likewise, memos. But ordinarily you would NOT want to do this.

■ QUALITY PRINT MODE?

If your printer has "draft" mode and "quality" mode, and if you've configured Printer Setup properly, answer YES to send the quality command to your printer.

■ FORMFEED AFTER EACH CHECK?

If you use a sheet-fed printer, with one check to a page, you'll want to answer YES, to make sure we start a new "page" after each check. For continuous-form checks, answer NO.

■ PAUSE BETWEEN CHECKS

If you feed them in manually, tell us to pause before printing.

PROBLEMS?

If the information we print isn't appearing where you want it to, press F9 to alter the layout. If the information isn't appearing AT ALL, check to be sure your printer is hooked up to your printer, your printer is on, and you've configured it properly in Program Setup.

NEED CHECKS?

Press F10 for a sales pitch.

COMPUTERIZED CHECK PRINTING FROM DELUXE COMPUTER FORMS

One of Managing Your Money's best features is its ability to print checks right from your printer. It's fast and easy, and saves your having to handwrite all the things we can write for you. (Not to mention that our handwriting may be better than yours.) Through our relationship with Deluxe Computer Forms, we are able to offer Managing Your Money customers personalized, sheet-fed, or continuous-form checks. Deluxe can produce them in only three days, or, if a special logo or background design is involved, as few as five — guaranteed fully compatible with this program and with your bank.

To order, call Deluxe toll free at 800-328-0304 (in Minnesota, 612-631-8500). Choose personal or business size checks (and window envelopes) — business-size are recommended, especially for sheet-fed printers — and please be certain to reference the Deluxe-Managing Your Money compatibility number: CO-5400 for faster service.

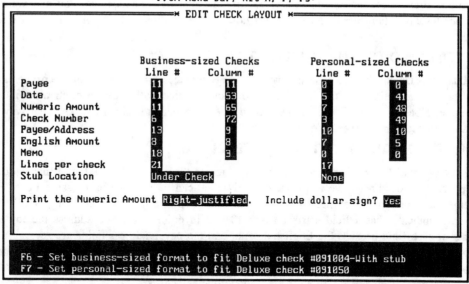

EDIT CHECK LAYOUT

STANDARD SETTINGS: F6 AND F7

Use this screen to adjust where we print things on your checks. Ordinarily, our standard settings should be fine — press F6 or F7.

F6 offers a choice of three different business-size styles. The first two are continuous-form checks with sprocket holes, one with a "stub" on which we'll print a recap of the check itself, the other without. The third is a one-to-a-page sheet-fed check.

F7 is for the standard personal-size check — but even if you're a person and not a business, I'd suggest ordering the larger checks.

CUSTOMIZING YOUR LAYOUT

It's easy to make adjustments to match almost any check format. Just start with the closest of our standard settings and then change our numbers one at a time. For example:

- To move something down 1 line lower, just add 1 to the line number on which we print it.

- If you don't want it to print at all, change its line number to 0.

- To move something a couple of spaces to the right, add 2 to its column number.

- If you want to move the date one space to the left, subtract 1 from its column number.

Don't worry too much about having things overlap accidentally. We won't let you do that. Just keep in mind that the payee/address field is 4 lines long and the English amount field (where we spell out the amount) is up to 2 lines long on a business-sized check and up to 3 lines long on a personal-sized check.

A little trial and error works wonders here. But since checks are expensive, you may want to do your tests on plain blank paper and just hold the results up to the light in front of a real check.

GETTING RID OF THE DUPLICATE PAYEE NAME

On business-size checks, we print the payee name two places: in the space for the payee name and then again, below, as the first line of the address that will show through the window envelope. Note that the "Payee" comes set to line 0 on personal-sized checks. That way, it doesn't duplicate the "Payee/Address" line further down.

LONGITUDE AND LATITUDE — TECH TALK

Most of you will be printing in tenths of inches across the page and in sixths of inches down the page. The coordinates we've provided (and which can be restored by pressing F6 or F7) assume that the top left corner of your check is at (1,1). So, coordinates of (13,14), for example, indicate that a field starts on line 13 and in column 14. We address the top left corner of each field because the English amount and the payee/address fields are several lines long: the English amount field can be up to 2 lines long on a business check and up to 3 on a personal check; the payee/address field is 4 lines long. The check length field is just for the check — if there's a stub, it will be the same length as the check.

We won't let you overlap; but, for your information, the date field is 8 characters wide, the check number 9, the numeric amount 14 right justified, the payee and payee/address fields 25, and the memo 50. On business-sized checks, the English amount can be up to 2x69. On personal-sized checks, it can be up to 3x40.

One last thing: on a business-sized check, if the English amount is only one line long (less than $100,000), we put it on the second line of its field and leave the first line blank. On a personal-sized check, we fill from the top and go down.

ABOUT CHECKFREE

CheckFree enables you to pay all of your bills electronically through its linkage to the Federal Reserve System. All you need is a checking account (your current one is fine) and a modem.

Before activating, you must register with CheckFree by sending in the application enclosed with this copy of Managing Your Money. About two weeks after you mail the form, you will receive written notice of your CheckFree account number and your "node" telephone number. Once you receive this information, you may activate CheckFree and begin using it.

Note: MECA is delighted to offer this link to CheckFree, just as it is delighted to provide compatibility with Lotus 1-2-3 or the HP LaserJet printer. But it neither endorses, profits from, nor takes any responsibility for your use of those or other fine products and services it supports.

```
                          <From Menu Bar, Alt-M, F>
┌─────────────────────────────────────────────────────────────────────────┐
│                       ═══* CHECKFREE ACTIVATION *═══                       │
│                             Personal Data                                  │
│   First EBONEEZER  MI . Last name SCROOGE                                  │
│   Addr1 3 TINY TIM LANE                    Soc. Sec. # 111-11-1111         │
│   Addr2                                    Home phone (305)222-2222        │
│   City  DICKENS                State OH Zip 33333-                         │
│                                                                            │
│                                                                            │
│                             From CheckFree                                 │
│        CheckFree ID 1234                   Node phone 555-5555             │
│                                                                            │
│                                                                            │
│                            Communications Info                            │
│        Communications port 1        Baud rate 1200      Tone/Pulse T      │
│        Optional modem initialization string glkagkakg                     │
│                                                                            │
│                                                                            │
│                        Your CheckFree Money Account                       │
│                   Your's        123-456-7                    ↑↓           │
│                                                                            │
├───────────────────────────────────────────────────────────────────────────┤
│   F7 - Make this a Business record                                        │
│   F1-Help                      F5-Add/OK                   Esc-Back up     │
└───────────────────────────────────────────────────────────────────────────┘
```

ACTIVATING CHECKFREE OR CHANGING ITS PARAMETERS

ARE YOU A BUSINESS?

If you're setting up a business account rather than a personal one, press F7 and we'll change the fields slightly.

FILL IN THE BLANKS

Then fill this in. If you don't know your communications port, it's probably 1 or 2. If neither of those works — but your modem is working otherwise — try 3 or 4.

MEMORIZE YOUR ID NUMBER!

To prevent unauthorized use, you will not be able to call CheckFree — or get back to this screen — without it.

GETTING SET UP EVEN BEFORE YOU GET YOUR ID NUMBER

If you'd like to get set up for CheckFree while you await your ID and "node" phone number, enter fake ones. But be sure to memorize your fake ID number (and write it down someplace), so you can get back in here to change it when the real one comes! Naturally, under no circumstances should you try calling CheckFree until you've established your account with them.

WE IGNORE PROGRAM SETUP'S MODEM SETUP

When dialing CheckFree, we ignore any modem instructions you may have entered in Program Setup. So if you need to dial 9 first, to get an outside line, for example, enter it (followed by a comma) in front of the CheckFree Node phone number — e.g., 9,879-2222.

CAUTION!

When you're ready, press F5. But note that you should definitely send your first few payment to yourself, as a test, and not send critical payments until you're confident that everything is working right. Only when you get your bank statement will you be sure you're getting the kind of "paper trail" for your payments you'll need, should you ever have to prove something to the IRS or a creditor. Banks are required to provide this detail, and most do, but not all, so it pays to go slow the first month.

DOUBLE CAUTION!

Once you've activated CheckFree for real, you can come back here to change something by selecting the View/Edit CF Setup menu option that will appear. But you'll find that three items are ordinarily frozen: your Social Security number, CF ID number, and the account you've chosen as your CheckFree account. An option will appear to unfreeze them (F6), but make changes ONLY after approval from CheckFree.

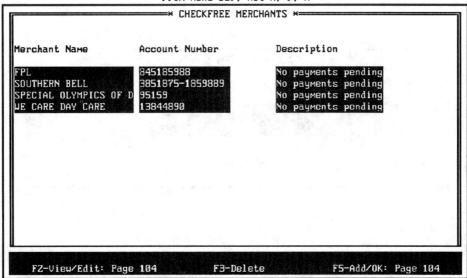

<From Menu Bar, Alt-M, F, M>

CHECKFREE MERCHANT LIST

This is where you maintain your list of CheckFree merchants (as CheckFree calls anyone you pay). To add a new one, press F5. To view or edit an existing one — F2.

HAVE WE JUST BROUGHT YOU HERE IN THE MIDST OF MAKING A PAYMENT?

If so, it's because the payee you told us to pay be CheckFree isn't on this list. You have two choices:

- Point to one of the merchants that IS on this list and press F10. We'll change the name of the payee on your transaction to the one you're pointing at and record the transaction.

- Press F5 to add whomever you're trying to pay to this list. THEN point to that newly created merchant and press F10 to record the transaction.

DELETE

We won't let you delete a CheckFree merchant once it's tied to a transaction on your Check Register. It must remain here until you go through the Close Out Previous Year procedure early next year. But no harm in having it stick around until then.

CHECKFREE LIMITS

A single CF merchant can have no more than 12 one-time payments pending. We won't let you enter another while 12 are on the CheckAlert Register waiting to be paid. Nor can a single CF merchant with a recurring payment pending — such as your monthly mortgage — be assigned a second recurring payment or any one-time payments.

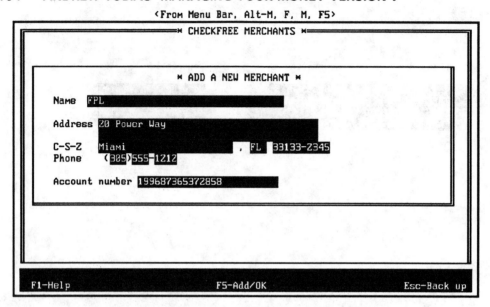

ADD OR EDIT A CHECKFREE MERCHANT

Fill in the blanks and we'll add this "merchant" (as CheckFree calls its payees) to your list. If you're here to edit an existing merchant, change anything you want.

Even if you're not ready to make a payment, we'll transmit your changes to CheckFree, so don't be surprised when we tell you "you have something to send."

The PHONE NUMBER has special importance, because it's what CheckFree looks to first in deciding where to send your payment. The phone number on your bill should be fine, or any other number, including 800-numbers, belonging to this merchant. But don't enter fake numbers, or your own phone number, thinking that it doesn't matter — it does.

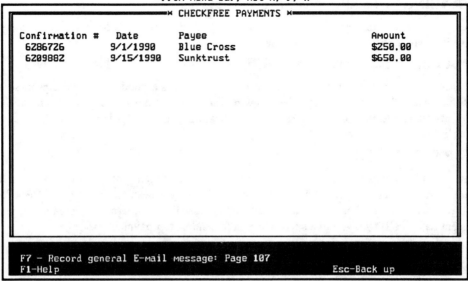

‹From Menu Bar, Alt-M, F, R›

CHECKFREE PAYMENT LIST: SENDING AN INQUIRY

These are all your past CheckFree payments, along with their transmission confirmation numbers. If there's a problem with one of them — typically, the merchant claims it never came — point to it and press F6. As you'll see, we make it very easy to send an inquiry. But in fairness to CheckFree, and for your own sanity, don't schedule payments to arrive at the last possible moment — and then send an inquiry if they're a day or two late. In the overwhelming majority of cases, the "problem" will resolve itself: The U.S. Mail will show up a little later than normal and/or the merchant, unused to CheckFree payments, will credit your account a few days later than it should have. It's not worth your time or CheckFree's to try to track down every such delay. You'll find that some payments, especially those that can be made by Electronic Funds Transfer (EFT) go like clockwork, while others do sometimes get delayed several days. Life is too short to turn each of these into a battle.

For questions or comments not tied to a specific transaction, use F7. You can send CheckFree a brief free-form message of any kind.

INCLUDE YOUR PREFERRED RESPONSE

Often, you will just get a postcard in response to your inquiry. (In a future version, we're working to get you a response by E-mail, direct into MYM.) But it's worth letting CheckFree know what's best. E.g. "Call 212-555-1212 — I have an answering machine" or "If possible, respond to Compuserve #70003,1234."

CHANGING AN EXISTING MESSAGE

When you record a message here, we add it to the Untransmitted E-Mail screen. Until you transmit it, you can view, change, or delete it there.

DO A PRINT SCREEN FOR YOUR FILE BEFORE TRANSMITTING

But once you do transmit it, we keep no record of it, so it's a good idea to do a print-screen of it, either now or, if you forget, when viewing it on the Untransmitted E-Mail screen. Stick the print-screen into the folder you keep for items waiting to be recorded in MYM. When the matter's resolved, toss it out.

STOP PAYMENTS

This screen is for payments that have been made. To stop a future payment, visit the CheckAlert Register and press F3 to delete it. If it's not yet been transmitted to CheckFree, we'll just delete it. If it has been transmitted, but at least five business days remain before the payment date, we'll take you to a special screen to send a stop-payment message.

If five business days do NOT remain before the scheduled payment date, but you want to try to stop payment anyway, call the CF Customer Service Line — 614-899-7500. For a fee of $15, which can sometimes be waived if you catch the transaction early enough, CF *may* be able to stop the payment.

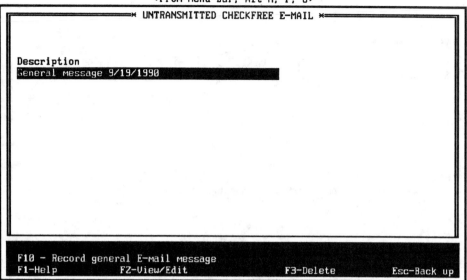

UNTRANSMITTED CHECKFREE E-MAIL

The florist just called to say they found your payment after all? Well, if you haven't yet transmitted your inquiry to CheckFree, you can delete it here — F3. If you've thought of something you meant to add — or decided not to be quite so sarcastic — press F2.

We show here any untransmitted stop-payment instructions you may have entered. To STOP a stop-payment (they delivered the goods after all, so you've decided to pay them after all), just delete it.

DO A PRINT SCREEN BEFORE TRANSMITTING

Once a message has been transmitted, of course, we can't "untransmit" it — nor do we keep a record of it (except for a stop payment) — so it's a good idea to press F2 and do a print-screen. Stick it into the folder you keep for items waiting to be recorded in MYM until the matter's resolved, just in case.

F10 FOR A GENERAL MESSAGE

Here's another place to send a free-form message to CheckFree. But if a particular transaction is involved, it's much better to point to that transaction on the CF CheckFree Register and press F6.

```
                        <Activate in FILE, Money Options>
┌─────────────────────══⊠ CheckAlert for 9/25/1990 ⊠══─────────────────────┐
│┌─────────────────────────────────────────────────────────────────────────┐│
││  Payee/Payor        Postponed Frequency              In/(Out)    CF      ││
││                               (46 times)               $0.00            ││
││  Busy Bank          █         Weekly (51 times)      $9,456.00          ││
││  Sunktrust          █         Monthly                $  650.00          ││
││                                                                         ││
││                                                                         ││
││                                                                         ││
││                                                                         ││
││  Any CheckFree transactions (♩) have already been paid by CheckFree.    ││
││  You may mark any non-CheckFree transactions you wish to postpone.      ││
││  Otherwise, they will be executed in their respective accounts.         ││
││                                                                         ││
│└─────────────────────────────────────────────────────────────────────────┘│
├─────────────────────────────────────────────────────────────────────────┤
│ F7 - Toggle postponed status        F9 - Rotate display                   │
│ F8 - View account balances: Page 110  F10 - Execute/Confirm transactions  │
└───────────────────────────────────────────────────────────────────────────┘
```

CHECKALERT: RECORDING OR POSTPONING TODAY'S TRANSACTIONS

F10 TO PROCEED

We've brought you here first to remind you that these items you scheduled for future payment (or receipt) are now due. When you press F10, we'll go ahead and record them.

All the transactions shown here come from your CheckAlert Register. Once you execute them, they appear on your real Check Register.

F7 TO POSTPONE

To postpone recording one, just point to it and press F7. You'd postpone a payment if, when you checked your account balance, you saw there wasn't enough cash on hand to make it (or if you were just feeling nasty and wanted to keep 'em waiting for their dough). You'd postpone a receipt if it had not, in fact, been received.

Press F9 to see which account a transaction will be recorded in (and then again to restore the normal display). Press F8 to check that account's balance.

Any items you do postpone will simply remain on your CheckAlert Register and show up again here the next time you start the program. If you've postponed so long that now TWO or more of the same item are due — the March rent AND the April rent, say — you won't see any special indication of that here. But we won't lose track. We'll just keep bringing you here each time you start the program to remind you the rent is due (April's rent, once you've paid March) until you get caught up.

ESCAPE NOT ACTIVE HERE

It's important that you deal with this somehow. But just postpone all your transactions (except CheckFree) if you'd rather deal with it later. And remember, of course, that once a transaction does move to your real Check Register, you can still edit or even delete it (except CheckFree). Either way, press F10 to proceed.

CAN'T POSTPONE CHECKFREE

CheckFree transactions are indicated by a checkmark in the righthand column. You can't postpone them, because you've already instructed CheckFree to make them. We just display them here to remind you that today's the day we'll be moving these transactions from your CheckAlert Register to your real I've-spent-it Check Register.

CHANGING OR DELETING

To change or delete a transaction, first postpone it here (so you can proceed), then visit the CheckAlert Register and work with it there.

```
                    <From Menu Bar, Alt-M, A, F8>
 ┌─────────────────── ✳ CheckAlert for 9/27/1990 ✳ ─────────────────┐
 │                                                                   │
 │   ┌────────────────────────────────────────────────────────┐    │
 │   │            ✳ VIEW MONEY ACCOUNT BALANCES ✳             │    │
 │   │                                                        │    │
 │   │   Name         Account #          Type        Balance  │    │
 │   │  Your's       123-456-7       ! Checking    $6,549.22  │    │
 │   │  Mine         122-333-4         Checking    $3,130.00  │    │
 │   │  Sunktrust    241               Savings     $9,800.00  │    │
 │   │  Visa         422-343-598-345   Charge          $0.00  │    │
 │   │                                                        │    │
 │   │                                                        │    │
 │   │       Speed scroll -                                   │    │
 │   │                                                        │    │
 │   └────────────────────────────────────────────────────────┘    │
 │                                                                   │
 ├───────────────────────────────────────────────────────────────┤
 │        F1-Help                              Esc-Back up          │
 └───────────────────────────────────────────────────────────────┘
```

VIEWING ACCOUNT BALANCES

Is there enough money in your account to make the payment? (To see which account you set the payment up to be drawn on, press F9 on the previous screen.) If you're not sure of your credit limit in an account, back up to the Menu Bar, select Money Accounts, and then press F2 to view the credit limit you entered.

```
                        <From Menu Bar, Alt-M, M>
 ┌──────────────────────────── MONEY ACCOUNTS ────────────────────────────┐
 │                                                                          │
 │   Name          Account #          Type          Balance   Last Chk #   │
 │                                                                          │
 │   Your's        123-456-7        ! Checking      $3,574.22        344    │
 │   Mine          122-333-4          Checking      $3,130.00       1215    │
 │   Sunktrust     241                Savings       $9,800.00               │
 │   Visa          422-343-598-345    Charge            $0.00               │
 │                                                                          │
 │                                                                          │
 │                                                                          │
 │                                                                          │
 │                                                                          │
 │   Speed scroll -                         ! indicates CheckFree account   │
 ├──────────────────────────────────────────────────────────────────────┤
 │   F9 - Rearrange accounts                                                │
 │   F10 - Visit this account: Page 117                                     │
 │                                                                          │
 │   F2-View/Edit: Page 113      F3-Delete     F4-Print    F5-Add/OK: Page 113 │
 └──────────────────────────────────────────────────────────────────────┘
```

MONEY ACCOUNTS

Choose a function and read HELP behind the next screen that appears. If you haven't been here before, you'll naturally want to start with F5 to add a new account. Once you do have accounts here:

CHANGING THE LAST CHECK NUMBER (F2)

Point to one of them and press F2 to change something about it — including the "Last Check Number" listed at far right, if you've gotten out of synch.

SEEING YOUR TOTAL AVAILABLE CASH AND CREDIT (F4)

Press F4 (repeatedly) for an Account Summary report that includes at the end a very helpful number you won't find elsewhere: your "total cash plus available credit" — i.e., the absolute maximum you could lay your hands on fast in an emergency (except for what you could borrow in a PORTFOLIO margin account).

GOING TO WORK WITH AN ACCOUNT (F10)

Point to an account and press F10 to visit its Check Register. (Of course, you can also just select Check Register from the MONEY menu and then switch to this account if it's not the one we've displayed.) Then, on the Check Register screen, press F10 again if you want to spend or receive money. (You can also do THAT directly by choosing Spend or Receive from the MONEY menu.) It's faster to work straight from the MONEY menu, but I kind of like to do it the old fashioned way: first see the list of my accounts; then pick one and see its check register; then spend or receive.

DELETING AN ACCOUNT (F3)

Deleting an account – *Careful!* – deletes all traces of it, including all its transactions and their budget allocations. (Any Quick List transactions specific to this account will be changed to "Global," in case you still want to use them.) We won't delete the account without first asking for confirmation. Should you delete one in error, and you haven't already saved your work, select Revert from the FILE menu. We won't let you delete your CheckFree account until you've successfully deactivated CheckFree.

<From Menu Bar, Alt-M, M, F3>

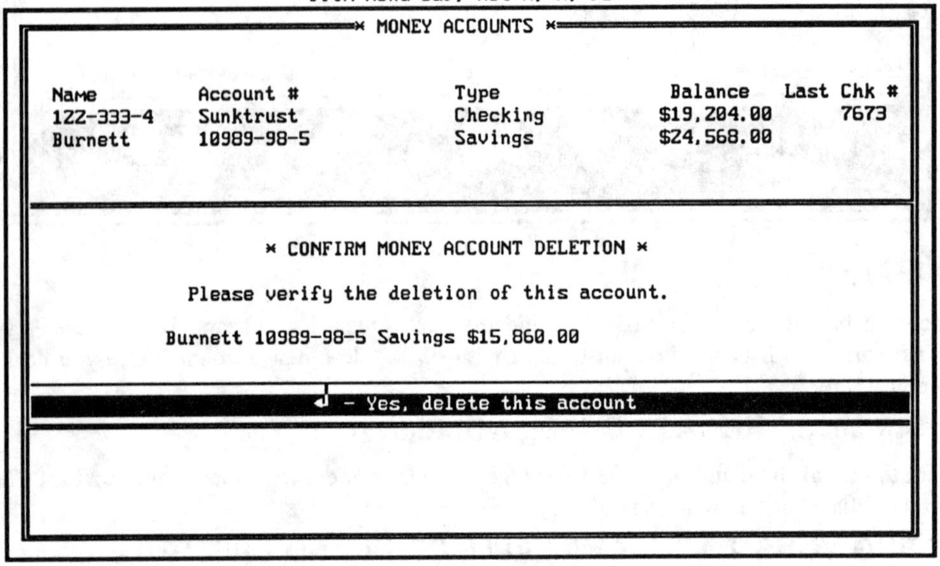
* MONEY ACCOUNTS *
Name Account # Type Balance Last Chk #
122-333-4 Sunktrust Checking $19,204.00 7673
Burnett 10989-98-5 Savings $24,568.00
* CONFIRM MONEY ACCOUNT DELETION *
Please verify the deletion of this account.
Burnett 10989-98-5 Savings $15,860.00
↵ - Yes, delete this account

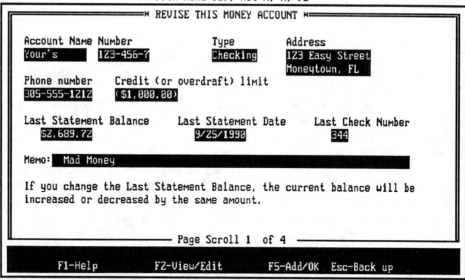

<From Menu Bar, Alt-M, M, F2>

```
══════════════════* REVISE THIS MONEY ACCOUNT *═══════════════

Account Name Number        Type       Address
Your's      123-456-7      Checking   123 Easy Street
                                      Moneytown, FL
Phone number  Credit (or overdraft) limit
305-555-1212  ($1,000.00)

Last Statement Balance    Last Statement Date   Last Check Number
    $2,689.72                 9/25/1990               344

Memo:  Mad Money

If you change the Last Statement Balance, the current balance will be
increased or decreased by the same amount.

──────────────── Page Scroll 1 of 4 ────────────────

     F1-Help         F2-View/Edit      F5-Add/OK  Esc-Back up
```

ADD OR EDIT A MONEY ACCOUNT

Fill in the blanks or revise whatever you've previously entered. When you're ready, press F5 to OK your entries. The only four fields you MUST fill in are the Account Name, Type, Last Statement Date, and Balance. But it's a good idea to fill in as many of the other fields as possible.

■ ACCOUNT NAME

I'm sorry we don't give you much space here. We hope to widen this field next year, but for now ask you to abbreviate as needed. You can use a name like "Mike's Checking" or "Sara's Visa," but it's probably better to use the name of the bank or credit card company. That way, if you ever use Transfer Money to write a check from one of your other accounts to this one, it will use the formal name. (Would First Federal accept a check made out to "Mike's Checking?" Maybe not.)

■ ACCOUNT NUMBER

This field should be plenty wide enough, though it's optional in case you don't want to bother with it.

■ TYPE

Keep track of as many accounts as you want. Checking accounts; "CMA" accounts linked to similarly tagged brokerage accounts; savings accounts; "money-market" accounts (which you may also tag checking or savings — the Fed doesn't know quite which they are, either); charge accounts; home equity accounts (best set up as loans if they're one-time things, but here if you'll be writing checks against them); and even "noncash" accounts (for things like depreciation and noncash charitable donations) and "cash" accounts for any family member brave enough to track all his or her expenditures. It's certainly NOT necessary to set up cash accounts to track every penny. But some will want to, at least until they've figured out where all the money's going.

Others will record only deductible outlays. If you do track cash outlays, toss your receipts along with your bills and such into a folder you keep by your machine. Every so often, clean out the folder (by paying your bills and recording these cash items) — but save the receipts for the IRS! The same goes for charge cards. Keep track of none of the accounts, all the accounts, or only your deductible transactions, depending on how closely you want to track your finances and analyze your budget. The idea is not to waste your time duplicating your monthly statement. When it arrives, however, it shouldn't take more than a few minutes to record the transactions you want to feed in for budget and tax purposes. (Or don't set up charge accounts at all. When you pay VISA, simply allocate the payment over several budget categories — business travel, personal travel, etc. This method provides less detail, but takes less time. Please see "How to Handle Credit Card Accounts" in your manual.) TAB into the choice box to see all the available Types and choose the one you want.

CAN'T CHANGE CMA TYPE

If you decide that the savings account you write checks on is really more of a checking account — or vice versa — it's easy to change the "Type" at any time. The same holds true for any other types — except CMAs. CMAs (Cash Management Accounts) are special because they link to "twins" in PORTFOLIO. You may have up to 9 such linked twins. If you set up one here, we will automatically set up its counterpart in PORTFOLIO. Anything you do that affects the cash balance in one will automatically affect the cash balance in the other. They'll always match. As a result, once you establish a set of CMA twins, you can't delete one without deleting the other; and you can't change the Type.

NO "CHECKFREE" TYPE

You'll notice that there's no such thing as a "CheckFree" type account, because this is not the place CheckFree users designate their CheckFree account. Instead, if you activate CheckFree, we present a list of all your existing accounts you have told CheckFree you'll be using. It's probably a Checking- or CMA-type account.

■ CREDIT (OR OVERDRAFT) LIMIT

Enter the size of your credit line, if any (we'll insist it be negative: it's the maximum negative balance the account allows you), both for your records and so we can include it in our Account Summary report (F4 on the Money Accounts screen), to figure your total available cash-and-credit — i.e., the maximum amount you could lay your hands on in an emergency.

■ LAST CHECK NUMBER

Enter the number of the last check you wrote. Leave this BLANK if it's a charge account or cash account — or blank it out if you accidentally entered one and we've begun numbering, inexorably, like the Sorcerer's Apprentice. Blanking it out here with the Space Bar is the way to stop us.

The ability to change "last check number" is handy because the program always sets it — until you reset it here — to the highest check number you've recorded. If you slipped one day and entered check "15003" when you meant 1503, we'd thereafter start you off in this account each day with #15004. If that ever happens, just select Money Accounts, press F2 to edit the one in question, and fix it here.

■ LAST STATEMENT DATE AND BALANCE

Enter the date and account balance of your most recent statement. (Then, to bring this account up-to-date with reality, you could visit it and record all the subsequent transactions you've made.) The balance for charge accounts and home equity accounts will be zero, if there's no outstanding balance, or NEGATIVE (because, typically, you owe money in these accounts). Enter a positive balance only if, for some reason, you've paid more than you owe and are sitting with a credit.

For a CMA linked to an existing portfolio, the balance comes from that portfolio, regardless of what you enter here. Thereafter, activity in one automatically affects the balance in the other, so they always agree.

■ MEMO

Put your account rep's name — or anything else — on the memo line (which F2 expands to epic length).

■ THE XXX TRICK TO SHARPEN CASH FORECASTING

To X-clude this account's balance from our cash forecast (Forecasting on the MONEY menu), put an XXX anywhere in its name (e.g., VISA-XXX). You'd do this for savings accounts you don't think of as available cash ("I'd sooner die than dip into that account") ... and for credit card and home equity accounts you don't normally pay off in full each month. (You owe the money, and that will be reflected as a liability in your Net Worth; but if you don't have to pay it back any time soon, other than a small monthly minimum, its negative balance doesn't cut into your available cash.)

<From Menu Bar, Alt-M, M, F4, F4>

```
9/21/1990                 Account Summary Report              Page 1
Jane Doe
--------------------------------------------------------------------

    !Account Name:    Your's           Account #:  123-456-7
     Type:            Checking
     Last Check Number:               344
     Credit limit:             ($1,000.00)
     Current Balance:           $2,524.22
     Last Reconciled Date:      9/19/1990
     Last Reconciled Balance:   $3,574.22
     Address:  123 Easy Street
               Moneytown, FL
     Phone Number:  305-555-1212
Mad Money
====================================================================
     Account Name:    Mine             Account #:  122-333-4
     Type:            Checking
     Last Check Number:              1215
     Current Balance:           $3,130.00
     Last Reconciled Date:      9/15/1990


PRESS ANY KEY TO CONTINUE OR ESC TO CANCEL....
```

ACCOUNT SUMMARY REPORT

When you print this report, we recap everything you've told us about your accounts — and total up your total cash on hand plus available credit. In an emergency, this is how much buying/borrowing power you could lay your hands on immediately. It's a number worth knowing — but I hope you never have to use it.

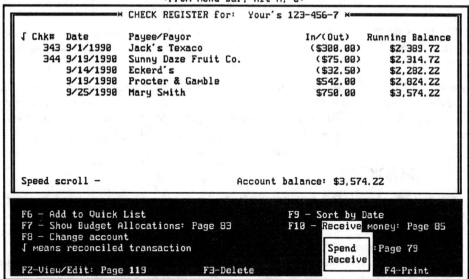

‹From Menu Bar, Alt-M, C›

CHECK REGISTER

This is a display of all the transactions you've made in this account as of this date. Any FUTURE transactions you may have recorded are not displayed here; they sit in the CheckAlert Register. When their day arrives, we display them on the CheckAlert screen. Those you approve for execution then get taken off the CheckAlert Register and recorded here, on your real Check Register. Even so, F4 lets you specify any date range. Our report will include future transactions if you use a future date.

CHOOSE THE RIGHT ACCOUNT (F8)

Check the top line of the screen to be sure this is the account you want to be working with. If not, press F8 and select it.

CHOOSE THE SORT ORDER (F9)

Ordinarily, you'll want to display your transactions by date. But press Ctrl-F and TAB into the Sort-By choice box to sort by Check Number, Payee, Amount, or Status. (Sorting by status is the same as sorting by date, except that it puts all reconciled transactions first.) These other ways of sorting can be quite useful — and they're fun! — but they will make your running balance sort of meaningless.

F4 will print your report in whatever order you've chosen to sort it.

RUNNING BALANCE

This column, though we display it no matter how you've sorted transactions, only really makes sense when you sort by date — it's the same as the running balance you used to keep in your handwritten checkbook (and perhaps still do), so that you know, at any time, how much is in your account. To see the Running Balance column if it's not already displayed, press F7.

CTRL-V — ALL PAYMENTS TO/FROM A PAYEE

Point to any transaction, press Ctrl-V, and we will search through all your accounts to display ALL the payments to (or from) this same payee (or payor) — and then even let you sort and print them.

However, we'll pull up only identical matches. SUNNY POOL SERVICE will be different from SUNNY POOL SERV CO — so, if you need to look in this account only, it may be better to use F9 here to sort by Payee. You'll see SUNNY POOL in all its variations. Or select MONEY's Report Generator to search on the "character string" SUNNY — and include any accounts you want, with any date range.

ADD TO QUICK LIST (F6)

The manual describes the advantages of MONEY's Quick List. I use it for most of my transactions; others will use it not at all, preferring to use Payee Search on the Spend and Receive Money screens. It's up to you. But a quick way to BUILD your Quick List is simply to enter a couple of months' transactions first and then, here, sort them by Payee (so all the duplicates will follow one after another) and go down the list pressing F6 for each Payee you want to include (skipping any duplicates, though there's no harm in including them by mistake).

Later, as you add new payees, just come here, point, and press F6 to add them to your list. Any transaction you add to the Quick List from this account will be "attached" to this account (though you can use it with other accounts if on the Quick List screen you choose to work with "All" transactions). To make one "global," visit the Quick List screen and edit it there.

CHECKFREE TRANSACTIONS — ALL CAPS

If you use CheckFree and this is your CheckFree account, you'll notice that, at CheckFree's request, CheckFree transactions are in all upper-case letters.

SHORTCUT TO SPEND/RECEIVE (F10)

It's really just as fast to press ESCape and then S or R, but for those of us who like to "stay within the account we're working with" and not return to the menu, it's nice to be able to press F10 here. And if you do enter Spend with F10 from here, ESCape there will take you back here, to the Check Register.

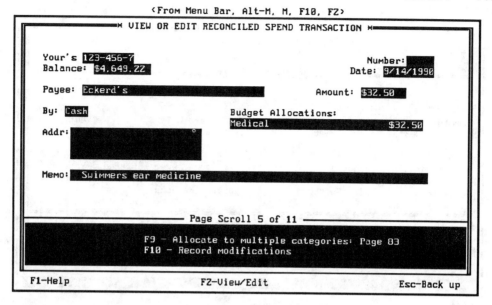

VIEW OR EDIT A TRANSACTION

If you couldn't remember what this transaction was about, you could come here to look at the Memo you tagged it with. Or, if you tagged it with the wrong memo, or entered the wrong amount or date or misspelled the payee or payor's name, you could change any of that here.

Press F9 to change your budget allocations, or to view any beyond the four we have room for here.

Press PgDn, PgUp, Home and End to Page Scroll thru the rest of your transactions, automatically recording any changes as you go (i.e., with Page Scroll, you don't have to press F10 each time).

RECONCILED TRANSACTIONS

If this is a transaction you've already reconciled — meaning that it was OK and made everything balance — you can't change the amount or date (or things could get OUT of balance!). But feel free to modify anything else, including the budget allocations.

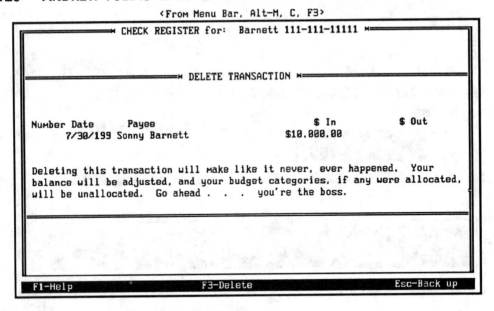

```
                          <From Menu Bar, Alt-M, C, F3>
┌──────────────────────────────────────────────────────────────────────┐
│ ╠══════════════════ ✕ CHECK REGISTER for:  Barnett 111-111-11111 ✕════╣
│
│ ╠═══════════════════════ ✕ DELETE TRANSACTION ✕═══════════════════════╣
│
│
│   Number Date     Payee                        $ In        $ Out
│           7/30/199 Sonny Barnett            $10,000.00
│
│
│   Deleting this transaction will make like it never, ever happened.  Your
│   balance will be adjusted, and your budget categories, if any were allocated,
│   will be unallocated.  Go ahead . . . you're the boss.
│
│
│
│
│
│
│
│
│   F1-Help              °          F3-Delete              Esc-Back up
└──────────────────────────────────────────────────────────────────────┘
```

DELETE A TRANSACTION

CAREFUL

Feel free to delete transactions you've entered by mistake, but think twice about deleting real transactions. Why would you want to do this?

VERY CAREFUL!

If you're deleting a mortgage payment, be advised that we don't undo the updated loan status. We don't turn back the hands of time. So if you should later need to re-enter this check, do it "by hand" — i.e., not with its Quick List transaction or CheckAlert (whichever of our two automated methods you chose). That way, you'll be able to re-record the payment without setting the hands of time ahead yet another month.

DELETING A CHECKFREE TRANSACTION

If this is one of those, you should have no reason to delete it, because if it's here on the Check Register, CheckFree presumably already paid it. But if you managed to get the payment stopped at the last minute (sometimes if you call CheckFree, even with fewer than five business days remaining, you can get a payment stopped), go ahead and delete it here. (To stop a CF payment when at least five business days do remain, point to it on the CheckAlert screen and press F3.)

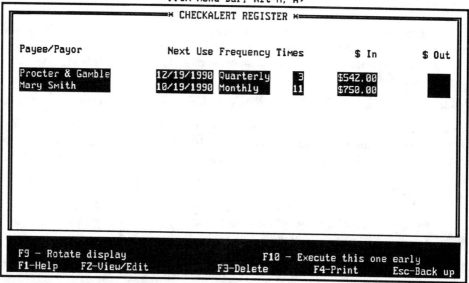

CHECKALERT REGISTER; CF STOP-PAYMENT INSTRUCTIONS

YOUR FUTURE TRANSACTIONS

Here are all the transactions you've entered for payment or receipt at some future date. When that date arrives, we will remind you of each the moment you boot up Managing Your Money. At that time, a single keystroke will approve them all (except those you choose to postpone) and record them for real on your Check Register. Those that were one-time future payments (or the last of a series) will then disappear from this register. Recurring payments that remain to be executed in the future will remain here — but with one fewer "time" remaining to be executed.

HAVE YOU JUST CONVERTED TO VERSION 7?

If you've just converted to Version 7 from an earlier version of Managing Your Money, note that any future transactions you had entered before the conversion WON'T show up here, and we WON'T remind you of them — they'll remain on your regular Check Register.

CHANGE ANYTHING YOU WANT (F2)

Point to any transaction and press F2 to change it, including the number of times in the future you want us to execute it. CheckFree payee names and addresses can't be changed here. Instead, visit the CheckFree Merchants list and edit them there.

ROTATE THE DISPLAY (F9)

If only your computer monitor were wider, we could show you everything on a single screen. Instead, F9 shows you the columns we couldn't fit — the Account Name and Number and, if this is a CheckFree transaction, its confirmation number (or "UNCONFIRMED" if it's not yet been transmitted successfully).

MAKE A PAYMENT OR RECORD A RECEIPT EARLY (F10)

Perhaps you don't WANT to wait till the first of the month this month to pay your rent. Just come here, point to the rent payment, and press F10. Bingo: it's done. (Then select Print Checks or Call CheckFree from the MONEY menu, unless you actually wrote the check by hand.)

DELETE (F3)

If you've moved to a new building, you obviously won't need to keep paying rent to the old landlord. You can delete him here with F3.

CHECKFREE STOP PAYMENTS (F3)

It's easy to delete an "UNCONFIRMED" CheckFree transaction — one you've not yet transmitted to CheckFree. Just do it. If the payment you want to delete IS one you've already transmitted to CheckFree (press F9 to check) ... and if more than five business days remain before it is due to be paid ... pressing F3 will take you to a Send-Stop-Payment screen. Your stop-payment instruction will be transmitted to CF the next time you call. Assuming the transmission succeeds, the confirmation number on this transaction will change to indicate the stop payment, and the amount of this transaction will change to ZERO. (Be sure to call CheckFree right away. They must receive your stop-payment instruction at least five business days in advance of the payment date!) If five business days do NOT remain before the scheduled payment date, but you want to try to stop payment anyway, call the CF Customer Service Line — 614-899-7500. For a fee of $15, which can sometimes be waived if you catch the transaction early enough, CF *may* be able to stop the payment. (If so, go ahead and execute this CheckAlert transaction, to move it onto the Check Register screen — but then delete it there.)

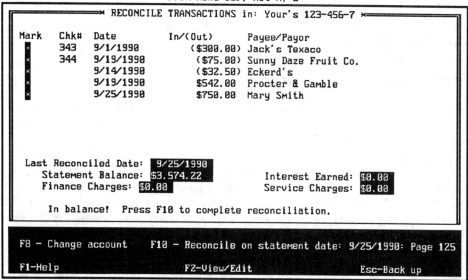

<From Menu Bar, Alt-M, E>

```
                    ╾══ RECONCILE TRANSACTIONS in: Your's 123-456-7 ╾══

  Mark   Chk#  Date         In/(Out)      Payee/Payor
    x    343   9/1/1990     ($300.00)     Jack's Texaco
    x    344   9/19/1990     ($75.00)     Sunny Daze Fruit Co.
    x          9/14/1990     ($32.50)     Eckerd's
    x          9/19/1990     $542.00      Procter & Gamble
    x          9/25/1990     $750.00      Mary Smith




      Last Reconciled Date:  9/25/1990
        Statement Balance:  $3,574.22          Interest Earned:  $0.00
         Finance Charges:  $0.00               Service Charges:  $0.00

        In balance!  Press F10 to complete reconciliation.


   F8 - Change account    F10 - Reconcile on statement date: 9/25/1990: Page 125

   F1-Help                    F2-View/Edit                Esc-Back up
```

RECONCILE AN ACCOUNT

CHOOSE THE RIGHT ACCOUNT – AND BE SURE IT'S SORTED SENSIBLY

If the account you want to reconcile is not already displayed, press F8 to select it. HINT: Your transactions will appear in whatever order you last sorted them. Sorting by Check Number usually makes reconciliation easiest.

ENTER YOUR BALANCE, FEES, AND INTEREST

When your monthly statement arrives, enter the "ending balance" as the Statement Balance at the bottom of the screen, along with any finance charges, fees or interest that you earned.

MARK THE TRANSACTIONS THAT HAVE CLEARED

Now press Ctrl-F to jump to the top of the screen and run down your list, putting an X beside any transaction your bank statement includes. Those left unmarked will remain unreconciled until next month.

HINT: To make this easy, we naturally display here only your UNreconciled transactions. If you've followed the last hint, you should be able simply to go down your bank statement in check-number order (and through your deposits by date), matching one against the other very quickly. Note that we "keep score" at the bottom of the screen as you go. Until the end, you'll ordinarily be out of balance. But once you've finished marking all the transactions that the bank knows about – so that you and the bank agree on what's gone in and out since you reconciled last month – you and the bank should again be in synch.

PRESS F2 TO MAKE CHANGES

If in comparing your statement with MYM you find you misentered a transaction — perhaps you entered $32.31 when you meant $31.32 — just point to it and press F2. (If you find it's the bank that goofed, call the bank!)

WHEN YOU'VE GOT IT, PRESS F10

Once you've marked everything the bank knows about, and entered the statement balance and any fees or interest you paid or received, press F10. We'll add a check mark under the "Reconciled" column on your Check Register.

PROBLEMS?

If this is your first attempt at reconciling, you may simply have entered the wrong "Last Statement Balance" when you set up the account. Select Money Accounts from the MONEY menu, point to this account, press F2 and correct it. Until you successfully reconcile, the "Last Statement Balance" we show should match the "beginning" balance on your bank statement.

Reconciling a statement is really a lot less mysterious than it seems. If you and your bank agree where things were as of the last statement — i.e., your "Last Statement Balance" matches their "beginning balance" — and if you agree what new money has gone in and out of your account this month, then you'll agree where you stand as of this statement. The only difference between your records and the bank's is that you know about some transactions the bank hasn't found out about yet — checks you've written recently that are reflected in YOUR current balance but not the bank's. (Those are the items you leave unmarked on this screen.) And the bank may know about a few that are news to you, like the $3.12 interest you earned or the $4.75 fee you were charged, which you must enter in the fields at the bottom of the screen.

CHARGE ACCOUNT AND HOME EQUITY ACCOUNT BALANCES

In reconciling charge accounts, note that your balance is most likely not $400, as shown on your statement, but MINUS $400 — the amount you owe.

‹From Menu Bar, Alt-M, E, F10›

```
╔══════════════════ ⊶ RECONCILED ACCOUNT ⊶═══════════════════╗
║                                                             ║
║   Now we'll adjust your balance for bank charges and interest earned.  You  ║
║   have entered $0.00 in finance charges, $0.00 in service charges, and $2.00 ║
║   in interest earned.                                        ║
║                                                             ║
║   First, press F9 to allocate bank charges and interest to categories.  ║
║   Then, press F10 and we'll:                                 ║
║                                                             ║
║      (1) Make an adjustment of $2.00 and change the account balance from  ║
║          $6,549.22 to $6,551.22;                             ║
║      (2) Mark your reconciled transactions with a √          ║
║                                                             ║
║                                                             ║
║                                                             ║
║                                                             ║
║                                                             ║
╚═════════════════════════════════════════════════════════════╝
```

F9 - Allocate bank charges and interest: Page 126

ALLOCATING FEES AND INTEREST

I hope that was easier than doing it with a pocket calculator.

If you've entered any interest earned, finance charges or fees paid, we want to allocate them to budget categories. Press F9 to do that the first time, after which we'll remember where these things go but always give you an opportunity to change them.

To blank out a choice you made in error, TAB into the choice box and select the very first choice on the list, the greyed blank.

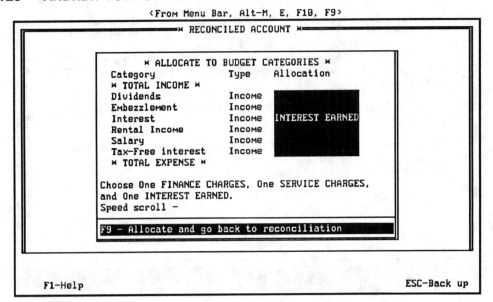

ALLOCATING BANK FINANCE CHARGES AND/OR INTEREST EARNED

If you want to allocate your interest earned and any finance charges and fees you've paid, you do it here. We've saved you the trouble of typing in the amounts; just find the proper budget categories, one at a time, TAB to the right-hand column, and use the choice box that appears to tell us what goes where.

Say you're trying to record a $32.11 service charge, and that you have a budget category called BANK CHARGES. Speed Scroll to that category, press TAB, and type S for "Service Charges." We'll dump your $32.11 into that budget bucket — and automatically allocate your service charges there from now on, each month, unless you change it.

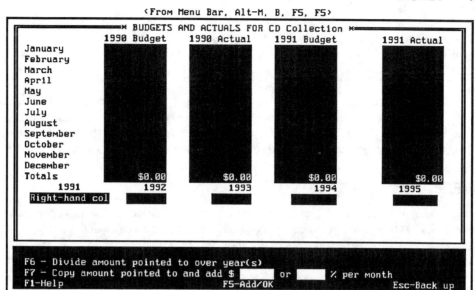

ENTERING YOUR BUDGET
MAKING YOUR BUDGET – THE EASY PART

The hard part of making your budget is knowing what it should be (see below for suggestions). The easy part is entering it here. One way to do it is simply to enter budget estimates for each month by hand. And for a few things, like tuition if it's paid all in a lump in September, you may want to do it.

But for most, there's an easier way. Say you spend $5,000 a year on SUPERMARKET STUFF. Just enter $5,000 in the first field (January of this year, even though it may now be March) and press F6. We'll put the proper amount in each month of this year – and also next year.

Note: Even though it's March, say, there's no harm in having budget numbers entered for the months that have already gone by. If you've turned on 5-YEAR BUDGETING, you'll see four more fields across the bottom of the screen, and we'll fill in those as well. Select Money Options from the FILE menu to turn it on. You can always switch it off later.

But wait! What if you're spending $5,000 a year now, but expect that to rise about half a percent a month with inflation and maybe a tad more indulgence on your part. Press Ctrl-L to jump to the last field on the screen, enter ".5" and then move the cursor back up to the current month. Press F7. See? You were budgeting at the rate of $5,000 a year as of the current month, but for each month thereafter we've now upped your budget by half a percent. Note that the inflation rate we let you enter (or the deflation rate if this is your TOBACCO category and you're weaning yourself off the stuff) is MONTHLY, so you'll ordinarily want to enter a very small number if any. Yes, we may have 5% or even 10% annual inflation – but ordinarily not 5% or 10% a month!

Note also that you can use F7 to inflate your spending a set number of dollars a month, if you like, rather than in percentage terms. You spend $300 a month on groceries now and figure that will be going up $5 a month. Just tell F7 and let it do the rest.

MAKE ANY MANUAL ADJUSTMENTS YOU WANT

Once you've taken advantage of our F6 and F7 shortcuts, you are of course free to fine-tune by hand. You may have entered $100 a month for charitable donations — which is correct for 22 of the 24 months shown here. But then just cursor to December of this year and next — the two months when you traditionally do most of your giving — and manually type $500 instead.

ENTERING ACTUALS

For the months that have already gone by, you have three choices: 1. Just leave the Actuals column blank. This will not give you a very close picture of how you're doing this year, so I recommend: 2. Just enter estimates — probably the same figure you have in the budget column for each month. Unless it's early in the year, this is what I'd recommend. But if you're ambitious: 3. Leave Actuals blank for now, but then go through your checkbook and credit card statements since the start of the year and use Spend Money to enter all those transactions, allocating them to their proper categories. If you do that, the Actuals for these months will fill up all by themselves — and be exactly accurate.

MAKING YOUR BUDGET — THE HARD PART

But how much DO you spend on groceries? And how much SHOULD you spend? As far as the "do" part is concerned, you can just take a guess; or you can look through your last couple of months' check stubs and receipts and take a more educated guess. The first year, you may not want to spend too much time trying to guess what you spend, because AFTER the first year, if you record your income and outgo in MYM, you'll know precisely — and, as part of the Close Out Previous Year process, we offer to make up next year's budget based on the past year's actual results (inflated or deflated, depending on your wishes).

The "should" part comes at the end of the process. After you've entered your budget for all the categories you can think of (going through last year's checkbook and credit card receipts and thinking where your dimes and ten dollar bills go will help think of them all), look at the Budget Categories screen to see how you're doing.

Are you making a "profit" (spending less than you earn)? Will there be enough cash coming in the door to pay for everything you've budgeted? And if the answer is yes, then the next question is: are you making enough of a profit? Does your budget include categories for saving? (If so, they should probably have an XX in the names you give them, so you can use F7 on the Budget Categories screen to see your totals with and without these "soft" categories.) The Retirement Planning and Tuition Planning sections of ANALYZE will help you to see what you need to put aside.

If, like most of us, you find there's not quite enough coming in to cover everything going out, plus the savings you'd like to accumulate, it makes sense to go back through your other budget categories and trim. But where you should trim — well, that's entirely up to you.

‹From Menu Bar, Alt-M, B›

```
════════════════════ ×= INCOME & EXPENSES:   TAX CATEGORIES ×═══════════════
   Budget
   Category              Type      Annual Total  Tax Category
   × TOTAL INCOME ×                  $2,042.00
   Dividends             Income        $542.00   Dividend Income        [B]
   Embezzlement          Income          $0.00   Not a Tax Category
   Interest              Income          $0.00   Interest Income        [B]
   Rental Income         Income      $1,500.00   Pre-Enact Act RE Inc   [E]
   Salary                Income          $0.00   Salary               [1040]
   Tax-Free interest     Income          $0.00   Not a Tax Category
   × TOTAL EXPENSE ×                 $3,137.50
   Automotive            Expense       $300.00   Not a Tax Category
   Child Care            Expense       $880.00   Child Care Expense [1040]
   Clothing              Expense       $350.00   Not a Tax Category
   Contributions         Expense         $0.00   Charity Contributions [A]
   Electrical            Expense         $0.00   Not a Tax Category
   Groceries             Expense        $75.00   Not a Tax Category

   Speed scroll —

 ┌──────────────────────────────────────────────────────────────────────────┐
 │ F6 — Empty all categories             F8 — Rotate to show: Annual Totals   │
 │ F7 — Exclude "X" categories           F9 — Summary graphs                  │
 │                                                                            │
 │ F2-View/Edit: Page 132     F3-Delete     F4-Print     F5-Add/OK: Page 134  │
 └──────────────────────────────────────────────────────────────────────────┘
```

BUDGET CATEGORIES:
YOUR LIST DISPLAYED THREE WAYS

BE SURE TO SEE ALL THREE DISPLAYS (F8)

There's a lot of power on this screen, but because we can't add four inches to the right side of your monitor, you've got to press F8 repeatedly to see it!

Hint: There's no need to jump down to the bottom of the screen to make a choice. Just keep pressing F8 and watch us rotate.

DELETE CATEGORIES YOU DON'T WANT (F3)

If you're here for the first time, it makes sense to run down our list of categories and delete any that definitely do not apply to you. Just press F3.

We won't let you delete a category once you've allocated actual transactions to it. To delete it anyway, first press F2, F10 to blank out the "Actuals" column with the Space Bar. Then come back and press F3.

As you run through our list, you'll find some categories you want to keep — but that you want to rename. Press F2 and then Ctrl-F or the Up Arrow and type in the new name.

If you decide to keep one of our sample categories, check to be sure you agree with its tax allocation. (Press F8 to see it.) Maybe in your line of work you can deduct something we assumed you couldn't.

ADD NEW CATEGORIES (F5)

Next, press F5 to add new budget categories. A new screen will appear for that purpose, complete with its own HELP.

Hint: Although this is the computer age, it may help to work out your budget by printing a list of our sample categories (F4) and playing around with it on paper.

VIEW OR WORK WITH A CATEGORY (F2)

F2 calls up a display of the category you've highlighted — including summary displays for TOTAL INCOME, TOTAL EXPENSE, and NET PROFIT.

SPEED SCROLL to any category just by pressing its first letter or two. Once there, you can enter or modify your budget for that category, see how your actual spending compares, change the tax treatment of the category — even draw graphs.

PAGE SCROLL

Note that when you do press F2 to view a category, you may then move directly from one to the next — without taking the time to record your changes each time, come back here, and select the next one — by using Page Scroll. It's a quick way to "page" through each of your budget categories.

REPORTS AND GRAPHS (F4 AND F9)

Press F4 to see our reports and F9 for graphs.

EXCLUDE XX AND XXX CATEGORIES (F7)

Use F7 to include or exclude from our three summary totals TOTAL INCOME, TOTAL EXPENSE, and NET PROFIT any categories that you've tagged with XX or XXX. As explained in the HELP you'll see when you press F5 to add a new category, these XX and XXX tags designate "spending" categories on savings and investments that don't actually make you any poorer. Want to see what your budgeted profit for the year is, excluding whatever you "spend" on your monthly mutual fund investment? Use F7.

- Note: This trick works on the display only. Reports you print WILL include XX and XXX categories in their totals, no matter how you have F7 set.

- Hint: There's no need to jump down to the bottom of the screen to make a choice. Just press F7 and we'll switch from one to the other.

IF OUR "ANNUAL TOTAL" COLUMN SEEMS WRONG

If the "Annual Totals" we show here seem wrong, it's because you have to understand what they represent. For each budget category we show the total of three things: (1) your ACTUAL expenditures through last month; (2) your BUDGETED expenditures for next month through the end of the year; (3) for this month, whichever's higher — your budget or the actual expenditures you've already recorded.

So if it's May and you've just set up a $1,000-a-month budget category, the annual total we show here will NOT be $12,000 (it will be $8,000).

<From Menu Bar, Alt-M, O, Income Summary, F2>

```
                                ═══* TOTAL INCOME *═══
            1990 Budget    1990 Actual      Difference     1991 Budget
January      $9,654.00     $10,654.00       $1,000.00        $782.41
February     $2,867.00      $2,867.00           $0.00        $786.33
March        $1,029.00      $1,045.00          $16.00        $790.30
April        $3,886.00      $3,886.00           $0.00        $794.30
May          $1,295.00      $1,395.00         $100.00        $798.34
June         $1,000.00      $1,000.00           $0.00        $802.41
July         $1,000.00      $1,000.00           $0.00        $806.52
August       $1,000.00      $1,000.00           $0.00        $810.67
September    $1,000.00      $3,042.00       $2,042.00        $814.86
October        $770.83          $0.00       ($770.83)        $819.08
November       $774.66          $0.00       ($774.66)        $823.35
December       $778.51          $0.00       ($778.51)        $827.65
Totals      $25,055.00     $25,889.00         $834.00      $9,656.22


          1991            1992            1993            1994            1995
 Right-hand col     $10,282.25      $10,980.72      $11,742.19      $12,000.00

                         ──── Page Scroll 1  of 26 ────
```

```
F9 - Graph Bar
```

VIEW BUDGET SUMMARY TOTALS

You can't change anything on this screen, since it's the total of the categories beneath it. And note that the F7 "Exclude" option on the previous screen affects the totals shown there only — not these, which include all your categories, regardless of how F7 is set.

‹From Menu Bar, Alt-M, B, F2, F10›

```
══════════════════ ✻ VIEW OR EDIT: Embezzlement ✻ ═══════════════════
                1990 Budget      1990 Actual       Difference      1991 Budget
   January        $1,000.00        $1,000.00           $0.00         $1,000.00
   February       $1,000.00        $1,000.00           $0.00         $1,000.00
   March          $1,000.00        $1,000.00           $0.00         $1,000.00
   April          $1,000.00        $1,000.00           $0.00         $1,000.00
   May            $1,000.00        $1,000.00           $0.00         $1,000.00
   June           $1,000.00        $1,000.00           $0.00         $1,000.00
   July           $1,000.00        $1,000.00           $0.00         $1,000.00
   August         $1,000.00        $1,000.00           $0.00         $1,000.00
   September       $1,000.00       $1,000.00           $0.00         $1,000.00
   October        $1,000.00                         ($1,000.00)       $1,000.00
   November       $1,000.00                         ($1,000.00)       $1,000.00
   December       $1,000.00                         ($1,000.00)       $1,000.00
   Totals        $12,000.00        $9,000.00        ($3,000.00)      $12,000.00
         1991           1992             1993             1994            1995
   Right-hand col   $12,000.00       $12,000.00       $12,000.00       $12,000.00

   ─────────────────── Page Scroll 3 of 26 ───────────────────

    F6 – Divide amount over years  [        ]            F9 – Graph Bar
    F7 – Copy amount and add $ [      ]  or  [      ]  % per month
    F8 – Change tax category: Page 133

    F1-Help                       F5-Add/OK                    Esc-Back up
```

VIEW OR EDIT A BUDGET CATEGORY
CHANGING THE NAME OR TAX CATEGORY

Here's a display of the budget category you selected. Change its name if you like by pressing Ctrl-F or the up arrow and typing over it. Change its tax category with F8. Transactions you've already entered will follow right along — they'll be tagged with the new budget category name and/or tax treatment.

PAGE SCROLL

Use PgDn, PgUp, Home, and End to Page Scroll thru your other categories, automatically recording any changes as you go.

CHANGING NUMBERS – CAREFUL

You can change any month's entry simply by typing over it or using our shortcuts, F6 and F7. That's fine for your "budget" numbers (one way to stay within your budget is to keep increasing it), but be careful about changing actuals. (To deter you, we make you press F10 first, to unfreeze them.) Say you had written checks to charity totaling $200 in May. The program would show that total. If you changed it to $750, WE'D BELIEVE YOU and that would become the new figure for May.

The extra $550 you dropped in could reflect the value of the Spiro Agnew autograph you donated to the historical society, or the cash you plan to tell the IRS you thrust upon the Salvation Army Santa. (In May?) But because you just dropped it in here like this, we WILL include it in your tax planning (so be careful not to stick in something crazy), but we WON'T give you any record of it when you go to print out all your deductible expenditures. How can we? We don't know what it is! (For help recording noncash expenditures like the donation of this autograph, see the tail end of HELP behind Spend Money.)

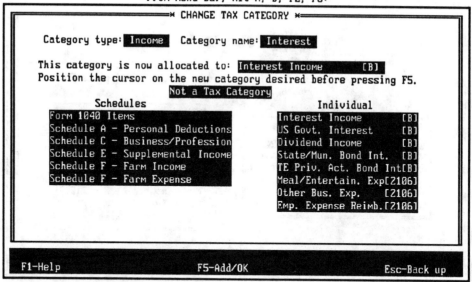

<CHANGE A TAX CATEGORY
━━━━━━━━━━━━━━━━━━━━━━━━━━━━━━━━

CHANGE A TAX CATEGORY

Goof in selecting a tax category for your LAKE HOUSE RENTAL income budget category? Just change it here. All the transactions you've dumped into that budget bucket will, in turn, be dumped into this new tax barrel.

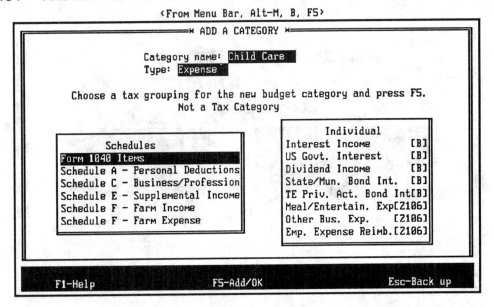

<From Menu Bar, Alt-M, B, F5>

```
═══════════════════ ✳ ADD A CATEGORY ✳ ═══════════════════

              Category name: Child Care
              Type: Expense

      Choose a tax grouping for the new budget category and press F5.
                      Not a Tax Category

    ┌─────────────────────────────┐    ┌─────────────────────────────┐
    │          Schedules          │    │          Individual         │
    │ Form 1040 Items             │    │ Interest Income        [B]  │
    │ Schedule A - Personal Deductions │ │ US Govt. Interest      [B]  │
    │ Schedule C - Business/Profession │ │ Dividend Income        [B]  │
    │ Schedule E - Supplemental Income │ │ State/Mun. Bond Int.   [B]  │
    │ Schedule F - Farm Income    │    │ TE Priv. Act. Bond Int[B]   │
    │ Schedule F - Farm Expense   │    │ Meal/Entertain. Exp[2106]   │
    └─────────────────────────────┘    │ Other Bus. Exp.    [2106]   │
                                        │ Emp. Expense Reimb.[2106]   │
                                        └─────────────────────────────┘

    F1-Help                 F5-Add/OK                 Esc-Back up
```

ADD A BUDGET CATEGORY; THE MEMO TRICK; XX AND XXX

This is the HELP both for adding a new budget category and for assigning it a tax treatment, should you choose to do that now. You'll find the tax treatment HELP at the end of this message.

WHAT YOU DO HERE

The only things you *must* do here are give your new category a name and, after you've named it, tell us whether it's Income (SALARY) or Expense (MAID'S SALARY). Answer NO to our next question and you can press F5 and be on your way. (Personally, though, I'd answer YES and not put off assigning this category a tax treatment and making up its budget.)

BUT GIVE IT SOME THOUGHT

You should take some time to plan your budget categories. A few will be Income categories, such as SALARY, your SPOUSE'S SALARY, RENT, if you receive it, ALIMONY, if you receive it, FREELANCE FEES, DIVIDENDS, INTEREST, and that monthly check from GRANDFATHER'S TRUST. The rest will be Expense categories. You can make them as broad or narrow as you like. Lump TRAVEL AND ENTERTAINMENT all in one ... or list PERSONAL TRAVEL, BUSINESS TRAVEL, PERSONAL ENTERTAINMENT, and BUSINESS ENTERTAINMENT as four separate categories. (Or even have HIS and HERS for each of these, which would make eight.)

THE MEMO TRICK FOR "SUB-CATEGORIES"

Managing Your Money does not provide for sub-categories as such. But if you did lump all your travel and entertainment expenses into one master category, there's a way you could still separate just HIS or HERS, or just TRAVEL or just ENTERTAINMENT. Namely: when you record a transaction, give it a unique "code" in the memo (in the second line, if you don't want it to appear on the check we print). That way, you can later tell the Report Generator to list and total only those TRAVEL AND ENTERTAINMENT expenses that include the "*HIS*" code. (I'd use the asterisks in my code so that memo-search didn't also include any other transactions with the letters h-i-s someplace in them, as in the word H-I-S-TORY.)

THE TAXCUT CONNECTION TRICK

Or, if you do go the "micro" route and use a lot of separate budget categories — eight of them in the his-and-hers business-and-personal travel-and-entertainment example above — there's a way to get reports that lump them all together. Namely, you can visit the TaxCut Connection on the TAX menu, even if you don't own the TaxCut Connection, and see how it allows you to group various categories together and print a report.

BUDGETING FOR SAVINGS: THE XX AND XXX TRICK

If you budget for expenditures that don't really make you poorer, like what you "spend" on Savings Bonds or on paying down your mortgage, include XX anywhere in the category name — SAVINGS BONDS-XX — and F7 we'll let you XX-clude it from the expenses that count against your Net Profit. (F7 on the Budget Categories screen Excludes or Includes these categories in your totals.) If it's a category that doesn't even tie up any cash, let alone make you poorer ... like what you budget to put in your money-market account each month (if you budget for this) ... use a triple XXX — MONEY MKT-XXX — and we'll also XXX-clude it from our analysis of your available cash. (Select Forecasting on the MONEY menu to see that analysis.) After all, "spending" $10,000 to build up the balance in your money market fund is a lot different from spending it on a weekend in Tokyo.

ASSIGNING A TAX TREATMENT

If you answer YES to our question about selecting a tax category, we pop up a set of choices. For a category like groceries, just move the cursor to NOT A TAX CATEGORY (if it's not already there) and press F5. But rent you receive goes on SCHEDULE E and medical bills go on SCHEDULE A. A quick look at last year's tax return will remind you how different items of income and expense are reported.

<From Menu Bar, Alt-M, B, F5, F5>

```
═══════════════════════✖ CHOOSE TAX CATEGORY ✖═══════════════════════

                    Category name: Child Care
                    Category type: Expense

     Position the cursor on the category desired before pressing F5.
          INCOME                      INCOME                    EXPENSE
     Salary             [1040] Moving Exp. Reimb. [1040] Alimony Paid        [1040]
     Salary - Spouse    [1040]                           Child Care Expense [1040]
     Other Income       [1040]          EXPENSE            FICA              [1040]
     State/Local Refunds[1040] IRA Contributions  [1040] FICA - Spouse      [1040]
     Alimony Received   [1040] IRA Payments/Spouse[1040] Early Withd Penalty[1040]
     Pensions/Annuities [1040] Keogh Payments     [1040] Tax Credits        [1040]
     Soc. Sec. Income   [1040] Keogh - Spouse     [1040]
     SS Inc. - Spouse   [1040] Federal Withholding[1040]
     Unemployment Comp. [1040] Fed. With. - Spouse[1040]
     IRA Distributions  [1040] Fed. Estimated Tax [1040]
     IRA Distrib./Spouse[1040]



        F1-Help              F5-Add/OK              Esc-Back up
```

ASSIGN A TAX CATEGORY

Position the cursor and press F5. Or, if you can't find the tax barrel you're looking for, back up (ESCape) and try looking for it on a different Schedule. There should be a place for everything, and your tax return from last year should be a guide. Items you don't find by name can generally be dumped into a more general category. Although lumped together here, we'll still keep them separate when it comes to printing your budget reports and the paperwork you'll need to prepare your taxes.

THE SCHEDULE E NIGHTMARE

For passive partnerships or actively-managed real estate holdings acquired after enactment of the Tax Reform Act of 1986 (October 23, 1986), choose Post-Enactment Passive Income (or Expense) or Post-Enactment Active Real Estate Income (or Expense). Those acquired before October 23 are Pre-Enactment.

For Real Estate to be active means that it is managed by you: you collect rents, see to repairs, screen tenants (and windows), etc. Active, non-real estate ventures are those in which you have material participation (like a law partnership).

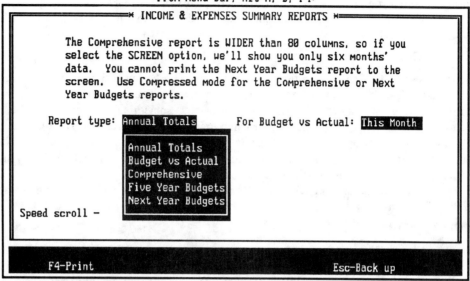

<From Menu Bar, Alt-M, B, F4>

```
═══════════════════════════╾✶ INCOME & EXPENSES SUMMARY REPORTS ✶═══════════════════════════

   The Comprehensive report is WIDER than 80 columns, so if you
   select the SCREEN option, we'll show you only six months'
   data.  You cannot print the Next Year Budgets report to the
   screen.  Use Compressed mode for the Comprehensive or Next
   Year Budgets reports.

   Report type: Annual Totals        For Budget vs Actual: This Month

                 Annual Totals
                 Budget vs Actual
                 Comprehensive
                 Five Year Budgets
                 Next Year Budgets
   Speed scroll -


      F4-Print                                        Esc-Back up
```

PRINTING HINTS

Fill in the blanks and press F4 (and then again, if we give you new choices to make). Stop printing once it's begun by pressing ESCape.

PRINTING ON PAPER

If printing or condensed printing doesn't work, visit Printer Setup by selecting Program Setup on the FILE menu.

If printing works but you're not thrilled with how the report looks, try printing it to disk and summoning it into our word processor, as described below. You can then make any changes you want and print it out from there.

To change the name we automatically print with today's date at the top of the report, select Program Setup from the FILE menu and then Preferences and change it there.

PRINTING TO THE SCREEN

Printing to the screen is fast and, except for reports over 80 columns, shows how your report will look on paper. The one drawback: you can't scroll back and forth through the report ... only "forth." But there's an easy solution. Just "print" the report to a file on your disk; then summon that file with Ctrl-W, our word processor, and view it — or edit it — any way you like.

PRINTING TO DISK

To send a report to the disk in drive a:, say, give it a filename like "A:REPORT.DOC". Then, to import the report into MYM-Write, just press Ctrl-W and tell F8 to summon a "directory of A:REPORT.DOC" and F2 to work with it. Of course, changes you make to a report with MYM-Write will not affect your actual data in Managing Your Money. [Floppy Users: If you run MYM on floppy disks, it's best to insert a blank disk in the drive you'll be printing to before you press F4, so as not to clutter your working disks. The drive you choose for this disk-swap should be the drive not in use by the disk that contains "3.chp," the file that's running the show.]

PRINT-TO-DISK HINT

Hard-drive users: It's fine to use a floppy disk for your reports, but easier just to save them to a file on your hard disk. Reports you don't plan to save permanently − "just-looking"-type reports − you might want to get in the habit of naming something very quick to type. No need to spend time thinking of some clever name each time! I use a one-keystroke file name: "A". Each new report by this name overwrites the last ... but that's good, because I didn't want to save them anyway, and this keeps my disk from getting cluttered with unwanted reports. To summon my just-looking-type report to the word processor (so I can scroll back and forth through it and use MYM-Write's "Find" feature), I need type just a single character in telling F8 the file to look for: A.

EXPORT FORMATS

When printing to disk, we offer three formats: our standard REPORT format, but also EXPORT and 1-2-3, for reports you can import into database or spreadsheet programs. (For help importing, please consult THEIR manuals or staff.) We recognize that our export capability is not entirely state-of-the-art. It will be better next year. TRY IT! With printing, a little trial and error is worth twice its weight in HELP.

```
                       <From Menu Bar, Alt-M, B, F4, F4>
┌─────────────────────────────────────────────────────────────────────────┐
│ 9/21/1990                Budget Category Annual Totals         Page 1     │
│ Jane Doe                                                                  │
│ ─────────────────────────────────────────────────────────────────────── │
│                                                                           │
│ Category              Type        Tax Pointer            Annual Total     │
│ Dividends             Income      Dividend Income    [B]    $14,713.00    │
│ Embezzlement          Income      Not a Tax Category        $12,000.00    │
│ Interest              Income      Interest Income    [B]         $0.00    │
│ Rental Income         Income      Pre-Enact Act RE Inc [E]   $1,500.00    │
│ Salary                Income      Salary          [1040]         $0.00    │
│ Tax-Free interest     Income      Not a Tax Category            $0.00     │
│ ─────────────────────────────────────────────────────────────────────── │
│ Total of Income Categories                                  $28,213.00    │
│ ─────────────────────────────────────────────────────────────────────── │
│ Automotive            Expense     Not a Tax Category         $1,562.42    │
│ Child Care            Expense     Child Care Expense [1040]    $880.00     │
│ Clothing              Expense     Not a Tax Category          $350.00     │
│ Contributions         Expense     Charity Contributions [A]      $0.00    │
│ Electrical            Expense     Not a Tax Category             $0.00     │
│ Groceries             Expense     Not a Tax Category           $75.00     │
│ Insurance             Expense     Not a Tax Category            $0.00     │
│                                                                           │
│ PRESS ANY KEY TO CONTINUE OR ESC TO CANCEL....                            │
└─────────────────────────────────────────────────────────────────────────┘
```

```
                              <From Menu Bar, Alt-M, L>
┌─────────────────────────════════* LOAN RECORDS *══════─────────────────────────┐
│ ┌─────────────────────────────────────────────────────────────────────────┐   │
│ │                                                                           │   │
│ │  Loan      Lender/    Borrowed/ Current               Annual Remain.      │   │
│ │  Date      Borrower   Lent      Balance    Type  For   Rate    PMts   Payment  Freq│
│ │  7/30/199  NorthWest     B      $15,000.00 Inte  Auto  11.000%  48       $0.00  M│
│ │  7/30/199  SunkTrust     L  $1,000,000.00 Mort  Other 15.000% 365  $12,635.65  M│
│ │                                                                           │   │
│ │                                                                           │   │
│ │                    * indicates Escrows included in Payment                │   │
│ │                                                                           │   │
│ └─────────────────────────────────────────────────────────────────────────┘   │
│ ┌───────────────────────────────────────────────────────────────────────────┐ │
│ │ F6 - Create CheckAlert transaction: Page 81                                 │ │
│ │ F7 - Create Quicklist transaction: Page 89                                  │ │
│ │ F8 - Record extra payment to principal (CheckAlert transactions): Page 148  │ │
│ │                                                                             │ │
│ │ F2-View/Edit: Page 145   F3-Delete    F4-Print    F5-Add/Save: Page 141     │ │
│ └───────────────────────────────────────────────────────────────────────────┘ │
└─────────────────────────────────────────────────────────────────────────────────┘
```

LOAN RECORDS

Here are your loans, both those you've taken out (your car loan and mortgage) and those you've made (the $2,000 you lent your daughter).

PRESS F5 TO ADD A NEW LOAN

There's a lot more help behind Adding a Loan, which you do with F5.

PRESS F6 OR F7 AFTER ADDING A NEW LOAN

Once you do add a new loan, you should definitely point to it here and press either F6 or F7 to create its linked transaction − either a CheckAlert transaction or a Quick List transaction. Although I am partial to the Quick List most of the time, I'd recommend your using CheckAlert for your mortgages. Easy as the Quick List is, for identical periodic transactions like your mortgage payment, CheckAlert is even easier. The CheckAlert choice here is available ONLY for mortgage-type loans, as you'll see if you try to use it with some other kind of loan.

ALWAYS USE A LOAN'S LINKED TRANSACTION TO MAKE PAYMENTS

To pay off or pay down a loan, always use its Quick or CheckAlert transaction, so we can update the status of the loan. (If you just use the Spend Money screen, we won't know you've made a payment.)

WELL, ALMOST ALWAYS. LATE PENALTIES

Late Penalties should be recorded separately, even if it means printing a separate check. Just go to Spend Money, write the check, and allocate it 100% to interest. DON'T use a mortgage loan's Quick transaction to record a late penalty, lest we confuse it for a repayment of principal.

MORTGAGE PRINCIPAL PRE-PAYMENTS — F8

Your normal monthly mortgage payment is $708.14 but you want to send an extra $1,000 this month to pay down the loan. How you do that depends on which kind of transaction you linked to the loan:

- If (despite my recommendation above) you've set up your mortgage with a Quick List transaction, making a principal prepayment is a snap. On the Quick List screen, simply boost the amount of your payment that month to include it. We assume that anything in excess of what you owe is a principal prepayment; so if you change the regular $708.11 monthly payment to $1,708.11, we'll assume that extra $1,000 is a principal prepayment and adjust your loan and your budget accordingly.

- If you set it up as a CheckAlert transaction (which is in other respects more convenient), you need to come here and press F8 to make an extra payment.

OUR LOAN SUMMARY REPORT — F4

The thing I like about this report is that at the end we summarize the total amounts you've borrowed and lent, and show the weighted average interest rate for each total. In my own case, I can see that my average borrowing cost is currently 10.31% and the average interest I'm charging is 14.45%. The only problem is that I am more likely to have to repay the money I've borrowed than to get back all the money I've lent.

VIEW OR EDIT A LOAN; PRINT AMORTIZATION SCHEDULE — F2

At any time, press F2 to check the status of your loan — or, with a mortgage, to see how it might look after 100 more payments or to print its amortization schedule.

RATE OR ESCROW CHANGES — F2

Should the rate on a Variable-Rate mortgage change, press F2 from this screen and then F6. We'll adjust the monthly payment AND your budget allocations for the months to come.

DELETING A MORTGAGE — F3

Deleting a mortgage also deletes its Quick or CheckAlert transaction and sucks budget allocations back out of the categories to which they'd been allocated.

LOAN BALANCES SHOW UP IN NET WORTH

Balances on loans here automatically sum to NET WORTH as assets (money you've loaned) or liabilities (money you owe).

AMORTIZATION SCHEDULE OFF BY A FEW PENNIES?

If your bank's amortization schedule varies from ours the difference is likely to be trivial. Ignore it! Or, if you can't stand the imprecision (they say your balance after 43 payments is $93,021.89 but we say it's $93,042.11) you'll have to set this up as a "Special" loan and forgo our automatic functions. Enter the monthly principal and interest in your budget by copying the bank's amortization schedule, and allocate each month's payment according to their printout. (I think this is a terrible waste of your time, but you're the boss.)

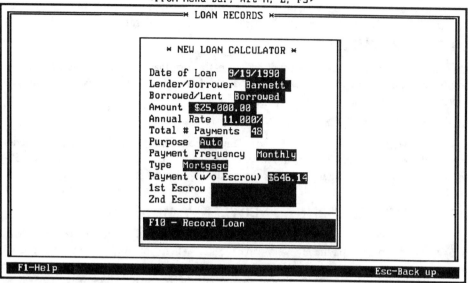

<From Menu Bar, Alt-M, L, F5>

```
════════════════════════ LOAN RECORDS ════════════════════════

                  ═ NEW LOAN CALCULATOR ═

           Date of Loan  9/19/1990
           Lender/Borrower  Barnett
           Borrowed/Lent  Borrowed
           Amount  $25,000.00
           Annual Rate  11.000%
           Total # Payments  48
           Purpose  Auto
           Payment Frequency  Monthly
           Type  Mortgage
           Payment (w/o Escrow)  $646.14
           1st Escrow
           2nd Escrow

           F10 - Record Loan

 F1-Help                                      Esc-Back up
```

ADD A NEW LOAN

■ DATE OF LOAN

If you're just taking it out now, it's today. If it's a loan from long ago, enter the date you first took it out. Once you record a loan, you can't change the date (unless you delete it and reenter it), so take a minute to find the original papers or to figure it out based on the number of payments left.

If you'd prefer, enter it with today's date anyway, but instead of calling it a 20-year $75,000 mortgage, set it up as a 17-year-five month $73,109 mortgage (or whatever it now is).

■ LENDER/BORROWER

Enter the name of the institution or person from whom you're borrowing or to whom you're lending.

■ BORROWED/LENT

I know. Neither a borrower or a lender be. But since you've apparently ignored that advice, tell us which you are here.

■ AMOUNT

Enter the original amount of the loan if you're setting it up with the original date; or enter the outstanding balance as of today if you're entering it as if it were a brand new loan today.

■ ANNUAL RATE

Enter the interest rate if this is an Interest-Only or Special type loan (see below), but LEAVE IT BLANK if it's a mortgage, and let us calculate it based on the term and monthly payment amount. It's possible that what your bank calls a 10.5% mortgage we will call 10.51% or 10.49% — that sort of thing — because some banks use a slightly nonstandard calculation or round things differently from others. It's more important that you enter the precise monthly payment (since the bank is expecting it) than the precise interest rate.

■ TOTAL PAYMENTS

If this is a 30-year loan and you set it up with the original loan date, then there are 360 monthly payments. (If you set it up with today's date, and have already made the first 17 payments on the loan, then it is a 343-payment loan.)

■ BIWEEKLY LOANS

These are a special case, as described below. Enter the number of MONTHLY payments this loan would have required if it were a conventional loan — i.e., 360 if it's based on a 30-year loan. We'll automatically change this to the actual number of biweekly payments when you press F10.

■ PAYMENT FREQUENCY — BIWEEKLY MORTGAGES

The only tricky one is Biweekly. It has a special meaning: namely, only those loans that have you pay half a monthly payment every two weeks. When you do, you're paying 26 half-month payments a year — the equivalent of 13 monthly payments instead of 12. It's a painless way of paying a little extra principal each month, and if your bank offers it, it's worth a hard look. You wind up paying off a 30-year loan in under 20! So if this is the kind of loan you have, choose BIWEEKLY as the frequency, and enter the exact payment the bank has told you to send every two weeks; but enter the "Total Number of Payments" as if it were a monthly loan and let us calculate the proper number for you.

If you have a regular monthly mortgage but your employer deducts payments from your biweekly paycheck, that's NOT a biweekly loan. It's a monthly loan. The simplest work-around is to set it up as a monthly loan with a CheckAlert transaction in a noncash account (because you're not actually going to write a check), and then just OK it each month when we pull it up on the CheckAlert screen. We'll credit your principal and interest budget categories accordingly, and both TAX and NET WORTH will be fed the proper numbers. As for your paycheck, just allocate this deduction to a Not a Tax Category budget bucket (so you don't double count the interest deduction) called something like "Mortgage Payment."

THREE TYPES OF LOANS

We handle three types of loans:

■ The familiar Mortgage type (good, too, for most auto loans) where the monthly payments are almost all interest at first, chipping away ever so slightly, but inexorably, at principal.

■ Interest-Only loans, like the $25,000 demand loan you've got with the bank at 1% over prime.

■ And Special loans, under which heading we include everything else that doesn't follow a standard mortgage amortization schedule — from the $2,000 your brother-in-law borrowed to any mortgage or auto loan calculated with a formula different from the standard one we use.

Special and Interest-Only loans are essentially the same for our purposes (so don't worry about accidentally mis-classifying one of them).

■ PURPOSE

Choose one. This is mainly for your records, but is also reflected in the breakdown of Liabilities in NET WORTH.

■ PAYMENT AND ESCROWS

Enter the amount the bank has you pay for the loan only. Any additional escrow amounts added into your monthly payment — typically, for insurance and property taxes — should be entered separately, below.

SPECIAL/INTEREST-ONLY: NOT ALL FIELDS ARE REQUIRED

If there's no stated interest rate or set payment schedule for the loan you made to your brother-in-law, just leave these fields blank. We only need them for mortgage loans.

RECORD THE LOAN — F10

Press F10 once to record the loan. (Press ESCape if you're not satisfied with our calculation and want to change something; we'll "unfreeze" the fields.) Then press F10 again to add the loan to your list.

■ On the Loan screen, be sure then to press F6 or F7 to create this loan's linked transaction — and always use that transaction to record payments on the loan. That way we can keep track of it.

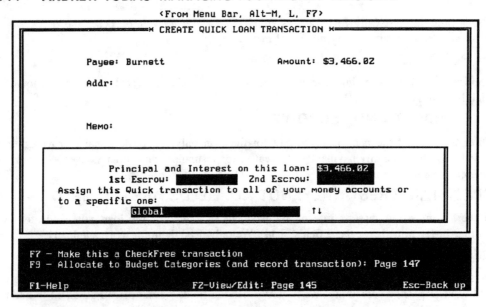

CREATE A QUICK LOAN TRANSACTION

Add whatever detail you want. If this is a mortgage, be sure to add escrow amounts, if any (one for taxes, one for insurance).

Use the arrow keys to choose the account you'll typically use to make this transaction (you can always come back and change it). When in doubt, choose "Global."

CHECKFREE

Press F7 to set this payment up for use with CheckFree, if you're a CheckFree user. Or, if you did set it up as a CheckFree payment, F7 here will offer to undo that. WHEN YOU'RE READY, PRESS F9.

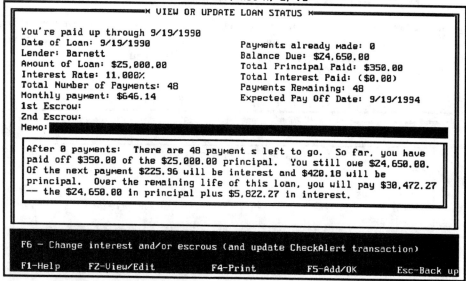

‹From Menu Bar, Alt-M, L, F2›

```
══════════════════════⊯ VIEW OR UPDATE LOAN STATUS ⊯══════════════
  You're paid up through 9/19/1990
  Date of Loan: 9/19/1990            Payments already made: 0
  Lender: Barnett                    Balance Due: $24,650.00
  Amount of Loan: $25,000.00         Total Principal Paid: $350.00
  Interest Rate: 11.000%             Total Interest Paid: ($0.00)
  Total Number of Payments: 48       Payments Remaining: 48
  Monthly payment: $646.14           Expected Pay Off Date: 9/19/1994
  1st Escrow:
  2nd Escrow:
  Memo:

  ┌────────────────────────────────────────────────────────────┐
  │ After 0 payments:  There are 48 payment s left to go.  So far, you have │
  │ paid off $350.00 of the $25,000.00 principal.  You still owe $24,650.00. │
  │ Of the next payment $225.96 will be interest and $420.18 will be │
  │ principal.  Over the remaining life of this loan, you will pay $30,472.27 │
  │ — the $24,650.00 in principal plus $5,822.27 in interest. │
  └────────────────────────────────────────────────────────────┘

  F6 — Change interest and/or escrows (and update CheckAlert transaction)

  F1-Help      F2-View/Edit        F4-Print       F5-Add/OK     Esc-Back up
```

VIEW OR UPDATE A LOAN

SPECIAL AND INTEREST-ONLY LOANS

For Special and Interest-Only type loans, all we do here is a recap (and let you change the memo). Press F6 to change the loan's linked transaction and/or set a new interest rate.

MORTGAGES

For mortgages, you can change the escrow amounts if the bank does and, if it's an adjustable-rate mortgage, the interest rate. If you haven't yet set up its linked transaction, you can also reset the number of "Payments already made" and press F6 to see the difference it makes. (Try it! Calculate your status as of the 10th or the 223rd payment. Then reset the number of payments and press F6 again.) We'll only record your changes for real if you press F5 (and save your work before quitting the program!). But if you do save changes, we automatically adjust everything, including your budget allocations for future months and, if the interest rate has changed, the amount of your linked CheckAlert or Quick transaction.

Note, also, that each time you execute the linked transaction created for a mortgage-type loan, the "You're paid up through ---" line at the top of the screen gets updated along with everything else.

CHANGING THE NAME, DATE, OR TERM

To change something even more fundamental, like the date of the loan, delete it entirely (F3 on the previous screen) and set it up again.

PRINT AN AMORTIZATION SCHEDULE — F4

To print an amortization schedule, if it's a mortgage, press F4. For a customized amortization schedule, where the interest rate changes a few times and you make occasional principal prepayments, select Loan Amortization from the ANALYZE menu.

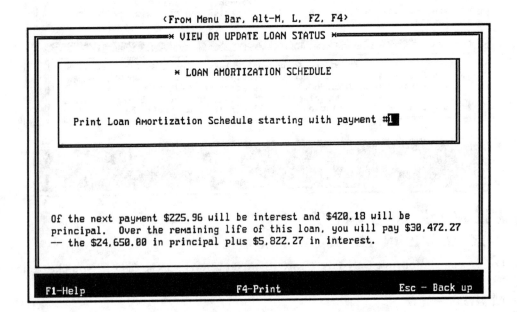

‹From Menu Bar, Alt-M, L, F2, F4›

```
═══════════════*× VIEW OR UPDATE LOAN STATUS *═══════════════

         ┌──────────────────────────────────────────────┐
         │          × LOAN AMORTIZATION SCHEDULE         │
         │                                               │
         │                                               │
         │  Print Loan Amortization Schedule starting with payment #█ │
         └──────────────────────────────────────────────┘




    Of the next payment $225.96 will be interest and $420.18 will be
    principal.  Over the remaining life of this loan, you will pay $30,472.27
    — the $24,650.00 in principal plus $5,822.27 in interest.

  F1-Help                    F4-Print                Esc — Back up
```

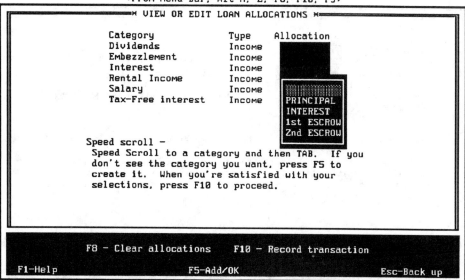

VIEW OR EDIT LOAN ALLOCATIONS
WHERE SHOULD WE ALLOCATE FUTURE LOAN PAYMENTS?

Tell us the budget categories into which you'd like us to dump this loan's principal, interest, and escrow amounts each time you use this linked transaction to make a payment. Presumably, they will be categories like MORTGAGE INTEREST and MORTGAGE PRINCIPAL, though you may have other names for them, or distinguish between home mortgage interest and rental-property mortgage interest, or between MAIN MORTGAGE INT and BEACH-HOUSE MORTGAGE INT. Escrows will probably belong to categories like INSURANCE and PROPERTY TAXES. But whatever your choices, once you tell us here and press F10, we'll never forget (unless you come back and change them).

IMPORTANT! IF IT'S A MORTGAGE, WE DO THE BUDGETING FOR YOU.

If this transaction is for a mortgage-type loan, when you press F10, we'll put the proper monthly budget figures into the categories you've selected, both for this year and for the years to come (and automatically adjust your budget should you later have occasion to change the interest rate or make an extra principal payment).

If you ever delete this transaction, the budget numbers we've dumped into these categories will get sucked back out (as we'll remind you on the warning screen before we let you proceed).

HOW TO MAKE YOUR CHOICES

The instructions are on the screen. Press F5 if you need to add a new category; F10 once you have assigned PRINCIPAL and INTEREST (and escrows, if any) to the proper budget categories.

```
                        <From Menu Bar, Alt-M, L, F8>
┌─────────────────────────────────────────────────────────────────────┐
│─────────────────────* EXTRA PAYMENT TO PRINCIPAL *────────────────────│
│                                                                       │
│     Date of loan: 9/19/1990      Payments already made: 0             │
│     Lender: Barnett              Balance due: $25,000.00              │
│     Amount of loan: $25,000.00   Total principal paid: $0.00          │
│     Interest rate: 11.000%       Total interest paid: $0.00           │
│     Total number of payments: 49 Payments remaining: 49               │
│     Mortgage payment: $646.14    Expected pay-off date: 9/19/1994     │
│     1st escrow: $0.00                                                 │
│     2nd escrow: $0.00                                                 │
│                                                                       │
│     Extra payment: $700.00    New number of payments remaining: 48    │
│                                                                       │
│     When you press F10, we'll generate a payment for the amount you've │
│     entered.  In addition, we'll change the remaining term of this    │
│     loan, rebudget principal and interest allocations and change the  │
│     CheckAlert transaction that pays it off.                          │
│                                                                       │
├───────────────────────────────────────────────────────────────────────┤
│  F8 - Change checking account from Your's 123-456-7                   │
│  F10 - Record extra payment to principal                              │
│  F1-Help                                              Esc-Back up      │
└─────────────────────────────────────────────────────────────────────┘
```

CHECKALERT: MORTGAGE PRINCIPAL PREPAYMENT

Prepaying principal can be a great investment. Not having to PAY 11% on money you've borrowed is as good as EARNING 11% — risk-free. And if it's an auto loan, say, that's not tax-deductible, then paying down the loan (if the bank allows it without penalty) is not just a risk-free but, in effect, a tax-free 11%.

Because this loan is linked to a CheckAlert transaction, you just tell us here how much of a principal prepayment you want to make. We'll record a payment — press F8 if we haven't selected the account you want to use to make it — and you can then print and mail in the check. (Be sure to mark it, "Principal Prepayment!")

Notice that when you TAB off the amount field, we automatically reduce the remaining number of payments (if, in fact, your principal prepayment is enough to make a difference). Also, though you can't see it, we adjust the amount of the final payment you'll need to make, which is probably now going to be some fraction of the normal payment.

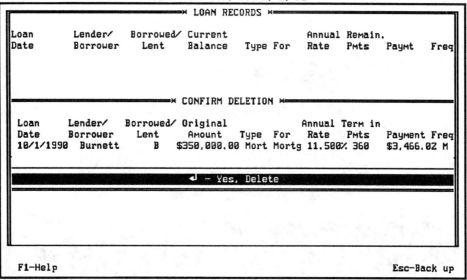

<From Menu Bar, Alt-M, L, F3>

DELETE A MORTGAGE

If you proceed with the deletion, this mortgage will disappear; your NET WORTH will no longer reflect it; and we will also delete the Quick List or CheckAlert transaction you linked to it, sucking all future budget allocations from the principal and interest budget buckets you assigned them to (if it's a mortgage-type loan).

Except in the case of payments by CheckFree — CheckAlert will not execute any of these future payments without your confirmation first. And you can change or delete any of them on the CheckAlert Register.

■ If this is a payment that does not recur regularly or that does, but with a different amount each time, you should probably choose "One-Time" here and, instead, add it to your Quick List. (To do that, just point to it on the Check Register screen and press F6.) It's fine to skip the address if you don't need it printed on the check or, with a credit card receipt, as part of the record you keep for the IRS.

<From Menu Bar, Alt-M, L, F6>

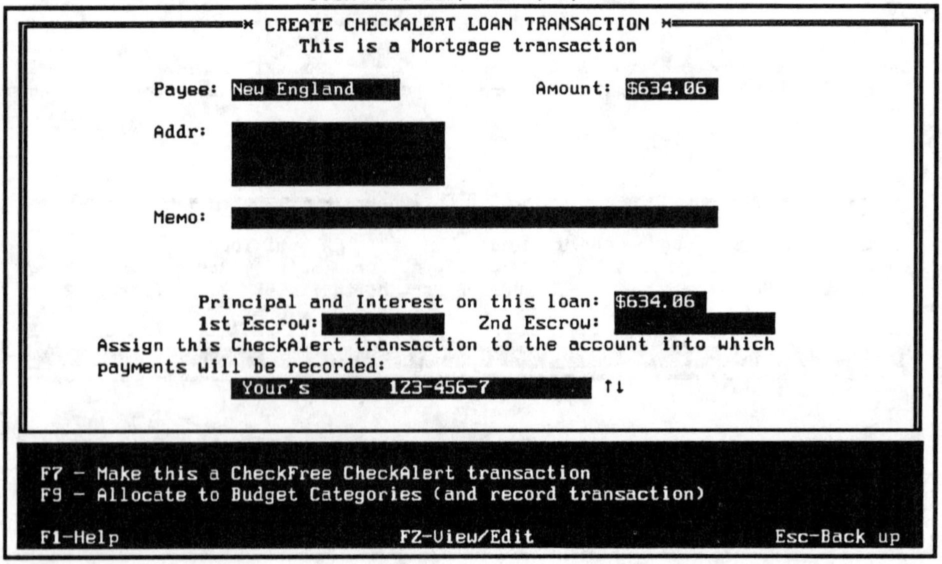
CREATE CHECKALERT LOAN TRANSACTION
This is a Mortgage transaction
Payee: New England
Amount: $634.06
Addr:
Memo:
Principal and Interest on this loan: $634.06
1st Escrow:
2nd Escrow:
Assign this CheckAlert transaction to the account into which
payments will be recorded:
Your's 123-456-7
F7 - Make this a CheckFree CheckAlert transaction
F9 - Allocate to Budget Categories (and record transaction)
F1-Help
F2-View/Edit
Esc-Back up

COMPLETING SPECIAL AND INTEREST-ONLY LOAN PAYMENTS

Is this payment interest only? A paydown or payoff of principal? Some of each? Tell us here and we'll allocate to your budget categories and update the balance of your loan.

<From Menu Bar, Alt-M, O>

```
========================* CASH FORECASTING *========
ALL CASH/SAVINGS/CHECKING  minus  ALL CHARGE ACCTS  equals   CURRENT CASH
        $15,454                          $0                     $15,454
                          Income        Expenses    Profit/Loss
This Month's Budget       $1,000          $220         $780
Your Actuals So Far       $3,042        $2,313         $730        PROJECTED
Over Budget               $2,042        $2,258                    ENDING CASH
Not Yet Spent/Rec'd          $0           $165                      $15,289
                         NEXT 11 MONTHS
             Budgeted   Income        Expenses    Profit/Loss   Cash at EOM
October                   $771          $866        ($95)        $15,194
November                  $775          $866        ($91)        $15,102
December                  $779          $866        ($88)        $15,015
January                   $782          $866        ($84)        $14,931
February                  $786          $866        ($80)        $14,851
March                     $790          $866        ($76)        $14,775
April                     $794          $866        ($72)        $14,704
May                       $798          $866        ($68)        $14,636
June                      $802          $866        ($64)        $14,572
July                      $807          $866        ($60)        $14,512
August                    $811          $866        ($55)        $14,457

F6 - Five-Year Forecasts: Page 153    F9 - Graph Bar    F10 - Graph Line
```

CASH FORECASTING

"Rich?" said the Texas millionaire. "Of course I'm rich. I just don't have any money!" He had oil wells and office buildings and limited partnership interests and a 200-karat diamond paperweight. He just didn't have $4 in his pocket for a pizza with peppers and extra cheese, and a Coke.

To avoid such situations, this screen displays your current and future cash positions, based on your budget, so you can spot trouble well in advance. It is divided into three sections — your current cash; the cash we project you'll have at the end of this month; and your cash at the end of each of the next 11 months. (If you've turned on the 5-year-forecasting Money Option on the FILE menu, F6 will take you to see that, too. Our Japanese version offers 250-year forecasting as well.)

CURRENT CASH

Across the top is your cash now: actual cash plus checking and savings account balances minus what you owe on your credit cards. Non-cash accounts and any others with XXX in their names are X-cluded. So if you have a savings account you never want to touch, name it, "B of A-XXX." A Visa you never pay off? Name it, "Visa-XXX."

So, let's say you have $2,348 on hand right now.

THIS MONTH'S ADJUSTMENTS

Next we show you four lines of information with regard to the current month. The first three lines are for your information only and do not figure into our calculation of your cash at the end of the month. They are: THIS MONTH'S BUDGET, YOUR ACTUALS SO FAR, and OVER BUDGET (which is the excess in all categories that are already over budget for the month). The fourth line — NOT YET SPENT/REC'D — is the one we use in our calculation.

It looks through all your income and expense categories and, for any where the actual amount you've spent or received is under budget, it grabs the difference on the assumption that by the end of the month you WILL spend or receive it. (It ignores those where you're already OVER budget, on the assumption that you won't be able to unspend the excess or, in the case of higher than budgeted receipts, won't have to give it back.)

Naturally, this is rough. But it's the most sensible assumption we can make, and the places we're off may tend to cancel each other out. What it leaves us with is an estimate of the additional cash we expect you to spend and receive for the rest of this month. Say there's $1,000 left to come in and $1,200 we expect to go out. That means you'll be $200 poorer by the end of the month, so we'd subtract that from the $2,348 you have on hand right now and show your PROJECTED ENDING CASH as $2,148.

The only income and expense categories we DON'T take into account in our calculation are any to whose names you've added an XXX. For example, if you put $250 a month into a money market fund, and you budget for that (MM FUND-XXX), we won't subtract $250 from your available cash each month, because that's what the $250 IS: available cash! The triple XXX in the category name tells Cash Forecasting to ignore it. (See below.)

NEXT 11 MONTHS

Based on your budgeted cash in and out, we then do the same for each of the 11 months that follow. If you forget to include TUITION or PROPERTY TAX, we'll have no way to take them into account. But if we do show you dipping into the red (numbers in parentheses), be sure you've got the credit you'll need to tide you over.

BUDGETING FOR SAVINGS – XXX

How your cash flow looks will depend in large part on how you budget for "savings and investments." If you don't have a SAVINGS budget category, then any cash build-up here is money available for investment. But if you do, then your cash position may be stronger than it looks. It depends on whether you've been socking your savings into a money market fund, Mayan art, or an IRA. All may be equally valuable, but only the money market fund is useful for paying the rent.

Hence our XXX and XX trick. Budget categories you want excluded from the cash flow analysis should have an XXX in their names. If you plan to "spend" $200 a month building up your savings account, call that budget category LIQUID SAVINGS-XXX. But the $200 you plan to "spend" on an IRA, even though it doesn't make you poorer, DOES reduce your available cash. Give that category just two XX's. We WILL let you exclude it from your profit-and-loss on the Budget screen, but NOT exclude it here.

ACCOUNT SUMMARY REPORT

If you're interested in this screen, there's another number on another screen that may interest you: your total available cash and CREDIT. Select Money Accounts from the MONEY menu and press F4 to order up an Account Summary report. At the tail end, you'll find our tally of this number. It includes every last dime you can lay your hands on in the next 10 minutes, except for borrowing power against securities you may own in margin accounts. Naturally, it's only as good as the credit-limit numbers you entered for each Money Account. But if you entered them properly, we'll tally them properly.

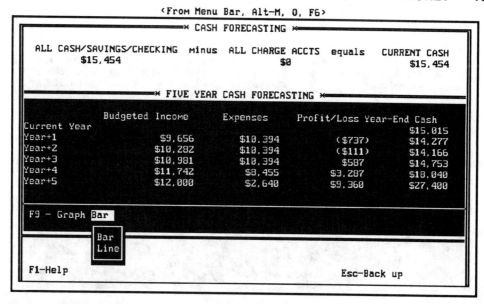

<From Menu Bar, Alt-M, O, F6>

```
                  ═══════✗ CASH FORECASTING ✗═══════

   ALL CASH/SAVINGS/CHECKING  minus  ALL CHARGE ACCTS  equals  CURRENT CASH
            $15,454                        $0                      $15,454


               ═══════✗ FIVE YEAR CASH FORECASTING ✗═══════

              Budgeted Income    Expenses    Profit/Loss Year-End Cash
   Current Year                                                $15,015
   Year+1            $9,656      $10,394        ($737)         $14,277
   Year+2           $10,282      $10,394        ($111)         $14,166
   Year+3           $10,981      $10,394         $587          $14,753
   Year+4           $11,742       $8,455       $3,287          $18,040
   Year+5           $12,000       $2,640       $9,360          $27,400


    F9 - Graph  Bar
                ┌──────┐
                │ Bar  │
                │ Line │
                └──────┘

    F1-Help                                           Esc-Back up
```

FIVE-YEAR CASH FORECASTING

Do the numbers at right grow every year? If so, we'll bet you have no teen-aged children. How your long-term cash flow looks will depend in large part on how you budget for "savings and investments." Be sure to read HELP behind the previous screen for an explanation of the "trick."

‹From Menu Bar, Alt-M, Y›

```
┌──────────────────────────────────────────────────────────────────┐
│ ┌──────────── ⊁ ACCOUNTS PAYABLE for:  Your's 123-456-7 ⊁════════┐ │
│ │                                                                │ │
│ │ Payee                   Mark Inv. Date  Due Date    Amt. Due     Pay Amt.
│ │ Graphic Representation    ▌  9/19/1990 12/19/1990  $1,000.00    $1,000.00
│ │ Design Associates         ▌  9/22/1990 10/22/1990  $4,325.00    $4,325.00
│ │
│ │
│ │
│ │
│ │
│ │
│ │
│ │
│ │ Speed scroll -
│ │
│ ├────────────────────────────────────────────────────────────────┤
│ │ F8 - Change Account              F10 - Pay marked Payables       │
│ │ F9 - Sort by Due Date                 on 9/19/1990  by Check     │
│ ├────────────────────────────────────────────────────────────────┤
│ │ F2-View/Edit: Page 156         F3-Delete            F4-Print     │
└──────────────────────────────────────────────────────────────────┘
```

ACCOUNTS PAYABLE

If you've turned on the Payables Money Option, one of the ways to pay a bill on the Spend Money screen is called "Payables." Choose it, and we won't spend your money at all — we'll move the transaction to this screen (and add this new liability to the liabilities side of your balance sheet in Your Net Worth). Then, when you're ready, come here and mark the ones you want to pay. For partial payments, just change the amount we show. Before you press F10, check the top of the screen to be sure we've selected the account you want to use to make the payment — press F8 if we've not.

Now, actually to print the checks, select Print Checks — you'll see these at the end of the list, ready to go. (Or, if you're a CheckFree user and selected that payment method, select Call CheckFree.) Once you do press F10:

- Payables you've only partially paid will remain, with the reduced amount-due. Those paid in full remain, with zero due, for quicker entry next time. (No need to retype the name and address; just press F2.) If you want to get rid of them, just point and press F3.

- Your Net Worth shows no change because, although your payables have shrunk, your bank balance has shrunk, too.

HANDY WAYS TO SORT — F9

One of the handiest ways to sort is by due date, so you can quickly spot the ... well, the embarrassments.

AGED PAYABLES REPORT — F4

It requires compressed printing because it's a wide report, but F4 will give you a list of your payables "with aging," so you can see which are over 30, 60, and 90 days due.

AN ALTERNATIVE WAY TO ENTER PAYABLES

The normal way to add a payable to this list when a new bill comes is to record it on the Spend Money screen (or your Quick List). Just choose "Payable" as your spending method. But it's also fine, once you've got some payables here, to use them over and over, as suggested above. Instead of deleting them, just leave them there, with you owing zero, until the next bill comes in. Then point and press F2 to enter the new amount and make any other needed changes. This is probably a clunkier way to do it than Spend Money or your Quick List, but it's just as good if you find it handy.

```
                    <From Menu Bar, Alt-M, Y, F2>
╔═══════════════════════════════════════════════════════════════╗
║═══════════════════* VIEW OR EDIT ACCOUNT PAYABLE *═════════════║
║                                                                 ║
║       Invoice Date: 9/19/1990      Due Date: ▓▓▓▓▓▓▓▓           ║
║                                                                 ║
║      Payee: Graphic Representation   Amount: $1,000.00          ║
║                                                                 ║
║      Addr: ▓▓▓▓▓▓▓▓▓▓▓▓▓▓▓▓▓▓                                   ║
║            ▓▓▓▓▓▓▓▓▓▓▓▓▓▓▓▓▓▓                                   ║
║            ▓▓▓▓▓▓▓▓▓▓▓▓▓▓▓▓▓▓                                   ║
║                                                                 ║
║     Terms: 30 days                                              ║
║                                                                 ║
║     Memo: ▓▓▓▓▓▓▓▓▓▓▓▓▓▓▓▓▓▓▓▓▓▓▓▓▓▓▓▓▓▓▓▓▓                     ║
║                                                                 ║
║                                                                 ║
║─────────────────── Page Scroll 1 of 1 ────────────────────────║
║ F9 - View/Edit budget allocations: Page 83                      ║
║                                                                 ║
║                                                                 ║
╚═══════════════════════════════════════════════════════════════╝
   F1-Help        F2-View/Edit             F5-Add/OK       Esc-Back up
```

VIEW OR EDIT AN ACCOUNT PAYABLE

Edit anything you like.

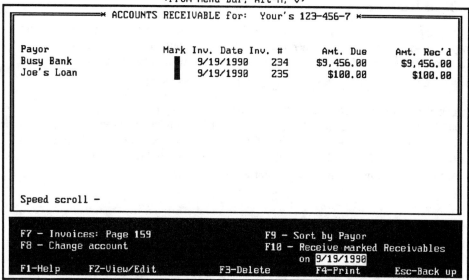

<From Menu Bar, Alt-M, V>

```
════════════╗ ✕ ACCOUNTS RECEIVABLE for:  Your's 123-456-7 ✕═══════════

 Payor                    Mark Inv. Date Inv. #      Amt. Due      Amt. Rec'd
 Busy Bank                 ▌   9/19/1990   234      $9,456.00      $9,456.00
 Joe's Loan                ▌   9/19/1990   235        $100.00        $100.00









 Speed scroll -

  F7 - Invoices: Page 159               F9 - Sort by Payor
  F8 - Change account                   F10 - Receive marked Receivables
                                              on 9/19/1990
 F1-Help      F2-View/Edit        F3-Delete        F4-Print        Esc-Back up
```

ACCOUNTS RECEIVABLE

If you've turned on the Receivables Money Option, one of the ways to record income — if you haven't actually received it yet, but it's now owed you — is called "Receivables." Choose it, and we'll enter the transaction on this screen. Your Net Worth will rise accordingly.

PRINT INVOICES — F7

Then, when you're ready, come here and mark any for which you want to print invoices (F7).

RECORD RECEIPTS — F10

As payments pour in, mark them off and press F10. (For partial payments, just change the amount we show.) But first check the top of the screen to be sure we've selected the account into which you want this money to go — press F8 if we've not. Once you do press F10:

- Receivables only partially paid will remain, with the reduced amount-due. Those paid in full remain, with zero due, for quicker entry next time. (No need to retype the name and address; just press F2.) If you want to get rid of them, just point and press F3.

- Your Net Worth shows no change because, although your Receivables have shrunk, your bank balance has ballooned by an equal sum.

HANDY WAYS TO SORT — F9

Two handy ways to sort are by due date — so you can quickly spot the worst offenders — and by amount — so you can focus your attention where it's most important.

AGED RECEIVABLES REPORT — F4

It requires compressed printing because it's a wide report, but F4 will give you a list of your Receivables "with aging," so you can see which are over 30, 60, and 90 days due.

INVOICE NUMBERS

If we're supplying them but you don't want them — or if we're not but you do — just select Money Options from the FILE menu and either blank out "Last Invoice Number," if you want us to stop, or enter "999," say, if you want us to start numbering from 1000 on.

AN ALTERNATIVE WAY TO ENTER RECEIVABLES

The normal way to add a Receivable to this list is to record it on the Receive Money screen (or your Quick List). Just choose "Receivable" as the receipt method. But it's also fine, once you've got some Receivables here, to use them over and over. Instead of deleting them, just leave them with zero due until these folks again owe you something. Then point and press F2 to enter the new amount and make any other needed changes.

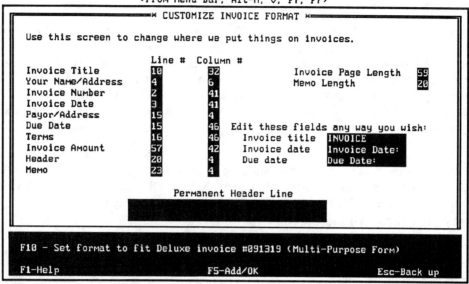

CUSTOMIZE INVOICE FORMAT

THE STANDARD DELUXE INVOICE

The simplest thing to do here is to order the Deluxe invoices we use as our standard and press F10 to set our format to match.

CUSTOMIZING YOUR OWN

But you can customize your invoices. For example, you can edit our headings. Instead of printing "INVOICE" on each of your invoices, you could have us print "Statement of Account." Instead of "Invoice Date:" you could have us print "As of:." Your "permanent header," if you use one, could be as simple as a line of dots or dashes. Or perhaps there's something you don't want to print at all. Just set its line and column numbers to 0, and they'll "print" in Never-Never land.

CHANGING YOUR NAME AND ADDRESS

To change the name and address we print on your invoice, select Preferences from Program Setup on the FILE menu. If you're printing on letterhead and don't want your name to appear twice, change it, temporarily, to asterisks, or some equally innocuous decoration, and leave your address blank.

MOVING THINGS AROUND

Note that an 8-1/2" x 11" sheet of paper is 80 columns wide (something you tell us to start printing in Column 1 will print flush left) and 66 lines deep. We'll beep if you ask us to do something impossible. For example, if your memos start on line 24 and you allow them 20 lines (which brings you to line 44), you'll find we won't let you set the "Total Amount Due" to print any earlier than line 45, lest it overlap the memo. With a little trial and error, you should be able to design a format you like. (Laser printers require a 3 line top and bottom margin, so adjust each line as necessary.)

INVOICE NUMBERS

If we're supplying them but you don't want them — or if we're not but you do — just select Money Options from the FILE menu and either blank out "Last Invoice Number," if you want us to stop, or enter "999," say, if you want us to start numbering from 1000 on.

CAUTION! MEMO LENGTH

The memo length is not only the printable length but the actual length we store in our memory. So, please be careful. If you shorten the memo, we'll shorten the memo for each of your receivables to that length.

‹From Menu Bar, Alt-M, G›

```
 File    Desk    Money    Tax    Insure    Analyze    Portfolio    Net Worth
```

```
                        × REPORT GENERATOR ×

        Report items between: 1/1/1990  and 12/31/1990
        (Optional payee search string:                    )
        (Optional memo search string:                     )


            F6 — Select money accounts: Page 163
            F7 — Select budget categories: Page 164
            F8 — Select tax categories: Page 165
            F9 — Report matching allocations: Page 170
            F10 — Report matching transactions: Page 168
```

```
 F1-Help                                              Esc-Back up
```

REPORT GENERATOR: MAIN SCREEN
GENERATE CUSTOMIZED REPORTS

Here is command central for MONEY's report generator. Don't miss other important MONEY reports, particularly those accessible from the Check Register and Budget Category screens. But the Report Generator lets you customize just about any kind of report you want.

STEP #1 — DECIDE WHAT TRANSACTIONS TO INCLUDE

If you don't instruct us otherwise, we'll include in your report all the transactions between whatever two dates you specify. But:

- F6 lets you include only those in selected Money Accounts.

- F7 lets you include only those allocated to certain budget categories.

- F8 lets you include only those belonging to selected tax categories.

- Optional PAYEE SEARCH lets you enter a "string" of characters — S-E-A-R-S, for example — and causes us to retrieve only transactions that include that string someplace in the payee/payor field.

- Optional MEMO SEARCH works the same way, only it searches the memo.

- The "date range" can be as narrow as a single day. Just set it to, say, 1/2/91-1/2/91.

ALL THESE RETRIEVAL CRITERIA WORK TOGETHER

Except for the date range — you do have to supply one of those — it's entirely up to you how many of these other retrieval criteria to impose, if any.

MEMO POWER

If you've coded the memos of all your transactions *HIS* and *HER*, you could enter "*HIS*" in the MEMO search field and thereby construct a report only of *HIS* transactions. Then you could do the same for hers. These reports could include all their transactions, or just those in certain budget categories — you name it.

You can "code" your memos any way you like. I've used asterisks in my example because to avoid having memo search retrieve extraneous transactions that had words like HERe, tHIS, wHERe, otHER and wHIStle in their memos.

Note that a single memo can include more than one such "code" (and that you may want to put it on the SECOND line of the memo, so it doesn't print out on your check). You can only search on one at a time. But after you're done reporting on things from the HIS and HERS angle, you might have some other way you want to see things.

I find this useful because I have several rental properties, with an overall budget category for each. If the plumber comes out to unclog a drain, the cost gets allocated to that property. But by including the word "Plumbing" in the memo, I can also get a report of all my plumbing expenditures for the year, regardless of (or grouped by) the properties they applied to.

STEP #2 — PRESS F9 OR F10

Once you've specified your retrieval criteria, no matter how narrow or broad, press F9 or F10 to continue.

F9 is for budget-and-tax-category ALLOCATION reports. It groups your transactions by budget and tax category. A transaction you split over six different budget categories will show up six times, with the proper amount for each category.

F10 is for TRANSACTION reports. It treats each transaction as just one, even if it was split over several income or expense categories. You can print your year's transactions by date, check number, payee, or even amount.

The simplest thing to do is try both (though F9 will ordinarily be the more useful) — and to try the sample report formats we've started you off with. But for the record, here is how F9 and F10 compare:

	F9-ALLOCATIONS	F10-TRANSACTIONS
On the next screen, you can Sort BY:	Payee/Payor Date Budget Category	Payee/Payor Date Check Number Amount
And then Sort your report by any of these... with Subtotals allowed for those starred (*):	*Type (Income or Exp) *Budget Category *Date *Payee/Payor Amount *Tax Category	*Account Account Number *Date *Payee/Payor Amount In Amount Out Check Number
And include, if you like:	Transaction detail Addresses Memos	Budget Allocations Addresses Memos
F10 - Help Index	Esc - Back up	PgUp, PgDn

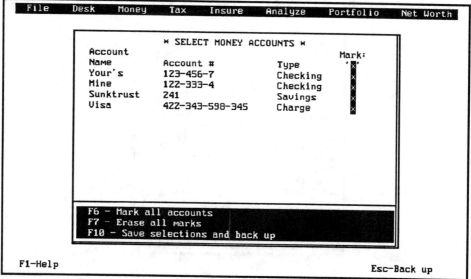

<From Menu Bar, Alt-M, G, F6>

| File | Desk | Money | Tax | Insure | Analyze | Portfolio | Net Worth |

× SELECT MONEY ACCOUNTS ×

Account Name	Account #	Type	Mark:
Your's	123-456-7	Checking	×
Mine	122-333-4	Checking	×
Sunktrust	241	Savings	×
Visa	422-343-598-345	Charge	×

F6 - Mark all accounts
F7 - Erase all marks
F10 - Save selections and back up

F1-Help   Esc-Back up

SELECT MONEY ACCOUNTS

If you'd like to exclude any of these accounts from your report, blank them out with the space bar. Or press F7 to blank out all of them and then mark the one(s) you do want to include.

<From Menu Bar, Alt-M, G, F7>

```
 File    Desk    Money    Tax    Insure    Analyze    Portfolio    Net Worth

                    ⋈ SELECT BUDGET CATEGORIES ⋈
                Budget                       Mark:
                Category              Type   'x'
                ⋈ TOTAL INCOME ⋈             x
                Dividends            Income  x
                Embezzlement         Income  x
                Interest             Income  x
                Rental Income        Income  x
                Salary               Income  x
                Tax-Free interest    Income  x
                ⋈ TOTAL EXPENSE ⋈            x
                Automotive           Expense x
                Child Care           Expense x
                Clothing             Expense x
                Contributions        Expense x

                F6 - Mark all categories
                F7 - Erase all marks
                F10 - Save selections and back up


  F1-Help                                        Esc-Back up
```

SELECT BUDGET CATEGORIES

If you'd like to exclude any of these categories from your report, blank them out with the space bar. Or press F7 to blank out all of them and then mark the one(s) you do want to include.

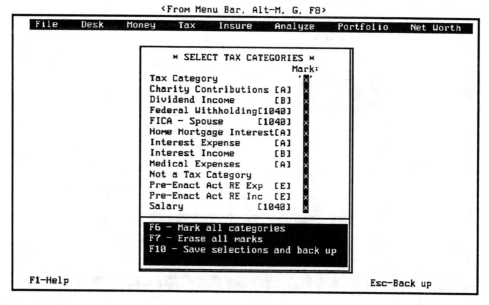

<From Menu Bar, Alt-M, G, F8>

SELECT TAX CATEGORIES

If you'd like to exclude any of these tax categories, blank them out with the space bar. Or press F7 to blank out all of them and then mark the one(s) you do want to include.

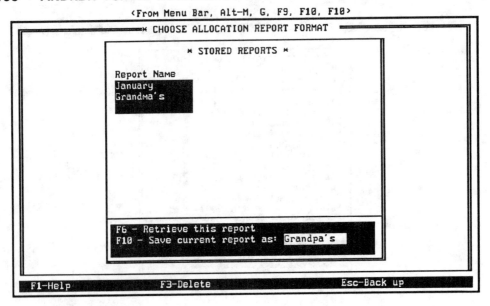

<From Menu Bar, Alt-M, G, F9, F10, F10>

STORED FORMATS

We've tried to give you a headstart. Point and press F6 to load each of our formats and see how it looks. Most require compressed printing to look decent. If you find one you ALMOST like, you can improve it easily on the previous screen. Then save it here with F10 with any name you like.

What we DON'T save here are the selection criteria you specified on your way in — the date range or portfolios or special codes you told us to retrieve. Those you have to respecify next time you want them.

<From Menu Bar, Alt-M, G, F10>

```
╔══════════× Extracted transactions between 1/1/1990 and 12/31/1990 ×═══════╗

   Date        Account      Account #   Payee/Payor        In        Out      #
   9/1/1990    Your's       123-456-7   Jack's Te                  300.00   343
   9/19/1990   Your's       123-456-7   Sunny Daz                   75.00   344
   9/14/1990   Your's       123-456-7   Eckerd's                    32.50
   9/19/1990   Your's       123-456-7   Procter &      542.00
   9/25/1990   Your's       123-456-7   Mary Smit      750.00
   9/19/1990   Your's       123-456-7   Barnett                   350.00   345
   9/13/1990   Mine         122-333-4   We Care D                  55.00  1214
   9/13/1990   Mine         122-333-4   Ellen's D               1,500.00  1215
   9/19/1990   Mine         122-333-4   We Care D       55.00
   9/19/1990   Mine         122-333-4   Loehman's                 350.00  1213



   F9 - Sort transactions by Date
   F10 - Select report formats: Page 168
   F1-Help                                             Esc-Back up
```

EXTRACTED TRANSACTIONS

These transactions meet all your criteria. Unless you press F9 to sort them, you'll find them grouped by account.

THE MAIN EVENT — F10

Ordinarily, you'll just pause briefly on this intermediate screen and then press F10 to proceed to your choice of report format. Be sure to read the HELP behind the report-format screen, as well.

TWO SUBSIDIARY THINGS YOU NEED *NOT* DO HERE:

- Use F9 to sort the display by date, payee, or budget category. This won't affect the report you print, but it may be useful in showing you whatever it is you're looking for.

- Point to one of the transactions and press Ctrl-V in case for some reason you want to see all other transactions involving this same payee or payor, regardless of any of the criteria you may have specified on the previous screen.

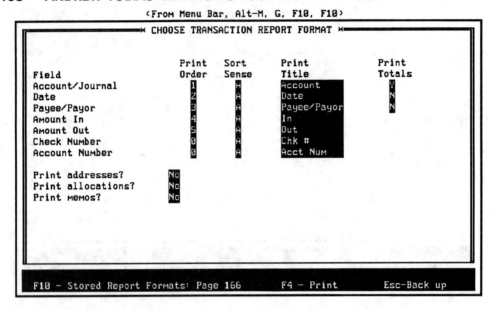

F10 – Stored Report Formats: Page 166

CUSTOMIZING "TRANSACTION" REPORTS

EASIER THAN IT LOOKS

F10 will take you to all the reports you're likely to need. If you like them, there's no need to read any further. Just press F10 and select one of our stored formats.

- Try F10 first. Get an idea of the reports we can print. If you find one you ALMOST like, come back here and make changes to it.

WHAT WE MEAN BY TRANSACTION REPORTS

Here's where you can get a report of all the transactions you chose to include, ordered by date, or check number, or payee — or even amount. At year's end, I find it extremely useful to print a hard copy of one of each. You'll be able to find virtually ANYTHING about your year's activity in seconds. If, on the previous screen, you chose to include just certain amounts or budget categories, only those will be included here. But if what you want is a report that subtotals your transactions by Tax Category and/or Budget Category and/or Type (i.e., income or expense), back out and use F9 to select "matching allocations." When you do, you'll find a different set of reports there.

DESIGNING YOUR OWN REPORT FORMAT

- ## PRIORITY

Assign "zero" as the priority for any of the fields you DON'T want to include in your report. Especially if your printer is not capable of compressed printing, you're going to want to limit the number of columns.

Number the other fields in order of importance. Try to be logical. (We'll help with error messages.) Do you want the main sort criterion to be date? If so we'll order all your transactions by date ... and for dates with more than one transaction, we'll break the tie based on the field you rate #2 — payee, probably.

■ ORDER

You'll almost always want to leave this set to A, for Ascending (A-Z, 1-10, January-December). But if you want to see your most recent transactions first, say, you could choose Descending order for the Date or the Check Number.

■ TITLE AS:

You don't have much room to be elegant, but if you can think of better headings than the ones we've used, be our guest.

■ PRINT TOTALS?

The main thing to remember here is that you probably want only one or two YESes, if any. It's unlikely you'd want a total by date or even by account. If you want a total at all here, it's probably by Payee. (On the ALLOCATION Report, you might want totals for tax and budget categories.)

■ Whatever you do total on should be the field to which you assign first priority.

■ If the heading you're totaling has just one item — one transaction for a particular payee, say — we don't clutter your report totaling it. We only show totals for the things that include more than one transaction (and thus need to be totaled).

■ PRINT MEMO, ETC?

The temptation is to answer YES, YES, YES. The problem is, these three additional items will all print UNDER each transaction, not in a column off to the far right (the 60-character memo field alone would take up much of the page) ... and that means you lose the ability to run your eye down the columns of the report. So ordinarily, you will want to answer NO.

STORED REPORT FORMATS — F10

Once you've devised a format you like, press F10, give it a description at the bottom of the screen, and press F10 to add it to your list. To retrieve it or one of the others, point and press F6.

■ It's the report format, not your selection criteria, that are being stored. If this is a report of just your Charitable Contributions (say), we don't know it. Next time you want to see them, you'll have to select that budget category again. But it doesn't take long.

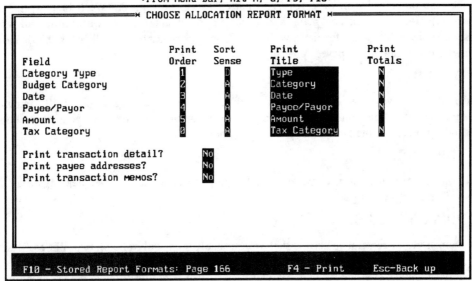

<CHOOSE ALLOCATION REPORT FORMAT>

From Menu Bar, Alt-M, G, F9, F10

Field	Print Order	Sort Sense	Print Title	Print Totals
Category Type	1	D	Type	N
Budget Category	2	A	Category	N
Date	3	A	Date	N
Payee/Payor	4	A	Payee/Payor	N
Amount	5	A	Amount	N
Tax Category	0	A	Tax Category	N

Print transaction detail?   No
Print payee addresses?   No
Print transaction memos?   No

F10 – Stored Report Formats: Page 166   F4 – Print   Esc-Back up

CUSTOMIZING "ALLOCATION" REPORTS

EASIER THAN IT LOOKS

F10 will take you to some perfectly decent reports we've stored to start you off with. Chances are, there's no need to read any further.

■ Try F10 first. Get an idea of the reports we can print. If you find one you ALMOST like, come back here and make changes to it.

WHAT WE MEAN BY "ALLOCATION REPORTS"

The purpose of this set of reports is to show you your transactions grouped and subtotaled by allocation – primarily, by budget and category. If what you really want instead is a report that shows all your transactions for the year in date, or check number order, or alphabetically by payee, back out and extract matching "transactions" instead of "allocations." We have a different set of reports there.

DESIGNING YOUR OWN REPORT

■ PRIORITY

Number the other fields in order of importance. Try to be logical. (We'll help with error messages.)

■ Assign "zero" as the priority for any of the fields you DON'T want to include in your report.

The broadest heading is "Category Type" – namely, Income or Expense – so it almost always makes sense, if you're including it, to place it first. It's a sensible way to organize your report, followed perhaps by tax and/or budget category and then Payee. (What would not make sense would be to give budget category a higher priority than, say, Category Type — just as it makes sense to sort the countries within a continent, but not the continents within a country.)

■ ORDER

You'll almost always want to leave this set to A, for Ascending (A-Z, 1-10, January-December). But if, under Category Type, you want to see Income before Expenses, have us alphabetize that one in descending order — I before E. We'll group all your income items first, all your expenses second.

■ TITLE AS:

You don't have much room to be elegant, but if you can think of better headings than the ones we've used, be our guest.

■ PRINT TOTALS?

The main thing to remember here is that you probably want only one or two YESes — perhaps a total for Type (total income, total expense) and then, within that, totals for each tax and/or budget category. Period. It's unlikely you'd want a total by date.

■ If you say yes to totals on one field, any field to which you've assigned a higher priority must be totaled, too.

■ If the heading you're totaling has just one item, we don't clutter your report totaling it — we only show totals for the things that include more than one transaction.

■ PRINT MEMO, ETC?

The temptation is to answer YES, YES, YES. The problem is, these three additional items will all print UNDER each transaction, not in a column off to the far right (the 60-character memo field alone would take up much of the page) ... and that means you lose the ability to run your eye down the columns of the report. So ordinarily, you will want to answer NO.

STORED REPORT FORMATS — F10

Once you've devised a format you like, press F10, give it a description at the bottom of the screen, and press F10 to add it to your list. To retrieve it or one of the others, point and press F6.

■ It's the report format, not your selection criteria, that are being stored. If this is a report of just your Charitable Contributions (say), we don't know it. Next time you want to see them, you'll have to select that budget category again. But it doesn't take long.

"AMOUNT" AND "DETAIL"

Because this is an "allocation report," the "amount" we'll show is just the portion allocated to each budget category. To include the full amount of the check or receipt — even though it's often same — answer "YES" to include "detail," which will also cause us to include the account name and number.

4

Tax

```
                        <From Menu Bar, Alt-T, 1>
        ═════════════════════ FORM 1040 ═════════════════════

   Filing Status: ▌ Joint ▐         Adjusted Gross Inc:      $38,133.33
   # Personal Exemptions:  4          Personal Exemptions:  ( $8,000.00 )
                                      Standard Deduction:   ( $5,200.00 )
   *Wages, Salaries:     $33,333.33  Taxable Income:         $24,933.33
    Sch. B Income:        $4,400.00
    Sch. C Gain/Loss:         $0.00  Tax (1989 Schedule Y):   $3,740.00
    Sch. D Gain/Loss:         $0.00   Tax Credits:          (     $0.00 )
    Sch. E Gain/Loss:       $400.00   Alternative Min. Tax:
    Sch. F Gain/Loss:         $0.00   Tax from Schedule SE:        $0.00
    Other Income:             $0.00  *Federal Tax Withheld: ( $6,666.67 )
   Gross Income:         $38,133.33  *Excess FICA Withheld: (     $0.00 )
    Adjustments:       (      $0.00  )>Tax Refund Due:        $2,926.67
   Adjusted Gross Income $38,133.33


                        Marginal Tax Bracket: ▌ 15.0% ▐

   ───────────────────────────────────────────────────────────────────
    F7 - Update all Tax Schedules with ▌ 1991 ▐      F8 - Update * items
    F10 - Calculate your tax
                    A, B, C, D, E, F - Go to Tax Schedules
    F1-Help                  F4-Print                   Esc-Back up
```

FORM 1040; OVERALL TAX HELP; STATE TAXES

This screen is an abbreviated Form 1040 and is home base for TAX. TAX provides all the tools you'll need to estimate your tax. Not only will it give you a good idea where you stand, it lets you play "what if," to help you stand someplace better. What if you got a $10,000 raise? What if you got a $9,000 facelift in January instead of December? F4 prints these estimates. (To calculate and print an actual, precise IRS-acceptable return, consider TaxCut, MYM's sister program, offered to registered users at a special price. Call 203-222-9150 for details.)

SIX STEPS TO ESTIMATING YOUR TAX:

1. Check the tax year we've got loaded. If in the righthand column, fifth line down, it says "Tax (1990 Schedule Y)" — and you're estimating your 1991 tax-year taxes — you'll first want to set us straight. Select Tax Tables & Parameters from the TAX menu.

2. Once you're sure you have the right year loaded, press F7 here on the Form 1040 screen to update everything based on your actual and budgeted income and outgo for the year.

    Or, if you prefer, visit each schedule in turn and do each one individually. Want to see Schedule A? Just press A. Likewise, B, C, D, E, and F. At least the first time, it's a good idea to do this even if you use F7 to update everything all at once.

3. Check the top left corner of this Form 1040 screen to be sure we have your correct Filing Status and number of Personal Exemptions. After you've calculated your taxes filing SINGLY, you can check to see whether it would make sense to get married.

4. Back up to the TAX menu and select 1040 Worksheet. Press F8 to update it (and/or do it by hand).

5.   Back up to the TAX menu again and visit the Self-Employment Tax and the Alternative Minimum Tax screens, pressing F8 on each to update them and see what tax, if any, you owe. When you return to Form 1040, those numbers will be reflected (but not before — we don't update them automatically).

6.   Now return to Form 1040 and press F10 to have us estimate your federal income tax.

The nice things about all this are that we do most of the calculating for you, and you can make change after change until you have everything the way you want it without having to recalculate anything or bloody even a single eraser.

So don't be put off by what may initially seem confusing (well, it is the tax code, after all); and don't bother with items, like the Alternative Minimum Tax or Moving Expenses, say, if you know they don't apply to you. Enter any numbers you want. Nothing you do in TAX will alter your real records in MONEY.

■   Note that with highlighted items on this screen like "Gross Income" and "Adjusted Gross Income," you can't type in estimates because they merely sum the preceding entries. Nor will they change each time you enter a new estimate on this screen — but they will change automatically each time you press F10 to calculate your tax, and each time you return to this screen from someplace else.

■   Note, too, that the tax we show you owing (or the refund due you) on the last line, is AFTER taking into account the withholding (and estimated tax payments) you've recorded and/or budgeted in MONEY. If you make a million dollars a year and have budgeted $300,000 in quarterly estimated tax payments for 1991 — but haven't made any yet — we'll show you due a refund. But to get it (and stay out of jail) you need to have paid the $300,000 you budgeted!

HOW AUTOMATIC "UPDATING" WORKS

Totals imported from MONEY with F7 and F8 are the sum of the transactions you've actually recorded up to this month plus the income and outgo you've budgeted for next month through year-end. For *this* month, we use your budget number in each income and expense catgeory — unless you've already exceeded it, in which case we go with the actual number.

But if the figure we come up with doesn't look right, because you know you make $36,000 a year and this thing is showing only $33,000 (maybe you forgot to enter a paycheck?), just type in the number you want to use. (If your Salary looks HIGH, it may be because it includes anything you dumped into the Moving Expense Reimbursement tax barrel.) If it appears we are not pulling up the right numbers from MONEY, be sure that you assigned your budget categories to the proper tax barrels.

ESTIMATING A FUTURE YEAR'S TAX

FILE's Money Options allows you to switch from pulling the current year's number into TAX in favor of pulling next year's numbers, based on your budget, instead.

SCHEDULE A WORKSHEETS

You'll find on Schedule A separate F-keys leading to "worksheets" for the Standard Deduction, Employee Business Expense, Investment Interest, and Moving Expenses. Entering or changing numbers there will update Schedule A, the aggregate of which, in turn, will be waiting for you here on Form 1040.

TAX CREDIT FOR PRIOR YEARS' ALTERNATIVE MINIMUM TAX

If you paid the alternative minimum tax in a past year but don't have to this year, you may actually be eligible to apply some of the prior AMT as a credit against this year's taxes. Check with your accountant or a good tax guide and, if so, calculate it with IRS form 8801 and include it along with any other tax credits you may have on the Tax Credit field.

FOOLING US INTO ESTIMATING YOUR STATE INCOME TAX

Many state and municipal income taxes are graduated in much the same way as the federal tax. So if you like, take one of the tax tables you DON'T need for your federal tax and adapt it. For HELP on how to do this — and its limitations — select Tax Tables and Parameters from the TAX menu and press F1 there.

For details on current tax rules, J.K. Lasser's inexpensive perennial, YOUR INCOME TAX, will ordinarily more than suffice.

```
                          <From Menu Bar, Alt-T, A>
╔════════════════════ ╌ SCHEDULE A - ITEMIZED DEDUCTIONS ╌ ═══════════════════╗
║                                                                              ║
║   *Medicine and Drugs:        $0.00   *Miscell. Deductions:         $0.00   ║
║   *Medical/Dental Expenses:  $800.00    Employee Bus. Expenses:      $0.00   ║
║    Total Medical:            $800.00    Total Miscellaneous:         $0.00   ║
║    Less Floor Amount:      $2,860.00    Less Floor Amount:         $762.67   ║
║     Allowable Medical:        $0.00      Allowable Misc.:            $0.00   ║
║                                                                              ║
║   *Consumer Interest:         $96.00   Casualty/Theft Losses:               ║
║    Limitation Percentage:    × 20%     Less Floor Amount:       $3,913.33   ║
║    Allowable Interest:       $19.20     Allowable Casualty:         $0.00   ║
║                                                                              ║
║   *State and Local Taxes:    $976.00   Investment Interest:         $0.00   ║
║   *Home Mortgage Interest:     $0.00   Moving Expenses:             $0.00   ║
║   *Charitable Contributions:$2,070.00  Other Miscellaneous:         $0.00   ║
║                                                                              ║
║   Total Deductions Entered:  $3,065.20     Standard Deduction:  $5,200.00   ║
║        We will use the  Standard Deduction  for your tax computation.        ║
╚══════════════════════════════════════════════════════════════════════════════╝
┌──────────────────────────────────────────────────────────────────────────────┐
│  F6-Standard Deduction worksheet:Page 180      F8-Update * items             │
│  F7-Employee Expenses worksheet:Page 181                                     │
│                                           F9-Investment Interest worksheet:Page 182│
│  F1-Help                                  F10-Moving Expenses worksheet: Page 183│
└──────────────────────────────────────────────────────────────────────────────┘
```

SCHEDULE A: ITEMIZED DEDUCTIONS

Here we tally your allowable deductions and see whether they exceed the standard deduction everyone gets to take. If so, you'll want to itemize your deductions. If not, we'll just apply the standard deduction.

Press F8 to pull from MONEY the sum of three things: your actual Schedule A expenditures up to this month; budgeted expenditures from next month on; and, for this month, the greater of your actual or budgeted expenditures. Change anything you want. Nothing you type here will alter your records in MONEY.

Now press:

- F6 if you or your spouse are over 64 or blind, or the standard deduction amount has changed.

- F7 if you have business expenses that your employer does or does not reimburse.

- F9 if you want to deduct investment interest (typically, interest paid to a broker).

- F10 if you moved during the year to take a new job.

Filling in these worksheets, whichever apply, will, in turn, fill in most of the remaining lines here on Schedule A.

Note that the STATE AND LOCAL TAXES deduction is the amount you'll actually pay (not owe) this year, including tax you may have paid this year for last year. It should include income and real estate taxes, but not sales tax.

Enter the full amount of your (unreimbursed) CASUALTY LOSSES. We subtract $100 and then 10% of your adjusted gross income. Only what remains, if anything, is deductible. (Alter this formula if the law changes by selecting Tax Tables & Parameters from the TAX menu.) If your loss is actually the sum of several different disasters, you must exclude yet another $100 for each extra one before figuring your deduction. It might also be wise to stop off at the store for a can of curse-remover.

If you have a scad of MISCELLANEOUS DEDUCTIONS, it may be you should be filling out Schedule C. Is some of your income from self-employment?

CONTRIBUTIONS over 30% or 50% of your adjusted gross income may not be deductible — you may have to carry the excess over to next year. Consult an accountant. To handle non-cash contributions, use a Non-Cash Account in MONEY as described in your manual.

There are five classes of INTEREST — consumer (auto, credit card), home-mortgage, investment (broker), passive-activity (Schedule E), and trade-or-business (C). Check a good tax guide if you're unsure which is which.

Not ALL home-mortgage interest is deductible, though most is. In 1990 you could deduct mortgage interest on any two of your residences on loans up to $1 million ($500,000, if married filing separately) used to buy, build, or substantially improve those residences (or to refinance an existing mortgage of like or greater amount) . . . and on home equity loans up to $100,000 ($50,000, filing separately) used for any purpose at all. Points are deductible in a lump if incurred to acquire or build a primary residence. For a refinancing or second home, they must be spread over the life of the loan. If you increased the debt on an existing home by more than $100,000 any time since 1986, consult a good tax guide.

<From Menu Bar, Alt-T, A, F6>

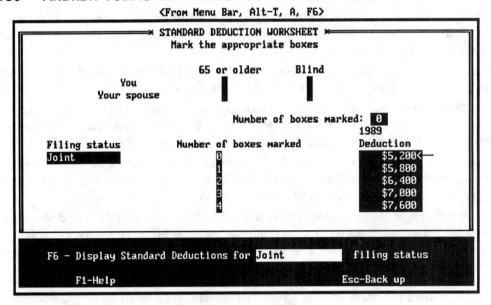

STANDARD DEDUCTION WORKSHEET

There are two uses for this screen:

1. If you or your spouse is over 64 or legally blind, check the appropriate box(es) so you get the extra standard deduction you're entitled to. (If you itemize your deductions, this does you no good.)

2. If Congress has changed the standard deduction, press Ctrl-L and TAB to select your filing status, if it's not already displayed to the right of F6; then press F6 to display the deduction. Type the correct new number over the one we've been using.

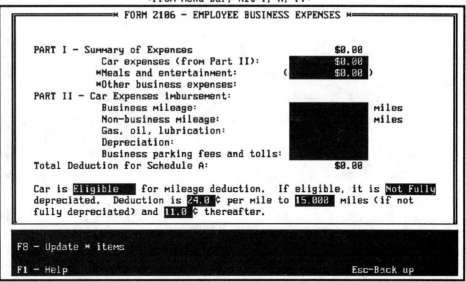

```
═══════════✳ FORM 2106 - EMPLOYEE BUSINESS EXPENSES ✳═══════════


   PART I - Summary of Expenses                        $0.00
           Car expenses (from Part II):                $0.00
          ✳Meals and entertainment:          (        $0.00 )
          ✳Other business expenses:
   PART II - Car Expenses imbursement:
           Business mileage:                                     miles
           Non-business mileage:                                 miles
           Gas, oil, lubrication:
           Depreciation:
           Business parking fees and tolls:
   Total Deduction for Schedule A:                     $0.00

   Car is Eligible   for mileage deduction.  If eligible, it is Not Fully
   depreciated.  Deduction is 24.0 ¢ per mile to 15,000 miles (if not
   fully depreciated) and 11.0 ¢ thereafter.


   F8 - Update ✳ items

   F1 - Help                                           Esc-Back up
```

FORM 2106 – EMPLOYEE BUSINESS EXPENSES

Unreimbursed employee business expenses are deductible, subject to certain thresholds and limitations, though you may have to persuade the IRS you had a good reason for not getting reimbursed. (If you're self-employed, this form does not apply to you. Enter your expenses on Schedule C.)

Pressing F8 draws from MONEY all the budget items you dumped into the starred tax barrels.

Part II of the screen takes the ratio of business miles to total miles driven and applies it to either the actual expenses you list or, if you're eligible, to the mileage formula – giving you credit for whichever is greater. You're not eligible for the mileage rate if your car is leased, you use more than one car at a time in your business or you take accelerated depreciation. Check the tax form or your accountant for further details.

On top of the mileage rate you get to deduct parking fees, tolls, and the business portion of interest and (non-gasoline) taxes. We do the calculations for you.

```
                          <From Menu Bar, Alt-T, A, F9>
┌──────────────────────────────────────────────────────────────────────┐
│                   ═══* INVESTMENT INTEREST DEDUCTION WORKSHEET *══      │
│                                                                        │
│                                                                        │
│                                                                        │
│        *This year's Investment Interest:            │ $0.00 │          │
│                                                                        │
│         Prior year's Disallowed Interest:           │       │          │
│                                                                        │
│         This year's Net Investment Income/Loss:     │       │          │
│                                                                        │
│                                                                        │
│         Allowable Investment Interest Deduction:      $0.00            │
│                                                                        │
│         Amount of Investment Interest being                            │
│               dissallowed this year:                  $0.00            │
│                                                                        │
│                                                                        │
├────────────────────────────────────────────────────────────────────── │
│    F8 - Update * item                                                  │
│                                                                        │
│    F1-Help                                     Esc-Back up             │
└──────────────────────────────────────────────────────────────────────┘
```

INVESTMENT INTEREST DEDUCTION WORKSHEET

Press F8 to summon the items you've dumped into the Investment Interest tax barrel; enter any prior year's disallowed carry-over (it's limited to the amount of taxable income you had that year); offset these with the investment income you've earned for the year (dividends, interest capital gains) – and we calculate the allowable investment interest deduction based on current tax law for 1990 and 1991. Make a note in the reminder pad to carry any excess over to next year. (And make a mental note in your investment strategy that investment income you realize up to the amount of this excess interest deduction is essentially tax-free.) The allowable deduction will be waiting for you back on Schedule A when you press ESCape.

Note: The regulations governing the five classes of interest are complex. Basically, they are: home-mortgage interest (see HELP for Schedule A), personal interest (auto loans, credit cards, etc.), investment interest (to buy securities), passive activity interest (partnership, Schedule E) and interest incurred on money borrowed to run your trade or business (Schedule C). When in doubt, the IRS looks at how you used the borrowed money to determine which type of interest it is. So be careful, keep good records, and check with your accountant if you are unsure which is which.

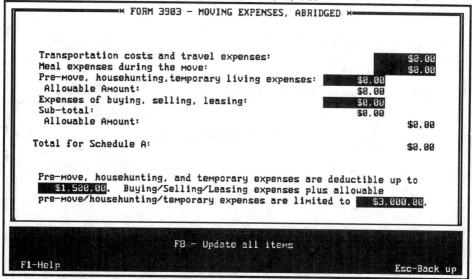

```
════════════════ FORM 3903 - MOVING EXPENSES, ABRIDGED ════════════════


     Transportation costs and travel expenses:              $0.00
     Meal expenses during the move:                         $0.00
     Pre-move, housand,temporary living expenses:     $0.00
      Allowable Amount:                               $0.00
     Expenses of buying, selling, leasing:            $0.00
     Sub-total:                                       $0.00
      Allowable Amount:                                    $0.00

     Total for Schedule A:                                 $0.00


     Pre-move, housand, and temporary expenses are deductible up to
      $1,500.00. Buying/Selling/Leasing expenses plus allowable
     pre-move/housand/temporary expenses are limited to  $3,000.00.


                          F8 - Update all items

     F1-Help                                         Esc-Back up
```

FORM 3903 — MOVING EXPENSES

Did you move to be closer to a new workplace? If so, and if — had you not moved — the commute would have been more than 35 miles longer than your old commute was to your old workplace — then you can ordinarily deduct your UNreimbursed moving expenses, up to the limits described on the screen.

Note: if your move involved a foreign location, or if you are a member of the Armed Forces, special, more liberal rules may apply. Check a good tax guide.

Press F8 if you actually took the trouble to assign your expenditures to budget categories that dump into the proper Form 3903 tax barrels (you'll find them in MONEY's Budget Categories section when you go to assign a budget category to a Schedule A tax treatment) ... or assemble your records and enter the correct totals by hand here.

Press ESCape and the deductible amount is waiting for you in its assigned seat on Schedule A. (AND NOW THAT YOU'VE MOVED, BE SURE TO LET US KNOW YOUR NEW ADDRESS!)

Note that any reimbursement you entered in a budget bucket that dumped into the "Moving Exp. Reimb. [1040]" tax barrel gets pulled up as part of *Salary* on the main Form 1040 screen.

<From Menu Bar, Alt-T, B>

```
═══════════════* SCHEDULE B - INTEREST AND DIVIDEND INCOME *═══════════════

    Interest Income:                                    $2,000.00

    Dividend Income:                                    $2,400.00

    Total Interest and Dividend Income:                 $4,400.00


    Tax Exempt Interest from Private Activity Bonds
    issued after 8/7/86:                                    $0.00

    Other Tax Exempt Interest:                              $0.00

    Total Tax Exempt Interest:                              $0.00


 F8 - Update all items              A, C, D, E, F - Go to Tax Schedules

 F1-Help                                            Esc-Back up
```

SCHEDULE B: INTEREST AND DIVIDEND INCOME

One of the IRS's simpler schedules. Just estimate your interest and dividend income and return to Form 1040. If you've been budgeting and recording interest and dividends (including a category for tax-free municipal bonds), F8 pulls up your actual receipts up to this month, the greater of this month's actual or budget, plus budgeted receipts through the end of the year. The tax-free portions are used for calculating tax on Social Security income and — in the case of private activity bonds — the Alternative Minimum Tax.

Once upon a time, the first $100 or $200 of dividends were free of tax. Should Congress reenact a dividend exclusion, you can, too. Just select Tax Tables & Parameters from the TAX menu and press F2. We will automatically subtract the exclusion here.

If you are a child under the age of 14 (or, for that matter, an adult under 14 — but not, as in my case, a child over the age of 40), investment income over $1,000 is taxed at your parents' top rate. Fill out Form 8615.

SCHEDULE C

<From Menu Bar, Alt-T, C>

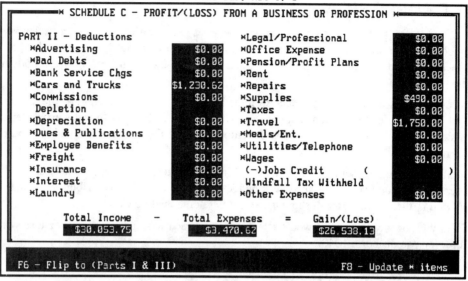

<From Menu Bar, Alt-T, C, F6>

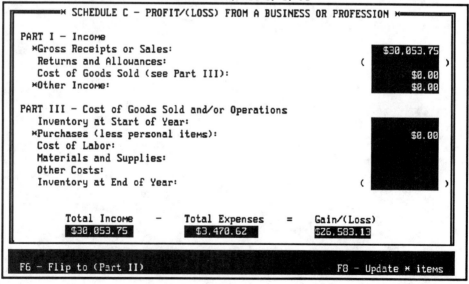

SCHEDULE C: PROFIT(LOSS) FROM A BUSINESS OR PROFESSION

Fill in the lines that apply to you, ignore the ones that don't — if you're a lawyer or graphologist, you probably don't carry an inventory or worry about "cost of goods sold" — and then go back to Form 1040. Be sure to press F1 to flip back and forth between both sides of the form.

Pressing F8 calls up your budget data from MONEY (actuals to last month, the greater of budget or actuals for this month, budget through the end of the year) for all starred items on both sides of the form. A few lines, like Inventory and, on the flip side, Depletion, you have to fill in yourself.

Naturally, our figures will be only as good as your budget and record-keeping. If you accidentally assigned your Freelance Fees budget bucket to the "IRA Distributions" tax barrel in MONEY, that's where it will show up — not here on Schedule C.

Make any changes you want (it won't affect your real records). Your net gain or loss will be waiting for you on Form 1040.

For thoughts on tracking your depreciation with a non-cash account in MONEY, please see your manual ("Non-cash Accounts").

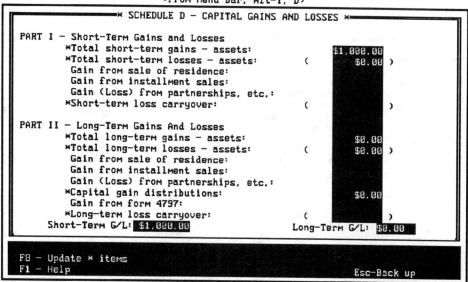

```
═══════════════✻ SCHEDULE D - CAPITAL GAINS AND LOSSES ✻═════════════

    PART I - Short-Term Gains and Losses
         ✻Total short-term gains - assets:              $1,000.00
         ✻Total short-term losses - assets:      (          $0.00 )
          Gain from sale of residence:
          Gain from installment sales:
          Gain (Loss) from partnerships, etc.:
         ✻Short-term loss carryover:              (                 )

    PART II - Long-Term Gains And Losses
         ✻Total long-term gains - assets:                    $0.00
         ✻Total long-term losses - assets:       (          $0.00 )
          Gain from sale of residence:
          Gain from installment sales:
          Gain (Loss) from partnerships, etc.:
         ✻Capital gain distributions:                        $0.00
          Gain from form 4797:
         ✻Long-term loss carryover:               (                 )
        Short-Term G/L: $1,000.00            Long-Term G/L: $0.00


   F8 - Update ✻ items
   F1 - Help                                          Esc-Back up
```

SCHEDULE D: CAPITAL GAINS AND LOSSES

If you've been tending your taxable portfolios in PORTFOLIO, F8 fills in most of this schedule for you. Naturally, portfolios you've labeled IRA/ Keogh or hypothetical won't show up here. Make changes if you like and then go back to form 1040. Nothing you type here will alter PORTFOLIO.

Gains or losses, realized or unrealized, on any assets you've tagged FUTURES CONTRACTS will show up here 40% short-term, 60% long-term, as per current law. We include unrealized gains because at year-end they must be "marked-to-market" (we help you do this as you start a New Year), so for tax planning purposes it makes sense to treat them as realized.

TO CHANGE THE CAPITAL GAINS TAX LAW, SELECT PORTFOLIO OPTIONS FROM THE FILE MENU.

〈From Menu Bar, Alt-T, E〉

```
╔══════════════════════════════════════════════════════════════════╗
║          ═══════════ SCHEDULE E - SUPPLEMENTAL INCOME ═══════════  ║
║                                                                    ║
║  Non-Real Estate Investments with Material Participation           ║
║          *Income:                                    $0.00         ║
║          *Expenses:                        (         $0.00)        ║
║  Actively-managed Real Estate Investments                          ║
║          *Pre-enactment Income:                  $1,500.00         ║
║          *Pre-enactment Expenses            (    $1,250.00)        ║
║          *Post-enactment Income:                     $0.00         ║
║          *Post-enactment Expenses:          (        $0.00)        ║
║           Prior year suspended loss:        (            )         ║
║  Passive Investments                                               ║
║          *Pre-enactment Income:                      $0.00         ║
║          *Pre-enactment Expenses:           (        $0.00)        ║
║          *Post-enactment Income:                     $0.00         ║
║          *Post-enactment Expenses:          (        $0.00)        ║
║           Prior year suspended loss:        (            )         ║
║                                                                    ║
║  Total Schedule E Gain/(Loss):                     $250.00         ║
║                                                                    ║
╠════════════════════════════════════════════════════════════════════╣
║  F8 - Update * items                                               ║
║  F1 - Help                                         Esc-Back up     ║
╚══════════════════════════════════════════════════════════════════╝
```

SCHEDULE E: SUPPLEMENTAL INCOME

You think I'm happy about this? I am not. But actually, it's not as bad as it looks. The trick is to assign your budget buckets to the proper tax barrels in MONEY. If you do that, pressing F8 here fills in the blanks, applies the proper phase-out percentages, nets this and that together (which is why things don't always just add up) and sends the proper number to Form 1040.

If you're confused, maybe we can help. The Tax Reform Act of 1986 was passed on October 23. Any investment real estate or limited partnerships you closed on before that date are "pre-enactment." Otherwise, they're "post-enactment."

All limited partnerships and all real estate holdings are "passive." But if you actively manage the real estate — collect rents and see to repairs, etc., and if your adjusted gross income is under $150,000, up to $25,000 in losses may be deductible without regard to the normal restrictions on passive losses. Fill in the blanks and we figure all this for you.

When in doubt call your accountant or the guy who sold you those passive losses in the first place. For thoughts on tracking your partnership losses with a non-cash account in MONEY, please see your manual.

```
                          ‹From Menu Bar, Alt-T, F›
╔════════════════════ ✳ SCHEDULE F - FARM INCOME, ABRIDGED ✳════════════════════╗
║                                                                                ║
║                                                                                ║
║                                                                                ║
║       Total Farm Income:                                    $15,800.00         ║
║                                                                                ║
║       Total Farm Expenses:                                   $7,200.00         ║
║                                                                                ║
║                                                                                ║
║       Net Farm Income/(Loss):                                $8,600.00         ║
║                                                                                ║
║                                                                                ║
║                                                                                ║
║                                                                                ║
║                                                                                ║
╠════════════════════════════════════════════════════════════════════════════════╣
║  F8 - Update both items                                                         ║
║                                                                                ║
║  F1 - Help                                             Esc-Back up              ║
╚════════════════════════════════════════════════════════════════════════════════╝
```

SCHEDULE F: FARM INCOME, ABRIDGED

We pull up and tally a summary of your income and expenses from the more detailed categories in MONEY.

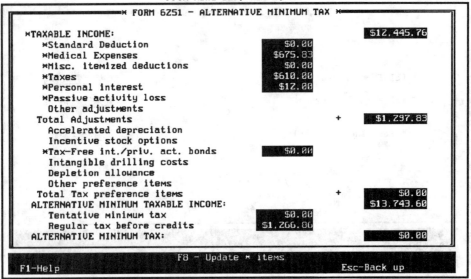

FORM 6251 – ALTERNATIVE MINIMUM TAX

Chances are, you're not subject to the Alternative Minimum Tax, but here's the place to find out. We add certain "adjustments" and "preference items" that don't count in figuring your regular taxable income, but do count in figuring the income subject to the alternative tax. That tax *rate* is low (currently, 21%), but it applies to a larger amount of taxable income. If the alternative minimum tax comes out higher than the regular income tax, then the excess is the AMT you owe. We display it on the last line of the screen and carry it over to Form 1040.

CAUTION!

Pressing F8 pulls the starred items from Schedules A, B, and E – not from MONEY or Form 1040! So be certain to update those schedules first, before coming here to press F8.

DON'T MISS THE AMT CREDIT...

If you owe AMT this year, it may serve to offset regular income tax in future years when no AMT is due. Or if you paid AMT in a prior year and none is due now, you may be able to claim a credit for a portion of the prior AMT you paid. Check with your accountant.

...AND FOREIGN TAX CREDIT

Note, too, that if you're due a foreign tax credit, most of it can serve to offset the AMT. We don't show that here.

CHANGING THE LAW

If the 21% AMT tax rate, exemptions, or other parts of the formula have changed, select Tax Brackets and Parameters from the TAX menu and make the same changes.

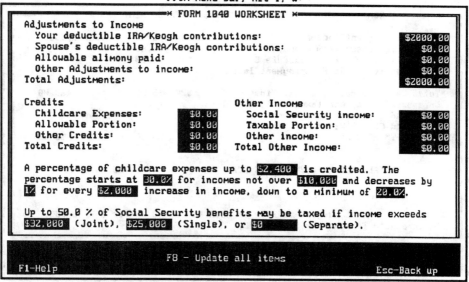

<From Menu Bar, Alt-T, W>

FORM 1040 WORKSHEET

Press F8 and then make any needed changes. When you return to Form 1040, everything here will be summarized there. If you allotted more to your deductible IRA budget bucket than will in fact be deductible, here's the place to change it. With IRAs, if either spouse is covered by a pension plan, the usual $2,000 limit decreases by 20 cents for each $1 by which adjusted gross income exceeds $25,000 for single taxpayers, $40,000 joint. MYM does not figure this for you.

OTHER ADJUSTMENTS TO INCOME pulls up only the "Penalties for Early Withdrawal [1040]" tax barrel. Any dependents, not just children, come under the **CHILDCARE CREDIT**. Also, if you have two or more, DOUBLE the figure we show as being the basis on which the credit is figured. Note: "Taxpayer" and "Spouse" Salary Budget Categories are needed in calculating "Childcare Expenses." **OTHER CREDITS** are any you've dumped into the "Tax Credits [1040]" tax barrel in MONEY (it's at the tail-end of the [1040] group of tax barrels), including the foreign tax credit.

SOCIAL SECURITY INCOME is taxed in accordance with the last boxes on the screen which, again, you can change. If you recorded tax-free interest in Schedule B, we know about it and include it in our calculation.

OTHER INCOME is fully taxed and here pulls up the budget items you dumped into these [1040] tax barrels: State & Local Tax Refunds, Alimony Received, Pension/Annuity Income, Unemployment Compensation, and IRA Distributions.

```
                    <From Menu Bar, Alt-T, S>
┌══════════× SCHEDULE SE - SOCIAL SECURITY SELF-EMPLOYMENT TAX ×══════════┐
│                                                                          │
│  Net Self Employment Income              Yourself      Your Spouse       │
│   ×Net Profit/(Loss) from Schedule F:       $0.00                        │
│   ×Net Profit/(Loss) from Schedule C:       $0.00                        │
│    Other Qualified  Self-Employment Income:                              │
│  FICA/RRTA TAX COMPUTATION                                               │
│   ×Total Social Security Wages, Tips:    $20,833.33         $0.00        │
│    Unreported Tips, etc taxed on Form 4137:                             │
│    Qualified US Government Wages:                                        │
│    Qualified Church Wages:                                               │
│  SELF-EMPLOYMENT TAX:                        $0.00         $0.00         │
│                                                                          │
│         TOTAL SELF-EMPLOYMENT TAX DUE:            $0.00                   │
│                                                                          │
│                                                                          │
│  The maximum amount subject to FICA or RRTA tax of 13.02% is $48,000.00. │
│  The threshold for the tax is $400.00.                                   │
└──────────────────────────────────────────────────────────────────────────┘
           F8 - Update × items
  F1-Help                                        Esc-Back up
```

SELF-EMPLOYMENT TAX

Fill out Schedules C and F before coming here, because F8 summons numbers from those schedules. MYM then figures your tax, knowing that income beyond the maximum is not taxed, and that wages on which you've already paid Social Security tax — which we get from MONEY, not from anything you may hypothetically have entered on Form 1040 — count toward the maximum. (If the tax rate or maximum taxable amount we show at the bottom of the screen has changed, select Tax Tables & Parameters from the TAX menu and press F2.)

A single, self-employed plumber in New York City who reports his 30th $1,000 of 1990 income is thus slated to pay around $150 of it in Social Security tax, $40 in NY City Unincorporated Business Tax, $40 in NY City Income Tax, $80 in NY State Income Tax, and $280 or so in Federal Income Tax, putting him in the 59% marginal tax bracket and leaving him $410, or just enough to garage his car in Manhattan for 18 nights (including the 16% parking tax, but no tips, wash, or wax). We believe in reporting every penny of income, but it's no surprise a lot of New York City drains get unclogged off the books.

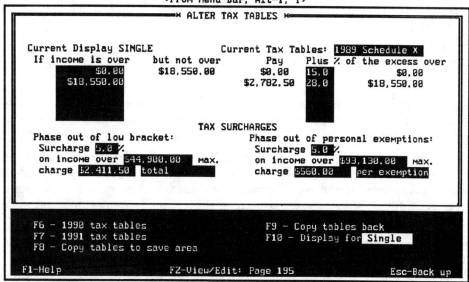

‹From Menu Bar, Alt-T, T›

ALTER TAX TABLES

We've made the tax tables and other parameters — press F2 to see the others — easily modifiable. Those shown here are for 1990 or 1991, depending on which year you loaded in (F6 or F7). When you get your new tax forms each year, use F10 to select YOUR tax table (Single, Joint, etc.) and compare it with the one you were sent. Type in any needed adjustments.

Note, however, that if you then load in a different year's numbers, any changes you've made are not retained. To spare your having to reenter the brackets, we've provided a "save area" with room for a single set of brackets. Press F8 to save the new brackets in that pouch and F9 to dump them back out. This is handy, too, if there's a hypothetical set of brackets you'd like to preserve — a set Congress is pondering, say, or Sweden's, if you'd like periodically to see how much better off you are living here.

The best way to learn to modify the tax brackets here is to play with the screen. Blank out everything with the Space Bar and then start from the top. Notice that when you enter the second line, WE supply the proper "but-not-more-than" figure for the first line. You'll quickly get the hang of it — and pressing F6 or F7 will always get you back to home base.

To change tax rules, press F2. (And if you switch tax years, do so again. We do not preserve tax-rule changes in the "save area").

ADAPTING A SET OF BRACKETS FOR YOUR STATE TAX ESTIMATE

Many state and municipal income taxes are graduated in much the same way as the federal tax. So, if you like, take one of the tax tables you DON'T need for your federal tax and adapt it.

Take, for example, the head-of-household table and type in your state tax brackets, instead. (In the text field, where it might now say "1991 Schedule Z," enter "California — 1991" so you remember what you've done.)

Now you can get a fix on your state income tax liability at any time by selecting "Head of House" as your Form 1040 filing status. The computer won't know you really file jointly and are merely out to see what you owe California. Our answer won't be exact, because your state may use a different personal exemption from Uncle Sam, and may treat other items differently, as well. But for most taxpayers it will be close.

If you live in a flat-tax state where the rate is, say, 3%, just type $0 and 3% in the boxes on the first line and then $1 and 3% on the second. Blank out everything else. If your state has more than 5 tax brackets, lump the first few into one. Use your state's tax table to figure the tax on the first $10,000, say — $430. Then divide by $10,000 (4.3% in this example) and there it is: instead of six little brackets, a single 4.3% bracket on the first $10,000. Enter $0 and 4.3% on our first line and the remaining 4 brackets on the remaining lines.

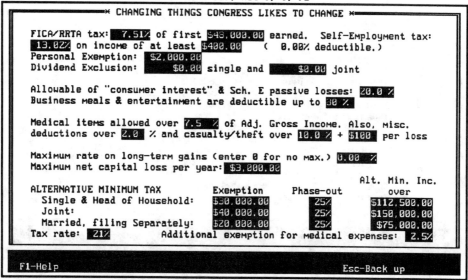

‹From Menu Bar, Alt-T, T, F2›

CHANGING THINGS CONGRESS LIKES TO CHANGE

Here are some key numbers for the tax year you've loaded. Don't let your child get at this and change everything without your knowing it, or we'll be giving you some pretty strange answers.

But if the tax code changes, you'll be able to accommodate most or all the change by modifying these boxes (and some others you'll find on the schedules or worksheets to which they apply). Note that your changes are retained only until you load in a different year's rules. If you then return to this year, be sure to reenter your changes.

If you've registered for the newsletter and Version 8 upgrade, we hope to keep you abreast of any necessary changes, and/or make them for you.

To change the capital gains law, visit Portfolio Options on the FILE menu.

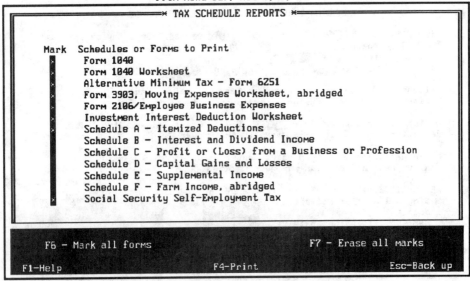

<From Menu Bar, Alt-T, 1, F4>

```
═══════════════════════╡ TAX SCHEDULE REPORTS ╞═══════════════════════

      Mark   Schedules or Forms to Print
             Form 1040
             Form 1040 Worksheet
             Alternative Minimum Tax - Form 6251
             Form 3903, Moving Expenses Worksheet, abridged
             Form 2106/Employee Business Expenses
             Investment Interest Deduction Worksheet
             Schedule A - Itemized Deductions
             Schedule B - Interest and Dividend Income
             Schedule C - Profit or (Loss) from a Business or Profession
             Schedule D - Capital Gains and Losses
             Schedule E - Supplemental Income
             Schedule F - Farm Income, abridged
             Social Security Self-Employment Tax


         F6 - Mark all forms                   F7 - Erase all marks

      F1-Help                  F4-Print                      Esc-Back up
```

PRINTING FORMS AND SCHEDULES

Fill in the blanks and press F4 or chicken out with ESCape. If printing or condensed printing doesn't work, select Printer Setup from Program Setup on the FILE menu.

‹From Menu Bar, Alt-T, X›

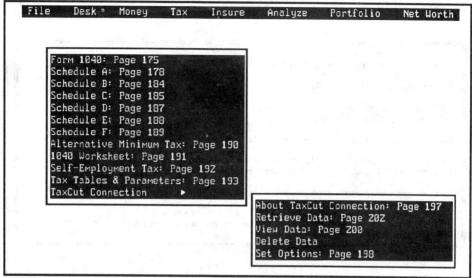

| File | Desk ° | Money | Tax | Insure | Analyze | Portfolio | Net Worth |

Form 1040: Page 175
Schedule A: Page 178
Schedule B: Page 184
Schedule C: Page 185
Schedule D: Page 187
Schedule E: Page 188
Schedule F: Page 189
Alternative Minimum Tax: Page 190
1040 Worksheet: Page 191
Self-Employment Tax: Page 192
Tax Tables & Parameters: Page 193
TaxCut Connection   ▶

About TaxCut Connection: Page 197
Retrieve Data: Page 202
View Data: Page 200
Delete Data
Set Options: Page 198

ABOUT TAXCUT CONNECTION

Andrew Tobias' TaxCut, Managing Your Money's award-winning sister program, helps you prepare your Form 1040 and up to 38 other forms and schedules. All print on plain blank paper in IRS-approved format, ready to sign and send.

TaxCut Connection is the link between MYM 7.0 and TaxCut. Here in MYM it extracts all your tax-related data and lets you make changes before exporting it to TaxCut. TaxCut can then import much of the data to the correct forms and schedules, and provide a list of the items it can't, with instructions for handling them. Even if you don't own TaxCut you may find the Connection useful for the special kinds of reports it lets you print. To use it, first select Set Options. Then select Retrieve Data.

- If you do just want to see what we can do, ignore the warning you'll get that "the TaxCut directory does not exist."

- If you have already run the retrieval process, select View Last Data to pick up where you left off, or, if you Retrieve Data again, to write a fresh set over what you had before.

- If disk space is very tight, you may wish to choose our Delete Data option, but ordinarily you would not.

- Note! Nothing you do in the TaxCut Connection affects your real MYM data in any way. So play all you like — and take several passes at this before finally exporting the results to TaxCut for real. Even then you can redo it — except that once you've done real work in TaxCut, a new import from MYM will overwrite it.

<From Menu Bar, Alt-T, X, S>

```
 File    Desk    Money    Tax    Insure    Analyze    Portfolio    Net Worth

                        ═══ SET OPTIONS ═══

   Please answer all the questions below.

   What tax year is your data in 90

   You'll find my current TaxCut data files in the following drive or
   directory:  C:\TAXCUT90
   ──────────────────────────MONEY DATA──────────────────────────
   Would you like to include budget data in this report?  Yes
   If so, would you like full detail of the data  Yes
   ──────────────────────────PORTFLIO DATA ──────────────────────
   Would you like to include portfolio data in this report? Yes
   If so, how does your broker report sale proceeds.  My broker reports
   Net   sale proceeds.


                        F10 - Save Options
```

TAXCUT CONNECTION: SET OPTIONS

WHAT TAX YEAR IS YOUR DATA?

As far as the IRS is concerned, every year is a new ball game. Do you want us to retrieve 1990 transactions? 1991? We'll ignore transactions from any year except the one you set here.

WHERE ARE YOUR TAXCUT DATA FILES

If you own TaxCut, they'll probably be in your c:\taxcut90 directory with the rest of the program, just as we've guessed. If you've renamed that directory or have them, say, on drive D: instead of C:, let us know.

If you don't own TaxCut, or haven't set it up yet for this year — you're just here to see what we can do — just let us go on thinking those files are in c:\taxcut90, and ignore the error message you'll get telling you we can't find them.

WHAT SHOULD WE RETRIEVE?

It's fine to set everything to YES ... but if you don't use our PORTFOLIO section, you obviously don't have to bother retrieving portfolio data. Or if you've already retrieved everything once but now want to get your Portfolio Data again, because something has changed, set Budget to NO and Portfolio to YES.

Saying YES to "Detail" for budget data instructs us to display every "unique payee" in each budget category. Say NO, and we'll pull up category totals only — except where the IRS needs to see detail, such as your W2 information and your Schedule B dividend and interest payors. It's fine to do it either way. Choosing NO just avoids some of the clutter. (Once you're looking at the display, Ctrl-V is available to elaborate on specific items for which you want more detail.)

THE CONCEPT OF "UNIQUE PAYEES"

For the purposes of the Connection, all transactions with identical names — and identical budget allocations — are aggregated into one. (Point to it on the display, press Ctrl-V, and we'll show you all its little components.) So instead of showing 26 biweekly payments to the orthodontist, we show one. It simplifies things.

BROKER'S METHOD OF REPORTING

Most brokers report to the IRS your total sales proceeds NET of commissions. A few have the incredibly annoying habit — in part because the IRS at one time required it — of reporting GROSS sales. You're then supposed to add the selling commission to the purchase price of each item (of all the convoluted ways of thinking!). We'll do this FOR you, to match the data sent to the IRS, if you set NET to GROSS. Press F10 to save these settings (you can always change them), and then select Retrieve Data.

RETRIEVE TAX DATA

Press F10 to retrieve the tax data you requested in Set Options.

Warning! — we'll overwrite the data retrieved in order to make room for this new extraction of tax data. You will lose any edits you may have made to the copy of the data we are working with.

BEFORE WE CONTINUE, A WORD ABOUT YOUR DATA

OK. We've "read" all the data you asked us to and put it into the form TaxCut requires. But before we wrap up MYM's side of the Connection (so you can go into TaxCut and actually import what we've done), we want to give you a chance to make changes.

Understand: any changes you make affect only the special transfer file we're going to create for TaxCut. Your original MYM data files are never altered by anything you do here.

If you DO want to change your real data, just back up and edit it in MONEY or PORTFOLIO. Then come back and Retrieve Data again. But what's your hurry? Why not at least see what we've done here?

VIEW TAXCUT CONNECTION SCREENS

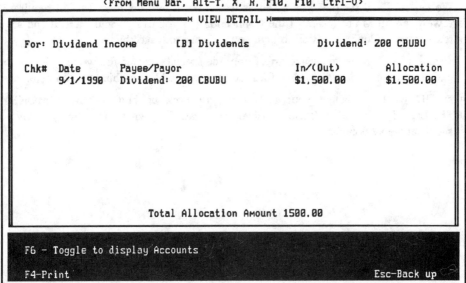

```
                    <From Menu Bar, Alt-T, X, R, F10, F10>
╔══════════════════════ VIEW BUDGET DATA TO BE EXPORTED ══════════════════════╗
║    Tax Category                                                              ║
║    Point       Budget Category       Payee                   Amount          ║
║                                                                              ║
║        ▐  Child Care Expense [1040]                                          ║
║        ▐       Child Care            We Care Day Care           $55.00       ║
║        ▐  Medical Expenses    [A]                                            ║
║        ▐       Medical               Eckerd's                   $32.50       ║
║        ▐  Dividend Income     [B]                                            ║
║        ▐       Dividends             Dividend: 100 IBM       $2,500.00       ║
║        ▐       Dividends             Dividend: 200 CBUBU     $1,500.00       ║
║        ▐       Dividends             Dividend: 25 WPPPS 9S99     $25.00       ║
║        ▐       Dividends             Procter & Gamble          $542.00       ║
║        ▐  Pre-Enact Act RE Inc [E]                                           ║
║        ▐       Rental Income         Mary Smith                $750.00       ║
║        ▐  Pre-Enact Act RE Exp [E]                                           ║
║        ▐       Rental Expense        Ellen's Design          $1,500.00       ║
║                                                                              ║
╠══════════════════════════════════════════════════════════════════════════════╣
║ Ctrl V   View Detail: Page 203        F8 - Flip to Sold Assets               ║
║ F6 - Consolidate Your Payees: Page 203                                       ║
║ F7 - Tax Category List: Page 204      F10 - Leave and Export                 ║
╠══════════════════════════════════════════════════════════════════════════════╣
║ F1-Help      F2-View/Edit      F3-Delete       F4-Print       Esc-Back up    ║
╚══════════════════════════════════════════════════════════════════════════════╝
```

```
                 <From Menu Bar, Alt-T, X, R, F10, F10, Ctrl-V>
╔═══════════════════════════════ VIEW DETAIL ═══════════════════════════════╗
║                                                                            ║
║   For: Dividend Income      [B] Dividends         Dividend: 200 CBUBU      ║
║                                                                            ║
║   Chk#  Date      Payee/Payor              In/(Out)       Allocation       ║
║         9/1/1990  Dividend: 200 CBUBU      $1,500.00      $1,500.00        ║
║                                                                            ║
║                                                                            ║
║                                                                            ║
║                                                                            ║
║                                                                            ║
║                                                                            ║
║                                                                            ║
║                                                                            ║
║                   Total Allocation Amount 1500.00                          ║
║                                                                            ║
╠════════════════════════════════════════════════════════════════════════════╣
║ F6 - Toggle to display Accounts                                             ║
║                                                                            ║
║ F4-Print                                                  Esc-Back up       ║
╚════════════════════════════════════════════════════════════════════════════╝
```

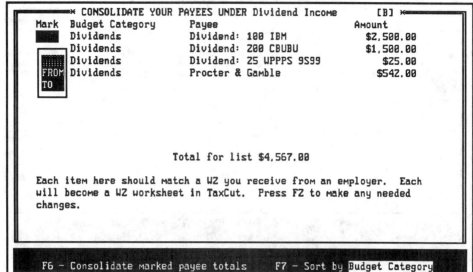

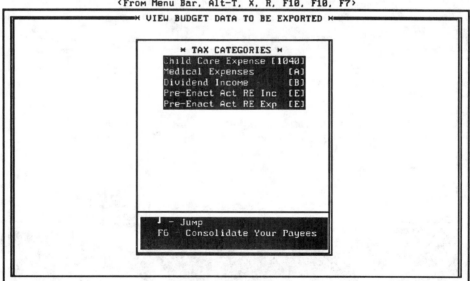

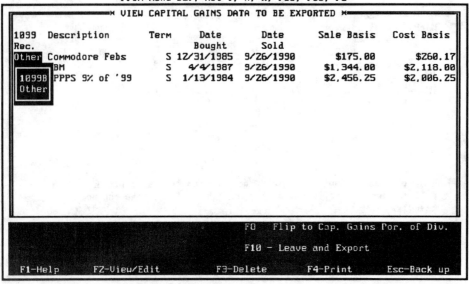

<From Menu Bar, Alt-T, X, R, F10, F10, F8>

```
═══════════* VIEW CAPITAL GAINS DATA TO BE EXPORTED *═══════════

1099   Description      Term    Date      Date      Sale Basis   Cost Basis
Rec.                            Bought    Sold
Other  Commodore Febs    S  12/31/1985  9/26/1990      $175.00      $260.17
       BM                S   4/4/1987   9/26/1990    $1,344.00    $2,118.00
1099B  PPPS 9% of '99    S   1/13/1984  9/26/1990    $2,456.25    $2,006.25
Other

                                    F8    Flip to Cap. Gains Por. of Div.

                                    F10 - Leave and Export

  F1-Help        F2-View/Edit         F3-Delete         F4-Print        Esc-Back up
```

<From Menu Bar, Alt-T, X, R, F10, F10, F8>

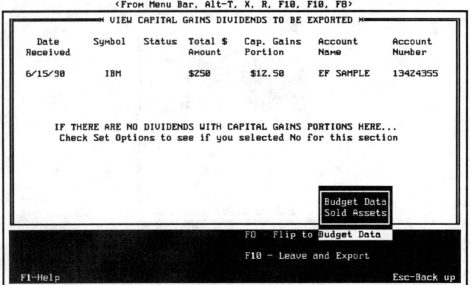

```
═══════════* VIEW CAPITAL GAINS DIVIDENDS TO BE EXPORTED *═══════════

  Date      Symbol   Status   Total $    Cap. Gains   Account     Account
Received                      Amount     Portion      Name        Number

6/15/90     IBM                 $250       $12.50      EF SAMPLE   13424355



    IF THERE ARE NO DIVIDENDS WITH CAPITAL GAINS PORTIONS HERE...
    Check Set Options to see if you selected No for this section



                                               Budget Data
                                               Sold Assets

                                    F8    Flip to Budget Data

                                    F10 - Leave and Export

  F1-Help                                                          Esc-Back up
```

```
┌══════════════════* VIEW OR EDIT UNIQUE PAYEE *══════════════════┐
│                                                                  │
│  Payee/Payor      Eckerd's                                       │
│  Budget Category  Medical                                        │
│  Amount               ███$32.50███                               │
│                                                                  │
│  Only the amount is modifiable, because for this type of category│
│  (unlike your W2 and Schedule B information) only the totals — not│
│  individual names — get passed through to TaxCut.  So don't worry│
│  about misspellings!  And if you've dumped this payee into the wrong│
│  budget category, don't worry about that either, so long as it's in│
│  the right TAX category.  (If it's not, just back up, print a list of│
│  the matching transactions using Ctrl-V, then edit the originals)│
│                                                                  │
│                                                                  │
│                  ────Page Scroll 2    of 8────                   │
├══════════════════════════════════════════════════════════════════┤
│                                                                  │
│                    F10 - Save Transaction                        │
│                                                                  │
│                       Esc-Back up                                │
└══════════════════════════════════════════════════════════════════┘
```

5

Insure

<From Menu Bar, Alt-I, Y>

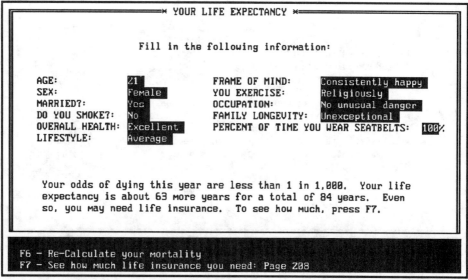

YOUR LIFE EXPECTANCY

Fill in the blanks and press F6. We claim no special accuracy here, but our calculations do attempt to incorporate much of the logic and data an actuary might use.

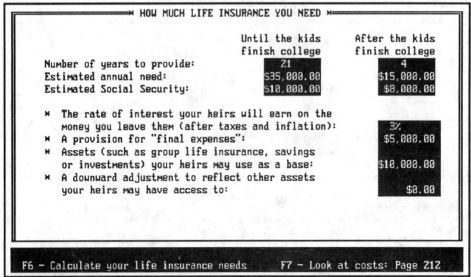

<From Menu Bar, Alt-I, H>

```
=*= HOW MUCH LIFE INSURANCE YOU NEED =*=

                              Until the kids      After the kids
                              finish college      finish college
  Number of years to provide:        21                  4
  Estimated annual need:      $35,000.00          $15,000.00
  Estimated Social Security:  $10,000.00           $8,000.00

  *  The rate of interest your heirs will earn on the
     money you leave them (after taxes and inflation):        3%
  *  A provision for "final expenses":                 $5,000.00
  *  Assets (such as group life insurance, savings
     or investments) your heirs may use as a base:    $10,000.00
  *  A downward adjustment to reflect other assets
     your heirs may have access to:                        $0.00


  F6 - Calculate your life insurance needs    F7 - Look at costs: Page 212
```

HOW MUCH LIFE INSURANCE YOU NEED

How much life insurance you should carry depends on how long and how well you'd like to provide for your heirs, and certain assumptions about the future. You will find that your needs vary greatly depending on the rate of interest you assume your heirs can earn on the money you leave them. This is particularly true when your needs go out over many years. A small change in your interest assumption makes a huge difference in the answer.

There's no way — or need — to get a precise figure. But filling in these blanks will give you a pretty good picture of your needs.

After getting a feel for how much coverage is required over various time periods and under various interest assumptions, you may well decide you can't afford as much insurance as you'd like. And so what you want to do is make the dollars you CAN allocate to life insurance stretch as far as possible. In the next section of this chapter we help you do just that.

But first fill in our blanks:

■ YEARS TO PROVIDE

In the left-hand box, enter the number of years left until your youngest child finishes school. If you have no kids, or all are grown, enter 0. (If you have no kids but plan to, you should still enter 0. Then redo the calculations when the baby is definitely on its way. Only if you are in questionable health does it make sense to secure extra coverage against the day you might have children.) In the right-hand box, enter the number of years, if any, you'd want to provide for your spouse or others AFTER the kids are grown. (Or from now on, if you have no kids or they already are grown.)

If you have no dependents (or elderly parents) to provide for, the correct answer in both these blanks is zero — you don't need life insurance.

If you do have dependents, and enter large numbers in these boxes, don't be surprised if the amount of insurance you need is also large. It takes a fortune to provide (say) $40,000 a year after taxes and inflation for 50 years. But do you really have to provide that long? Might 15 years be enough? Might your spouse remarry long before the kids are grown? Or be supported by the kids once they are? Or find a better paying job?

■ ANNUAL NEED

In the event of your death, what would it take to replace you financially? UNTIL the kids are grown, the figure might be around 75% of your current after-tax pay (not 100% because there would be one fewer mouth to feed, body to clothe, etc.). AFTER the kids are grown the figure might be 60%. Think about it and enter any figures you want. One thing you DON'T have to allow for here is inflation — we deal with that further down.

■ SOCIAL SECURITY

From your estimated annual need we subtract the amount Social Security might be expected to kick in. It may be fair to assume that Social Security benefits will remain about constant in current dollars — that Congress will not raise them, except to keep pace with inflation, nor slash them drastically.

Thus, it's reasonable to enter in these boxes the after-tax benefit your heirs would get if you died today. The more they'd get, the less insurance you need.

And just how much would your spouse receive if you died today?

Currently a widow or widower typically received $8,000 to $16,000 a year if caring for one child, $10,000 to $21,000 if caring for more than one. Those without dependent children receive no benefits until they reach their 60s — currently about $5,000 to $10,000 a year. The exact amounts depend on how long and how much you've been paying into the system. For a more precise estimate, write your local Social Security office.

Chances are you're at or near the top of the range. But because benefits are not likely to FULLY to keep pace with inflation,

■ RATE YOUR HEIRS WILL EARN

After taxes and inflation your heirs would be doing well to earn 3% over the long term. (During the Seventies, it was all too easy to earn a NEGATIVE return.) Take a guess. Indeed, take several. The beauty of the computer is that it allows you to experiment.

■ FINAL EXPENSES

For burial, grief-induced family illness, and the like. The rule of thumb is 50% of your gross salary.

■ ASSETS TO USE AS A BASE

If you have $5 million in T-bills, chances are you don't need ANY life insurance. Enter here your net worth exclusive of any assets it would be awkward for your heirs to unload (like the house).

This is also the place to include life insurance you may already have under group policies at work. (If you could be sure of dying at work, you'd be able to count on hefty worker's compensation benefits, too. Death in a commercial plane crash is even better.)

■ DOWNWARD ADJUSTMENT

Have your children wealthy grandparents who would be willing to see them through any emergency? This is a perfectly legitimate reason to make a downward adjustment in your life insurance needs.

Other to consider: your spouse could remarry, in which case the "number of years" you entered on the first line might be reduced; your spouse might significantly increase his or her earnings, which would reduce or eliminate the income gap ("annual needs") you were looking to life insurance to fill.

When you're all done, press F6.

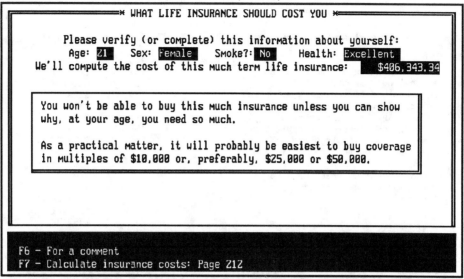

‹From Menu Bar, Alt-I, W›

SPECIFY HOW MUCH INSURANCE TO PRICE

Make any changes you like and then press F6 for a comment (if we have anything to say), followed by F7 to calculate your cost.

<From Menu Bar, Alt-I, W, F7>

```
═════════════════════════════M LIFE INSURANCE COSTS M═════════════════════════

          Annual premiums based on age for $406,343.34 of term insurance:

                                               Age        Premium
  These low rates are based on a                25       $226.77
  reversionary term policy that                 26       $226.77
  requires you to requalify every ten           27       $226.77
  years.  If you don't, the rates go            28       $226.77
  much higher ... although, of                  29       $316.16
  course, you are free to apply for             30       $320.23
  cheaper coverage elsewhere.  To see           31       $326.32
  a set of rates that do not involve            32       $336.48
  a physical exam for                           33       $338.51
  requalification, press F6.  For               34       $346.64
  more general information, please              35       $356.80
  press F1.                                     36       $364.92
                                               37       $377.11
                                               38       $393.37



  F7 - For information after age 69: Page 215
```

F7 - For information after age 69: Page 215

WHAT LIFE INSURANCE SHOULD COST

These rates are for RENEWABLE TERM insurance and are offered as benchmarks, only. If you're already paying even less, great. Premiums on whole life — not illustrated here — start out several times higher but remain level for the whole of your life. We believe most families are better served buying term insurance and investing the difference.

If you ARE interested in a good universal life policy (a more modern form of whole life), one of your best bets may be USAA Life, in San Antonio, which does all its business by phone. Call 800-531-8000; in Texas, 800-292-8000. Ask, also, about USAA term insurance. But understand that we have absolutely no connection with any of the companies listed in this section of Managing Your Money, nor can we provide any assurance as to their future rates or service. Not all the products they offer may be good ones, by any means, and many companies not listed here offer attractive policies as well.

Renewable term insurance is plain vanilla insurance. If you die, they pay. It gets more expensive as the odds of your dying increase. "Renewable" (to age 65 or 70) means you can't be dropped from the policy, so long as you pay the premiums, no matter how your health may deteriorate. Most companies offer a "waiver-of-premium" rider that keeps your policy in force should you become disabled.

If you're hardy, consider "reversionary term." These plans start out dirt cheap and allow you to requalify every few years by passing a physical. Should your health deteriorate, sharply higher rates apply.

If you expect to keep your policy in force a long time, consider a mutual insurer like the Prudential. Dividends will significantly lessen the rise in rates in the later years of the policy.

If you're in the market for a large policy (premiums in excess of $500 a year), you may wish to let an independent insurance agent well versed in life insurance do your shopping for you. Just be clear in explaining what you want: the cheapest possible renewable term insurance. Buy in bulk. Four $50,000 policies cost far more than one $200,000 one.

Call InsuranceQuote (800-972-1104) and SelectQuote (800-343-1985) to be mailed rates and descriptions of a handful of low-cost policies each will recommend at no cost to you (but a commission if you buy).

Here are some companies that MAY offer low term insurance rates (but ALWAYS shop around):

UNDER $100,000:

Savings Bank Life Insurance (if you live or work in MASS, NY, or CONN)

Savers Life (call 800-223-7608, or 212-753-6531 in NY

or write c/o AIG Life, 70 Pine St., NYC 10270)

$100,000 AND UP:	HOME OFFICE
AMICA Life	Providence
Bankers National Life	Parsippany, NJ
Bankers Security Life	New York
Berkshire Life	Pittsfield, MA
Executive Life	Beverly Hills
First Colony Life	Lynchburg, VA
ITT Life	Minneapolis
N. Amer. Co. for Life Ins.	Garden City, NY
Old Line Life	Milwaukee
Protective Life	Birmingham, AL
Southwestern Life	Dallas
Transamerica Life	San Francisco
USAA Life	San Antonio

And/or ask your local independent insurance agent to shop for you.

SHOULD YOU DROP YOUR WHOLE LIFE POLICY?

Although we're not wild about whole life (and other investment-oriented insurance products), it doesn't necessarily follow that you should drop coverage already purchased. You've paid the front-end sales charge; dropping the policy won't get it back.

To get a sense of how good an investment it will be from here on out ... or to evaluate a new policy you are considering ... you need to break it into two elements: the insurance portion of the package and the investment portion. To do this, subtract from each year's premium what you'd pay for an equivalent amount of term coverage. (Subtract a little more to reflect special features or flexibility the whole life plan may offer.) What you're left with is the estimated cost of the investment element of your policy.

Now go to the Investment Analysis section of ANALYZE and enter the current surrender value of the policy, if any, as CASH OUT this year. It is, in effect, the amount you're investing with the insurer. Add to that this year's premium. Then, for each subsequent year, enter the projected premium you'd pay (as adjusted above) as CASH OUT, and dividends you'd receive as CASH IN.

Do this for 5 years and then pretend you surrendered your policy. Enter the projected surrender value 5 years from now as your CASH IN. Calculate the internal rate of return on your investment. Is it attractive? Good! Not attractive? Well, that tells you something. (Although remember: in most cases this is largely or fully a tax-free return, which makes it better than it seems.)

Now enter the 6th through 10th years of the projection and see how you'd fare after 10 years. And after 15 and after 20. This process will take time. But if you're careful in entering the data, you'll have a better sense of the value of what may be one of your largest investments. What you won't know is whether you'll actually get the rate of return that, typically, is "illustrated but not guaranteed" in insurers' projections. The fact that they may always have met their projections in the past, during decades of gradually rising interest rates, does not mean they'll meet them in the future, should interest rates trend back toward historically more normal levels.

Another approach: calculate how much you'd save each year with term insurance and what those savings could grow to in an IRA. Compare that with the surrender value of the policy after a like period. Remember, IRA contributions may be deductible; insurance premiums ordinarily are not. But IRA withdrawals are taxable; life insurance cash value ordinarily is not. One last note: If you wouldn't "buy term and invest the difference" − if you'd *squander* the difference − then buy whole life, like the man says.

INSURANCE COSTS AFTER AGE 69

Term insurance becomes very expensive past the age of 60 or 65 for the simple reason that the insurer might actually have to pay off!

Most term policies don't allow purchase past 65 or renewal past 69, which is why we don't show rates beyond 69. Others allow renewal all the way to 100, but at a price. The same company that charged $500 for $100,000 of insurance to a male of 50 charged him $3,730 at 70 and $15,175 (!) at 85.

Ordinarily, you wouldn't renew term insurance much beyond 60 unless you knew you were in poor health, with the policy all too likely to pay off in a few years. But with decent planning, by the time term insurance does become prohibitive, YOU WON'T NEED IT. The kids will be grown, the mortgage paid off, and your assets substantial. (See ANALYZE's Retirement Planning section.)

If you are one who CAN'T save, then whole life or universal life may be for you. But bear in mind that many who buy whole life policies DROP them after just a year or two — losing not just their insurance coverage, but a good chunk of savings, too.

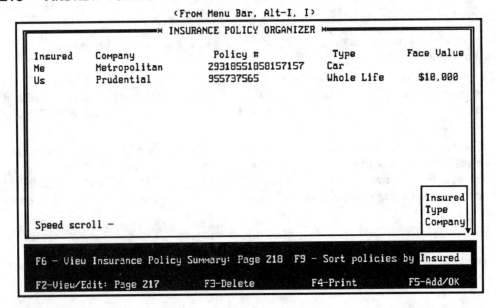

INSURANCE POLICY ORGANIZER

Here's a summary of your policies.

To add a new one, press F5. To see an existing one in more detail, highlight it and press F2. To sort them differently, press F9. To see a summary, press F6.

Three policies to consider if you don't have them:

1. An umbrella liability policy. If you've got much in the way of assets, it's worth paying the roughly $100 a year that buys $1 million in coverage. If you have a big skating party and everyone falls through the ice, it could come in handy. Talk to an insurance broker about this.

2. Disability. Financially, it can be a tragedy even worse than death. Talk to several life insurance agents (shop around).

3. Insurance for your computer. If you claim you use it for business, it may not be covered by your homeowner's policy. Check with a broker or call SAFEWARE at 800-848-3469 (614-262-0559 in Ohio), which sells a policy from American Bankers of Florida.

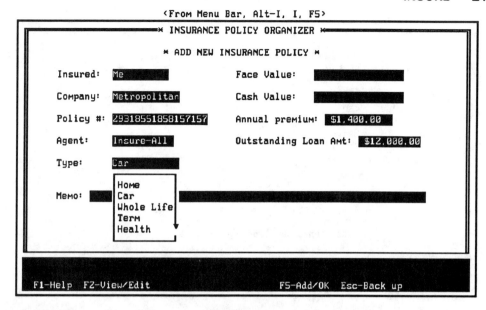

‹From Menu Bar, Alt-I, I, F5›

ADD OR EDIT AN INSURANCE POLICY

Fill in the blanks. "Insured" is the person or thing covered by the policy. Aetna may be the company, but who's your agent? Cash value and outstanding loan balance apply only to whole life policies (which includes universal life and any others that build savings, not just provide insurance).

Cash value sums to NET WORTH, but *policy loan balances don't.* They're picked up when you record them in the Loan Records section of MONEY.

Press F2 to note such things as who owns the policy (important with life insurance), the beneficiary, payment and expiration dates, and details of coverage ("fire, not flood," "20% co-insurance," "auto rentals, too").

```
                       <From Menu Bar, Alt-I, I, F6>
╔══════════════════════════════════════════════════════════════════╗
║  ┌───────────────────*  INSURANCE POLICY SUMMARY  *───────────┐   ║
║  │                                                            │   ║
║  │       Policy Type              Total Premium               │   ║
║  │                                                            │   ║
║  │       Life                        $150                     │   ║
║  │       Car                       $1,400                     │   ║
║  │       Home                          $0                     │   ║
║  │       Health                        $0                     │   ║
║  │       Accident                      $0                     │   ║
║  │       "Other"                       $0                     │   ║
║  │                                                            │   ║
║  │               Life Insurance Summary                       │   ║
║  │                                                            │   ║
║  │       Total coverage:          $10,000                     │   ║
║  │       Total cash value:        $10,000                     │   ║
║  │       Total loans outstanding:      $0                     │   ║
║  │                                                            │   ║
║  └────────────────────────────────────────────────────────────┘  ║
║                                                                    ║
║  F1-Help                                          Esc-Back up      ║
╚══════════════════════════════════════════════════════════════════╝
```

INSURANCE POLICY SUMMARY

Here's a little summary of your coverage. Total cash value, if any, sums to NET WORTH as one of your assets, but *policy loans, if any, do not* because we expect you to set those up as loans in MONEY, and THAT'S where they get picked up as liabilities by NET WORTH.

VITAL RECORDS

The following screens help "keep your affairs in order." They're also a sort of checklist. You have no will? No Social Security numbers for your kids? Your passport is about to expire? You haven't designated someone to take charge when YOU are about to expire? Some of it's rather morbid (sorry), but in an emergency, a little planning and organization go a long way. If you're married, the same holds true for your spouse. Each of you should have a vital records log. F8 flips between the two and F7 spares retyping items that are the same.

The screens seem one-dimensional — who ever heard of entering an address on a single line? — but F2 makes all the difference in the world, as when (to put it in technical terms) the Wizard of Oz jumps from black-and-white to color. Addresses can have three lines; you can add ten children beyond those we give you slots for; you can give full instructions for the care and feeding of each of your pets.

But you needn't bother to use F2 to attach addresses and phone numbers to the key people you list (your lawyer, etc.). If you already have them in the Card File, we can make up a little "directory" for you automatically as part of our comprehensive report — F4.

DON'T MISS THE POWERFUL REPORT CAPABILITY HERE

We organize everything you've entered (ignoring the stuff you've left blank), including all the "icebergs" you've attached with F2. But we also offer a comprehensive "inter-chapter" report of your own design, as you'll see when you press F4. You should probably print such a report periodically, so you, your spouse, and your attorney always have a copy, just in case. It might be a good idea to enter a note in the Reminder Pad, reminding you to print this report semi-annually, so it's always fairly current.

It's crucial to understand that this is not a legal document. It is no substitute for a will, nor for a power of attorney should you become incapacitated, nor a legally binding grant of your corneas to the Eye Bank, nor a legally binding instruction to your physician to keep you on or take you off life support. For those kinds of documents, consult an attorney. Finally, don't be shy. In the line for your obituary, which you can expand with F2 to epic length, you should enter awards you've won, charities you've supported, military service — anything you think might be of help to your heirs or the local reporter who, in the sad confusion of the moment, might not remember it all.

```
                          <From Menu Bar, Alt-I, V>
┌──────────────────────────────────────────────────────────────────────┐
│══════════════ ✷ VITAL RECORDS - OWNER'S RECORD PAGE 1 ✷══════════════ │
│                                                                        │
│ My legal name is:  ████████████                                        │
│ My date of birth:  ███████████      My Social Security #: ███████████  │
│ My legal address:  ████████████                                        │
│ I ▐don't▌ have a will.                                                  │
│   My most recent will is dated: ████████████                           │
│   It is located: ███████                                               │
│ The executors of my estate are: ██████████████████████                 │
│                                                                        │
│ My attorney: ███████████████        My doctor: ███████████████         │
│ My life insurance agent: █████████                                     │
│ My broker: █████████████            My banker: ███████████             │
│ My employer: ███████████            My secretary: █████████            │
│                                                                        │
│ I am a citizen of: ██████████              My blood type is: ██████    │
│ My passport #: ███████████   Expires: ████████                         │
│ Driver's license #: ███████         Expires: ████████                  │
│                                                                        │
├────────────────────────────────────────────────────────────────────── │
│ F6 - Second Page                          F8 - Spouse's record         │
│ F7 - Same as spouse                                                    │
│                                                                        │
│ F1-Help          F2-View/Edit            F4-Print       Esc-Back up    │
└──────────────────────────────────────────────────────────────────────┘
```

```
                        <From Menu Bar, Alt-I, V, F6>
┌──────────────────────────────────────────────────────────────────────┐
│══════════════ ✷ VITAL RECORDS - OWNER'S RECORD PAGE 2 ✷══════════════ │
│                                                                        │
│ My nearest of kin: ██████████████    Relationship: ██████████          │
│                                                                        │
│ Father: ██████████████              Mother: ██████████████             │
│                                                                        │
│ Children:  ████████████       Soc. Sec.: ████████████                  │
│            ████████████       Soc. Sec.:                               │
│            ████████████       Soc. Sec.:                               │
│            ████████████       Soc. Sec.:                               │
│            ████████████       Soc. Sec.:                               │
│ Other key  ████████████       Relationship:                            │
│ Relatives: ████████████       Relationship:                            │
│            ████████████       Relationship:                            │
│            ████████████       Relationship:                            │
│            ████████████       Relationship:                            │
│            ████████████       Relationship:                            │
│            ████████████       Relationship:                            │
│            ████████████       Relationship:                            │
│                                                                        │
├────────────────────────────────────────────────────────────────────── │
│ F6 - Third Page                           F8 - Spouse's record         │
│ F7 - Same as spouse                                                    │
│                                                                        │
│ F1-Help          F2-View/Edit            F4-Print       Esc-Back up    │
└──────────────────────────────────────────────────────────────────────┘
```

〈From Menu Bar, Alt-I, V, F6, F6〉

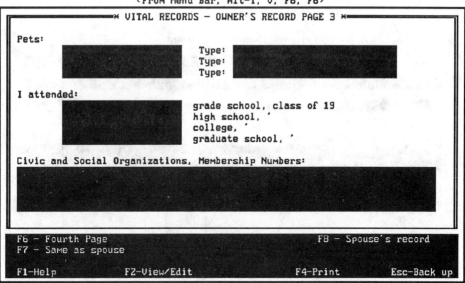

```
╔════════════════ ✕ VITAL RECORDS — OWNER'S RECORD PAGE 3 ✕ ═══════════════╗

  Pets:
                                        Type:
                                        Type:
                                        Type:

  I attended:
                                        grade school, class of 19
                                        high school, '
                                        college, '
                                        graduate school, '

  Civic and Social Organizations, Membership Numbers:




  ════════════════════════════════════════════════════════════════════════
   F6 - Fourth Page                              F8 - Spouse's record
   F7 - Same as spouse

   F1-Help            F2-View/Edit              F4-Print        Esc-Back up
```

〈From Menu Bar, Alt-I, V, F6, F6, F6〉

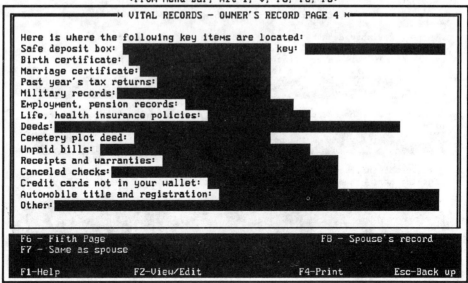

```
╔═══════════════ ✕ VITAL RECORDS — OWNER'S RECORD PAGE 4 ✕ ═══════════════╗

  Here is where the following key items are located:
  Safe deposit box:                             key:
  Birth certificate:
  Marriage certificate:
  Past year's tax returns:
  Military records:
  Employment, pension records:
  Life, health insurance policies:
  Deeds:
  Cemetery plot deed:
  Unpaid bills:
  Receipts and warranties:
  Canceled checks:
  Credit cards not in your wallet:
  Automobile title and registration:
  Other:

  ════════════════════════════════════════════════════════════════════════
   F6 - Fifth Page                               F8 - Spouse's record
   F7 - Same as spouse

   F1-Help            F2-View/Edit              F4-Print        Esc-Back up
```

`<From Menu Bar, Alt-I, V, F6, F6, F6, F6>`

```
━━━━━━━━━━━━━━━━━━※ VITAL RECORDS - OWNER'S RECORD PAGE 5 ※━━━━━━━━━━━━━━━━

  I have made the following provisions in the event
     - illness should render me incompetent:
  ████████████████████████████████████████████████████████████████████████

     - my life can only be sustained by "extraordinary means:"
  ████████████████████████████████████████████████████████████████████████

  I ██████████████████████████        my bodily organs:██████████████████


  This additional information may be of help in compiling my obituary:
  ████████████████████████████████████████████████████████████████████████

  These are my wishes with respect to funeral arrangements:
  ████████████████████████████████████████████████████████████████████████

  My clergyperson:████████████████████████████████████████████

━━━━━━━━━━━━━━━━━━━━━━━━━━━━━━━━━━━━━━━━━━━━━━━━━━━━━━━━━━━━━━━━━━━━━━━━━━━
  F6 - Final Page                                F8 - Spouse's record
  F7 - Same as spouse

  F1-Help          F2-View/Edit              F4-Print        Esc-Back up
```

`<From Menu Bar, Alt-I, V, F6, F6, F6, F6, F6>`

```
━━━━━━━━━━━━━━━━━━※ VITAL RECORDS - OWNER'S RECORD PAGE 6 ※━━━━━━━━━━━━━━━━

  Finally, you should be aware of the following assets, liabilities,
  promises and commitments I've made or that have been made to me; pending
  deals, special wishes and other important items that are not recorded
  elsewhere in this program or in my will:
  ████████████████████████████████████████████████████████████████████████

  Notes to myself on the current contents of my will and possible changes to
  discuss with my attorney:
  ████████████████████████████████████████████████████████████████████████

  A letter of instructions to be read in the event of my death (if you enter
  anything here, it will be printed as an introduction to the Vital Records
  Report):
  ████████████████████████████████████████████████████████████████████████
  ████████████████████████████████████████████████████████████████████████

━━━━━━━━━━━━━━━━━━━━━━━━━━━━━━━━━━━━━━━━━━━━━━━━━━━━━━━━━━━━━━━━━━━━━━━━━━━
  F7 - Same as spouse                            F8 - Spouse's record

  F1-Help          F2-View/Edit              F4-Print        Esc-Back up
```

<From Menu Bar, Alt-I, V, F4>

```
╔══════════════════════════════════════════════════════════════╗
║                     ━━━━ ✕ VITAL RECORDS REPORTS ✕━━━━         ║
║                                                                ║
║    Print the Vital Records Report for:  Owner                  ║
║                                                                ║
║      From Insure,   Insurance Policy Report                    ║
║                                                                ║
║      From Card File,                                           ║
║            each record special coded   , under the heading Key People    ║
║            each record special coded   , under the heading Relatives     ║
║            each record special coded   , under the heading Beneficiaries ║
║                                                                ║
║      From Reminder Pad,    All pending reminders               ║
║                                                                ║
║      From Net Worth,    Your Net Worth Corporate              ║
║                                                                ║
║      From Money,    Account Summary,     Loan Summary          ║
║                         Aged Payables,    Aged Receivables     ║
║                                                                ║
║      From Portfolio,                        Report            ║
║                         Current Financial Reminders           ║
║                                                                ║
╠════════════════════════════════════════════════════════════════╣
║  F1-Help                  F4-Print                  Esc-Back up ║
╚════════════════════════════════════════════════════════════════╝
```

VITAL RECORDS REPORTS

This screen lets you pull together an amazingly complete report. You may just want to mark the first box, the highlighted Vital Records report, and leave it at that. We'll print your entries, icebergs and all, in a form we think your spouse or executor would find very helpful if anything terrible ever happened to you.

We'll print just your report, just your spouse's, or both. Print to disk, and you can make changes with your word processor. But on top of the Vital Records report, you can use this screen to order a host of "supporting schedules." Actually, they're all just reports you could get elsewhere in MYM. But this screen relieves you of all the running around. Presuming you have enough paper and that it doesn't jam, you'll have a full report waiting for you when you get back from lunch. (If you do have a printer that occasionally jams, or are not quite sure what you're getting into, it might be wise to select only a few reports at a time.)

When you give the go-ahead, MYM will visit the database of each chapter you've selected, printing the requested information as it goes. If you have your data on floppies, it will prompt you for the file it needs (so you can't take off for lunch, after all).

Mark the reports you want us to print with an X (or anything else). But if you want us to print a report of key people from your Card File, don't use X's; use the Card File codes you want us to fetch. And tell us what heading to print above each group of names and addresses.

If your Card File is not in shape for this right now, just press Ctrl-C and use the F7 shortcut there to QuickEdit special codes. And note that the Card File distinguishes between upper- and lower-case letters, so if you ask us to print the R's here, it will skip past those coded "r."

The Reminder Pad report lists ALL your pending reminders, appointments, and projects, so, if worse came to worst, those you left behind would have some help in trying to wind things down.

If you include your Net Worth report, we'll update it on the way in, to be sure it reflects your numbers from other sections, and save our work as we leave.

The other reports are fairly self-explanatory. Or just give them a try. If we haven't offered one you want, or in the format you want it, just wait until we're done and then go print it individually.

Remember, you can preface the Vital Records report with a "letter of instructions." It's the last item we ask you for in Vital Records. So if you already follow my practice of periodically printing four sets of MONEY reports — by payee, by date, by check number, and by budget category — you could just say so in this letter. "Oh, and honey, you'll find all my transactions for the year in the manilla folder I keep with pending bills, etc., beside the computer." Your lawyer may wonder why you're calling him honey, but the reports should be highly useful in settling your affairs.

If you have no hard disk, you'll find we can't include any of the MONEY reports if you print to disk. Otherwise...

If you print to disk, we'll put each report you choose in a file name that begins with VR (Vital Records) and has an extension, as follows:

Insurance Policy Report	VRINS.RPT
Card File Report	VRADDRA.RPT
Card File Report	VRADDRB.RPT
Card File Report	VRADDRC.RPT
Reminder Summary Report	VRREM.RPT
Networth Report	VRNET.RPT
Account Summary Report	VRACCT.RPT
Loan Summary Report	VRLOAN.RPT
Aged Payable Report	VRPAY.RPT
Aged Receivable Report	VRREC.RPT

6

Analyze

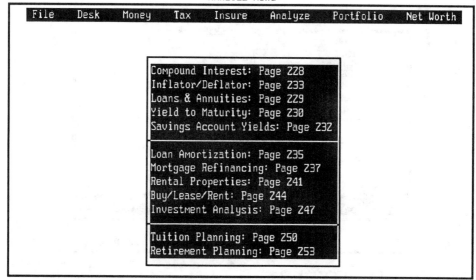

⟨ANALYZE Menu⟩

| File | Desk | Money | Tax | Insure | Analyze | Portfolio | Net Worth |

Compound Interest: Page 228
Inflator/Deflator: Page 233
Loans & Annuities: Page 229
Yield to Maturity: Page 230
Savings Account Yields: Page 232

Loan Amortization: Page 235
Mortgage Refinancing: Page 237
Rental Properties: Page 241
Buy/Lease/Rent: Page 244
Investment Analysis: Page 247

Tuition Planning: Page 250
Retirement Planning: Page 253

COMPOUND INTEREST, LOAN, ANNUITY, AND YIELD CALCULATIONS

This HELP applies to four different sections of ANALYZE:

1. Compound Interest

2. Loans & Annuities

3. Yield to Maturity

4. Savings Account Yields

To a normal human, they seen rather different, so we've given each its own menu selection and display. But underneath they're all one, and so all attached to a single HELP message. Just scroll down to the one you want.

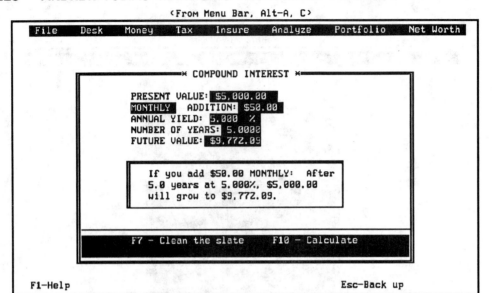

COMPOUND INTEREST

Want to know what $1 will grow to in 83 years at 4.5% interest? Or how long it will take to reach $1 million at that rate? Or how many dollars a week you'd have to set aside to get there in 18 years? Just fill in the blanks.

PRESENT VALUE is the amount you start out with. It could be zero or a million bucks; the computer will believe anything. FUTURE VALUE is what that sum will grow to at a given interest rate and over a given number of years. (For 20 years, nine months, enter "20.75" years.) Will you be adding to the pot along the way? If so, tell us how much and how often. Otherwise, enter zero. ANNUAL YIELD is the annual rate at which your money will grow.

Enter any FOUR of the variables. If all five lines are filled in, just blank out one with the Space Bar. When you're ready, press F6. The program solves for the fifth variable.

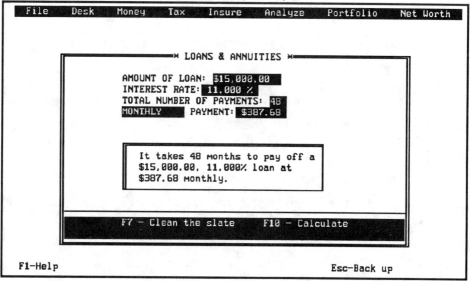

<From Menu Bar, Alt-A, L>

```
 File    Desk   Money   Tax   Insure   Analyze   Portfolio   Net Worth
```

```
                    ═══ × LOANS & ANNUITIES ×═══
             AMOUNT OF LOAN: $15,000.00
             INTEREST RATE: 11.000 %
             TOTAL NUMBER OF PAYMENTS: 48
             MONTHLY      PAYMENT: $387.68


             ┌─────────────────────────────────┐
             │ It takes 48 months to pay off a │
             │ $15,000.00, 11.000% loan at     │
             │ $387.68 monthly.                │
             └─────────────────────────────────┘


              F7 - Clean the slate    F10 - Calculate
```

F1-Help   Esc-Back up

LOANS AND ANNUITIES

Enter any three of the variables. If all four are filled in, just blank one out with the Space Bar. When you're ready, press F6. The program solves for the fourth variable.

Want to know the payments on a $75,000 25-year mortgage at 10.25%? Fill in the blanks. The interest rate on a $1,000 loan repayable over four years at $28.53 a month? Fill in the blanks.

TO PRINT A CUSTOMIZED AMORTIZATION SCHEDULE, BACK UP TO THE MENU AND SELECT LOAN AMORTIZATION.

This display is written for "loans" but applies equally well to annuities. Want to know the monthly income a $40,000 7% annuity would throw off for 25 years? Or how long $100,000 earning 12% would last if you withdrew $20,000 a year? Fill in the blanks. With an annuity, YOU are making the loan — to an insurance company — and it is making monthly payments to YOU. Most pay as long as you live. With this screen you can at least see how long that has to be in order for the annuity to outperform a conventional fixed-term investment.

Note also that with an annuity, your proceeds are taxed as you withdraw them; with a tax-free bond (say), they are never taxed. This is an argument against tying up your funds in an annuity (as is the fact that the alluring interest rate you're quoted may be guaranteed only for a year or so).

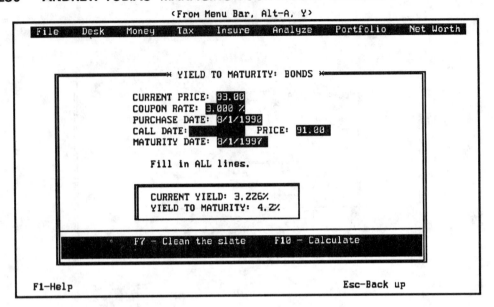

```
                      <From Menu Bar, Alt-A, Y>
 ┌──────────────────────────────────────────────────────────────┐
 │  File   Desk   Money   Tax   Insure   Analyze   Portfolio   Net Worth │
 │                                                                │
 │       ┌──────────── YIELD TO MATURITY: BONDS ────────────┐     │
 │       │                                                  │     │
 │       │   CURRENT PRICE: 93.00                           │     │
 │       │   COUPON RATE: 3.000 %                           │     │
 │       │   PURCHASE DATE: 8/1/1990                         │     │
 │       │   CALL DATE:          PRICE: 91.00               │     │
 │       │   MATURITY DATE: 8/1/1997                         │     │
 │       │                                                  │     │
 │       │      Fill in ALL lines.                          │     │
 │       │                                                  │     │
 │       │       ┌──────────────────────────────┐           │     │
 │       │       │  CURRENT YIELD: 3.226%        │           │     │
 │       │       │  YIELD TO MATURITY: 4.2%      │           │     │
 │       │       └──────────────────────────────┘           │     │
 │       │                                                  │     │
 │       ├──────────────────────────────────────────────────┤     │
 │       │  ·   F7 - Clean the slate     F10 - Calculate    │     │
 │       └──────────────────────────────────────────────────┘     │
 │                                                                │
 │  F1-Help                                    Esc-Back up        │
 └──────────────────────────────────────────────────────────────┘
```

YIELD TO MATURITY

Bonds are issued in multiples of $1,000, but their prices are quoted in cents on the dollar. A bond selling at "93" is selling for 93 cents on the dollar — $930. A bond selling at "129-1/2" is selling for $1,295. Be sure to enter the prices as quoted — 93, not $930. A bond's stated rate of interest is its COUPON RATE.

The Bulova "sixes of 1992," listed in the paper as "6s92," pay 6% interest on $1,000 — $60 a year in $30 semi-annual installments — until they mature in 1992. But trading at 71 when I first started using this example years ago, their CURRENT YIELD was 8.45% ($60 interest on a $710 bond).

Meanwhile, Bulova was promising to redeem the bond at par — 10 cents on the dollar — in 1992. To grow from $710 to $1,000 in 3 years (this was back in 1989) is to grow at better than 12% a year. Blend that in with the current yield and you have YIELD TO MATURITY. (YTM is less than the simple total of 8.45% and 12% because, while your $710 is growing at 12%, the interest on that $710 is not.)

If you don't know the precise MATURITY DATE, guess. July 1 couldn't be too far off. For the exact date, check your brokerage statement or call your broker.

Be careful, in evaluating bonds, to check their call provisions. A bond that matures July 1, 2020 may in fact be callable in 1993. Just as you might pay off your mortgage early to refinance at a lower rate, so do bond issuers "call" their bonds, when allowed to, if THEY can refinance at a lower rate.

So in addition to calculating YIELD TO MATURITY, it's even more important to calculate YIELD TO CALL. Simply enter the call date and price. (Not all bonds are callable, but those that are often are callable at a small premium over par — at "102," say. This little sweetener is supposed to make you feel better seeing the last 18 years of high interest you'd been counting on go down the drain.)

We don't ask you to enter a "maturity price" because we know all bonds are slated to pay 100 cents on the dollar — $1,000 per bond — at maturity.

<From Menu Bar, Alt-A, S>

```
 File    Desk    Money    Tax    Insure    Finance    Portfolio    Net Worth


              ╞══ EFFECTIVE YEILD: SAVINGS ACCOUNTS ══╡

              Daily Compounding

              ANNUAL INTEREST RATE:  6.500 %
              EFFECTIVE ANNUAL YIELD:  6.715 %
              Fill in ONE line.




              F7 - Clean the slate      F10 - Calculate


  F1-Help                                        Esc-Back up
```

SAVINGS ACCOUNT YIELDS

You know how bank ads offer 8% interest and then, in larger type, tell you that it's an "effective annual yield" of 8.33%? This is because the bank compounds your interest daily. It gives you one day's worth of 8% annual interest each day — and for the rest of the year even THAT little bit of interest is earning interest. So the annual interest RATE is 8%, but the EFFECTIVE ANNUAL YIELD is 8.33%. This is the more meaningful number and the one we work with throughout Managing Your Money. If you tell us 8% is the annual yield on an investment, we will assume you really MEAN 8%. Namely, that $100 will grow after a year to $108 — not to $108.33. And if you tell us that $100 has grown to $108 in a year and ask us to figure what Annual Yield that represents, we'll tell you 8%.

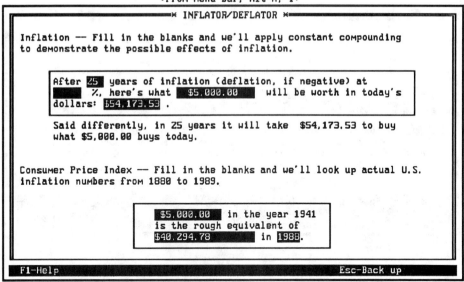

<From Menu Bar, Alt-A, I>

═══════════ ✳ INFLATOR/DEFLATOR ✳═══════════

Inflation — Fill in the blanks and we'll apply constant compounding
to demonstrate the possible effects of inflation.

After **25** years of inflation (deflation, if negative) at
▇▇▇ %, here's what ▇**$5,000.00**▇ will be worth in today's
dollars: **$54,173.53** .

Said differently, in 25 years it will take $54,173.53 to buy
what $5,000.00 buys today.

Consumer Price Index — Fill in the blanks and we'll look up actual U.S.
inflation numbers from 1800 to 1989.

▇**$5,000.00**▇ in the year 1941
is the rough equivalent of
$40,294.78▇▇▇ in **1988**.

F1-Help   Esc-Back up

INFLATOR/DEFLATOR

Want to know whether you're REALLY doing better than your Dad did, earning $32,000 when the best he ever earned, back in '57, was $7,800? Here's the place to find out. (Except that we don't take into account changing tax brackets — just inflation.)

It took inflation of just over 4% to push Richard Nixon into imposing wage and price controls in 1971. It was a dumb move, but you can see from the first set of boxes why he felt something had to be done.

<From Menu Bar, Alt-A, M>

```
 File   Desk   Money   Tax   Insure   Finance   Portfolio   Net Worth
```

```
============= MORTGAGE AMORTIZAION =============

 Loan Date    Type      Principal   # Payments   Interest   Payment
 6/15/90     MONTHLY    $315,000       360        9.800 %

Fill in the Loan Date and Type, and then leave ONE of the remaining four
fields blank.  Press F2 to calculate the empty field, and then press F2
again to see what happens if you modify your principal payments or the
interest rates during the term of this loan.


 F7 - Clean the slate           F10 - Calculate the remaining field
```

F1-Help   Esc-Back up

<From Menu Bar, Alt-A, M, F10>

```
 File   Desk   Money   Tax   Insure   Analyze   Portfolio   Net Worth
```

```
============= LOAN AMORTIZATION =============

 Loan Date    Type      Principal     # Payments   Interest   Payment
 6/15/1990   MONTHLY   $315,000.00       360        9.800%   $2,717.91

Fill in the Loan Date and Type, and then leave ONE of the remaining four
fields blank.  Press F6 to calculate the empty field, and then press F6
again to see what happens if you modify your principal payments or the
interest rates during the term of this loan.


 F8 - Convert from MONTHLY   to BI-WEEKLY
 F10 - Modify principal payments or interest rates: Page 236
```

F1-Help   F4-Print   Esc-Back up

CUSTOMIZED LOAN AMORTIZATION

This screen and the next allow quick calculations that would be all but impossible without a computer. It is essentially for mortgages, but would apply to auto loans and others that follow the same standard format: constant periodic payments that are almost entirely interest at first but tilt increasingly toward principal.

THE FIRST SCREEN – SETTING UP THE LOAN

Start by telling us about your loan – when you took it out (or plan to) and what kind of loan it is (monthly-payment loans are the most common, but yours might be different). Then fill in any three of the remaining four blanks and let us calculate the fourth. As soon as we have, use the space bar to blank one of them out again, change one or more of the others, and recalculate. You can try as many scenarios as you like. You can also press F8 to see the effect of a biweekly payment schedule, if it's offered in your area, on a standard monthly mortgage. Pressing F8 repeatedly switches back and forth between the two.

You'll notice that with a biweekly-type loan your PAYMENT is half the monthly amount – but because you make 26 payments a year you're in effect paying 13 months' interest each year, and thus paying down the loan a lot faster than would otherwise have been the case. A 30-year 360-payment monthly loan might require not 720 biweekly payments, but just – well, try it and see. You might be surprised.

When you're ready, press: F4 to print an amortization schedule; F6 to see the additional tricks we can perform (see below); or ESCape to unfreeze the loan you just entered so you can try another.

<From Menu Bar, Alt-A, M, F10, F10>

```
╔══════════════════════════ LOAN MODIFICATION ══════════════════════════╗
║                                                                        ║
║   Loan Date    Type       Principal   # Payments   Interest   Payment  ║
║   6/15/1990   MONTHLY    $315,000.00      360        9.800%  $2,717.91 ║
║─────────────────────────────────────────────────────────────────────── ║
║            Fill in any fields you want to modify.                      ║
║  After ▓▓▓▓ payments, increase payment by ▓▓▓▓▓▓▓▓▓▓ to $0.00         ║
║  and/or change interest rate to ▓▓▓▓ %                                 ║
║                                                                        ║
║  After ▓▓▓ more payments, increase payment by ▓▓▓▓▓▓▓▓ to $0.00       ║
║  and/or change interest rate to ▓▓▓▓ %                                 ║
║                                                                        ║
║  After ▓▓▓ more payments, increase payment by ▓▓▓▓▓▓▓▓ to $0.00       ║
║  and/or change interest rate to ▓▓▓▓ %                                 ║
║                                                                        ║
║  After ▓▓▓ more payments, increase payment by ▓▓▓▓▓▓▓▓ to $0.00       ║
║  and/or change interest rate to ▓▓▓▓ %                                 ║
║                                                                        ║
║   This loan will be paid off after 360 payments on 6/15/2020.         ║
║   After 0 payments, your remaining principal will be $315,000.00      ║
╚════════════════════════════════════════════════════════════════════════╝
   F7 - Clean the slate                      F10 - Re-calculate
   F1-Help                    F4-Print       Esc-Back up
```

THE SECOND SCREEN — CUSTOMIZING IT

Now we give you a chance to play a bit. To begin with, enter a number in the last blank on the screen ("After _____ payments ..."). You'll see that after 10 years' payments on a 30-year mortgage, say — 120 payments in all — you'll have made barely a dent in the principal due.

But what if this were not a steady, regular loan? What if the interest rate changed every so often? What if you occasionally prepaid some of the principal? We have provided the sections in the middle of the screen for you to enter up to four such twists and turns in your scenario. You can leave them all blank or use just the first or the first few. If you do want to indicate some sort of change to the loan, tell us, first, after how many payments it occurs. Then tell us how much extra you'll be paying, if anything, and/or whether the interest rate has changed. It's perfectly okay to leave one of these two items blank. But if you do indicate an extra payment, you must tell us whether you'll be making it Once or Regularly. (If you forget to tell us, we'll beep and flash a "see help" message when you press F6.)

Press F6, and we'll show you your new monthly payment and, at the bottom of the screen, the new number of payments the loan requires from start to finish.

Press F4 to see how the loan is amortized, taking into account whatever twists and turns you may have thrown in to complicate it.

NOTE: Mortgage computations may vary slightly from lender to lender, so don't be alarmed if our amortization schedule varies slightly from your bank's. We use the most common calculation (based on a 360-day year).

‹From Menu Bar, Alt-A, M›

```
═══════════════════╣ MORTGAGE REFINANCING ╠═══════════════════

              Your discount rate  5.00  %

        Current Financing                Suggested Refinancing
Principal remaining  $160,000.00    Principal    $200,000.00
Interest rate           12.0 %      Interest rate      9.50 %
Payments remaining      300         Payments due       360
Payments/year            12         Payments/year      12
                                    Points             2.5
                                    Other Closing Costs 3,000
                                    Prepayment Penalty

            Interest and points are  deductible
            Points are deductible  over the life mortgage
            Sell the property after  5  years.

            Your current or projected tax bracket  %

┌──────────────────────────────────────────────────────────┐
│ F7 - Clean upper slates          F10 - Compare financing costs │
│ F1-Help                                     Esc-Back up    │
└──────────────────────────────────────────────────────────┘
```

MORTGAGE REFINANCING: DATA ENTRY; YOUR DISCOUNT RATE

Tell us the particulars of your current mortgage and the one you're considering — which may be for a lesser, equal, or greater amount — and we try to respond with a sensible analysis, in English. But to do that, we have to know what money is worth to you, also known as your "discount rate."

■ YOUR DISCOUNT RATE

If you'd just as soon have $1.05 a year from now as $1 today, then your discount rate is around 5%. If you say, Heck, no!, you wouldn't part with a dollar today if all you'd get back in a year were $1.05, then your discount rate is higher than 5%.

Basically, your discount rate is the best after-tax return you expect to earn on your money. If it's a 7% municipal bond, then you might set your discount rate at 7%. If you're convinced you can make your money grow at 25% a year, after tax, by reinvesting it in your business, then 25% is your discount rate. If all you'd do with an extra $10,000 or $20,000 is put it in a passbook savings account that earned 3% after tax, then that's your discount rate.

But unless you're wealthy, it's not QUITE this simple. You may think the most you can earn on your money after tax is 7%, say — but if you're paying 18% on your credit card balance, then you could actually "earn" 18% after tax by paying it off. Your discount rate is at least 18%. (You're in no position to be lending me $1 to get back $1.07 if borrowing that dollar is going to cost you $1.18!) If you were starving, your discount rate would be all but infinite. Almost NO promised return a year from now would be high enough to make it worth your giving up the $1 that stands between you and a loaf of bread.

Choose any number you want — try several. There IS no one precise measure of your own personal discount rate. The beauty of the computer is that it lets you try out a whole range of assumptions in seconds.

■ PRINCIPAL REMAINING

Your current principal is the balance owing on your mortgage. Not the original $100,000, but the mere $98,222 that, after dozens of payments, you now owe. The new principal can be the same, more, or less. It should be whatever amount you're actually thinking of borrowing.

If you currently have both a first and a second mortgage, break the analysis into two parts. Compare, first, refinancing just the $70,000 first mortgage with $70,000 of the $150,000 you plan to borrow. Print out our analysis of that much. Then compare, say, refinancing your $25,000 second mortgage (or whatever balance is left on it) with the remaining $80,000 of the $150,000 you actually plan to borrow. Print out that analysis. Then combine the results with our calculator. Or a pencil.

■ INTEREST RATE

Fill these in. But if one loan is variable and the other fixed, the analysis is harder. What you may want to do, after you do this once with the current numbers, is raise the variable rate to the kinds of levels you think it might realistically average over the next five or ten years. Or pretend the fixed rate is actually 1% or 2% lower than it is, in recognition that you're not just getting a loan, you're locking the bank in for 20 or 30 years, while it is locking you in, typically, for just one. The advantage is hard to quantify, but it's definitely worth 1%, maybe more.

■ PAYMENTS REMAINING

How many payments remain on your current mortgage? How many would be due on the new one?

■ PAYMENTS/YEAR

Most mortgages require 12 payments a year. How about these?

■ POINTS, CLOSING COSTS, PENALTIES

Tell us how many points, if any, you'd pay to refinance (typically 2 or 3, meaning 2% or 3% of the value of the loan) and what other closing costs (legal fees, etc.) and prepayment penalties there might be.

■ DEDUCTIBILITY

On a mortgage refinancing, the points you incur are deductible, but only proportionally over the life of the loan. (If it's $3,000 of points on a 30-year loan, just $100 is deductible each year. Should you pay it off early, the balance of the points may then be deducted.)

Home mortgage interest and points are ordinarily deductible. If the loan amount exceeds the cost of your home plus improvements (unless the excess is for medical or education expense), check with your accountant.

■ **SELL THE PROPERTY AFTER __ YEARS**

Whether it makes sense to incur the expense of refinancing depends largely on the length of time over which you'll be spreading that expense. Unless you expect to hold the property for the full life of the loan, use this box to try different assumptions.

■ **YOUR TAX BRACKET**

This comes straight from our TAX 1040 screen – unless you contemplate borrowing so much new money that the enormous interest deductions will knock you down to a much lower bracket. If that's the case, use a reasonable average of your current bracket and the bracket you'd be in if you refinanced. (To see the effect of a big home interest deduction, visit TAX and enter it on Schedule A.)

Ready? Press F6 for our analysis.

<From Menu Bar, Alt-A, M, F10>

```
┌────────────────────────────────────────────────────────────┐
│                 ═══ COMPARISON OF FINANCING COSTS ═══        │
│  ┌──────────────────────────────────────────────────────┐   │
│  │ By the time you sell, after 10 years, you'll have paid down │
│  │ $23,923.76 under your current financing, or $13,139.87 under the │
│  │ proposed refinancing.  These figures, discounted back to today's │
│  │ dollars, are taken into account in the following analysis. │
│  │                                                        │   │
│  │ By taking out a smaller loan, you are in effect spending an extra │
│  │ $5,000.00 up front, in today's dollars, to pay down your balance. │
│  │ Since the after-tax interest rate on the new mortgage is higher than │
│  │ your assumed discount rate — meaning that it costs you more to │
│  │ borrow money than you think it's worth — you are wise to be paying │
│  │ down the loan.  Over the life of your current financing, the total │
│  │ you'd be paying to own your home, after taxes and discounted back to │
│  │ today's dollars, would be $154,306.08.  If you refinanced, the cost │
│  │ would be $142,007.58.  This includes as an initial cost of │
│  │ refinancing your immediate $5,000.00 cash outflow for reducing the │
│  │ size of your debt.  So, refinancing is definitely worth considering. │
│  └──────────────────────────────────────────────────────┘   │
├────────────────────────────────────────────────────────────┤
│ F1-Help                                      Esc-Back up     │
└────────────────────────────────────────────────────────────┘
```

MORTGAGE REFINANCING: OUR ANALYSIS

If you find this confusing, it may help to go back to the previous screen and re-read the HELP message that explains your discount rate. Note that whenever your after-tax cost of borrowing is lower than your discount rate — meaning that it costs you less to borrow money than you think it's worth — it makes sense to borrow (or to rethink your discount rate). And vice versa.

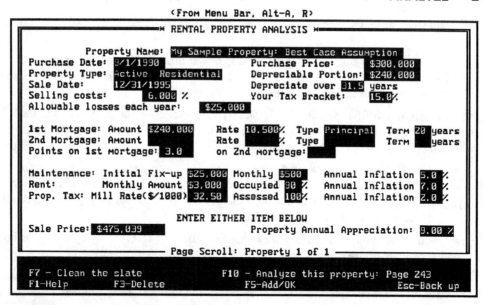

<From Menu Bar, Alt-A, R>

```
════════════════════════════ RENTAL PROPERTY ANALYSIS ════════════════════════

            Property Name: My Sample Property: Best Case Assumption
Purchase Date: 9/1/1990              Purchase Price:      $300,000
Property Type: Active  Residential   Depreciable Portion: $240,000
Sale Date:     12/31/1995            Depreciate over 31.5 years
Selling costs:      6.000 %          Your Tax Bracket:    15.0%
Allowable losses each year:    $25,000


1st Mortgage: Amount $240,000   Rate 10.500%  Type Principal  Term 20 years
2nd Mortgage: Amount            Rate      %   Type            Term    years
Points on 1st mortgage: 3.0    on 2nd mortgage:


Maintenance: Initial Fix-up $25,000 Monthly $500  Annual Inflation 5.0 %
Rent:         Monthly Amount $3,000 Occupied 90 %  Annual Inflation 7.0 %
Prop. Tax: Mill Rate($/1000) 32.50 Assessed 100%  Annual Inflation 2.0 %

                       ENTER EITHER ITEM BELOW
     Sale Price: $475,039              Property Annual Appreciation: 9.00 %

────────────────── Page Scroll: Property 1 of 1 ──────────────────

 F7 - Clean the slate         F10 - Analyze this property: Page 243
 F1-Help        F3-Delete           F5-Add/OK              Esc-Back up
```

RENTAL PROPERTY ANALYSIS: DATA ENTRY

Enter your estimates and we do the rest. You can give this property a name and save its particulars (F5), along with those of others you own. Or save 3 or 4 analyses for each:

> 123 Elm − Best Case
>
> 123 Elm − Sell '92
>
> 123 Elm − 6% Inflation

When you do, just use PgDn and PgUp to move among them.

Your ALLOWABLE LOSS is currently the $25,000 limit set by Congress − per year, not per property − less $1 for every $2 by which your adjusted gross income exceeds $100,000 (thus falling to zero above $150,000).

Note that we allow separate inflation estimates for how fast maintenance costs will rise, how fast you plan to raise the rent, and how fast you expect property tax rates to rise. If you don't know the PROPERTY TAX RATE but have an idea of the actual tax, just divide it ("it runs around $1,200 a year") by the price of the property in thousands (100, say) and you have your answer ($12 per $1,000). If you use this method, enter "100%" in the "assessed valuation" box. (For property tax inflation, enter ZERO if you expect the tax to rise no faster than the property appreciates. We figure the tax each year based on each year's appreciated value, so the tax will go up even if the rate doesn't.)

We can't accommodate every financing scheme, but do have room for first and second mortgages, both of the conventional "Principal and Interest" type (where the principal repayments start out tiny but grow imperceptibly every month) and of the "Interest Only" type (where all the principal is due in a lump at the end). If you're assuming a mortgage, enter only the UNpaid balance, and only the years remaining until it's paid off.

POINTS are charged by the lender at the outset of the loan. Each point is equal to 1% of the loan.

Few rental properties are fully OCCUPIED 100% of the time. Enter your estimate — 100% or some lesser number — here. (And try to get ample security deposits from your tenants so if they do run out on you in the middle of the night all's not lost.)

If you plan MAJOR FIRST-YEAR EXPENDITURES to improve the property, add them to the purchase price and we'll depreciate them as we do the property. A landlord may deduct MINOR INITIAL FIX-UP expenses, as well as regular maintenance costs, as incurred.

What makes real estate such a favored investment is that you get to depreciate it for tax purposes even while it may be appreciating in real life. Tell us how much of the purchase price you'll be depreciating (land is not depreciable) and over how many years (currently, 27.5 for residential properties, 31.5 for commercial).

You may estimate the sale price either with a specific number ($150,000) or by telling us how fast it will appreciate (7.5%).

In calculating your after-tax gain, we lower your basis by the amount of the depreciation you've claimed. (If you sell a $100,000 house for $125,000 but claimed $20,000 of depreciation in the meantime, your taxable gain is $45,000, not $25,000.)

If you tag the property "active," we allow a tax loss up to $25,000 in our calculations; zero for "passive." If you tag it "personal," we allow neither losses nor depreciation nor a deduction for maintenance or initial fix-up, but deduct points fully the first year. With either "commercial" or "residential," we do allow those deductions, but spread your points over the life of the loan.)

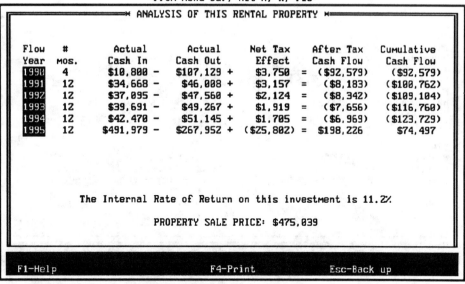

<From Menu Bar, Alt-A, R, F10>

RENTAL ANALYSIS: RESULTS

Here is how your investment develops, year by year, complete with its internal rate of return. Since different tax brackets affect the after-tax cash flows and the internal rate of return, you might want to back up and change your tax bracket. To view the investment apart from tax consequences, enter zero as your tax bracket. To see the details underlying these numbers, press F4.

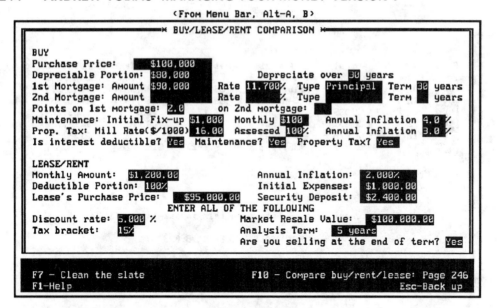

<From Menu Bar, Alt-A, B>

```
╔══════════════════ ⊁ BUY/LEASE/RENT COMPARISON ⊁ ══════════════════╗

 BUY
 Purchase Price:        $100,000
 Depreciable Portion: $80,000          Depreciate over 30 years
 1st Mortgage: Amount $90,000     Rate 11.700%  Type Principal  Term 30 years
 2nd Mortgage: Amount             Rate       %  Type            Term    years
 Points on 1st mortgage: 2.0      on 2nd mortgage:
 Maintenance: Initial Fix-up $1,000  Monthly $100  Annual Inflation 4.0 %
 Prop. Tax: Mill Rate($/1000) 16.00  Assessed 100%  Annual Inflation 3.0 %
 Is interest deductible? Yes  Maintenance? Yes  Property Tax? Yes

 LEASE/RENT
 Monthly Amount:    $1,200.00       Annual Inflation:  2.000%
 Deductible Portion: 100%           Initial Expenses:  $1,000.00
 Lease's Purchase Price:  $95,000.00  Security Deposit:  $2,400.00
                    ENTER ALL OF THE FOLLOWING
 Discount rate: 5.000 %             Market Resale Value:  $100,000.00
 Tax bracket:   15%                 Analysis Term:   5 years
                                    Are you selling at the end of term? Yes

╠════════════════════════════════════════════════════════════════════╣
  F7 - Clean the slate          F10 - Compare buy/rent/lease: Page 246
  F1-Help                                             Esc-Back up
╚════════════════════════════════════════════════════════════════════╝
```

BUY/LEASE/RENT: DATA ENTRY

Should you buy a house or rent an apartment? Buy a car or lease it? The decision could be as simple as, "Hey, I like the convenience of leasing." End of discussion. But the mathematical answer is more complicated.

On this screen you tell us about the thing you might buy, lease, or rent. On the next, we show you how the alternatives compare. The only difference between leasing and renting, for our purposes, is that with leasing, we assume you own the item at the end of the period. With renting, you don't.

Tell us what you'd pay for the item; what portion, if any, you'd depreciate (business and investment items only) and over how many years. We don't handle accelerated depreciation here. A 5-year item we simply depreciate 20% each year. But the difference is not large.

If you'd borrow money to own the item, describe the loan(s). (Your auto loan is a "first mortgage.") Most home and auto loans are of the standard "principal and interest" type. But will the interest be deductible? Points are the up-front fee a bank may charge — each point equals 1% of the loan. Currently, points are immediately deductible on your own home (except refinancings), but amortized over the life of the loan otherwise.

To get the PROPERTY TAX RATE, divide the actual tax ($1,200 yearly, say) by the price of the property in thousands (100, say) and you have your answer: $12 per thousand. Enter "100%" as the "assessed valuation." We figure the tax on each year's appreciated value, so enter ZERO inflation if you expect the tax to rise no faster than the property appreciates.

In the LEASE/RENT section, fill in the blanks that apply (inflation is more likely to apply to rent than to lease payments); tell us the item's purchase price at the end of the lease (which will be the same as its "resale value," below, unless the lease says otherwise); and enter any initial expense or down payment. (If your security deposit earns decent interest, ignore it: It's not really a cost of renting, just a savings account. Otherwise, enter it and we'll factor in the cost of having that money lie dormant.)

Finally, tell us your discount rate (the after-tax return you think you could earn on this money if it weren't tied up in a down payment), your tax bracket, the length of the lease or the length of time over which you'd like us to make the rental analysis, and your estimate of the item's market value at that the end of that time.

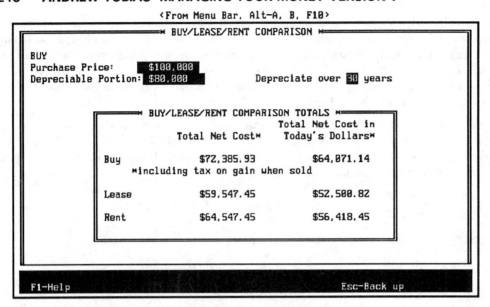

‹From Menu Bar, Alt-A, B, F10›

BUY/LEASE/RENT: OUR ANALYSIS

At left we show the total cost (after taking tax benefits into account) of your three alternatives, buying, leasing, or renting. With buying, the "cost" we show might actually be negative − a profit − if, at the end of the period, the value of the item you own has risen. That's one reason people put up with the hassles of ownership.

But what about the "time value of money" − the cost of tying up money now that could otherwise be making you a fortune in the stock market? If money has no time value to you, so your "discount rate" is zero, then the right-hand column will be identical to the left. But if you figure you'd rather have a dollar today than have to wait a year for it − that, in fact, if you've got to wait a year you want $1.10 (after taxes), then your discount rate is 10%. That changes the right-hand column dramatically, because it includes the cost to you of tying up money by purchasing rather than renting or leasing.

Forgetting questions of convenience, etc., THE BEST ALTERNATIVE IS THE ONE FOR WHICH THE TOTAL COST ("discounted back to today's dollars" in the right-hand column) IS LOWEST. Because the future is uncertain, be sure to try out several different scenarios. The idea is not to get one seemingly precise answer, but a feel for the range of possibilities.

<From Menu Bar, Alt-A, U>

```
================= * INVESTMENT ANALYSIS *=================

        ----- ACTUAL CASH -----         ------ REPORTED FOR TAXES ------
           Out          I                          Ordinary      Long-term
  Year  (Invested)  (Received)    Deductions        Income         Gains
  1     $15,000.00                $12,000.00
  2                   $350.00      $3,000.00         $350.00
  3                 $1,200.00                      $1,200.00
  4                 $2,000.00                      $2,000.00
  5                $28,000.00                      $3,000.00     $25,000.00




                  Your Tax Bracket: 15.0%


   F7 - Clean the slate          F10 - Display Analysis Summary: Page 248
   F1-Help     F3-Delete      F4-Print      F5-Add/OK: Page 250     Esc-Back up
```

INVESTMENT ANALYSIS: DATA ENTRY

If you invest $10,000 and get $15,000 back in four years it's not hard to figure what's happening. But what if you invest $10,000 this year and get a $15,000 tax deduction (the promoter swears it will stand up with the IRS) ... $10,000 next year and get an $11,500 deduction ... and then in the third year receive a $15,000 long-term capital gain? What kind ofreturn is that?

This screen allows you to input your estimates of cash flows for as many years as you like (number them 1991, 1992... or 1, 2, 3...). First enter the year; then your ACTUAL cash outlay for the year and any cash you expect to receive. Then, in the right-hand columns, enter the tax deductions and taxable income you estimate — which may be very different from the actual cash income or outgo. (We give you separate columns for "Ordinary Income" and "Long Term Gains," even though both currently receive the same tax treatment, in case that should change.)Repeat this procedure for each year. Then Press F10 to see our calculations of what they'll mean to you.

We pull you tax bracket from TAX. But type over it any other number you want to try. What you want here is your total marginal tax bracket (including local income tax) — namely, the proportion of each incremental $1,000 you have to pay in taxes.

<From Menu Bar, Alt-A, V, F5>

```
╔══════════════════════ INVESTMENT ANALYSIS ══════════════════════╗
║                                                                  ║
║     ───── ACTUAL CASH ─────      ────── REPORTED FOR TAXES ────── ║
║          Out         In                   Ordinary    Long-term  ║
║   Year (Invested)  (Received)   Deductions  Income       Gains   ║
║                                                                  ║
║   ╔═══════════════ ADD NEW CASH FLOW LINE ═══════════════╗       ║
║   ║       Out         In                  Ordinary  Long-term ║  ║
║   ║Year (Invested)  (Received)  Deductions  Income     Gains  ║  ║
║   ║ ██    ████        ████        ████       ████      ████   ║  ║
║   ╚═══════════════════════════════════════════════════════╝     ║
║                                                                  ║
║              Your Tax Bracket: 34.0%                             ║
╠══════════════════════════════════════════════════════════════════╣
║                        F5-Add/Save                               ║
╚══════════════════════════════════════════════════════════════════╝
```

<From Menu Bar, Alt-A, V, F10>

```
╔══════════════ INVESTMENT ANALYSIS SUMMARY ══════════════╗
║                                                          ║
║   Cash Flow    Reportable      After-Tax     Cumulative  ║
║     Year     Income/(Loss)    Cash Flow      Cash Flow   ║
║      1       ($12,000.00)    ($13,200.00)   ($13,200.00) ║
║      2        ($2,650.00)       $747.50     ($12,452.50) ║
║      3         $1,200.00      $1,020.00     ($11,432.50) ║
║      4         $2,000.00      $1,700.00      ($9,732.50) ║
║      5        $28,000.00     $23,800.00      $14,067.50  ║
║                                                          ║
║    The Internal Rate of Return on this investment is 21.4%. ║
║                                                          ║
╠══════════════════════════════════════════════════════════╣
║   F1 - Help                            ESC - Back up     ║
╚══════════════════════════════════════════════════════════╝
```

INVESTMENT ANALYSIS: RESULTS

On this screen, we tell you four things:

1. The net income or loss you'll have to report to Uncle Sam each year.

2. Each year's net cash inflow or outflow after giving effect to taxes. (If you pay out $100 in cash but get a $600 deduction and are in the 33% bracket, you're actually $100 cash ahead.)

3. Your cumulative cash flow. (After three years of this you'd be $300 ahead and minutes away from the audit.)

4. Your internal rate of return.

Internal rate of return is a complicated but crucial calculation. It tells you, in effect, what rate of interest you would have had to earn after tax to match the results you got from this deal. It adds up all the cash you invest (and tax you incur), takes into account the varying time periods involved, and compares that with all the cash you receive (and tax you save).

Internal rate of return (IRR) can boil a very complicated deal down to: "Gee, on average the return you've gotten (or are projected to get), including all the tax benefits, would be about the same as if your cash had been earning 8% after tax someplace." Or 80%. Or -18%. I could explain it more technically — the discount rate that sets the sum of all the cash flows to zero — but you get the idea. It's a way of averaging the return from a series of uneven cash inflows and outflows, giving much more weight to the early flows than to the later ones because of the time value of money.

1st IMPORTANT NOTE: When you do an internal rate of return calculation on a deal that involves tax savings, those savings are treated as if they are real cash. Which they are . . . but this assumes your only alternative was to pay that money to the IRS and not invest in some other tax favored scheme. In other words, at least a portion of the "return" is not an economic profit the tax shelter promoter made for you, but simply his way of taking credit for the money that would otherwise have gone to Uncle Sam. To calculate the strict economic merits of a deal, set your tax bracket to zero and look at it that way.

EVEN MORE IMPORTANT NOTE: There can actually be more than one right answer to IRR equations. If your investment involves money out in the early years and money back in the later years, it will be straightforward and we should handle it fine. But if in the first year, after tax benefits, you actually make money (so your initial investment is actually a negative number), or if there are a lot of "sign changes" over the years — net cash inflows followed by net cash outflows followed by inflows, outflows, inflows — the answer you get, while technically correct, may be garbage. Always trust common sense over technically correct garbage.

```
                    <From Menu Bar, Alt-A, T>
┌─────────────────────────────────────────────────────────────┐
│   File    Desk    Money    Tax    Insure    Analyze    Portfolio    Net Worth │
│                                                               │
│              ═══════ ⊭ TUITION PLANNING ⊭ ═══════              │
│                                                               │
│       Your child's name:                    SARA              │
│                                                               │
│       Today's annual cost of college:       $15,000.00        │
│                                                               │
│       Annual college-cost inflation:        10 %              │
│                                                               │
│       Years until your child enters college: 14               │
│                                                               │
│       Years your child will be in college:  4                 │
│                                                               │
│       Present savings:                      $6,800.00         │
│                                                               │
│       Annual yield:                         7.800 %           │
│                                                               │
│   ┌───────────────────────────────────────────────────────┐  │
│         F10 - Calculate a college plan: Page 252              │
│                                                               │
│     F1-Help                              Esc-Back up          │
└─────────────────────────────────────────────────────────────┘
```

TUITION PLANNING: DATA ENTRY

■ YOUR CHILD'S NAME

If you supply it, we'll include it in the report we print (and help you keep things straight if you've got more than one child).

■ TODAY'S ANNUAL COST OF COLLEGE

Dartmouth is one thing, UCLA another — and UCLA if you're a California resident, still a third. Tell us what it would cost to send your 3-year-old to the school of your choice today. Remember, the cost of tuition, room, board, books, trips home, etc., may be offset, in part, by scholarships, student loans, and part-time and summer jobs. Include here only what you figure would be the NET annual cost you'd have to bear.

■ ANNUAL COLLEGE-COST INFLATION

The rate at which the cost of college will rise. Who knows? But by trying a few different assumptions here, and, in a minute, in the box for "Annual Yield," you'll get a very good feel for the range of possibilities you face.

■ THE NUMBER OF YEARS BEFORE YOUR CHILD STARTS COLLEGE

If you have more than one child, calculate their costs one at a time. Unless you have more than five kids, you can use the five memories of the on-line calculator (Ctrl-N) to jot down the results for each and then add "a+b+c+d+e" to come up with a truly staggering total.

■ NUMBER OF YEARS YOUR CHILD WILL ATTEND

The most common answer is 4, but what about medical school? Or, for that matter, prep school? If the annual costs of these (today) vary widely, do the calculation for each separately. Where we say "college," just picture the words "grad school" or "military school" — the computer won't care. Use the memories of our on-line calculator (Ctrl-N) to jot down the costs of each and then add them together.

■ PRESENT SAVINGS

Enter here whatever savings you've already earmarked for college, if any. Caution: If you have five kids and a total of $12,000 presently saved for their education, don't enter the full $12,000 for each child — split the $12,000 up (any way you want) among the five of them. Otherwise, you'll be double- (or in this case quintuple-) counting your nest egg.

■ ANNUAL YIELD

Enter the after-tax rate of return you think you'll earn on the money you save for college. Presumably, somewhere between 2% and maybe 10%, unless you have a really golden touch. The beauty of the computer is that in seconds you can try out four or five different assumptions to get a feel for the range of possibilities. Note that the yield from money you give your children, or place in certain kinds of trusts, may be taxed at a very low rate, if at all. Check with your accountant or attorney to learn the latest rulings.

‹From Menu Bar, Alt-A, T, F10›

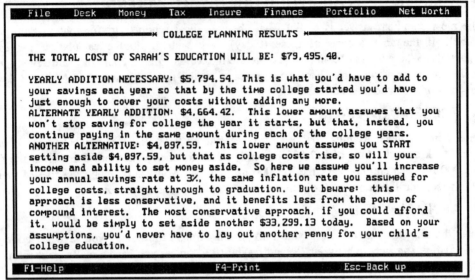

File	Desk	Money	Tax	Insure	Finance	Portfolio	Net Worth

```
========================= ⋈ COLLEGE PLANNING RESULTS ⋈ =========================

THE TOTAL COST OF SARAH'S EDUCATION WILL BE: $79,495.40.

YEARLY ADDITION NECESSARY: $5,794.54. This is what you'd have to add to
your savings each year so that by the time college started you'd have
just enough to cover your costs without adding any more.
ALTERNATE YEARLY ADDITION: $4,664.42.  This lower amount assumes that you
won't stop saving for college the year it starts, but that, instead, you
continue paying in the same amount during each of the college years.
ANOTHER ALTERNATIVE: $4,097.59.  This lower amount assumes you START
setting aside $4,097.59, but that as college costs rise, so will your
income and ability to set money aside.  So here we assume you'll increase
your annual savings rate at 3%, the same inflation rate you assumed for
college costs, straight through to graduation.  But beware:  this
approach is less conservative, and it benefits less from the power of
compound interest.  The most conservative approach, if you could afford
it, would be simply to set aside another $33,299.13 today.  Based on your
assumptions, you'd never have to lay out another penny for your child's
college education.
```

F1-Help	F4-Print	Esc-Back up

TUITION PLANNING: RESULTS

I can understand your needing help here. Chances are, we show you needing to set aside vast amounts of money. Starting early helps. Sending your child to an in-state school helps. Expecting your child to earn a good chunk of the cost through part-time and summer jobs is more than reasonable, and good experience − I loved it. Not to mention scholarships and student loans.

You can increase the after-tax return on your college funds by giving those funds to your child. But check with your accountant on the latest regulations and pitfalls.

The interest on Savings Bonds purchased after 1989 is entirely tax-free if, when redeemed, the proceeds of the bonds are used for a child's tuition and your income is below a certain level. (The level rises with inflation − check your local bank for details.)

NOTE: Our calculations assume that you make your contributions at the end of each year. If you made them at the beginning, you'd need to put away a little less.

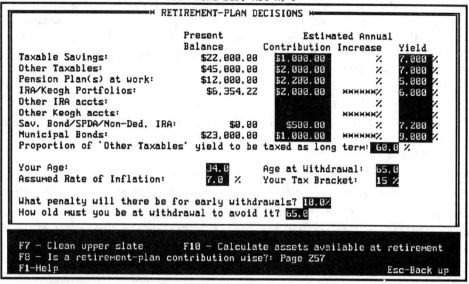

‹From Menu Bar, Alt-A, P›

RETIREMENT PLANNING

It's impossible to predict the future with accuracy, but important to plan for it in broad strokes. By entering a variety of assumptions here, you will begin to get a pretty good feel for where you're headed. For each class of assets, enter:

- The amount you have now (if we haven't entered it for you);

- The additions, if any, you expect to make each year;

- The rate at which those additions might grow (if you expect your earnings to increase 8% a year with inflation and seniority, you might also expect your retirement savings to increase at that rate, also — or even more, if the kids are almost finished draining your pockets);

- And the pre-tax "yield" you think that class of asset might generate — namely, income plus appreciation (pre-tax because we'll figure the tax ourselves).

Now here are the classes of assets:

TAXABLE SAVINGS includes savings accounts, CD's, T-bills — most interest-bearing instruments. Their annual yield is 6%, 8% — whatever they pay.

OTHER TAXABLES is a catch-all for stocks and other investments that may throw off income, like dividends or rent, but that may also appreciate.

"ANNUAL YIELD" here means income PLUS capital appreciation. But will it come mostly from dividends and short-term gains? Or from long-term appreciation? It gets even dicier when you consider that an asset growing at 10% a year and held 30 years before being taxed will be worth substantially more than a series of assets appreciating at 10% but sold — and taxed — every year. But the idea here is not to pretend to be precise, just to get a sense of ballparks and scenarios. So in the field a few lines down labeled **PROPORTION OF**

"OTHER TAXABLES" YIELD TO BE TAXED AS LONG-TERM, just enter a guess. We assume that whatever proportion you enter as "long-term" is entirely untaxed until withdrawal. If you have all your money in diamonds you plan to hold until retirement, enter 100% in this field. If it tends to be in things that yield 5% and appreciate at 5% and that you'll hold onto until retirement (paying no capital gains along the way), enter 50%. But if it's in things you buy and sell every year or two, so that both the income and the appreciation are taxed regularly, enter 0% or close to it.

PENSION PLANS include the value of 401K Salary Reduction Plans and/or profit-sharing and other pension plans in which you may have a interest. We subject these amounts to tax only at withdrawal.

IRA/KEOGH ACCOUNT values are drawn in from any you may have entered in PORTFOLIO. We provide a second line for other IRA and Keogh accounts set up elsewhere. As with pensions plans, we subject these amounts to tax only at withdrawal.

NON-DEDUCTIBLE IRAs are treated like SAVINGS BONDS and SPDAs (Single Premium Deferred Annuities). The appreciation they earn is shielded from tax until withdrawal, at which time *only* the appreciation — not your original investment or annual contribution — is taxed.

MUNICIPAL BONDS are tax-free securities. (True, they may have local or alternative-minimum tax implications, but we ignore these and leave them entirely untaxed.)

We assume annual contributions are made at the end of each year but that withdrawals are made at the beginning. So if you're 40 now and withdraw your money at 42, you'll have made two annual contributions — but earned just one year's interest on the first and none on the second.

```
════════ ASSETS AVAILABLE AT YOUR RETIREMENT ══════════
HERE'S HOW YOUR ASSETS WOULD LOOK:              Adjusted for
                               AT 65.0        3.0% Inflation
Taxable Savings:                   $0              $0
Other Taxables:                    $0              $0
Pension Plan(s) at work:           $0              $0
IRA/Keogh Portfolios:          $6,354          $2,542
Other IRA accts:                   $0              $0
Other Keogh accts:                 $0              $0
Sav. Bond/SPDA/Non-Ded. IRA:       $0              $0
Municipal Bonds:                   $0              $0

TOTAL AVAILABLE:               $6,354          $2,542

   By taking advantage of a deductible IRA/Keogh, you put away $0 that
   would have otherwise gone in taxes, and your savings grew free of
   tax.  The $6,354 you accumulated, although taxable as you withdraw
   it, compares with $6,354 you would have accumulated (after tax)
   otherwise.

F6 - Plan for withdrawals over 10  years    F9 - Retirement Analysis graphs
F1-Help                                              Esc-Back up
```

ASSETS AVAILABLE AT RETIREMENT

Inflation may vary dramatically over the years ahead. So, too, your tax bracket and investment success. Still:

■ Whatever your tax bracket when you retire, it probably won't be much HIGHER than when you were working. (Or if it is, you could move to a state with no income tax, if any remain by then, to soften the blow.)

■ It usually makes sense to save for retirement under the shelter of a tax- deferred plan. (To see if it does for you, press ESCape after you leave this HELP and then F7.) Under such plans, long-term gains get no special treatment — and losses won't reduce your taxes. So unless you're a very adept trader, invest tax-sheltered funds in safe, high-yielding securities and make risky investments with your taxable funds. Losses will be cushioned by a tax deduction; gains may be lightly taxed when long-term, depending on the mood of Congress.

■ The more you put away now, the more you'll have at retirement. (Note: In our calculations we assume contributions are made at the end of the year but that withdrawals are made at the beginning. So if you're 40 now and 42 at withdrawal, you'll have made two annual contributions — but earned just one year's interest on the first and none on the second.)

<From Menu Bar, Alt-A, P, F10, F6>

```
╔═══════════════ ANNUAL INCOME AFTER RETIREMENT: AGE 74.0 TO 74.0 ═══════════════╗
║                                                                                ║
║  Assuming your money continued to appreciate, if you withdrew it all over 10   ║
║  years, your pre-tax income would be $635 a year (plus Social Security --      ║
║  see HELP).  Because of inflation, that would equal about $254 in today's      ║
║  dollars in the first year, and -- with inflation's continued erosion --       ║
║  $195 in the last year.  (To keep your buying power constant, you could        ║
║  withdraw fewer dollars at first, to have more later on.)                      ║
║                                                                                ║
║  It's tough to say what tax brackets will look like in the future.  But if     ║
║  they are adjusted to keep pace with inflation, then yours would be about      ║
║  15%.  Thus, at age 65.0, your annual income after tax would be $540, or       ║
║  $216 in today's dollars.  By age 74.0, your after-tax income would be $540    ║
║  (you're in the 15% bracket now), or $166 in today's dollars (inflation        ║
║  rages on).                                                                    ║
║                                                                                ║
╚════════════════════════════════════════════════════════════════════════════════╝
        F6 - Re-calculate your withdrawals over  10  years
  F1-Help                                               Esc-Back up
```

ANNUAL INCOME AFTER RETIREMENT

When it comes to withdrawing funds from your retirement plan(s), you should talk to a competent accountant or tax attorney to set a strategy that will minimize − or at least not maximize − taxes. If you can afford to, you'll want to delay withdrawing funds as long as possible. That way, your money continues to grow tax free.

With Keogh and "401K" Salary Reduction Plans, but not IRAs, you may currently withdraw your funds all at once subject to favorable "5-year-forward" income averaging. Say you withdrew $150,000. From an IRA, most of that would be taxed at the maximum tax rate. But from a Keogh Plan, it would be taxed as if your total income were $30,000 for each of the next 5 years. Use TAX to see the difference between the tax on $150,000 and five times the tax on $30,000. (In the days when tax brackets were more steeply graduated, it was larger than it is now.) And check to see if the law has changed.

NOTE: The income we project for your retirement does not include Social Security benefits. Retirees currently get from $6,000 to $11,000. It's reasonable to think Congress will not raise this, except to keep up with inflation (how could it afford to?), nor lower it dramatically (how could it get reelected?). Chances are, your Social Security, after tax, will be the rough equivalent of $6,000 or $7,000 a year in today's purchasing power.

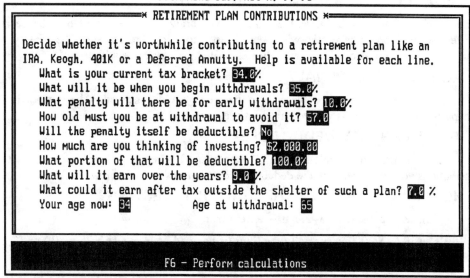

‹From Menu Bar, Alt-A, P, F8›

```
═════════════════════✳ RETIREMENT PLAN CONTRIBUTIONS ✳═════════════════════

  Decide whether it's worthwhile contributing to a retirement plan like an
  IRA, Keogh, 401K or a Deferred Annuity.  Help is available for each line.
     What is your current tax bracket? 34.0%
     What will it be when you begin withdrawals? 35.0%
     What penalty will there be for early withdrawals? 10.0%
     How old must you be at withdrawal to avoid it? 57.0
     Will the penalty itself be deductible? No
     How much are you thinking of investing? $2,000.00
     What portion of that will be deductible? 100.0%
     What will it earn over the years? 9.0 %
     What could it earn after tax outside the shelter of such a plan? 7.0 %
     Your age now: 34          Age at withdrawal: 65


                           F6 - Perform calculations
```

IS A RETIREMENT PLAN CONTRIBUTION WISE?

This screen is designed to help you decide whether to make a retirement plan contribution this year, not whether to contribute every year. Next year, come back and look again. It's in no sense meant to be exact. Try several different assumptions to get a range of scenarios.

■ YOUR CURRENT TAX BRACKET

On this line, enter your approximate income tax bracket. If you're not sure of it, visit TAX and fill in our Form 1040. When you do, we display your tax bracket in the lower left corner of the screen. To that number, add in your marginal state and local income tax bracket, if any, as well. We assume the number you enter here to be your tax bracket all the way to withdrawal. So if you're a grad student in the 0% tax bracket soon to be a Yuppie paying 28%, it would be more realistic to enter 28% here. (But if you're in a low tax bracket this year, consider contributing to an IRA but not deducting the contribution. Why get little or no tax benefit this year and subject your contribution to pay a hefty tax at withdrawal?)

■ YOUR TAX BRACKET AT WITHDRAWAL

Who knows? On the one hand, tax brackets could easily rise between now and then. On the other hand, there are four reasons they might be lower:

1. You could retire to a lower-tax state.

2. If you do retire, or semi-retire, your income (and thus your tax bracket) may fall.

3. Favorable income-averaging rules may apply at withdrawal, as they currently do on some retirement plans (not IRAs). With an expanding population of elderly voters, expect some special tax breaks.

4. You need not withdraw the money all at once. The withdrawals you make in your 70's and 80's and 90's might not be heavily taxed.

■ PENALTY FOR EARLY WITHDRAWALS

Probably 10%. But note that if you do have to withdraw money early, it may be because you've lost your job or have otherwise been thrust into a low tax bracket. The penalty will smart — but you may also be in a lower than estimated tax bracket at withdrawal.

■ AGE TO AVOID PENALTY

Probably 59.5 — though as people live longer, this could conceivably be extended. But perhaps not on contributions you've already made.

■ IS THE PENALTY DEDUCTIBLE?

It's not now. It probably won't be then. But note that it's not levied on the nondeductible contributions you've made, only the deductible contributions and all appreciation.

■ HOW MUCH ARE YOU THINKING OF INVESTING?

Enter as little as you want. Or as much — except that:

- If it's an IRA, $4,000 is currently the limit (if you and your spouse both work) or $2,250 (if one of you doesn't) or $2,000 (if you're single).

- If it's a 401K-type salary reduction plan, around $7,500 plus inflation is the limit (or a portion of your income, whichever is less).

- If it's a Keogh Plan, $30,000 is ordinarily the limit (or 20% of your net income from self-employment, whichever is less).

■ WHAT PORTION OF YOUR CONTRIBUTION IS DEDUCTIBLE?

If it's a Keogh plan contribution, it's likely to be 100% deductible. If it's an investment in a single-premium deferred annuity, none of it's deductible. If it's a contribution to a company-sponsored retirement plan, it may be 100% deductible; but many company plans allow nondeductible contributions in excess of the deductible amount. (If so, consider this two separate decisions: first whether to contribute the maximum amount you can deduct; then, whether to invest additional, nondeductible funds.)

For IRAs, the rules currently state that contributions are fully deductible if neither spouse is covered by a pension plan (or Keogh plan). Otherwise, the contributions are fully deductible only if your adjusted gross income is under $25,000 (single) or $40,000(joint).

One dollar of the $2000-per-worker allowable deduction is phased out for every $5 by which income exceeds those levels — which means the deduction phases out altogether once income exceeds $35,000 (single) or $50,000 (joint).

■ WHAT WILL IT EARN OVER THE YEARS?

Can you buy zero-coupon bonds that compound at 10% to maturity? At 11%? At only 7%? Or might you invest this money in a no-load mutual fund you're convinced can average a 15% annual return? (Few can.) Or even 20%? (Dream on.)

■ WHAT COULD IT EARN WITHOUT THE SHELTER OF THIS PLAN?

Ordinarily, this number is going to be lower than the last one, because we're looking for a rough estimate of the *after-tax* return you'd expect. Maybe 4%, after tax, 6% in a savings account or 7% from a municipal bond or 12%, after tax, from a good mutual fund that earned 18% before tax.

But maybe you think you can earn 20% a year, after tax, playing the market. Fine. If your alternative for this money is a tax-deferred annuity the insurer hopes will grow at 12% (but only guarantees will grow at 4%), and so you have entered 12% in the box above, we'll do some lightning fast calculations and tell you what you knew already: you'd be better off earning 20% after tax than 12% tax-deferred.

With any of these plans, once the money is in, it grows tax-free until withdrawn. At withdrawal, non-deductible contributions are not taxed (but their appreciation is). If you stretch your withdrawals, each is considered a proportionate blend of deductible and non-deductible contributions. The purpose of this is to drive you crazy.

```
                  <From Menu Bar, Alt-A, P, F8, F6>
 ╔══════════════════════════════════════════════════════════════════════╗
 ║ ══════════════╗ RETIREMENT PLAN CONTRIBUTIONS ╗══════════════          ║
 ║ Decide whether it's worthwhile contributing to a retirement plan like an║
 ║ IRA, Keogh, 401K or a Deferred Annuity.  Help is available for each line.║
 ║    What is your current tax bracket? 34.0%                             ║
 ║    What will it be when you begin withdrawals? 35.0%                    ║
 ║    What penalty will there be for early withdrawals? 10.0%             ║
 ║    How old must you be at withdrawal to avoid it? 57.0                 ║
 ║    Will the penalty itself be deductible? No                           ║
 ║    How much are you thinking of investing? $2,000.00                   ║
 ║    What portion of that will be deductible? 80.0 %                     ║
 ║    What will it earn over the years? 9.0 %                             ║
 ║    What could it earn after tax outside the shelter of such a plan? 7.0 %║
 ║    Your age now: 34           Age at withdrawal: 65                     ║
 ║                                                                        ║
 ║ ┌────────────────────────────────────────────────────────────────────┐║
 ║ │The $2,000.00 you are thinking of contributing to an IRA-type investment│║
 ║ │this year would grow to $17,614.28 after all taxes and penalties by age│║
 ║ │65.0.  That compares with $10,751.55 investing outside the shelter of such│║
 ║ │a plan.  You should therefore seriously consider investing in this    │║
 ║ │tax-sheltered plan.                                                   │║
 ║ └────────────────────────────────────────────────────────────────────┘║
 ║                                                                        ║
 ║ F1-Help                   F4-Print                  Esc-Back up        ║
 ╚══════════════════════════════════════════════════════════════════════╝
```

7

Portfolio

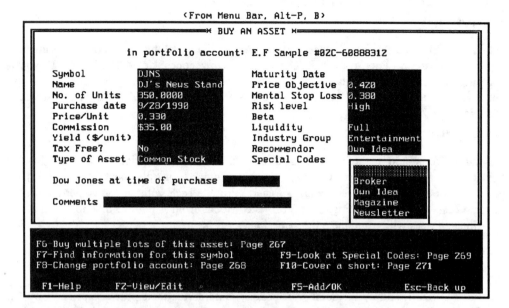

<From Menu Bar, Alt-P, B>

```
========================* BUY AN ASSET *=========================

              in portfolio account: E.F Sample #02C-60888312

   Symbol          DJNS              Maturity Date
   Name            DJ's News Stand   Price Objective    0.420
   No. of Units    350.0000          Mental Stop Loss   0.380
   Purchase date   9/28/1990         Risk level         High
   Price/Unit      0.330             Beta
   Commission      $35.00            Liquidity          Full
   Yield ($/unit)                    Industry Group     Entertainment
   Tax Free?       No                Recommendor        Own Idea
   Type of Asset   Common Stock      Special Codes

   Dow Jones at time of purchase                        Broker
                                                        Own Idea
   Comments                                             Magazine
                                                        Newsletter


   F6-Buy multiple lots of this asset: Page 267
   F7-Find information for this symbol        F9-Look at Special Codes: Page 269
   F8-Change portfolio account: Page 268      F10-Cover a short: Page 271

   F1-Help       F2-View/Edit             F5-Add/OK          Esc-Back up
```

BUY AN ASSET (OR COVER A SHORT)

Here's where you build a profile of the asset you're adding to your portfolio.

THREE STEPS TO ADDING AN ASSET

1. Check the top of the screen to be sure we're about to add it to the RIGHT portfolio. (If not, just press F8 and select the proper one.)

2. Fill in as many of the blanks as you can. (See below.) You can always make changes later. And don't miss these shortcuts:

    ■   If you've bought this same asset previously, just enter its symbol and press F7. If we already know anything about it, we'll fill in many of the blanks for you.

    ■   If you're here to enter several lots of the same asset, press F6 after supplying the information common to all (symbol, name, etc.). We'll take you to a screen that speeds multiple entry.

3. When you're ready, press F5. We'll record your new asset and get set to add another. If there IS no other you want to add, just press ESCape and you're through.

NOTE: Initially, we put the asset you've added at the END of the list on the Display Assets screen. To put it in order, press F7 on that screen; or just wait until we do it for you as part of some other operation.

HOW TO FILL IN THE BLANKS

■ SYMBOL

Where possible, use the actual stock, bond, option, or mutual fund symbol. (Consult your broker, Standard & Poor's STOCK GUIDE, or Dow Jones News Retrieval.) If you're compiling a portfolio of rare stamps, assign any symbols you'll find easy to remember — just not stock symbols. "AL-1924" is fine for your Abraham Lincoln 1924 classic ... but "AL" alone is Alcan Aluminum.

■ NAME

Anything. We pay no attention, other than to include it when we print Schedule D. But the Update Prices screen will sort by name, so you may wish to use the same abbreviations the newspaper does, to make price- updating easier. (Precede each with an N-, A-, B-, O-, etc., or some other symbol, to distinguish NYSE-listed stocks from Amex from bonds from OTC, and Update Prices will group them the same way!)

■ No. OF UNITS

■ For STOCKS, just enter the number of shares.

■ For BONDS, multiply the number of bonds — and divide their purchase price — by 10. This conforms to the way bond prices are quoted (as a percentage of their $1,000 face value). Instead of saying you bought one bond for $1,000, enter 10 at $100. Should you buy "100,000 Iowa 13's of 2000 at 112" (paying, that is, $112,000 for 100 State of Iowa bonds that promise $130 each in annual interest until redeemed for $1,000 each in the year 2000), you'd enter 1,000 units, 112 as the price, and 13 as the yield.

■ For OPTIONS (a put or call on 100 shares of stock), enter each one as "100" to conform to the way prices are quoted. Instead of saying you bought one IBM call for $350, which you did, say you bought 100 at $3.50.

■ For FUTURES CONTRACTS, the same applies. Don't say you bought one contract on 5,000 bushels of beans, say you bought 5,000 units at $7.56 each (the price per bushel). That way you'll conform to the way prices are quoted — and it will also bring home to you the enormity of the risk you've assumed. (Though this will plunge your cash balance much deeper into the red than it actually is, because you only had to put up a tiny fraction of the contract price, it will not throw off your Net Worth, because the asset value of this portfolio will be equally large, reflecting all those beans.)

■ For ANYTHING ELSE use whatever system makes sense. For a house: one unit at $175,000 (or 1,000 units at $175). Enter gold and silver by the ounce, because that's how prices are quoted.

■ PURCHASE DATE

Use the "trade" date (the day you made the transaction) not the "settlement" date (the day your cash was due).

- ## PRICE PER UNIT

As per "No. of Units," above.

- ## COMMISSION

If you don't know exactly, just guess and correct it later.

- ## YIELD

If your asset pays no dividend or interest (or rent), enter zero or just leave this space blank. Otherwise, enter the annual yield per unit. Such as, ".25" for 25 cents a share, or "12.5" for a 12.5% bond or "7200" for a house you've rented out at $600 a month ($7,200 annually).

- ## TAX FREE?

Enter "Yes" ONLY for municipal bonds or other assets whose cash distributions are not subject to tax. For everything else, enter "No," even though they may be assets in a tax-sheltered portfolio. (Assets that are federally tax free but subject to local income tax you might wish to assign a special code, for retrieval separately later.)

- ## TYPE

Choose one. (Note: closed-end mutual funds may be mutual funds, but they trade like stocks. If you want Managing the Market to update their prices when you call Dow Jones, be sure to choose "Common Stock" as the Type.)

- ## MATURITY DATE

For bonds or CD's — we'll remind you as expiration looms (Financial Reminders on the PORTFOLIO menu) and allow you to sort by maturity (F7 on the Display Assets screen).

- ## PRICE OBJECTIVE

If you enter one, we'll remind you when you reach it.

- ## MENTAL STOP LOSS

Likewise. Of course, if you like you can enter REAL stop loss orders with your broker.

- ## RISK

Short-term Treasury obligations entail virtually no risk. But 30-year Treasury bonds do entail risk, because if interest rates rocket, long-term bonds (even safe ones) will plunge. All stocks entail some risk, but some entail a lot. By categorizing your assets this way, you allow us to show you the risk distribution of your portfolio(s).

- ## BETA (OR VALUELINE)

This is a measure of a stock's (or portfolio's) volatility relative to the market as a whole. A stock that moves with the market has a beta of 1. A ponderous blue chip that goes up or down only half as fast has a beta of one half (.5). A stock that zooms and craters at every turn may have a beta of 3 or 4. If you care about betas — I don't — find a place to look them up, and fill them in. Otherwise, settle for your own risk classification (above), which amounts to much the same thing.

Or use this box to enter VALUE LINE rankings, if you're a Value Line fan. The heading will still say "Beta," but you and I will know. Value Line ranks stocks from 1 to 5 for timeliness. If you enter those rankings here, you will be able to determine, for example, the proportion of your assets ranked 1 or 2 for timeliness.

■ LIQUIDITY

Fully liquid assets are readily converted to cash. Illiquid assets (a better term might be "frozen") include partnership interests, stock in a family business, "letter stock" — that sort of thing. Semi-liquid assets are those you can sell, but not right away or all at once, such as 250,000 shares of a stock that normally trades 200 shares a day, a certificate of deposit that doesn't mature for six months, a Renoir or a parcel of land.

■ INDUSTRY GROUP

Choose one. If you don't find anything that fits, which, I fear, is all too likely, choose "Other" or assign a Special Code.

■ RECOMMENDOR

Likewise.

■ INDEX

If you enter the current Dow Jones Average (or some other index), we'll thereafter be able to compare the performance of this asset with that of the index.

■ COMMENTS

"Supposed to earn $10 a share next year." With F2, you'll be able to keep a running notes on your broker's excuses for this stock.

■ SPECIAL CODES

Here's what makes your program so flexible. Press F9 and read HELP there to see what I mean.

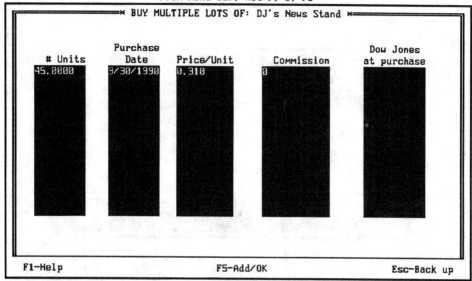

BUY MULTIPLE LOTS OF THE SAME ASSET

Fill in the blanks for each lot; press F6 to record the lot of 'em. Note that a "lot" (or "tax lot") is any discrete purchase. If you buy 50 shares in the morning at $12 and 50 more share that afternoon at $12.125 — or 50 more at $12 the next day — the second 50 is a separate lot from the first.

<From Menu Bar, Alt-P, B, F8>

```
╞══════════════════════════ BUY AN ASSET ══════════════════════════╡

        ┌─────── * SELECT PORTFOLIO ACCOUNT TO WORK WITH * ───────┐
        │ Portfolio      Account #          Type                  │
        │ E.F Sample     02C-60888312       Taxable               │
        │ Fidelity Funds 8A-3563-GG-91837   IRA/Keogh             │
        │ Wine Cellar    Downstairs         Taxable               │
        │                                                         │
        │                                                         │
        │                                                         │
        │                                                         │
        │ Speed scroll —                                          │
        ├─────────────────────────────────────────────────────────┤
        │              ↵ — Select portfolio                        │
        └─────────────────────────────────────────────────────────┘

    F1-Help              F5-Add/OK                    Esc-Back up
```

SELECT PORTFOLIO ACCOUNT

Highlight the portfolio you want to work with and press the ENTER key.

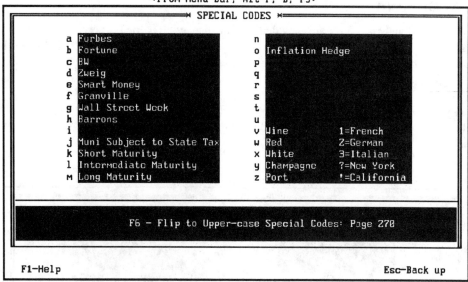

F6 - Flip to Upper-case Special Codes: Page 270

SPECIAL CODES LIST

HOW TO USE THIS SCREEN

We've provided 52 tags for you to assign any way you like — 26 lowercase letters and 26 capital letters. Code stock tips from three services you subscribe to a, b, and c, so you can quickly separate and compare their performances. If you've set up a portfolio for your stamp collection, you could have codes for "Plate Blocks," "Commemoratives," and "First Day Covers." You are limited only by your imagination. This screen is just a scratch pad to jot down what each code stands for, to refresh your memory later. Press F6 to toggle back and forth between upper- and lower-case codes.

SAMPLES

Note that we've started you off with some sample codes, just to show you how this could work. You'll probably want to get rid of them and use a coding scheme more to your liking. If so, blank ours out with the Space Bar.

SHORTCUT FOR ASSIGNING SPECIAL CODES

Once you've recorded your assets, it's easiest to make changes and assign additional codes on the Update Prices screen. You'll see any you've assigned sitting there in the right-hand column.

THE SPECIAL CODES % DISPLAY

To see the percentage of your assets tagged with each code, select Analyze Assets from the PORTFOLIO menu and then press F6, F6, F8 for our "Special Codes % Display."

40 ADDITIONAL CODES

Only the 52 alphabetic codes are included in that display. But for purposes of retrieval you can also use the 40 non-alphabetic characters on your keyboard as codes. Just find someplace to note them on the screen. (Remember, this is a scratch pad; it can be messy.)

THE F9 TOGGLE SHORTCUT

When you are through, you can naturally press ESCape to back up. But you'll find that F9, the key that brought you here, will also flip you back out. For typists like me, it's handy to be able to tap in and out with a single key.

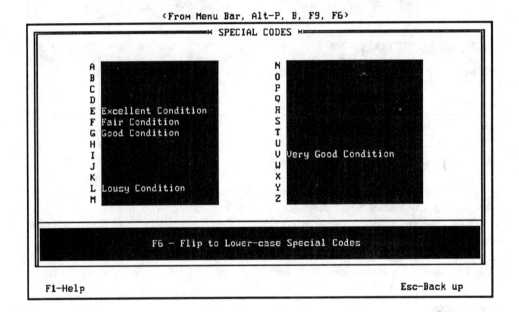

<From Menu Bar, Alt-P, B, F9, F6>

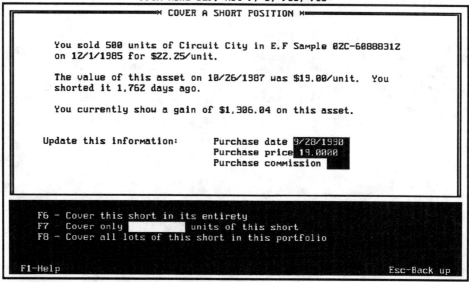

<From Menu Bar, Alt-P, B, F10, F10>

```
═══════════════════════ ✳ COVER A SHORT POSITION ✳ ═══════════════════════

    You sold 500 units of Circuit City in E.F Sample 02C-60888312
    on 12/1/1985 for $22.25/unit.

    The value of this asset on 10/26/1987 was $19.00/unit.  You
    shorted it 1,762 days ago.

    You currently show a gain of $1,306.04 on this asset.


    Update this information:      Purchase date  9/28/1990
                                  Purchase price 19.0000
                                  Purchase commission



    F6 - Cover this short in its entirety
    F7 - Cover only              units of this short
    F8 - Cover all lots of this short in this portfolio

  F1-Help                                              Esc-Back up
```

COVER A SHORT POSITION

Fill in the blanks and press a key. Your cash balance will be increased or decreased to the extent of your profit or loss; your short position will move to the "Sold Assets" list (meaning it's a position you've closed out); the profit or loss will show up in our capital gains calculations and, at year's end, in the Schedule D attachment we print.

<From Menu Bar, Alt-P, S>

```
═══════×═ SELL ASSETS IN PORTFOLIO: E.F Sample #0ZC-60888831Z ×══════════

    #          Purchase  Current    Total     Gain      Simple  Annual.
 Units Symbol   Price     Price     Value   (Loss) Term Apprec. Apprec.
   201 CBUBU      2.41     45.00    $9,045   $8,515 ×  1605.5%      %
   100 CBUBU     45.00     45.00    $4,500   ($35)S     -0.8%    0.0%
    45 DJNS       0.31      0.31      $14     ($0)S      0.0%    0.0%
   164 HI-INCOME 12.22     18.09    $2,960    $960 L     48.0%   27.2%
   100 IBM       64.13    112.00   $11,200   $4,602 L    69.8%    6.6%
   160 MAGELLAN  12.16     21.27    $3,394   $1,394 L    69.7%   12.2%
    75 WPPPS 9S99 79.50    98.25    $7,369   $1,350 L    22.4%    3.1%




 Speed scroll -                    × under Term indicates aggregate asset.
───────────────────────────────────────────────────────────────────────
 F6 - Sell asset: Page 273          F8 - Change portfolio account: Page 268
 F7 - Enter short sale with symbol:

 F1-Help                 F2-View/Edit                      Esc-Back up
```

CHOOSING AN ASSET TO SELL

Here is a list of all the assets you own in this portfolio. If the one you want to sell is in a different portfolio, press F8 to switch to that portfolio. Then highlight the asset with the cursor and press F6.

Or press F7 to sell a stock short (i.e., sell it even though you *don't* own it, hoping it will decline in price before you buy it back.)

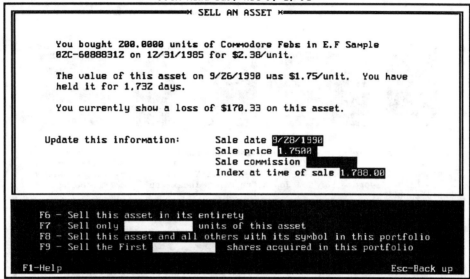

‹From Menu Bar, Alt-P, S, F6›

```
═══════════════════════════✹ SELL AN ASSET ✹═══════════════════════════

   You bought 200.0000 units of Commodore Fabs in E.F Sample
   02C-60888312 on 12/31/1985 for $2.38/unit.

   The value of this asset on 9/26/1990 was $1.75/unit.  You have
   held it for 1,732 days.

   You currently show a loss of $170.33 on this asset.


   Update this information:       Sale date  9/28/1990
                                  Sale price  1.7500
                                  Sale commission
                                  Index at time of sale  1,788.00


   F6 - Sell this asset in its entirety
   F7 - Sell only            units of this asset
   F8 - Sell this asset and all others with its symbol in this portfolio
   F9 - Sell the First            shares acquired in this portfolio

 F1-Help                                                  Esc-Back up
```

SELL AN ASSET (OR ENTER A SHORT SALE)

We display a recap of your position and invite you to fill in the blanks. Should you accidentally sell something you didn't mean to, or all your shares when you meant to sell just some of them, never fear. You can "unsell" anything. Just display your "Sold Assets" (select Display Assets from the PORTFOLIO menu and press F9); then highlight the one in question and press F6. If you're selling a BOND, we provide a field for you to enter the accrued interest, if any, you received along with the sale proceeds.

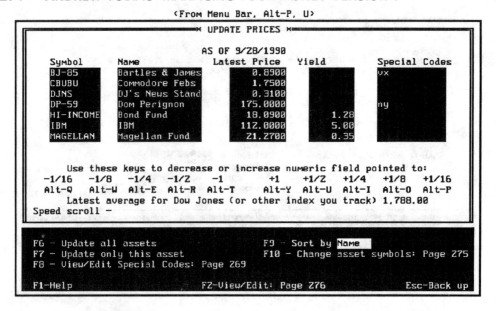

```
                    <From Menu Bar, Alt-P, U>
┌──────────────────────────────────────────────────────────────────────┐
│                     ═══════ UPDATE PRICES ═══════                       │
│                                                                        │
│                         AS OF 9/28/1990                                 │
│       Symbol      Name          Latest Price   Yield    Special Codes   │
│       BJ-85       Bartles & James    0.8900              vx             │
│       CBUBU       Commodore Febs     1.7500                             │
│       DJNS        DJ's News Stand    0.3100                             │
│       DP-59       Dom Perignon     175.0000              ny             │
│       HI-INCOME   Bond Fund         18.0900     1.28                    │
│       IBM         IBM              112.0000     5.00                    │
│       MAGELLAN    Magellan Fund     21.2700     0.35                    │
│                                                                        │
│       Use these keys to decrease or increase numeric field pointed to:  │
│     -1/16   -1/8   -1/4   -1/2   -1      +1    +1/2  +1/4  +1/8  +1/16  │
│     Alt-Q   Alt-W  Alt-E  Alt-R  Alt-T   Alt-Y Alt-U Alt-I Alt-O Alt-P  │
│       Latest average for Dow Jones (or other index you track) 1,788.00  │
│   Speed scroll -                                                        │
└──────────────────────────────────────────────────────────────────────┘
┌──────────────────────────────────────────────────────────────────────┐
│  F6 - Update all assets             F9 - Sort by Name                   │
│  F7 - Update only this asset        F10 - Change asset symbols: Page 275│
│  F8 - View/Edit Special Codes: Page 269                                 │
│                                                                        │
│  F1-Help              F2-View/Edit: Page 276            Esc-Back up      │
└──────────────────────────────────────────────────────────────────────┘
```

UPDATE PRICES

HOW TO UPDATE PRICES, YIELDS, SPECIAL CODES

To change a Price, Yield, or Special Code, simply type over the old one. Then press F6 or F7.

■ To update just a few items, it's fastest to press F7 after each one, then press ESCape to leave.

■ If you're updating many, skip that and press F6 when done.

THE ALT-QWERTYUIOP SHORTCUT

The top row of the keyboard — QWERTYUIOP — allows you to change prices even more easily. Down three eighths? Hold down the Alt key and press "W" three times fast. Up a half? Press "U" — or, if you prefer to think in eighths, 4 fast "O"s. You'll find the legend for this in the middle of the screen.

LATEST DOW JONES AVERAGE

Note the blank we give you for the current Dow Jones average. Actually, you can use it for any index you choose to compare yourself with — just be consistent and always use the same one. Update it here before doing an analysis, and, if you've included index levels in recording your purchases and sales, we'll compare the performance of your assets with that of the index over the same period of time.

This is a powerful feature, so it's worth deciding early just which index you'll want to use, and then sticking to it. (Less important is to get the index precisely right. If you enter 1840 when the Dow's really 1846.37, our comparison will be off, but only slightly. And do you really know where the Dow was at the precise moment you bought your asset?)

SPECIAL CODES

Want to see how your assets break down between Inflation, Deflation, and Prosperity hedges? Run through your assets adding I's, D's and P's, or any other unused code letters (press F8 to see which are free). Then select Analyze Assets from the PORTFOLIO menu, F6, F6, F8. Voila!

OTHER IMPORTANT TRICKS!

Don't miss F2, F9, and F10 on this screen either. F2 let's you view ALL LOTS of this asset in ALL PORTFOLIOS, if you keep track of more than one.

F9 sorts your assets by name (or symbol) — handy if you want to update prices in the same order the paper lists them. (Precede each NYSE name with a 1, say, each NASDAQ name with a 2, and so on . . . when you sort by name, your securities will be grouped by the page of the paper their prices are on.)

F10 will come in handy when Time Warner is acquired by Tofutti International and changes its symbol again.

PRESS F6 TO CORRECT OUR ANNUALIZED APPRECIATION NUMBERS

The annualized appreciation numbers we show throughout this chapter are based on the holding period as of the last price update, NOT today's date. So if one ever seems screwy, it's probably because you haven't updated prices in a long time (or because you just entered a purchase from long ago and had not yet updated it to the current price). Press F6 here and the annualized appreciations we show will be completely up-to-date.

```
                       <From Menu Bar, Alt-P, U, F10>
┌──────────────────────── UPDATE PRICES ────────────────────────┐
│                                                                │
│          ┌───────────── CHANGE ASSET SYMBOL ─────────────┐     │
│          │  The symbol to be changed:  IO-U               │     │
│          │  The new symbol should be:  IO-U2              │     │
│          ├───────────────────────────────────────────────┤     │
│          │ F6 - Change this asset symbol in all portfolios│     │
│          └───────────────────────────────────────────────┘     │
│                                                                │
│   Note:  After you press F6, the new symbol will be out of order here │
│   -- but only until the next time you visit.  To change anything else │
│   about this asset, such as its name, highlight it on the Display │
│   Assets screen and press F2.                                  │
│                                                                │
│                          Esc-Back up                           │
└────────────────────────────────────────────────────────────────┘
```

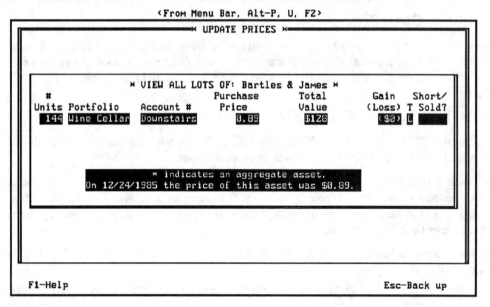

‹From Menu Bar, Alt-P, U, F2›

VIEW ALL LOTS

A quick way to see all the GM you've got scattered among your portfolios, including sold lots and short sales. For shorts, in the "purchase price" column we show the current price — what you'd pay if you covered — and, under "total value," the size of your position. In the box below, we show the price as of the last time you updated it (remember, you have to press F6 or F7 on the previous screen before a new price "takes"). If the only items here are shorts, you'll see the sale price of the lot most recently recorded.

<From Menu Bar, Alt-P, R>

```
╔════════════════════════════ * RECORD INCOME *═════════════════════════════╗
║  #              Purchase   Latest                                          ║
║ Units  Symbol     Date     Price   Portfolio    Account#        Type       ║
║  144 BJ-85      12/24/1985    0.89  Wine Cellar  Downstairs      Taxable    ║
║  200 CBUBU      12/31/1985    1.75  E.F Sample   0ZC-60888312    Taxable    ║
║  100 CBUBU      12/31/1985    1.75  E.F Sample   0ZC-60888312    Taxable    ║
║   50 CC          9/28/1990   22.25  E.F Sample   0ZC-60888312    Taxable    ║
║  450 CC          9/28/1990   22.25  E.F Sample   0ZC-60888312    Taxable    ║
║   45 DJNS        9/30/1990    0.31  E.F Sample   0ZC-60888312    Taxable    ║
║   12 DP-59       3/17/1960  175.00  Wine Cellar  Downstairs      Taxable    ║
║  164 HI-INCOME   5/5/1984    18.09  Fidelity Fun 8A-3563-GG-91   IRA/Keogh  ║
║  100 IBM         6/7/1982   112.00  E.F Sample   0ZC-60888312    Taxable    ║
║   12 IBM         4/4/1987   112.00  E.F Sample   0ZC-60888312    Taxable    ║
║  160 MAGELLAN    3/3/1983    21.27  Fidelity Fun 8A-3563-GG-91   IRA/Keogh  ║
║   25 WPPPS 9S99 1/13/1984    98.25  E.F Sample   0ZC-60888312    Taxable    ║
║   75 WPPPS 9S99 1/13/1984    98.25  E.F Sample   0ZC-60888312    Taxable    ║
║                                                                            ║
║                                                                            ║
║ Speed scroll -                        * indicates aggregate asset.         ║
╚════════════════════════════════════════════════════════════════════════════╝
            F10 - Record income: Page 278

  F1-Help                                              Esc-Back up
```

RECORD INCOME: SELECT THE ASSET THAT PRODUCED IT

Just point to the asset that produced this income and press F10. If you have more than one lot of this asset, it ordinarily doesn't matter which you point to — so long as it's in the right portfolio.

If you have three separate lots of GE in your Shearson account and four in your separate Shearson profit-sharing account (not to mention the two in your Schwab account) ... and if this dividend applies to both your profit-sharing accounts, be sure to point to any one of those four lots before pressing F10. You'll find a lot more help on the next screen.

DIVIDENDS ON SHORT SALES

If you are short a stock, you don't get the dividend it pays — you PAY it. So on the next screen be sure to use a minus sign to report any dividends your brokerage statement shows were debited against your account. We'll debit them, too. For a tip on reporting short-sale dividends on your tax return, see HELP behind View Income.

```
                  <From Menu Bar, Alt-P, R, F10>
┌─────────────────────────────────────────────────────────────────┐
│┌──────────────────────── RECORD INCOME ────────────────────────┐│
││  #            Purchase  Latest                                 ││
││ Units  Symbol   Date    Price   Portfolio   Account#     Type  ││
││ 144 BJ-85     12/24/1985   0.89 Wine Cellar Downstairs   Taxable││
││ 200 CBUBU     12/31/1985   1.75 E.F Sample  0ZC-6088831Z Taxable││
││ 100 CBUBU     12/31/1985   1.75 E.F Sample  0ZC-6088831Z Taxable││
││                                                                ││
││                                                                ││
││ ┌───────── ENTER INCOME from Commodore Febs ─────────────────┐ ││
││ │                          o                                 │ ││
││ │ Date received ┌──────┐ Amount ┌─────┐  Status ┌──────────┐ │ ││
││ │               └──────┘        └─────┘         └──────────┘ │ ││
││ ├──────────────────────────────┬─────────────────────────── ┤ ││
││ │     F10 - Continue recording │ I received cash            │ ││
││ │                              │ Broker held for me         │ ││
││ │                              │ Automatic Reinvestment      │ ││
││ │                              └─────────────────────────── ┘ ││
││                                                                ││
││ Speed scroll -               * indicates aggregate asset.     ││
││                                                                ││
│└────────────────────────────────────────────────────────────────┘│
│ F1-Help                                           Esc-Back up     │
└─────────────────────────────────────────────────────────────────┘
```

RECORD DIVIDENDS AND INTEREST

If you received a dividend or interest (or your broker received it for you, or it was automatically reinvested in the purchase of new shares), record the details here. (This is NOT the place to record so-called "stock dividends," the nontaxable little stock splits we describe in the HELP behind Split Stocks on the PORTFOLIO menu.)

To avoid asking you questions when they don't apply, we've split this job into two or three steps. Ordinarily, especially once you're set up, recording a dividend or interest payment will involve just a very few keystrokes.

■ STEP #1 – THE PRELIMINARY INFO

Tell us the date you received this income, the total amount (not amount per share), and its "status" — did you actually get it in cash? is your broker holding it in your account? was automatically reinvested in more shares? Then press F10.

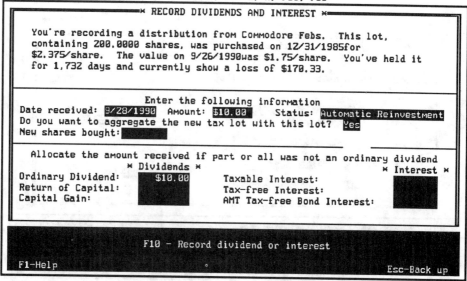

<From Menu Bar, Alt-P, R, F10, F10>

```
═════════════════ ✕ RECORD DIVIDENDS AND INTEREST ✕ ═════════════

 You're recording a distribution from Commodore Febs.  This lot,
 containing 200.0000 shares, was purchased on 12/31/1985for
 $2.375/share.  The value on 9/26/1990was $1.75/share.  You've held it
 for 1,732 days and currently show a loss of $170.33.


                     Enter the following information
Date received: 9/28/1990  Amount: $10.00    Status: Automatic Reinvestment
Do you want to aggregate the new tax lot with this lot? Yes
New shares bought:

  Allocate the amount received if part or all was not an ordinary dividend
                  ✕ Dividends ✕                              ✕ Interest ✕
Ordinary Dividend:      $10.00       Taxable Interest:
Return of Capital:                   Tax-free Interest:
Capital Gain:                        AMT Tax-free Bond Interest:


                     F10 - Record dividend or interest

 F1-Help                          °                          Esc-Back up
```

■ STEP #2 — THE DETAILS

If you told us this income was reinvested in new shares, tell us how many ... and, also, whether to aggregate the new shares with the original ones. You can always disaggregate them later, so answer YES! Otherwise, all we need to know here is that we've guess right about the nature of this income. If it came from a stock, we guess it was all an ordinary dividend. (But was it?) If it came from a bond, we guess it was all taxable interest — unless it came from a bond you tagged as being "tax-free."

If we've guess wrong about any of this, which is not unlikely, just enter the correct amounts in the correct fields. We'll adjust everything else accordingly. For example, if you've received a $100 dividend from your mutual fund but now tell us that $40 of it represented a capital gains distribution, you'll see we automatically lower the ordinary part to $60.

■ Capital gains distributions will be noted as such on the statement your mutual fund sends. (Only the portion of a mutual fund distribution that represents long-term gains is considered a capital gains distribution.)

■ Tax-free interest comes from municipal bonds.

■ AMT tax-free interest does, too, but is subject to the Alternative Minimum Tax.

When you're satisfied we've got the details right, press F10.

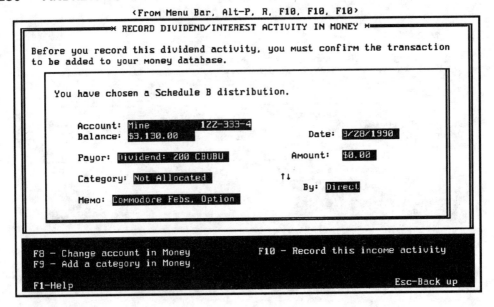

<From Menu Bar, Alt-P, R, F10, F10, F10>

```
============= RECORD DIVIDEND/INTEREST ACTIVITY IN MONEY =============

Before you record this dividend activity, you must confirm the transaction
to be added to your Money database.

    You have chosen a Schedule B distribution.

        Account:  Mine          122-333-4
        Balance:  $3,130.00                    Date:  9/28/1990

        Payor:   Dividend: 200 CBUBU           Amount:  $0.00

        Category: Not Allocated              ↑↓
                                              By:  Direct
        Memo:  Commodore Febs. Option


   F8 - Change account in Money        F10 - Record this income activity
   F9 - Add a category in Money

   F1-Help                                                   Esc-Back up
```

■ STEP #3 — THE ALLOCATION

If the income you recorded was held by your broker or reinvested (so there's no cash to deposit), and if it had no Schedule B tax consequence (so there's no budget allocation necessary), then there IS no Step #3. Otherwise, we ask you to verify the MONEY account into which you'll deposit this cash.

■ If we seem to be about to deposit your cash to the wrong checking or savings account, just press F8 to select the right one. (If you HAVE only one, you won't see F8.)

And, if it's a taxable dividend or interest payment, we ask which budget category to allocate it to.

■ Ordinarily, you'd type "D" for Dividends or "I" for Interest and we'd Speed Scroll straight there. But you may have used different category names, which is fine. Just type the first letter or two.

■ If you need to set up a new budget category on the fly, just press F9. First we'll add it; then you can allocate this income to it.

■ There's no need to allocate capital gains distributions to a budget category. We record them for you on the View Income screen and include them in PORTFOLIO's tax estimation, which flows to TAX.

When you're satisfied, press F10. You're done!

WHAT WE DO WITH YOUR INCOME

Dividends and interest you receive in cash are added to the MONEY account you specified. Dividends your broker credits you with (which you presumably record just once a month, from your brokerage statement), are added to your portfolio cash balance.

With dividends that are automatically reinvested, we purchase the new shares (without lowering your cash balance; the purchase required no cash) and, assuming you told us to, aggregate them with the original shares. If you have more than one batch of these shares, be sure you highlighted the one you want the reinvestment attached to. Or record this dividend in pieces, splitting it proportionally over your various batches.

The capital gains distribution portion of any mutual fund dividend, whether received in cash or reinvested, we show as realized long-term gains in our capital gains analysis here in PORTFOLIO and on the capital-gains distribution line of Schedule D in TAX.

The return-of-capital portion of any dividend (also known as a liquidating dividend) is the portion that need not be reported as income — but that lowers the basis of your shares. If you have 250 shares of XYZ in this portfolio (three separate tax lots that you bought at three different prices); and if you record a $200 dividend for this stock of which, say, $125 represented nontaxable return of capital, you'd enter $125 in the "return of capital" box and we would automatically reduce the purchase price of each of your XYZ shares in this portfolio by 50 cents to reflect their new, lower, basis. ("Basis" is tax talk for "adjusted cost." Usually, it's just what you actually paid. But if you inherited the asset or depreciated it or received returns of capital from it, as in this case, the basis is adjusted.)

- **Note:** We will display dividends in IRA/Keogh and Hypothetical portfolios on the View Income screen. But TAX will, naturally, ignore them.

- **Note also:** If you're recording a dividend on a sold asset (because the dividend arrived after you sold it), you won't be allowed to aggregate it or to allocate a portion to Return of Capital.

- **Final Note:** You may prefer to rely on your monthly or year-end brokerage statements for tallying dividends and interest, rather than record them stock-by-stock. If so, just adjust your portfolio cash balances every so often to reflect the receipt of this new money (with a corresponding budget allocation in MONEY) and skip this screen altogether. (NOW he tells us!)

TO "SEE" YOUR DIVIDEND, SELECT "VIEW INCOME" FROM THE PORTFOLIO MENU

DIVIDENDS ON SHORT SALES

If you short a stock, you don't get the dividend it pays — you PAY it. Be sure to use a minus sign in recording them here. We'll debit your cash balance accordingly. For a tip on reporting short-sale dividends on your tax return see HELP behind View Income.

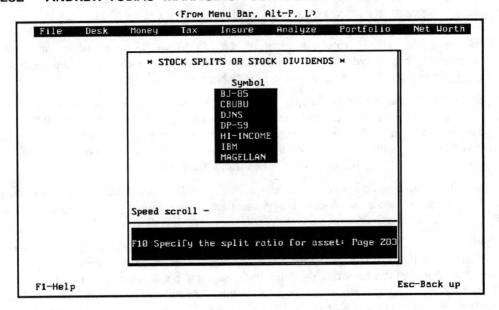

〈From Menu Bar, Alt-P, L〉

STOCK SPLITS

Find the stock you want and Press F6. The excitement and a longer help message follow.

<From Menu Bar, Alt-P, L, F10>

```
 File    Desk    Money    Tax    Insure    Analyze    Portfolio    Net Worth
```

```
            × SPECIFY SPLIT OR DIVIDEND RATIO ×

      You are entering a stock split or dividend for BJ-85.

      Verify or change the split or dividend ratio:

            2.0000    -for-1.0000

            Round down fractional shares? No

                 F10 - Execute the split
```

```
F1-Help                                          Esc-Back up
```

SPECIFY SPLIT RATIO

With a 4-for-1 stock split you have 4 quarters instead of $1. You're not a penny richer. With a 6% stock dividend, which is nothing more than a tiny stock split, you have 106 shares for every 100 you had before; but so does everyone else. The total pie hasn't grown, nor your share of it. It's just been divided into slightly thinner slices. No income tax is due on a stock dividend because it isn't worth anything.

Even so, splits are fun — and must be taken into account. Simply enter the correct ratio in the spaces provided — 3-for-1, 5-for-4, 5-for-1.00, 1-for-10 (called a "reverse" split, and often the beginning of the end) — and press F6. Ordinarily, you'll want to round down to the lowest whole share, because that's what happens in the real world. They send you a check for the difference. If you'll be getting a fractional share instead, answer "No."

THIS IS ORDINARILY NOT THE PLACE TO RECOGNIZE STOCK RECEIVED THRU DIVIDEND REINVESTMENT PLANS.

Those are real, taxable dividends which you could have taken in cash but used to buy more shares. For that, select Record Income from the PORTFOLIO menu. The one exception is for nontaxable portfolios (Hypothetical or IRA/Keogh) where taxes are not a factor. As described in the manual, it may be handier to come here and use the "stock split method" for recording these distributions than to record them separately.

<From Menu Bar, Alt-P, P>

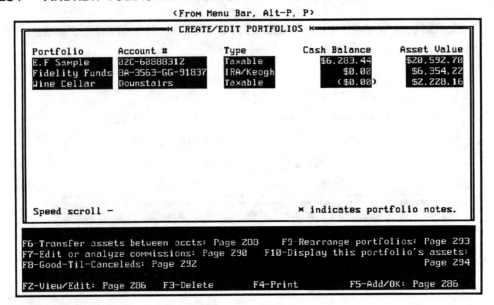

═══════════════ ✳ CREATE/EDIT PORTFOLIOS ✳═══════════════

Portfolio	Account #	Type	Cash Balance	Asset Value
E.F Sample	02C-60888312	Taxable	$6,283.44	$20,592.70
Fidelity Funds	8A-3563-GG-91837	IRA/Keogh	$0.00	$6,354.22
Wine Cellar	Downstairs	Taxable	($0.00)	$2,228.16

Speed scroll —   ✳ indicates portfolio notes.

F6-Transfer assets between accts: Page 288   F9-Rearrange portfolios: Page 293
F7-Edit or analyze commissions: Page 290   F10-Display this portfolio's assets:
F8-Good-Til-Canceleds: Page 292   Page 294

F2-View/Edit: Page 286   F3-Delete   F4-Print   F5-Add/OK: Page 286

PORTFOLIO ACCOUNTS

SETTING UP A PORTFOLIO

First set up a portfolio (F5); then fill it with the assets you own by selecting Buy Assets from the PORTFOLIO menu and by "buying" them.

ADJUSTING ITS CASH BALANCE

Then come back here and type in your correct current Cash Balance. This balance will then rise and fall automatically as you buy and sell assets in the future. From time to time you'll have to edit the Cash Balance to match your monthly brokerage statement: to account for cash you add or withdraw, account fees and so on. But don't think of this as a weakness in the program; the idea is not to mimic your brokerage statement to the penny, which would just waste your time (who needs two monthly statements?). The idea is to analyze things your brokerage statement does not (such as − F7 − the commissions you've been paying!).

■   It's possible to have a negative cash balance − known as "margin debt" − if you owe your broker money. But if you don't owe anything, because you've paid for your purchases in full, just zero out the negative balance we show.

ADJUSTING *CMA* CASH BALANCES

If you've set up one or more of your portfolios as a CMA account, linked to a checking account in MONEY, you'll see you CAN'T adjust the cash balance here. That's because any money you added to or withdrew from the account should be recorded in MONEY, either as a receipt (perhaps you transferred $5,000 from one of your other accounts to this one; record that as a Transfer in MONEY) or else as an expenditure (perhaps you wrote a $3,208.13

check against this account to pay this year's property tax; record that on MONEY's Spend Money screen.)

MAKING OTHER CHANGES — F2

To change the Name or Account Number of a portfolio, point to it and press F2. You can't edit a portfolio's Asset Value, because this is merely the sum of the assets (but not the cash) it contains.

You can't change a portfolio's Type directly, either, but there's an indirect way. First, set up a new portfolio of the proper type, giving it a slightly different name if need be. Then use F6 on this screen to transfer all the assets to it. Finally, delete the old portfolio.

DELETING PORTFOLIOS — F3

It's almost never a good idea to delete a portfolio (F3) — at least not if you had any activity in it this year.

PRINTING REPORTS — F4

We don't show totals for the columns on this screen, but it's easy to see them: Just press F4 and print a Portfolio Summary. (You needn't actually print it — just display it on the screen.) As you'll see, we total up all but your hypothetical portfolios. Or use F4 to print a detailed report of all your assets, by portfolio.

TRANSFERRING ASSETS — F6

Use F6 if you instruct Merrill Lynch to deliver your 10,000 shares of IBM to your account at Shearson, Lehman, Hutton. Use F9 if, now that that's your primary account, you'd like it to be listed first on the screen.

COMMISSIONS — F7

Use F7 both to "QuickEdit" and to analyze your brokerage commissions — and please read its HELP, also. It could save you money!

```
                      ‹From Menu Bar, Alt-P, P, F5›
╔═══════════════════════════════════════════════════════════════╗
║ ═══════════════════✳ CREATE/EDIT PORTFOLIOS ✳═════════════════ ║
║                                                                 ║
║        ╔═══════════════════════════════════════════════╗        ║
║        ║          ✳ ADD A NEW PORTFOLIO ✳              ║        ║
║        ║                                               ║        ║
║        ║  Portfolio (broker) Name  ███████████████     ║        ║
║        ║  Account Number           ████████████████    ║        ║
║        ║  Type of Portfolio        ██████              ║        ║
║        ║  Initial Cash Balance     ████ ┌──────────┐   ║        ║
║        ║                                │Taxable   │   ║        ║
║        ║  Memo:        ████████████     │IRA/Keogh │   ║        ║
║        ║                                │Hypothetical│ ║        ║
║        ║                                │CMA1      │   ║        ║
║        ║                                │CMA2     ▼│   ║        ║
║        ║                                └──────────┘   ║        ║
║        ╚═══════════════════════════════════════════════╝        ║
║                                                                 ║
║ F1-Help        F2-View/Edit          F5-Add/OK      Esc-Back up ║
╚═══════════════════════════════════════════════════════════════╝
```

ADD OR EDIT A PORTFOLIO

Here you add a new portfolio or edit the details of one you added previously. Set up as many portfolios as you like:

- Normal Taxable portfolios (including up to nine cash-management accounts — CMAs — linked to checking accounts in MONEY)

- IRA/Keogh-type tax-sheltered portfolios

- Hypothetical portfolios

■ PORTFOLIO NAME

This would typically be "Paine Webber," but could be "Dad's Portfolio" or "British Coins" so far as we're concerned.

■ ACCOUNT NUMBER

Ordinarily, you'd just enter your real account number. But we don't care.

■ TYPE OF PORTFOLIO

Just type your choice — T, I, H, or C. If you choose C, you'll have to type the whole thing — CMA1. And of course you'll have to choose one not already in use. If you already HAVE a CMA1, make this one CMA2. (We'll beep at you if you goof.)

If you're adding a new CMA, we'll flash a warning and then lead you through adding it's counterpart in MONEY. (You can't link a new CMA to an existing MONEY account.) It just requires filling in a few more fields. You'll notice that the cash balances of the two linked accounts will be identical — always — because changing one affects the other. The "memo" will be identical, too. For all practical purposes, they are ONE account, shared by MONEY and PORTFOLIO.

The other way to set up a CMA is to do it first in MONEY. That's fine, too. Once you do, it will be sitting here all filled out and ready to use.

■ CASH BALANCE

If this actually is a brand new account, and not just new to Managing Your Money, enter as the Initial Cash Balance whatever amount you've sent to open it.

If you're here to set up an existing account, don't worry about the initial balance. Leave it at zero and go "buy" the assets the account contains, with the original purchase dates and prices. Once you have, we'll show a huge negative cash balance — the cost of all those purchases. So then just type in the correct cash balance, as shown on your brokerage statement.

We adjust the cash balance automatically when you buy or sell things, or record a dividend; but if you actually send your broker a check, or hand him a suitcase full of $20 bills, we don't know about it unless you tell us. Adjust the cash balance at any time simply by typing over it, either here or on the Portfolio screen. Have you added $5,323 to your account by sending a check in that amount to pay for your 200 shares of W. R. Grace? Fine. Add $5,323 to the number we show as the cash balance in this Portfolio. The same holds true for withdrawals you make, margin interest you are charged and account fees. Adjust your cash balance accordingly.

■ If it's a CMA, account for those withdrawals simply by "Spending" the money in MONEY. Your cash balance here will be reduced automatically. To record a receipt, visit MONEY's Transfer Money screen and tell us you transferred $5,323 from one of your other accounts to this CMA account.

■ MEMO

Use the memo field — which F2 will expand to 1000 acres — for anything you want, including the name of your broker and her assistant; the office manager; the promises they've made you; the instructions you've given them — and so on. Chances are, it will be a very happy, profitable relationship. But in case it's not, having detailed, dated notes on your conversations won't hurt.

If it's an IRA, use the memo to keep a running tally of each year's non-deductible contribution, if any — a handy record that will save you time and taxes when you begin your withdrawals. Or if you have begun withdrawals, here's a place to note the minimum amounts you've been advised the law requires you to withdraw.

■ PAGE SCROLL

If you're here to look at or change an existing portfolio, you'll see our familiar Page Scroll at the bottom of the screen. Use PgUp and PgDn to run through various portfolios.

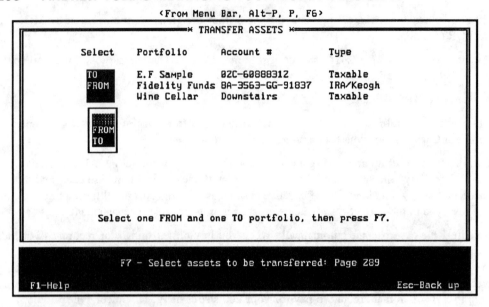

```
                       <From Menu Bar, Alt-P, P, F6>
┌─────────────────────────────────────────────────────────────────────┐
│═══════════════════════════ ✕ TRANSFER ASSETS ✕ ═══════════════════════│
│                                                                       │
│        Select     Portfolio     Account #          Type               │
│                                                                       │
│        ▐TO  ▌     E.F Sample     02C-60888312       Taxable           │
│        ▐FROM▌     Fidelity Funds BA-3563-GG-91837   IRA/Keogh         │
│                   Wine Cellar    Downstairs         Taxable           │
│        ▐▓▓▓▓▌                                                         │
│        ▐FROM▌                                                         │
│        ▐TO  ▌                                                         │
│                                                                       │
│                                                                       │
│                                                                       │
│            Select one FROM and one TO portfolio, then press F7.       │
│                                                                       │
│                                                                       │
└─────────────────────────────────────────────────────────────────────┘
         F7 - Select assets to be transferred: Page 289
  F1-Help                                              Esc-Back up
```

TRANSFER ASSETS

Should you ever merge two IRA accounts into one, or transfer stocks back from your discount broker to Merrill Lynch, this screen and the one that follows will save a ton of work. Here, tell us the accounts to transfer between. Press F7 and you'll be asked to specify just which assets you want transferred.

```
                    <From Menu Bar, Alt-P, P, F6, F7>
 ┌─────────────────────────────────────────────────────────────────────┐
 │═════════════ SELECT ASSETS TO BE TRANSFERRED ── Status: ═════════════│
 │                                                                       │
 │            #           Purchase  Current     Total                    │
 │   Select  Units Symbol   Price    Price      Value      Status        │
 │                                                                       │
 │   ███████ 163.63 HI-INCOME  12.22   18.09   $2,960      Unsold        │
 │           159.58 MAGELLAN   12.16   21.27   $3,394      Unsold        │
 │                                                                       │
 │                                                                       │
 │                                                                       │
 │                                                                       │
 │          ╳ indicates an aggregate.  It will be moved as a whole.      │
 │                                                                       │
 └─────────────────────────────────────────────────────────────────────┘
 ┌─────────────────────────────────────────────────────────────────────┐
 │   F6 - Rotate to show Gain/Loss                                       │
 │   F7 - Transfer marked assets  FROM: Fidelity Funds #8A-3563-GG-91837 │
 │                                  TO: E.F Sample #0ZC-60888312          │
 │   F1-Help                                                Esc-Back up   │
 └─────────────────────────────────────────────────────────────────────┘
```

SELECT ASSETS TO BE TRANSFERRED

Assets you mark will be magically transferred when you press F7. The cash balances of your accounts won't change because no cash is involved. Ordinarily, it's not a good idea to transfer sold assets. If they were sold in your Merrill Lynch account, switching to a different broker won't change the fact (or Merrill's reporting to the IRS) that they were sold in the Merrill account. (If we're not displaying the sold/unsold status for you, press F6 to see it.)

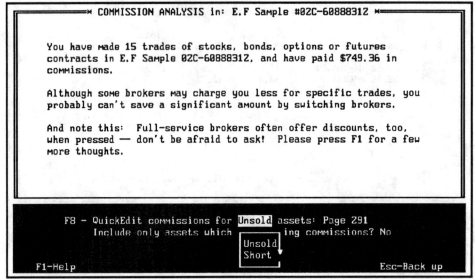

‹From Menu Bar, Alt-P, P, F7›

COMMISSION ANALYSIS

For this calculation we've used a simplified, representative discount commission schedule. Because most discounters charge a minimum of $30 or more per trade, small traders may realize no savings. Nor, if you're spending only $200 or $300 a year on commissions, is there much reason to make a change. But for active traders the savings can be significant.

The two largest discount brokers are Charles Schwab & Co. and Fidelity Brokerage. Both are open 24 hours a day and have 800 numbers. Check the Wall Street Journal ads for discounters that offer even better deals; but also be sure to compare financial strength and the level and range of services offered. Most accounts are insured, but the last thing you want is to have yours frozen while they straighten things out.

One wrinkle: Some of your trades may be reported with no commission (just a small service charge, if that). Instead, the confirm will show that the price has been marked up or down a fraction of a point. To reflect that here, you'd want to enter the price not as $13 and the commission as zero, as the broker did, but as $12.75 and $250 (if it was a quarter-point mark-up on 1000 shares) — which it was. Press F8 to QuickEdit your commissions.

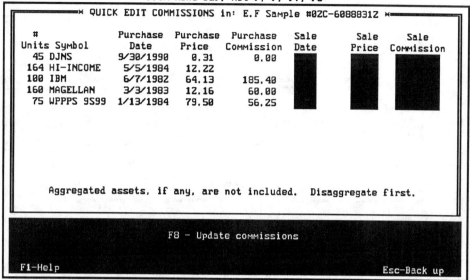

⟨From Menu Bar, Alt-P, P, F7, F8⟩

```
━━━━━━━━━━━✕ QUICK EDIT COMMISSIONS in: E.F Sample #0ZC-60888312 ✕━━━━━━━

   #                 Purchase  Purchase  Purchase   Sale      Sale     Sale
 Units Symbol          Date     Price    Commission Date      Price    Commission
   45  DJNS           9/30/1990  0.31      0.00
  164  HI-INCOME      5/5/1984   12.22
  100  IBM            6/7/1982   64.13    185.40
  160  MAGELLAN       3/3/1983   12.16     60.00
   75  WPPPS 9S99     1/13/1984  79.50     56.25




          Aggregated assets, if any, are not included.   Disaggregate first.



                              F8 - Update commissions


 F1-Help                                                          Esc-Back up
```

QUICKEDIT COMMISSIONS

If you like to record trades as you make them, so you're up-to-the-minute, come here when the confirms arrive a week later and record the commission. Include the extra little service charges many brokers add — typically, $1 or $2 per trade (though it sure mounts up for them) along with the tiny SEC fee levied on sales of listed securities. See HELP behind the previous screen for a thought on commissions disguised as mark-ups.

Come here also if, after having complained a commission's too high, you receive a corrected confirm with a lower one. (Yes, with many brokers, if you're a good customer, you can do this. Just don't tell them where you got the idea.)

```
                        <From Menu Bar, Alt-P, P, F8>
==========================* CREATE/EDIT PORTFOLIOS *==========================


          * GOOD-TIL-CANCELEDS in: E.F Sample #02C-60888312 *

                    #                      Buy/        GTC
                 Units        Symbol       Sell        Price
                    25        IBM          Buy         $11.20








   F1-Help         F3-Delete         F4-Print        F5-Add/OK       Esc-Back up
```

GOOD-TIL-CANCELEDS

This is no more than a pad on which to jot down the good-til-canceled orders you place.

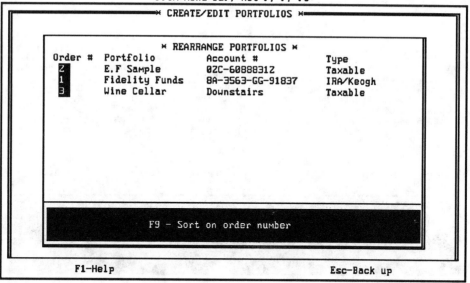

<From Menu Bar, Alt-P, P, F9>

REARRANGE PORTFOLIO ORDER

Type 1 next to the portfolio you'd like us to list first, 2 next to the second, and so on. Then press F9. Arrange your portfolios any way you like — flexibility is our middle name.

<From Menu Bar, Alt-P, D>

```
━━━━━━━━━× DISPLAY UNSOLD ASSETS IN PORTFOLIO ── ASSET NAME: ×━━━━━━━━━

                      E.F Sample #0ZC-60888312

   #                                 Purchase    Gain       Simple  Annual.
Units       Symbol      Name           Date    (Loss) Term  Apprec. Apprec.
 201.0000 CBUBU     Commodore Febs  12/31/1985  $1,480 ×    279.0%       %
  45.0000 DJNS      DJ's News Stand 9/30/1990     ($0)S       0.0%    0.0%
 163.6263 HI-INCOME Bond Fund        5/5/1984    $960 L      48.0%   27.2%
 100.0000 IBM       IBM              6/7/1982   $4,602 L     69.8%    6.6%
 159.5780 MAGELLAN  Magellan Fund    3/3/1983   $1,394 L     69.7%   12.2%
  75.0000 WPPPS 9S99 WPPPS 9% of '99 1/13/1984  $1,350 L     22.4%    3.1%



Speed scroll −                      × under Term indicates aggregate asset.

```

```
 F6-Rotate to show Original Cost       F9-Work with Sold   assets: Page 298
 F7 Sort by Symbol                     F10-Buy  Assets: Page 263
 F8-Change portfolio account: Page 268
                                       Alt-F1-Select assets to aggregate: Page 304

 F2-View/Edit: Page 296        F3-Delete: Page 297              F4-Print
```

DISPLAY ASSETS

GETTING THE DISPLAY YOU WANT

This powerful screen allows you to see a lot of different things different ways:

1. Check the name of the portfolio at the top of the screen. To work with a different one, press F8.

2. Use F9 if you'd prefer to see your short positions or the assets you've sold.

3. Press F6 repeatedly to rotate among our three different displays (you need not jump into the choice box to do this). Ordinarily, you'll want the "Current Value" display; but to check a commission or a purchase date or a fractional number of shares, just flip-flip-flip with F6.

4. Use F7 to sort your assets any of seven ways. (Remember, TAB jumps you into the choice box to see the last couple of choices.) Ordinarily, you'll want to sort by symbol; but if you own bonds, it can be helpful to sort in order of their maturity. Or if you want to focus on the most important holdings, sort by Total Value. And so on.

Note: If you've just added an asset, it will be at the end of the list. Use F7 to put it in order. Whatever the order, use Speed Scroll to jump to any symbol. When you press F4 to print, we'll print in whatever order you've sorted.

AGGREGATING SEPARATE TAX LOTS

If you have two or more tax lots with the same symbol, point to one of them, press Alt-F1 and read HELP to see what we can do. To view or dis-aggregate an aggregated set of tax lots, point and press F2. Aggregates here are denoted by an asterisk in the Term column (because they may be part long-term, part short-term).

SHORTCUT

F10 on this screen is just a way to go straight to the Buy (or Sell) screen.

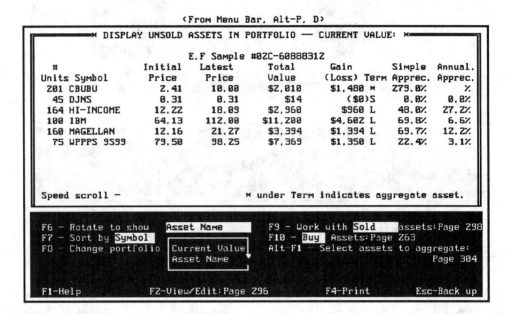

```
                             <From Menu Bar, Alt-P, D>
┌──────────────────────────────────────────────────────────────────────────┐
│═══════════════ ✳ DISPLAY UNSOLD ASSETS IN PORTFOLIO — CURRENT VALUE: ✳ ════│
│                                                                            │
│                        E.F Sample #0ZC-60888312                            │
│     #                Initial   Latest    Total       Gain         Simple  Annual.│
│  Units  Symbol        Price    Price     Value     (Loss) Term   Apprec.  Apprec.│
│   201  CBUBU           2.41     10.00    $2,010     $1,480 ✳     279.0%       %│
│    45  DJNS            0.31      0.31       $14       ($0)S        0.0%    0.0%│
│   164  HI-INCOME      12.22     18.09    $2,960       $960 L      48.0%   27.2%│
│   100  IBM            64.13    112.00   $11,200     $4,602 L      69.8%    6.6%│
│   160  MAGELLAN       12.16     21.27    $3,394     $1,394 L      69.7%   12.2%│
│    75  WPPPS 9S99     79.50     98.25    $7,369     $1,350 L      22.4%    3.1%│
│                                                                            │
│                                                                            │
│                                                                            │
│  Speed scroll -                     ✳ under Term indicates aggregate asset.│
└──────────────────────────────────────────────────────────────────────────┘
┌──────────────────────────────────────────────────────────────────────────┐
│  F6 - Rotate to show  Asset Name      F9 - Work with Sold    assets:Page 298│
│  F7 - Sort by Symbol                  F10 - Buy  Assets:Page 263           │
│  F8 - Change portfolio │Current Value│ Alt-F1 — Select assets to aggregate:│
│                        │Asset Name  ↓│                       Page 304       │
│                                                                            │
│  F1-Help          F2-View/Edit:Page 296          F4-Print      Esc-Back up │
└──────────────────────────────────────────────────────────────────────────┘
```

```
                         <From Menu Bar, Alt-P, D, F2>
┌──────────────────────────────────────────────────────────────────────────┐
│                        ═══ VIEW OR EDIT ASSET ═══                          │
│                                                                            │
│    Symbol            DJNS              Maturity Date                        │
│    Name              DJ's News Stand   Price Objective   0.420             │
│    No. of Units      45.0000           Mental Stop Loss  0.380             │
│    Purchase date     9/30/1990         Risk Level        High              │
│    Price/Unit        0.310             Beta                                 │
│    Commission        $0.00             Liquidity         Full              │
│    Yield ($/unit)                      Industry Group    Entertainment     │
│    Tax Free?         No                Recommendor       Own Idea          │
│    Type of Asset     Common Stock      Special Codes                       │
│                                                                            │
│    Dow Jones (or the index you follow) at time of purchase                 │
│    Comments                                                                 │
│    Current Price for assets with this symbol is $0.310                     │
│                                                                            │
│                       ─── Page Scroll 1 of 7 ───                          │
├────────────────────────────────────────────────────────────────────────┤
│                                                                            │
│    F6 - Update just this asset           F9 - Look at Special Codes: Page 269 │
│    F7 - Update all assets with this symbol                                  │
│                                                                            │
│    F1-Help        F2-View/Edit                  F4-Print      Esc-Back up   │
└────────────────────────────────────────────────────────────────────────┘
```

VIEW OR EDIT AN ASSET

Edit anything just by typing over it; then choose F6 or F7. (Or PgDn to save your work and Page Scroll to your next asset.)

If you use F7 to "update all assets with this symbol," as you normally would, we will update the items that are common to all. Obviously NOT the date or price or number of shares or commission, but everything else except "recommendor" (in case the first bunch of shares were bought on the recommendation of a newsletter, while the second time it was your own bright idea) and "comments" (in case you use this line to, for example, time-stamp your order and record the verbal confirmation number your broker may give you for that specific trade).

For a refresher on what each classification means, choose HELP for "Buy an Asset" from the Help Index.

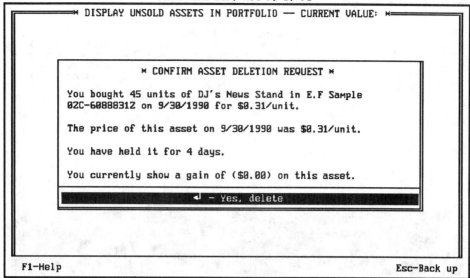

<From Menu Bar, Alt-P, D, F3>

CONFIRM DELETION OF ASSET OR SHORT

Deleting an asset or short is different from selling (or covering) it. When you delete an asset or short, it's as though you never bought or shorted it in the first place. It will vanish, and whatever paid for it (nothing, in the case of a short) will be restored to your cash balance. You'd use this feature, for example, if you thought you had bought 100 shares of So-and-So, only to find that your broker never did manage to execute the trade. Or if your child accidentally entered a whole bunch of nonsense stocks while you were in the kitchen fixing a snack.

<From Menu Bar, Alt-P, D, F9>

```
╔══════════════════════════════════════════════════════════════════════╗
║                  ══╼ DISPLAY SOLD ASSETS IN PORTFOLIO: ╾══             ║
║                                                                        ║
║                        E.F Sample #0ZC-6088831Z                        ║
║      #              Purchase    Sale      Total      Gain      Simple   Annual. ║
║   Units Symbol        Price     Price    Proceeds   (Loss) Term Apprec. Apprec. ║
║     100 CBUBU          2.38      1.75       $175      ($85)  L  -32.7%   -8.0%   ║
║      50 CC            19.00     22.25     $1,113      $131   S   13.7%    2.7%   ║
║      12 IBM          168.00    112.00     $1,344     ($774)  L  -36.5%  -12.2%   ║
║      25 WPPPS 9S99    79.50     98.25     $2,456      $450   L   22.4%    3.1%   ║
║                                                                        ║
║                                                                        ║
║                                                                        ║
║                                                                        ║
║   Speed scroll —                                                       ║
║                                                                        ║
╠════════════════════════════════════════════════════════════════════════╣
║  F6 - Unsell asset: Page 300       F9 - Work with [Short] assets: Page 301 ║
║  F8 - Change portfolio account: Page 268                                  ║
║                                                                           ║
║  F2-View/Edit: Page 299          F3-Delete              F4-Print          ║
╚════════════════════════════════════════════════════════════════════════╝
```

SOLD ASSETS

Here are the assets that USED TO BE in this portfolio. You may press: F8 to view the sold assets in a different portfolio, F4 to print the list, F2 to view or change the details of one of the sales, F6 to "unsell" the asset, if the sale didn't go through, after all. It will be as if the sale never took place. (You'd also "unsell" it temporarily if the sale did go through but you need to correct some of the PURCHASE information you had entered. In that case, unsell it; correct it on the Unsold Assets screen; then select Sell Assets to sell it again, now that it's correct.)

Press F3 to delete one of the sales altogether. It will disappear; whatever profit or loss you showed will be cut from both our tax calculations AND your cash balance. It's not clear why you'd want to do this, but we aim to please.

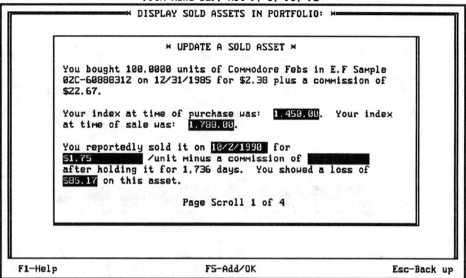

‹From Menu Bar, Alt-P, D, F9, F2›

═══════ ✕ DISPLAY SOLD ASSETS IN PORTFOLIO: ✕ ═══════

✕ UPDATE A SOLD ASSET ✕

You bought 100.0000 units of Commodore Febs in E.F Sample
02C-60888312 on 12/31/1985 for $2.38 plus a commission of
$22.67.

Your index at time of purchase was: `1,450.00`. Your index
at time of sale was: `1,788.00`.

You reportedly sold it on `10/2/1990` for
`$1.75`   /unit minus a commission of `          `
after holding it for 1,736 days. You showed a loss of
`$85.17` on this asset.

Page Scroll 1 of 4

F1-Help   F5-Add/OK   Esc-Back up

UPDATE A SOLD ASSET

Correct anything you want and press F5.

‹From Menu Bar, Alt-P, D, F9, F6›

```
╒══════════ × DISPLAY SOLD ASSETS IN PORTFOLIO: ×══════════╕
│                                                          │
│   ┌──────────────── × UNSELL A SOLD ASSET ×───────────┐  │
│   │                                                    │  │
│   │ You bought 100.0000 units of Commodore Febs in E.F Sample │
│   │ 02C-60888312 on 12/31/1985 for $2.38/unit.         │  │
│   │                                                    │  │
│   │ You sold it on 9/26/1990 for $1.75/unit after holding it for │
│   │ 1,730 days.                                        │  │
│   │                                                    │  │
│   │                                                    │  │
│   │ You showed a loss of $85.17 on this asset.         │  │
│   │                                                    │  │
│   ├────────────────────────────────────────────────────┤  │
│   │          ↵ - Unsell this sold asset                │  │
│   └────────────────────────────────────────────────────┘  │
│                                                          │
│                                                          │
│   F1-Help                               Esc-Back up      │
╘══════════════════════════════════════════════════════════╛
```

UNSELL A SOLD ASSET

Press the Enter key if you really want to undo this sale. The asset will return to your portfolio; the cash you received for it will be subtracted from your cash balance. If you've come here to "uncover" a short sale you'd previously covered, we'll restore it to your portfolio and remove from your cash balance whatever profit or loss you made covering it.

<From Menu Bar, Alt-P, B, F10>

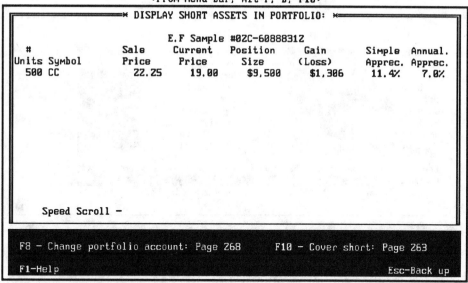

SHORT POSITION DISPLAY

If you do much short-selling (selling something you don't own in the hope it will fall in price before you buy it back), you know how confusing your monthly brokerage statements can be. You never quite know (sometimes your broker doesn't, either), whether the market value and cash balances shown include the value of your shorts or add in your current profit on the shorts or ...

Rather than duplicate this confusion, we've given shorts this separate screen. To sell a stock short, select Sell Assets from the PORTFOLIO menu. We'll show here the current size of your position (but not include it in your portfolio asset value); your gain or loss on the position (which we do include in our capital gains analysis); and express that gain or loss as a percentage of the size of your original position, dubiously meaningful though such percentages may be.

When you cover a short (F10), the profit or loss will be added to your cash balance and included as a realized short-term gain or loss in all tax calculations and recordkeeping (if this is a taxable portfolio).

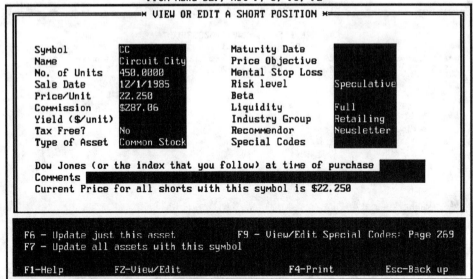

<From Menu Bar, Alt-P, D, F9, F2>

```
==================× VIEW OR EDIT A SHORT POSITION ×==================

   Symbol          CC              Maturity Date
   Name            Circuit City    Price Objective
   No. of Units    450.0000        Mental Stop Loss
   Sale Date       12/1/1985       Risk level          Speculative
   Price/Unit      22.250          Beta
   Commission      $287.06         Liquidity           Full
   Yield ($/unit)                  Industry Group      Retailing
   Tax Free?       No              Recommendor         Newsletter
   Type of Asset   Common Stock    Special Codes

   Dow Jones (or the index that you follow) at time of purchase
   Comments
   Current Price for all shorts with this symbol is $22.250


   F6 - Update just this asset.          F9 - View/Edit Special Codes: Page 269
   F7 - Update all assets with this symbol

   F1-Help          F2-View/Edit                F4-Print          Esc-Back up
```

VIEW OR EDIT A SHORT POSITION

Edit anything you like simply by typing over the old information. Then choose F6 or F7.

<From Menu Bar, Alt-P, S, F7>

ENTER A SHORT POSITION

Enter a short as you would a regular purchase. We know the yield will be negative (you don't get it, you pay it), so don't use a minus sign. For a refresher, go to the HELP behind adding a (regular) new asset.

Throughout PORTFOLIO, shorts are given no value (only, in places, a "position size" — the number of shares times their price). When we total up the value of everything you own, shorts neither increase it nor decrease it. When we show the distribution of your portfolio by risk, special code, or anything else, shorts do not figure in the calculation.

What we do track carefully is your gain or loss on each position. These figure in all gain/loss calculations. For "percentage gains," we divide the gain by the original size of your short position. If you shorted 100 shares of a $50 stock that's now $40, that's a $1,000 gain on what was a $5,000 position, or 20%. I'm not saying this is logically airtight, but it gives you some feel for what's happening. We could call it a $1,000 gain on a ZERO investment, which it sort of was, but then what percent gain do we show — a zillion?

Short sales have NO EFFECT on your cash balance. When you cover a short, the gain or loss is added to your cash balance in the account.

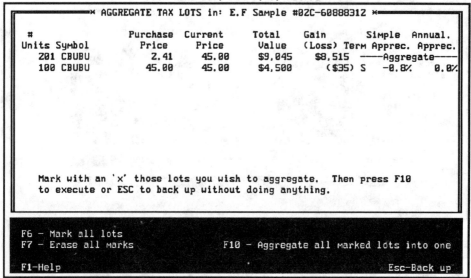

AGGREGATE TAX LOTS

Except for tax purposes, it's usually more convenient to think of all your GM shares as one block than as a lot of little chips. So typically here you'd press F6 to mark all the lots and then F10 to aggregate them. But never fear: to disaggregate them, you need only point to the newly aggregated block on the Display Assets screen and press F2 to View or Edit — or disaggregate — them.

Note that with dividend reinvestments, we will do the aggregation for you automatically if you ask us to when you record the dividend, and, when you go to view the aggregate block, we offer a special way of calculating its performance.

But which of your tax lots become the ducklings, and which the mother duck? For most purposes, it doesn't matter. But for the "Original Cost" analysis we do when you go to View an aggregate (point to it on the Display Assets screen and press F2), you want to be sure to attach reinvested dividends to their initial big block purchases and not the other way around.

Whichever lots you mark here, the one closest to the top of the list becomes the mother duck. All those marked beneath it aggregate to it. So use F7 on the previous screen to sort by date (presumably) before coming here. That way, the initial purchase will be at the top of the list.

```
╔═══════╗ VIEW AGGREGATED LOTS OF THIS ASSET in: E.F Sample #02C-60888312 ╔═══════╗

    #               Purchase   Current     Total     Gain       Simple  Annual.
  Units  Symbol       Price      Price     Value    (Loss) Term Apprec. Apprec.
   200   CBUBU         2.38      10.00     $2,000    $1,480  L  284.4%   32.8%
     1   CBUBU        10.00      10.00        $10     ($0)   S    0.0%    0.0%




              Total Cost          Market Value        Simple Appreciation
               $530.33             $2,010.00               279.0%


  F6 - Mark all lots                      F9 - Show  Total Cost
  F7 - Erase all marks                    F10 - Disaggregate marked lots

  F1-Help                    F4-Print                        Esc-Back up
```

VIEW AGGREGATED TAX LOTS OF THIS ASSET

Here are the chips that make up your block. If you want to edit one, first disaggregate it from the rest. Then go view it separately, as you would any other tax lot. Make changes if you like. When you're done, you can always point to it and press Alt-F1 to aggregate it again.

Note that when you disaggregate, this asset winds up at the end of your list. You can take a moment to re-sort the list, or else just wait til we do it for you as part of some other operation.

F9 here lets you see performance two different ways. Press Ctrl-L to jump there and try both choices:

TOTAL COST

With Total Cost we show at the bottom of the screen the total you paid for this block — the cost of ALL the chips, even if some of them seemed to be "free" because they were automatic dividend reinvestments. (They were NOT free: you could have taken the cash instead of using it to buy these extra shares.) And we show their current value. Comparing the two, we show the gain or loss in simple percentage terms.

ORIGINAL COST

But for aggregates that are the result of dividend reinvestments, many people, quite reasonably, would prefer to think of it as if they had made just a single investment way back when — that their total cost was just that initial purchase. To see the calculation this way, choose Original Cost and press F9.

We will assume that tax lot to which you attached the other lots was the "real" investment and that all the others on this screen were "free." At the bottom of the screen, we'll show the

COST of just the initial shares, but the VALUE of all the shares. And we'll tell you the annualized growth rate that represents.

How has this mutual fund done compared with the rate you could have gotten on a savings account? For this to work, it's important to aggregate all the dividend reinvestments to the right tax lot — namely, the original shares. If you've let us do the aggregation for you as, over the quarters and years you've recorded dividend reinvestments in this chapter, we've done it right.

But if you've aggregated the shares yourself, or disaggregated what we've done and then reaggregated yourself, you might accidentally have attached the initial 200 shares you bought to one of the 8-share dividend reinvestments — on which, accordingly, we'll show a truly world-beating annualized gain. So be sure to read HELP on the aggregation screen to see what attaches to what!

"Original Cost" is a sensible way to look at how your mutual fund (or other dividend-reinvesting asset) has performed. It obviously makes no sense when you've aggregated, say, 100 shares of GE you bought in 1986 with 100 more you purchased this past March. The "Original Cost" annualized appreciation we'd show in that case would be meaningless, since the second lot of shares was unquestionably a separate investment.

Where you may have to improvise a bit is with a mutual fund in which you reinvest your dividends — but in which you occasionally also buy new shares. (If you buy them weekly, forget trying to track the performance of each little purchase; just use our Total Cost display and whatever performance statistics your fund sends out each quarter.)

Say you bought 200 shares of the fund in 1986, have aggregated the little reinvestments, and now buy 100 more. What do you do when you get a notice that your 300 shares have been credited with 8.361 new shares? (Because the fund itself is not fool enough to keep all your tax lots separate: it now thinks of your having one 300 share lot.) If it's important to you to try to track the "Original Cost" performance of each block, one option is to give the first a symbol like MAGELLAN, but call the next MAGELLAN2 — and so on. When you get a dividend reinvestment notice, divide it pro-rata among your two or three "original" blocks, and record each of those dividends separately, thus aggregating each little duckling to the proper duck.

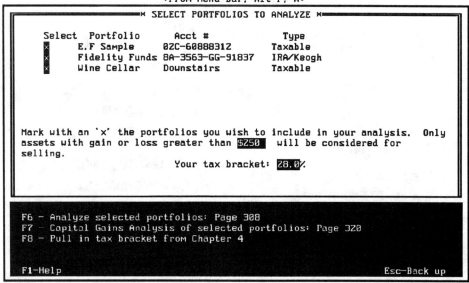

SELECT PORTFOLIOS TO ANALYZE

To look at only one portfolio, place an X beside it and proceed. But if you're keeping track of several, this feature allows you to lump them together any way you like.

You reach most of our analyses by pressing F6. For capital gains, press F7. We won't waste your time suggesting sales of tax lots with gains or losses below $250 (or any other number you specify — just move the cursor down and type in the cutoff you want). Type over our guess at your tax bracket, or press F8 to summon it from TAX.

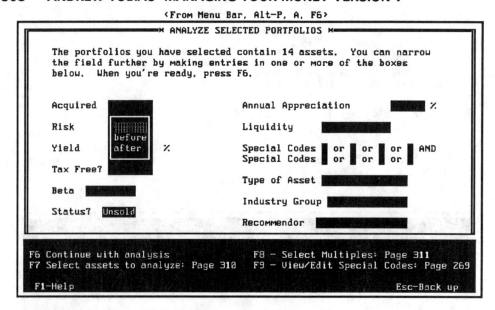

ANALYZE SELECTED PORTFOLIOS

NARROWING THE FIELD

Ordinarily, you'll just breeze right pass the screen. Press F6 without doing a thing. But for those of you with a multitude of assets (mazeltov!), here's a way to specify exactly which ones you want to include in the analysis.

Note: With AGGREGATES, we look to the "mother duck" to see whether it meets your criteria, even if its ducklings don't. If you prefer, disaggregate them first and we'll subject each lot to your criteria.

Note: You may specify as many different criteria as you like.

Remember: to blank out a choice that's already showing, just TAB into the choice box, arrow up to that first greyed choice, and press the Enter key.

■ ACQUIRED BEFORE/AFTER

Want to include only assets bought since you switched brokers? Or before the divorce proceedings were filed? Just let us know.

■ RISK

Want to consider only assets you've categorized as risky, to focus on the real hot spots in your portfolio . . . or all BUT the risky ones? We'll weed out any assets that don't meet your criteria.

■ YIELD

Should you wish to consider only stocks that pay a dividend of at least 5.5%, or bonds that yield less than ".01%" — like your zero-coupon bonds — use this field.

■ TAX FREE?

To view and analyze ONLY your municipal bonds, enter "Yes." To EXCLUDE them, enter "No." Otherwise, leave this blank.

■ BETA

Leave this blank, and your securities will be analyzed regardless of the betas you've assigned them. Beta — a measure of a stock's volatility — is much the same as "risk," above, only quantified.

■ STATUS?

This is the one box on this screen you cannot leave blank. Ordinarily, you'll want to leave it set at UNSOLD, to look only at the things you own. But you can look at the things you used to own by choosing SOLD or at BOTH sold and unsold. To see your open short positions, which we do not mix with your open longs, set this to SHORT. Once shorts are covered, you'll find them among your other closed-out transactions on the "Sold" screen.

■ ANNUAL APPRECIATION

Should you wish to consider only assets that have appreciated above or below some annualized rate, let us know. (Remember: a stock that rises 3% in a week has appreciated at a very dramatic annualized rate.)

■ LIQUIDITY

Should you wish to consider only your fully liquid assets (or your illiquid ones), let us know.

■ SPECIAL CODES

This is a tricky one (unless you leave it blank). Enter from one to four special codes on the top line, and we'll weed out assets not possessing AT LEAST ONE of them. If you enter codes in the SECOND LINE AS WELL, we'll weed out assets not possessing at least one code from EACH LINE. So to look only at securities recommended by Tom, Dick, or Harry, enter their codes on the first line. To look only at the FOREIGN securities they've recommended (assuming you've assigned foreign securities a code), put that special code on the second line.

■ TYPE OF ASSET

If you want to look only at your common stocks, say, or your preferred stocks, tell us. To look only at your common AND preferred stocks, enter "Multiple" and press F8.

■ INDUSTRY GROUP

If you want to look only at your oil stocks, say, or your autos, tell us. To look only at your oils AND autos stocks, enter "Multiple" and press F8.

■ RECOMMENDOR

If you want to look only at stocks that were your own ideas, tell us. To look only at those you learned of from magazines and newsletters, enter "Multiple" and press F8.

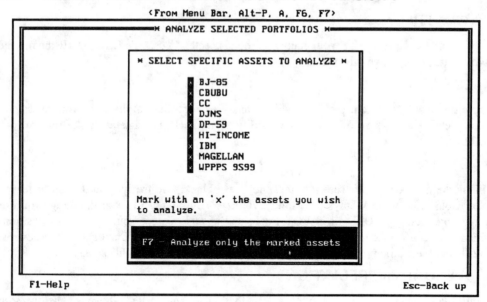

SELECT ASSETS TO ANALYZE

To limit your analysis to just certain stocks, select them here and press F7. (If you're trying to see all lots of just one asset, it's easier and will usually suffice just to point to it on the Update Prices screen and press F2.)

```
                    <From Menu Bar, Alt-P, A, F6, F8>
             ═══════════╳ SELECT MULTIPLES TO VIEW ╳═══════════
   ┌──────────────────────────────────────────────────────────────┐
   │     Type of Asset        Industry Groups                       │
   │   ▪ Common Stock        ╳ Agribusiness     ╳ Health Care       │
   │   ▪ Preferred Stock     ╳ Aircraft         ╳ Heavy Construction│
   │   ▪ Mutual Fund         ╳ Airline          ╳ High Tech         │
   │   ▪ Savings Bond/SPDA   ╳ Automotive       ╳ Housing           │
   │   ╳ Bond                ╳ Banking          ╳ Insurance         │
   │   ╳ Option              ╳ Capital Goods    ╳ Mining            │
   │   ╳ Futures Contract    ╳ Chemicals        ╳ Oil & Gas         │
   │   ╳ Real Estate         ╳ Clothing         ╳ Packaged Goods    │
   │   ╳ Tax Shelter         ╳ Conglomerate     ╳ Railroads         │
   │   ╳ Metals/Collectibles ╳ Defense          ╳ Retailing         │
   │   ╳ Other               ╳ Electric Utility ╳ Telephone Utility │
   │   ▪ Special Coded       ╳ Entertainment    ╳ Textiles          │
   │                         ╳ Food             ╳ Other             │
   │                         ╳ Forest Products                      │
   ├────────────────────────────────────────────────────────────────┤
   │                                                                  │
   │                    F9 - Select marked items                      │
   │                                                                  │
   ├──────────────────────────────────────────────────────────────────┤
   │  F1-Help                                          Esc-Back up      │
   └──────────────────────────────────────────────────────────────────┘
```

SELECT "MULTIPLES" TO ANALYZE

Isn't this nice? Just mark the ones you want to include and press F9.

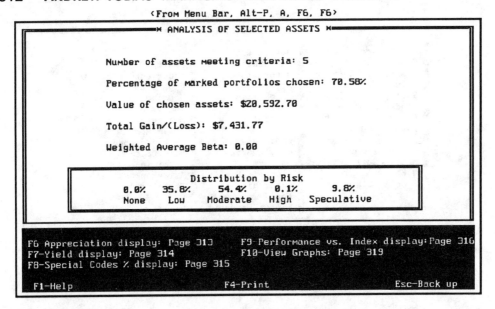

‹From Menu Bar, Alt-P, A, F6, F6›

ANALYSIS OF SELECTED ASSETS

Here's an overview of the assets you've selected. If "Percentage of Marked Portfolios Chosen" shows 99.9% instead of 100%, it's a rounding error. If it shows 134% (say), you've chosen to look not just at the 100% of the assets currently in this portfolio but also at those that have been sold.

The weighted average beta will make sense only if you assigned ALL your assets a beta (those left blank count in the average as zero, which is almost surely too low).

Press F6 for our Appreciation Display, F7 for the Yield Display, or F8 to see your assets (not shorts) summarized by Special Code.

Compare your Performance Versus Index and check your portfolio's Internal Rate of Return (F9). Or view your holdings in the Aggregate (F6, F10), with all lots of the same asset lumped together.

Press F4 to print a Report or F10 to view Graphs, if you have a graphics card. I find one of the graphs — "By Asset Type" — particularly handy.

<From Menu Bar, Alt-P, A, F6, F6, F6>

```
===================M APPRECIATION DISPLAY M===================

   #              Purchase  Current    Total      Gain         Simple   Annual.
Units Symbol       Price     Price     Value    (Loss) Term   Apprec.  Apprec.
   45 DJNS          0.31      0.31       $14      ($0)  S       0.0%     0.0%
  100 IBM          64.13    112.00   $11,200    $4,602  L      69.8%     6.6%
   75 WPPPS 9S99   79.50     98.25    $7,369    $1,350  L      22.4%     3.1%
  200 CBUBU         2.38     10.00    $2,000    $1,480  L     284.4%    32.8%
    1 CBUBU        10.00     10.00       $10      ($0)  S       0.0%     0.0%




===============================Totals/Averages================================
  421                                $20,593    $7,432         56.5%

  Speed scroll -                          M under Term indicates aggregate asset.

  F7-Yield display:Page 314         F9-Performance vs. Index display:Page 316
  F8-Special Codes % display:Page 315   F10-Aggregate display:Page 318

  F1-Help                         F2-View/Edit                    Esc-Back up
```

APPRECIATION DISPLAY

This is the APPRECIATION display. Don't miss the others. Note that when you first buy a stock you have an immediate short-term loss because of the commission. (If you pay $1,250 for 100 shares of a $12 stock, I'm sorry — that's a $50 loss.) Where a number is too large to fit in the display, we substitute but keep the real number in mind. For shorts, rather than show an infinite return on a $0 investment, we base it on the size of your original position.

Note the important difference between simple and annualized appreciation. It's great to have a stock up from $20 to $30 — 50% — but less so if it took 13 years to get there. It's lovely to have a stock appreciating 900% a year — but less so if it's been growing at that rate for only the three days since you bought it $1 cheaper. As for losses, note that 100% is the most of a thing you can lose and thus the largest loss you'll see. To be sure our annualizations are up-to-date, select Update Prices from the PORTFOLIO menu first and press F6.

To see the internal rate of return for your overall investment in these assets (not counting dividends, interest or taxes), press F9 (here or on the previous screen) and look in the bottom right corner of the display, where we show weighted average Annualized Appreciation. To print this report: ESCape, F4.

<From Menu Bar, Alt-P, A, F6, F6, F7>

```
══════════════════════════╴╴ YIELD DISPLAY ╴╴══════════════════════════
                                                                      Total
  #
Units  Symbol      Yield       Total      %   Portfolio  Purchased   Return
   45  DJNS        $0.00       $0.00     0.0%  E.F Sample  9/30/1990    0.0%
  100  IBM         $5.00     $500.00     4.5%  E.F Sample  6/7/1982    14.4%
   75  WPPPS 9S99   $9.00     $675.00     9.2%  E.F Sample  1/13/1984   14.4%
  200  CBUBU        $0.00       $0.00     0.0%  E.F Sample 12/31/1985   32.8%
    1  CBUBU        $0.00       $0.00     0.0%  E.F Sample  9/28/1990    0.0%


══════════════════════════╴Totals/Averages╴══════════════════════════
  421                     $1,175.00     5.7%


  Speed scroll -                         ╳ indicates an aggregate asset.
```

```
F6 Appreciation display: Page 313   F9 Performance vs. Index display: Page 316
F7-Yield Summary Analysis           F10-Aggregate display: Page 318
F8-Special Codes % display: Page 315

F1-Help                      F2-View/Edit                      Esc-Back up
```

YIELD DISPLAY

This is the YIELD display: in dollars per unit (which you can change most easily on the Update Prices screen), dollars for the whole lot, and as a percentage of current value.

■   Press F7 for another bit of analysis (available if any asset has a positive yield).

■   Press ESCape, F4 to print a report.

For shorts, we show yields as negative, because you don't get dividends, you pay them.

The last column, "Total Return," is included by popular demand even though it is not exactly an orthodox measurement. It is the sum of the asset's annualized appreciation (press F6 to see it) plus the current yield as a percentage of the original purchase price. A stock you bought 12 months ago at $10 that paid a 50 cent dividend and that was now $11 would show a total return of 15% — 10% annualized appreciation plus a 5% yield.

‹From Menu Bar, Alt-P, A, F6, F6, F8›

```
══════════════════════════ SPECIAL CODES PERCENT DISPLAY ══════════════════════════

       a Forbes                  25.3%   n                             0.0%
       b Fortune                  0.0%   o Inflation Hedge             0.0%
       c BW                       0.0%   p                             0.0%
       d Zweig                    0.0%   q                             0.0%
       e Smart Money              0.0%   r                             0.0%
       f Granville                0.0%   s                             0.0%
       g Wall Street Week         0.0%   t                             0.0%
       h Barrons                  0.0%   u                             0.0%
       i                          0.0%   v Wine          1=French      0.0%
       j Muni Subject to State Tax 25.3% w Red           2=German      0.0%
       k Short Maturity           0.0%   x White         3=Italian     0.0%
       l Intermediate Maturity    0.0%   y Champagne     7=New York    0.0%
       m Long Maturity           25.3%   z Port          !=California  0.0%

          As each asset can have many codes, the total may exceed 100%
```

```
 F6 Appreciation display: Page 313   F9 Performance vs. Index display: Page 316
 F7-Yield display: Page 314          F10-Aggregate display: Page 318
 F8-Flip to codes A-Z

 F1-Help                                               Esc-Back up
```

SPECIAL CODES AS A PERCENT OF THE WHOLE

The quickest way to assign and reassign codes to your assets is to select Update Prices from the PORTFOLIO menu. Then come here to see the percentage of your assets to which each code applies — the percentage you've coded as "foreign" or as "recommended by Paine Webber" or as "inflation hedges" or as "exempt from California tax." (Shorts are not included in this analysis.) Press F8 to see capital-letter codes.

<From Menu Bar, Alt-P, A, F6, F6, F9>

```
═════════════════════* PERFORMANCE VS. INDEX DISPLAY *═════════════════

      #                 Original Price    Simple Apprec.      Annual Apprec.
  Units Symbol          Asset    Index    Asset    Index      Asset    Index
    288 BJ-85           0.45              0.0%       %         0.0%       %
     45 DJNS            0.31              0.0%       %         0.0%       %
     12 DP-59           6.85              2,454.7%   %        13.4%       %
    164 HI-INCOME      12.22  1,400.0     48.0%    27.7%      27.2%     16.2%
    100 IBM            64.13    777.0     69.8%   130.1%       6.6%     26.5%
    160 MAGELLAN       12.16  1,788.0     69.7%     0.0%      12.2%      0.0%
     75 WPPPS 9S99     79.50  1,270.0     22.4%    40.8%       3.1%     19.3%
    200 CBUBU           2.38             284.4%      %        32.8%       %
      1 CBUBU          10.00              0.0%       %         0.0%       %
═══════════════════════════════Totals/Averages══════════════════════════
  1,044                                  67.9%    55.0%       9.0%      6.0%


  Speed scroll -                    The current Index value is 1,788.00
```

```
F6-Appreciation display: Page 313    F8-Special Codes % display: Page 315
F7-Yield display: Page 314           F10-Aggregate display: Page 318

F1-Help           F2-View/Edit              F4-Print        Esc-Back up
```

PERFORMANCE VS. INDEX

This is pretty neat. Your broker calls and says your account is up 22%. You say, yeah, but how does that compare with the market as a whole? Whatever he says, the truth is, he doesn't know. To know, he'd have to compare the performance of each of your assets from the time you bought it with the performance of the market over the same time — and then weight those performances according to how much you had invested in each. That's what we do here, with a modified Internal Rate of Return calculation. So you really know. Just compare the two summary numbers beneath the right-most columns. (Any assets to which you assigned no time-of-purchase index number we assume performed no better or worse than the index. If NO index numbers are showing, select Update Prices to be sure you entered a current index level.)

Under Original Price, we show the price of the asset and the level of the index on the purchase date. Under Simple Appreciation, we show the amount by which each has grown or shrunk since.

To get the Weighted Average SIMPLE Appreciation for the portfolio as a whole, we subtract its total cost from its total current value and express that gain or loss as a percentage of its total cost. But, unlike the Annualized Appreciation columns at far right, no account is taken of the time you've held your assets.

Under ANNUALIZED Appreciation, we show for each asset its compounded annual appreciation — an asset that doubled in 10 years had simple appreciation of 100% but compounded annual growth of just 7.2% — and we show the same for its index. But note:

1. The annualized appreciation numbers we show throughout this chapter are based on the holding period as of the last price update. So if one ever seems screwy, it's probably

because you haven't updated its price in a long time. Select Update Prices and press F6 to bring all the holding periods up to today's date.

2.   Shorts are ignored in calculating portfolio and index performance.

3.   We take commissions into account even though we don't show them. You may think a stock that's gone from $5 to $6 has made you 20% — but not if you paid a $50 commission to buy it. (It's up even less if you take into account the commission you'll have to pay to sell it.)

<From Menu Bar, Alt-P, A, F6, F6, F6, F10>

```
========================= AGGREGATE DISPLAY ==========================
    #              Avg Cost      Total      Total      Total      % of Total
 Units  Symbol     Per Unit      Value      Yield   Gain/(Loss)   Selected
   288  BJ-85        $0.45        $128        $0        ($0)        0.4%
   201  CBUBU        $2.41      $2,010        $0      $1,400        6.9%
    45  DJNS         $0.31         $14        $0        ($0)        0.0%
    12  DP-59        $6.85      $2,100        $0      $2,018        7.2%
   164  HI-INCOME   $12.22      $2,960      $210        $960       10.1%
   100  IBM         $64.13     $11,200      $500      $4,602       38.4%
   160  MAGELLAN    $12.16      $3,394       $55      $1,394       11.6%
    75  WPPPS 9S99  $79.50      $7,369      $675      $1,350       25.3%




============================Totals/Averages==========================
  1044             $16.30     $29,175    $1,440     $11,804

Speed scroll —

```

```
  F1-Help                      F4-Print                   Esc-Back up
```

AGGREGATION DISPLAY

This is the AGGREGATE display. Separate purchases of the same asset are lumped together. (Of course, within any single portfolio, you may already have aggregated some of your tax lots. But if you haven't, or if you want to see the holdings in several different portfolios aggregated as one, this display is quite handy.) To return to the YIELD or APPRECIATION displays, you'll have to back up, reselect the portfolios you want to include, and come around for another look.

The last column compares the value of each asset to the total current value of the portfolio(s) you've chosen. (If you've chosen to look at sold assets as well, or only sold assets, the column could total way over 100% — which is one reason we don't total it.)

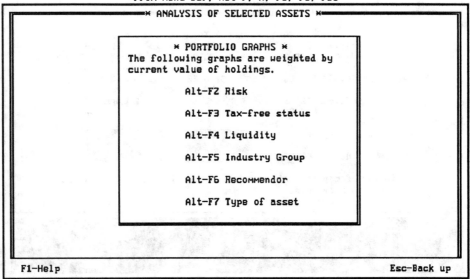

<From Menu Bar, Alt-P, A, F6, F6, F10>

```
╔══════════════════ ✳ ANALYSIS OF SELECTED ASSETS ✳ ══════════════════╗
║                                                                      ║
║            ┌──────────────────────────────────────────┐             ║
║            │          ✳ PORTFOLIO GRAPHS ✳             │             ║
║            │  The following graphs are weighted by      │             ║
║            │  current value of holdings.                │             ║
║            │                                            │             ║
║            │         Alt-F2 Risk                        │             ║
║            │                                            │             ║
║            │         Alt-F3 Tax-free status             │             ║
║            │                                            │             ║
║            │         Alt-F4 Liquidity                   │             ║
║            │                                            │             ║
║            │         Alt-F5 Industry Group              │             ║
║            │                                            │             ║
║            │         Alt-F6 Recommendor                 │             ║
║            │                                            │             ║
║            │         Alt-F7 Type of asset               │             ║
║            └──────────────────────────────────────────┘             ║
║                                                                      ║
║ F1-Help                                                  Esc-Back up ║
╚══════════════════════════════════════════════════════════════════════╝
```

PORTFOLIO GRAPHS

We have six ways of representing the data you have extracted. Take a look at each. (Remember: "Alt-F2" means "hold down the Alt key while you press F2.) To print one of our graphs, just view it, ready your printer, and press the Print-Screen key.

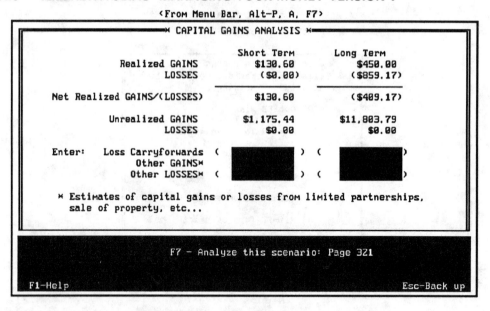

‹From Menu Bar, Alt-P, A, F7›

CAPITAL GAINS ANALYSIS

Here's a tally of all your gains and losses so far this year in these portfolios ... and a summary of your unrealized "paper" gains and losses. UNrealized gains and losses on assets you've tagged futures contracts are counted as realized (and automatically treated as 40% short-term, 60% long-term gain) because they're taxed whether you've realized them or not. (To change the long-term/short-term proportion, if Congress has, select Portfolio Options from the FILE menu.) But so long as there's no distinction between long- and short-term gains, it doesn't really matter.

Before you press F7, enter any capital loss carryforwards from prior years. (Currently, no more than $3000 in capital losses can be deducted from income in any given year. The excess is carried forward.) Enter, also, any capital gains or losses we don't know about — such as your $4,200 share of a partnership's short-term loss, or the $50,000 you made selling HOT-TO-TROT, your two-year-old.

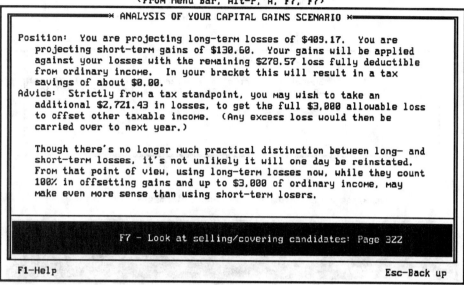

⟨From Menu Bar, Alt-P, A, F7, F7⟩

```
╔══════════════════➤ ANALYSIS OF YOUR CAPITAL GAINS SCENARIO ➤══════════════════╗
║                                                                                ║
║  Position:  You are projecting long-term losses of $409.17.  You are           ║
║     projecting short-term gains of $130.60.  Your gains will be applied         ║
║     against your losses with the remaining $278.57 loss fully deductible        ║
║     from ordinary income.  In your bracket this will result in a tax            ║
║     savings of about $0.00.                                                     ║
║  Advice:  Strictly from a tax standpoint, you may wish to take an               ║
║     additional $2,721.43 in losses, to get the full $3,000 allowable loss       ║
║     to offset other taxable income.  (Any excess loss would then be             ║
║     carried over to next year.)                                                 ║
║                                                                                 ║
║     Though there's no longer much practical distinction between long- and       ║
║     short-term losses, it's not unlikely it will one day be reinstated.         ║
║     From that point of view, using long-term losses now, while they count       ║
║     100% in offsetting gains and up to $3,000 of ordinary income, may           ║
║     make even more sense than using short-term losers.                          ║
║                                                                                 ║
║════════════════════════════════════════════════════════════════════════════════║
║             F7 - Look at selling/covering candidates: Page 322                  ║
║════════════════════════════════════════════════════════════════════════════════║
║                                                                                 ║
║  F1-Help                                                         Esc-Back up    ║
╚════════════════════════════════════════════════════════════════════════════════╝
```

ANALYSIS OF YOUR CAPITAL GAINS

For 1988 and beyond — until Congress changes it, which it will — long-term gains are treated no better than any other kind of ordinary income. (To reflect the inevitable change, when it comes, select Portfolio Options from the FILE menu. You should at least be able to jerry-rig an approximation until our annual upgrade is ready. But our "Advice" messages won't reflect your change.)

The main thing to remember is that taxes should never dictate your investment strategy. This is particularly true when it comes to selling to take a loss. If you bought a stock at 20 that's now 15, you might save taxes by selling it for a loss . . . but if it was a good buy at 20, it might be an even better value at 15. You don't want to get into the habit of buying high and selling low. So if you DO sell for a tax loss, consider one of three strategies:

1. Immediately buy something you consider roughly equivalent. Swap Ford for GM, say, or one AA-rated long-term municipal bond for another.

2. Wait 31 days (the IRS requires it) and then buy back what you sold. Hopefully it won't have zoomed in the meantime. Or,

3. To guard against just that, buy the extra shares FIRST, wait 31 days, and THEN sell the original ones. (Identify them by instructing your broker to sell "Versus Purchase" their acquisition date.) In that case, the hope is they won't fall further during the month you've doubled up.

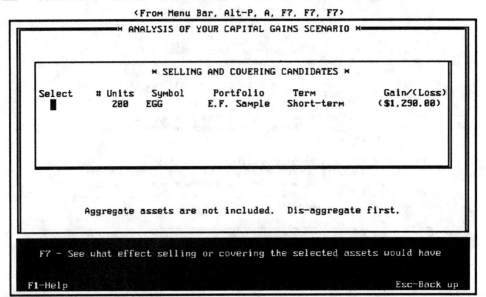

```
            <From Menu Bar, Alt-P, A, F7, F7, F7>
╔══════════════════════════════════════════════════════════════╗
║ ┌─────────────── ⋇ ANALYSIS OF YOUR CAPITAL GAINS SCENARIO ⋇───────────┐║
║ │                                                                       │║
║ │  ┌─────────────────────────────────────────────────────────────┐     │║
║ │  │             ⋇ SELLING AND COVERING CANDIDATES ⋇              │     │║
║ │  │ Select  # Units  Symbol   Portfolio    Term       Gain/(Loss)│     │║
║ │  │   █       200    EGG      E.F. Sample  Short-term ($1,290.00)│     │║
║ │  │                                                             │     │║
║ │  │                                                             │     │║
║ │  │                                                             │     │║
║ │  └─────────────────────────────────────────────────────────────┘     │║
║ │                                                                       │║
║ │       Aggregate assets are not included.  Dis-aggregate first.         │║
║ └───────────────────────────────────────────────────────────────────────┘║
║ ┌───────────────────────────────────────────────────────────────────────┐║
║ │  F7 - See what effect selling or covering the selected assets would have│║
║ └───────────────────────────────────────────────────────────────────────┘║
║   F1-Help                                                   Esc-Back up    ║
╚══════════════════════════════════════════════════════════════╝
```

SELLING AND COVERING CANDIDATES

Try as many combinations of possible sales (and short covers) as you want and see the effect on your taxes. Don't worry. Nothing you do here will actually change your PORTFOLIO records in any way, or show up in TAX. Only if you actually decide to go sell something will a real change be made.

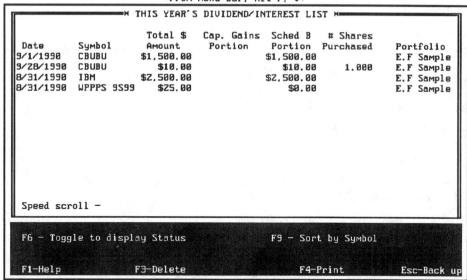

<From Menu Bar, Alt-P, V>

THIS YEAR'S DIVIDENDS AND INTEREST

SORT – AND PRINT – NINE WAYS

Here are your dividends and interest, which you can sort (F9) – and then print – nine ways. (TAB into the choice box and arrow down to see them all.)

CAPITAL GAINS PORTION

In the fourth column, we break out the capital-gains-distribution portion of your income, if any, if this is a mutual fund distribution. You'll find the total amount flows into our tax calculations for Schedule D.

SCHEDULE B PORTION

In the fifth column we break out the taxable dividends-plus-interest that – for taxable portfolios – will flow to Schedule B. (We show these also for income you've recorded for IRA/Keogh and Hypothetical portfolios, but never fear: We don't actually count them where we shouldn't. The IRA/Keogh income is accorded no tax consequence in TAX; hypothetical income is ignored by both TAX and NET WORTH.)

SHARES PURCHASED

The sixth column applies only to dividend reinvestments.

ACCRUED INTEREST

If any of the income you've recorded represents accrued interest you've received (or paid) on the sale (or purchase) of a bond, we let you know by displaying "ACC" in what is otherwise an invisible seventh column to the right of # Shares Purchased.

THE F6 TOGGLE

Press F6 to see the status of this money or the portfolio it came from.

RETURNS OF CAPITAL, TAX-FREE INTEREST, AMT INTEREST

Returns of capital and tax-free interest, being untaxed, show up only in the Total Amount column. But they are broken out on the reports we print. Likewise, "AMT" interest — which is free of regular tax but subject to the Alternative Minimum Tax.

PRINT — COMPRESSED, IF POSSIBLE!

Press F4 to print your list as sorted.

- The most practical report is usually the one you'll get when you've sorted by "Portfolio." If your printer is capable of it, choose compressed printing.

To print a list of all your accrued interest paid, say, to back up your tax return to the IRS, sort by Accrued Interest and print that way. All your accrued interest paid and received will be listed first. (Print to disk and then use Ctrl-W to delete all the entries that do not apply.)

Printing to screen is quite a jumble, because there are so many different columns — more, even, than on our display — so if possible, use compressed printing and print on paper.

DELETING: CAUTION

Deleting an entry will remove it from our tallies in MONEY. And if it was a capital gains distribution that we told Schedule D and this chapter's capital gains analyzer about, it will reduce those numbers.

But deleting does *not* reverse our other actions: if it was a dividend we added to your portfolio cash balance, deleting it here won't reduce the cash balance; if it involved a return of capital that lowered the basis of your shares, it won't restore their basis; if it was reinvested in new shares, it won't delete those shares. So before deleting, make a note of the adjustments you'll want to make "by hand."

DIVIDENDS ON SHORT SALES

If you sell stocks short, you PAY dividends, not receive them. Any such dividends should be entered as negative, and so should show up with minus signs here. They will DECREASE the Schedule B dividend income we tell TAX about. But to avoid unnecessary hassle with the IRS, it's a good idea to report your dividend income in full, and then show this negative dividend income on a separate line, clearly labeled: "Dividend PAID on short sales."

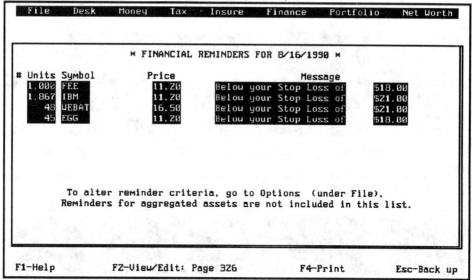

<From Menu Bar, Alt-P, F>

| File | Desk | Money | Tax | Insure | Finance | Portfolio | Net Worth |

× FINANCIAL REMINDERS FOR 8/16/1990 ×

# Units	Symbol	Price	Message	
1,000	FEE	11.20	Below your Stop Loss of	$18.00
1,867	IBM	11.20	Below your Stop Loss of	$21.00
48	WEBAT	16.50	Below your Stop Loss of	$21.00
45	EGG	11.20	Below your Stop Loss of	$18.00

To alter reminder criteria, go to Options (under File).
Reminders for aggregated assets are not included in this list.

| F1-Help | FZ-View/Edit: Page 326 | F4-Print | Esc-Back up |

FINANCIAL REMINDERS

This is a highly customizable feature which you can have us display automatically the first time each day or only on demand.

To set your options, please select Portfolio Options from the FILE menu. On the first screen you see there; then press F10 for the rest.

We'll remind you of options nearing expiration, bonds soon to mature, assets that have reached your goals or mental stop-loss points, and assets that are soon to qualify for long-term tax treatment (assuming there's enough of a gain or loss to warrant your attention).

<From Menu Bar, Alt-P, F, F2>

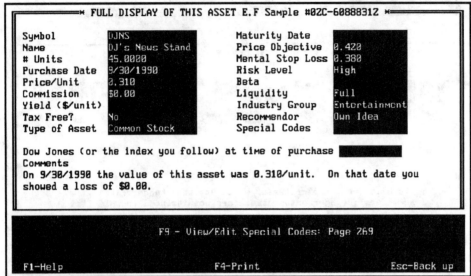

```
╺═══════╸ FULL DISPLAY OF THIS ASSET E.F Sample #02C-60888312 ╺═══════╸

  Symbol          DJNS                 Maturity Date
  Name            DJ's News Stand      Price Objective   0.420
  # Units         45.0000              Mental Stop Loss  0.380
  Purchase Date   9/30/1990            Risk Level        High
  Price/Unit      0.310                Beta
  Commission      $0.00                Liquidity         Full
  Yield ($/unit)                       Industry Group    Entertainment
  Tax Free?       No                   Recommendor       Own Idea
  Type of Asset   Common Stock         Special Codes

  Dow Jones (or the index you follow) at time of purchase
  Comments
  On 9/30/1990 the value of this asset was 0.310/unit.  On that date you
  showed a loss of $0.00.


                  F9 - View/Edit Special Codes: Page 269


   F1-Help                      F4-Print                    Esc-Back up
```

FULL DISPLAY OF THIS ASSET

If you want to take some action — sell the asset or change one of its attributes — select Sell
Assets from the PORTFOLIO, point to the one in question and press F2 to view/edit or F6 to
sell it. To change its symbol, price, yield, or special codes — or to see all lots with this same
symbol select the Update Prices screen.

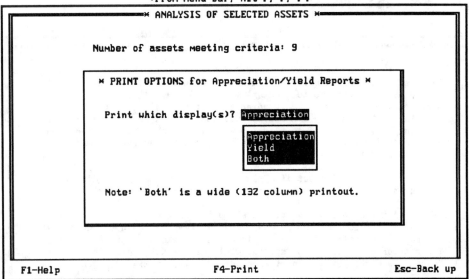

‹From Menu Bar, Alt-P, P, F4›

PRINTING REPORTS

Make any choices we may give you here (depending on the screen you came from) and then press F4.

If you've come here from the PORTFOLIO screen ("Create/Edit Portfolios"), you'll see that the "All Assets" report includes all your portfolios. To get a report of just ONE portfolio's assets, select Display Assets or, for a variety of others, select Analyze Assets. For customized reports or a Schedule D, select the Report Generator.

If you've come here from DISPLAY ASSETS, note that we print in whatever order you sorted your assets. There are seven ways to sort them, so you may want to print at least a couple of different ways — once alphabetized by symbol, say, and then again by Total Value or by gain/loss. (Ordinarily, you'd say "No" to our offer of Full Detail, which provides an entirely different kind of report.)

If you've come here from VIEW AN ASSET there are no choices, we just print a glorified print-screen. (To print a report of all your assets in this detailed format, back up to Display Assets, press F4 to print, and answer "Yes" to our offer of Full Detail.)

If you've come here from ANALYZE ASSETS, you get your choice of an Appreciation report, Yield report or, if you have a wide printer, Both.

BULLISHNESS INDEX

<From Menu Bar, Alt-P, I>

```
════════════════════════════ ✳ BULLISHNESS INDEX ✳ ════════════════════════════


                                     PREFACE
     The best stock-market advice for almost everyone is to buy shares in one
     or two or three good no-load mutual funds and leave it at that.  Invest
     more heavily when the world is going to end; hold off buying new shares
     when the market is rosy and almost everybody is making money at it.  Over
     the long run, you should do fine.  Over the long run, stocks have always
     outperformed safer investments, because over the long run the market
     "pays" you to take the extra risk.

     But there's no doubt about it:  playing the market yourself, directly,
     without aid of professional mutual fund managers, is enticing.

     If you do throw your own darts, here's a little hocus-pocus for today,
     Sunday, September 2nd, 1990.  None of it is reason enough to buy or sell,
     not buy or not sell.  And none of it alone is likely to yield a profit.
     The cost of commissions and spreads would very likely cancel out any
     "edge" you might get playing these odds.  Still, it may help you to know:


     PgDn - Next Page          Esc-Back up          F6  - Change date to 9/2/1990
```

<From Menu Bar, Alt-P, I, Page 2>

```
═══════════════════════════ ✳ A LOOK AT THE CALENDAR ✳ ═══════════════════════════


     At the risk of sounding like a fortune cookie, Fridays are, more often
     than not, good days for the stock market.  So if you're selling, you might
     want to wait until near the close of trading to see if you can get an
     extra eighth or quarter.  And if you're buying, you might want to buy
     right at the opening bell — or wait until Monday afternoon to see if you
     can save a few dollars if the price softens a bit.

     Of course, this should only be a very minor consideration.  If a stock, or
     the market, is sliding, it may very well continue to slide, or even
     plunge, on a Friday.








     PgDn - Next Page          Esc-Back up          PgUp - Previous Page
```

<From Menu Bar, Alt-P, I, Page 3>

```
╔══════════════════════════════════════════════════════════════════╗
║══════════════════════ ✕ PRESIDENTIAL CYCLE ✕══════════════════════║
║ This is the second year of the current presidential term.  Typically, the ║
║ market does best in the second half of a presidential term.  In the first ║
║ half, the president likes to get the pain out of the way so that he, or at ║
║ least a successor from his party, can look good for the election.           ║
║                                                                            ║
║ This is by no means foolproof — and it didn't work very well during the    ║
║ Reagan presidency.  But Yale Hirsch found that over the century and a half  ║
║ beginning with 1832, annual gains and losses in the market pretty much      ║
║ canceled each other out if you looked at just the first two years of each   ║
║ presidential term ...  but that they totaled a whopping 515% in the second  ║
║ half of each term.                                                          ║
║                                                                            ║
║ That's not 515% "compounded," which wouldn't be very impressive over such   ║
║ a long time period.  Rather, it's a total of 515% worth of annual gains in  ║
║ each of those years, or about 7%, on average (plus dividends).  That may     ║
║ not seem like much; but $10,000 compounded at 7% for 75 years (all the       ║
║ "good" years of the presidential terms) would grow to $1,600,000, which is  ║
║ a lot better than seeing it grow barely at all.  (Again, all this ignores    ║
║ dividends and is very rough.) So if past patterns hold — as they only       ║
║ sometimes do!  — the next few months might be kind of dull, pending a       ║
║ strong market ahead.                                                        ║
╠══════════════════════════════════════════════════════════════════╣
║ PgDn - Next Page          Esc-Back up          PgUp - Previous Page ║
╚══════════════════════════════════════════════════════════════════╝
```

<From Menu Bar, Alt-P, I, Page 4>

```
╔══════════════════════════════════════════════════════════════════╗
║═════════════════════ ✕ YESTERDAY'S MARKET ACTION ✕═══════════════════║
║                                                                            ║
║ Odds are, if it was up yesterday (especially if it closed strong in the     ║
║ last few minutes of trading) it will be up today.  And vice versa.  But we  ║
║ won't weight your answer very heavily in our calculation (which you should   ║
║ not weight very heavily in any event!), because the impact here is kind of   ║
║ like the impact of a light breeze on a supertanker.  Sure, the breeze may    ║
║ affect its short-term course a little.  But ocean currents will affect it    ║
║ more — and the pilot in the wheelhouse could easily be about to drop off     ║
║ some cargo and then head back in precisely the opposite direction.  Trying   ║
║ to guess the course of the pilot in the stockmarket's wheelhouse would be    ║
║ a lot easier if he didn't seem to take such pleasure in confounding those    ║
║ who do.                                                                     ║
║              How did the market do yesterday?                               ║
║                                            ┌─────────────┐                  ║
║                                            │ Strong Gain │                  ║
║                                            │ Decent Gain │                  ║
║                                            │ Nothing Much│                  ║
║                                            │ Ouch        │                  ║
║                                            │ Mayday      │                  ║
║                                            └─────────────┘                  ║
╠══════════════════════════════════════════════════════════════════╣
║ PgDn - Next Page          Esc-Back up          PgUp - Previous Page ║
╚══════════════════════════════════════════════════════════════════╝
```

330   ANDREW TOBIAS' MANAGING YOUR MONEY VERSION 7

<From Menu Bar, Alt-P, I, Page 5>

```
╔══════════════════════════════════════════════════════════════════╗
║┌────────────────────────── INTEREST RATES ──────────────────────┐ ║
║│                                                                 │ ║
║│ By far the most important influence on stock prices is the      │ ║
║│ direction of interest rates.  When interest rates are rising    │ ║
║│ or expected to head up, stocks generally head down -- or will.  │ ║
║│ When the perceived direction of interest rates is down, stocks  │ ║
║│ generally head up.  But even this is tricky.  To begin with,    │ ║
║│ it's all but impossible to predict interest rates.  But even    │ ║
║│ if you could, the market doesn't always follow this rule.  A    │ ║
║│ glaring example?  During the Depression, interest rates were    │ ║
║│ exceptionally low but stocks were even lower.                   │ ║
║│                                                                 │ ║
║│ (One reason?  With deflation instead of inflation, "real"       │ ║
║│ interest rates were actually higher than they seemed.)          │ ║
║│                                                                 │ ║
║│ Lately, the general level of interest rates seems to be      .  │ ║
```

Rising
Peaking
Falling
Bottoming
Unchanged

```
║│                                                                 │ ║
║└─────────────────────────────────────────────────────────────────┘║
║                                                                    ║
║ PgDn - Next Page          Esc-Back up          PgUp - Previous Page║
╚══════════════════════════════════════════════════════════════════╝
```

<From Menu Bar, Alt-P, I, Page 6>

```
╔══════════════════════════════════════════════════════════════════╗
║┌─────────────── DIVIDENDS RELATIVE TO BOND YIELDS ──────────────┐ ║
║│                                                                 │ ║
║│ The 30-year US Treasury bond is yielding ███ %, while the S&P   │ ║
║│ 500 index is currently yielding ███ % in dividends and selling  │ ║
║│ at a price/earnings ratio of ███.                               │ ║
║│                                                                 │ ║
║│ Leave any of these blank, if need be, or use rough estimates.   │ ║
║│ You'll find the 30-year Treasury bond yield in the financial    │ ║
║│ pages of almost any newspaper; the S&P numbers, in the MARKET   │ ║
║│ LABORATORY section of BARRON'S.  (Look for the little table     │ ║
║│ called INDEXES' P/E's AND YIELDS and ignore the "Earns Yield"   │ ║
║│ number you'll see there.  It's the "Divs Yield" we want.)       │ ║
║│                                                                 │ ║
║│ The less stocks yield relative to bonds, the less attractive    │ ║
║│ they are and the less likely to rise, other things being        │ ║
║│ equal.  Also, when they sell at a high multiple of their        │ ║
║│ earnings, they may have less room to rise than they otherwise   │ ║
║│ might -- though if earnings have been battered by a recession,  │ ║
║│ the price/earnings multiple may be high (because there are no   │ ║
║│ earnings) even though stocks are cheap (assuming the recession  │ ║
║│ will end some day).                                             │ ║
║│                                                                 │ ║
║└─────────────────────────────────────────────────────────────────┘║
║                                                                    ║
║ PgDn - Next Page          Esc-Back up          PgUp - Previous Page║
╚══════════════════════════════════════════════════════════════════╝
```

<From Menu Bar, Alt-P, I, Page 7>

```
========× STOCK PRICES RELATIVE TO BOOK VALUE ×========

In the same BARRON'S table you will find a number comparing the total
current market value of the 500 Standard & Poor's stocks with their total
book value (abbreviated:  "Mkt to Book, %"):  ████  %.  Although book value
is an iffy measure at best — it unrealistically inflates the value of
some things and drastically understates the value of others — it is
nonetheless a benchmark against which to judge whether the market is cheap
or dear.  Historically, when the market has sold around book value, it's
been a bargain.  When it's sold at well over double book value, it's been
time to take cover.

Of course, if things were that pat and simple, you could just look at a
few of these ratios and make an awful lot of money.  It's not that pat and
simple, and, as with all aspects of this bullishness index, is not meant
to be given much weight.  But if you have BARRON'S handy, fill this in.
```

PgDn — Next Page   Esc-Back up   PgUp — Previous Page

<From Menu Bar, Alt-P, I, Page 8>

```
========× CONSIDER YOUR SOURCE ×========

I was thinking of buying because (mark any that apply):

▌ A large brokerage firm just added it to the "buy list"
  for its retail clients.

▌ I hear a large brokerage firm is about to recommend it.

▌ I heard about it from a friend who was real excited.

▌ It was recommended last night on Wall Street Week.

▌ It just goes up and up!

▌ I hear they've come up with a cure for ██████
  or are about to announce a major  ███ discovery.

▌ Nobody's recommending it, but it sure seems to
  represent good value.
```

PgDn — Next Page   Esc-Back up   PgUp — Previous Page

<From Menu Bar, Alt-P, I, Page 9>

═══════════════════ ✳ TODAY'S BULLISHNESS INDEX ✳ ═══════════════════

Taking all these factors into account, and weighting their relative
importance, we'd say today ranks as a slightly better day to be selling
than buying. Assuming, that is, the asset in question is likely to move
with the market. (Gold stocks, by contrast, often move opposite to the
market.) In fact, since this is a computer program, we'll stick our necks
out even further -- more for fun than anything else -- and assign this day
a 5.0 on a scale from 0 to 10, where 0 is apocalyptic; 5, neutral; and 10,
the buying opportunity of a lifetime.

How seriously should you take this information? Not very seriously at
all. But if after examining all the more important considerations you
really can't make up your mind whether or not to buy (or to sell) -- as I
often can't -- using this information to decide should work at least as
well as tossing a coin, possibly a tad better. Over long periods of time,
that "tad" could mount up.

PgUp - Previous Page   Esc-Back up

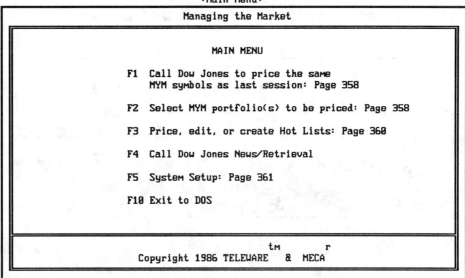

```
                        <Main Menu>
                      Managing the Market

                          MAIN MENU

            F1  Call Dow Jones to price the same
                MYM symbols as last session: Page 358

            F2  Select MYM portfolio(s) to be priced: Page 358

            F3  Price, edit, or create Hot Lists: Page 360

            F4  Call Dow Jones News/Retrieval

            F5  System Setup: Page 361

            F10 Exit to DOS


                                  tm        r
            Copyright 1986 TELEWARE    &  MECA
```

MANAGING THE MARKET

Managing the Market is an optional program that allows you to call Dow Jones News Retrieval and automatically update your portfolios. You may also use it to create "Hot Lists" to check only a few key prices or to use DJNR's many other services: check the weather or movie reviews, look up historical stock prices, see the up-to-the-minute status of your American Express account, book airline reservations, search the last five years' Wall Street Journal and other media, send MCI mail — and more.

Managing the Market stores all the text you receive from Dow Jones so you can hang up the phone fast and peruse it at your leisure. You can also print it or transfer important data to a spreadsheet program like Lotus 1-2-3.

Managing the Market is available to registered owners of Managing Your Money for $79.95. To order, call MECA Order Processing at 203-222-9150.

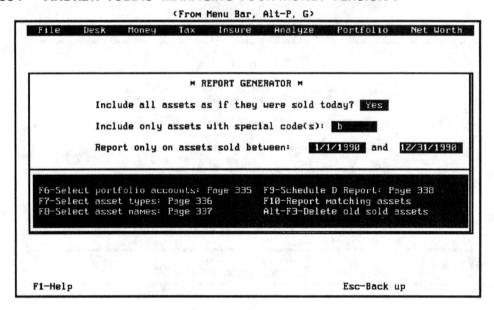

‹From Menu Bar, Alt-P, G›

```
  File    Desk    Money    Tax    Insure    Analyze    Portfolio    Net Worth

                        ⊁ REPORT GENERATOR ⊁

         Include all assets as if they were sold today?  Yes

         Include only assets with special code(s):  b

         Report only on assets sold between:  1/1/1990  and  12/31/1990


     F6-Select portfolio accounts: Page 335    F9-Schedule D Report: Page 338
     F7-Select asset types: Page 336           F10-Report matching assets
     F8-Select asset names: Page 337           Alt-F3-Delete old sold assets




     F1-Help                                         Esc-Back up
```

REPORT GENERATOR: SPECIFYING THE ASSETS TO INCLUDE
WHAT IT DOES

The Report Generator can produce a Schedule D you can attach to your tax return (F9) and reports of your own design (F10). But unlike the many reports you can get elsewhere in PORTFOLIO — primarily on the Display Assets and Analyze Assets screens (don't miss those!) — the Report Generator works only with closed-out positions ... assets you've sold (or shorts you've covered).

PRETEND THEY'RE SOLD ANYWAY

For your Schedule D, it's only closed-out positions you would want to report. (Except for futures contracts, you only pay tax on a gain, or get to deduct part of a loss, if it's REALIZED ... not if it's just a paper profit or loss.) But for most other reports, you will probably want to include positions you still hold, not just those you've closed out. And we make it easy. Just select YES on this screen, and we'll pretend, for the purposes of your report only, that you've sold everything as of today. (Well, actually as of the LAST PRICE UPDATE.)

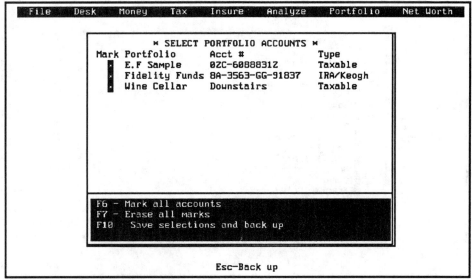

‹From Menu Bar, Alt-P, G, F6›

NARROW THE FIELD

But perhaps you don't want to include all your assets. F6, F7, and F8 allow you to narrow the field. (And they work cumulatively, so if you use F6 to select just two of your four portfolios and then F7 to limit your report to bonds, we'll report only on bonds from those two portfolios.) And, as you see, you may also specify up to 8 special codes, and a date range. Only assets with one of those codes, and sold within that date range, will be retrieved for your report (including assets you instruct us to treat as if sold today, if today falls within the date range).

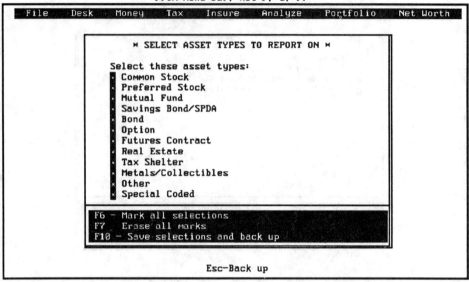

‹From Menu Bar, Alt-P, G, F7›

File   Desk   Money   Tax   Insure   Analyze   Portfolio   Net Worth

⋇ SELECT ASSET TYPES TO REPORT ON ⋇

Select these asset types:
- Common Stock
- Preferred Stock
- Mutual Fund
- Savings Bond/SPDA
⨯ Bond
- Option
- Futures Contract
- Real Estate
- Tax Shelter
⨯ Metals/Collectibles
⨯ Other
- Special Coded

F6 - Mark all selections
F7   Erase all marks
F10 - Save selections and back up

Esc-Back up

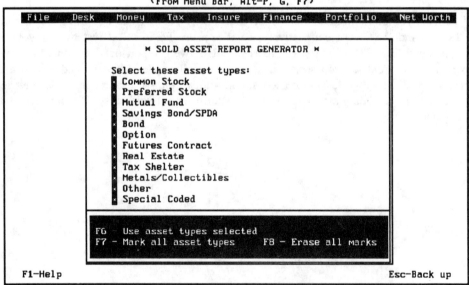

‹From Menu Bar, Alt-P, G, F7›

File   Desk   Money   Tax   Insure   Finance   Portfolio   Net Worth

⋇ SOLD ASSET REPORT GENERATOR ⋇

Select these asset types:
- Common Stock
- Preferred Stock
- Mutual Fund
- Savings Bond/SPDA
⨯ Bond
- Option
- Futures Contract
- Real Estate
- Tax Shelter
⨯ Metals/Collectibles
⨯ Other
- Special Coded

F6 - Use asset types selected
F7 - Mark all asset types   F8 - Erase all marks

F1-Help   Esc-Back up

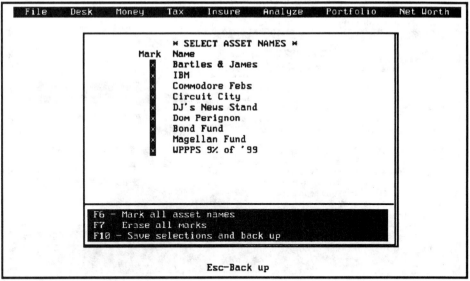

<From Menu Bar, Alt-P, G, F8>

INCLUDE COMMENTS?

These are the memos you're invited to attach to any asset, and can run many lines in length. As a result, you'll sometimes want to include them but often not, because they're printed beneath each asset and thus make it difficult to "run your eye down" each column of the report.

PRESS F9 OR F10 TO PROCEED

Whichever you choose, you'll find help behind the next screen.

```
                        <From Menu Bar, Alt-P, G, F9>
╔═══════════════════ ⨯ OTHER GAINS AND LOSSES ⨯═══════════════════╗
║  Basis for reporting sale proceeds:                              ║
║  ██████████████████████████████████                             ║
║  ┌─────────────────────────────────────────────────┐           ║
║  │ Gross Proceeds/Cost Plus Expense of Sale         │           ║
║  │ Net Proceeds/Cost                                │           ║
║  └─────────────────────────────────────────────────┘           ║
║  Short-term gain from sale or exchange of your home: ██████████  ║
║  Short-term gain from installment sales: █████████████████████   ║
║  Net short-term gain or (loss) from partnerships,                ║
║                   S corporations, and fiduciaries: ███████████   ║
║  Short-term capital loss carryover: ███████████████              ║
║                                                                  ║
║  Long-term gain from sale or exchange of your home: ███████████  ║
║  Long-term gain from installment sales: ████████████             ║
║  Net long-term gain or (loss) from partnerships,                 ║
║                   S corporations, and fiduciaries: ███████████   ║
║  Capital gain distributions:                       $0.00         ║
║  Gain from form 4797: ███████████████████████████████            ║
║  Long-term capital loss carryover: ███████████████               ║
╠══════════════════════════════════════════════════════════════════╣
║  F10 - Continue with Schedule D                                  ║
║                                                                  ║
║  F1-Help                                          Esc-Back up    ║
╚══════════════════════════════════════════════════════════════════╝
```

REPORT GENERATOR: SCHEDULE D
BROKER'S METHOD OF REPORTING

Most brokers report to the IRS your total sales proceeds NET of commissions. A few have the incredibly annoying habit — in part because the IRS at one time required it — of reporting GROSS sales. You're then supposed to add the selling commission to the purchase price of each item (of all the convoluted ways of thinking!). We'll do this FOR you, to match the data sent to the IRS, if you change NET to GROSS. Fill in any other fields that may apply and press F10 to proceed.

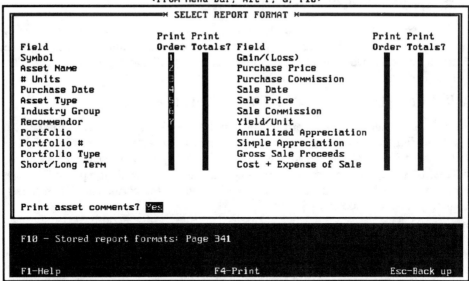

<From Menu Bar, Alt-P, G, F10>

CUSTOMIZED REPORTS & SCHEDULE D

TRY OUR STANDARD FORMATS

The simplest thing to do here is press F10 and try one of our standard report formats.

DESIGN YOUR OWN

But it's easy to design (and then save) formats of your own. Just number those items you want to include — just a few unless you have a three-foot wide screen! — assigning numbering them in order of importance. As a practical matter, the key thing is which you choose to be #1, because it will not only appear in the first column, it will dictate the organization of the whole report. Do you want it organized alphabetically by name or symbol? Designate Name or Symbol #1 in the print order. In order of date of purchase? Enter your 1 beside that field. In order of gross sale proceeds? Enter your 1 beside THAT field. It's not unlike Tic Tac Toe, where whoever gets to go first controls the game — only more so.

Only when there is a "tie" does the #2 field dictate the order. (If you made Symbol #1 and Date #2, we'd start with your shares in AAPL and run through ZW ... but if you had several lots of ZW, we'd order them by date.)

TOTALS

Except on fields where it would make no sense, we give you an opportunity to have us print totals and subtotals.

- If you request a total for one field, any field you've assigned a higher priority must be totaled, too. (Don't worry; we'll remind you.)

- Ordinarily, you'd want totals for just the first and possibly the second item on your list.

WE RESHUFFLE WHILE YOU'RE GONE

Don't be surprised, when you come back from trying out a report, to find that while you were off printing we were straightening things up here. You may have numbered your items "5, 2, 9, 3" (you can leave gaps, we just look to see the order). But when you return, you'll find we've reordered them to match your ranking.

HAVE FUN, BUT DON'T GET FRUSTRATED

There are about 7 million report formats you can devise. (Well, not literally. Literally, there are probably billions.) So have as much fun with this as you want. But don't lose sight of the fact that all the reports you actually NEED are probably already available, standard, on PORTFOLIO's Display and Analyze screens and here with our standard reports. We hope the Report Generator lets you fine tune them to your liking — but customizing formats is NOT something you have to bother with!

AN EASY EXAMPLE

Say you like one of our Portfolio Reports, but instead of using the Name of the asset you'd like to use the Symbol. Just blank out whatever number we'd placed beside Asset Name and enter that same number beside Asset Symbol instead. Presto: you've got your new format.

HINT

If you're designing a report from scratch, don't number 1,2,3..., number 2,4,6... or even 3,6,9... That way, when you realize you forgot something and decide to wedge it between two others, you'll have room.

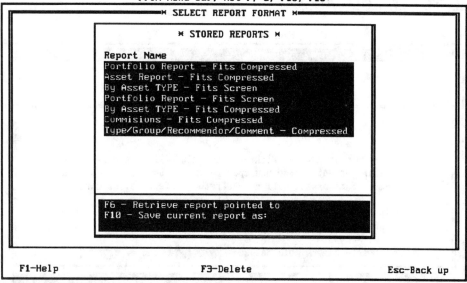

‹From Menu Bar, Alt-P, G, F10, F10›

```
═══════════════════╾ SELECT REPORT FORMAT ╾═══════════════════

              ╾ STORED REPORTS ╾

    Report Name
    Portfolio Report - Fits Compressed
    Asset Report - Fits Compressed
    By Asset TYPE - Fits Screen
    Portfolio Report - Fits Screen
    By Asset TYPE - Fits Compressed
    Commisions - Fits Compressed
    Type/Group/Recommendor/Comment - Compressed




    F6 - Retrieve report pointed to
    F10 - Save current report as:


 F1-Help                    F3-Delete              Esc-Back up
```

STORED FORMATS

We've tried to give you a headstart. Point and press F6 to load each of our formats and see how it looks. Most require compressed printing to look decent. If you find one you ALMOST like, you can improve it easily on the previous screen. Then save it here with F10 with any name you like. What we DON'T save here are the selection criteria you specified on your way in — the date range or portfolios or special codes you told us to retrieve. Those you have to respecify next time you want them.

DELETE OLD SOLD ASSETS

```
                    <From Menu Bar, Alt-P, G, Alt-F3>
 ┌────────────────────────────────────────────────────────────────┐
 │  File   Desk   Money   Tax   Insure   Analyze   Portfolio   Net Worth │
 ├────────────────────────────────────────────────────────────────┤
 │                                                                  │
 │                                                                  │
 │   ┌──────────────────────────────────────────────────────────┐  │
 │   │                                                            │  │
 │   │              × DELETE OLD SOLD ASSETS ×                    │  │
 │   │                                                            │  │
 │   │  WARNING:  This is a very tricky option.  It will delete all assets │
 │   │  sold within the date range you specify (e.g., between 1/2/85 and   │
 │   │  12/31/88).  Such assets will not be recoverable.  So, be careful.  │
 │   │                                                            │  │
 │   │  The only time it makes sense to delete sold assets is when space is │
 │   │  tight.  Otherwise, just leave them.                        │  │
 │   │                                                            │  │
 │   │  Delete assets sold between: [        ]   and  [        ]   │  │
 │   ├──────────────────────────────────────────────────────────┤  │
 │   │      Alt-F3 - Proceed with the deletion, as specified      │  │
 │   └──────────────────────────────────────────────────────────┘  │
 │                                                                  │
 └────────────────────────────────────────────────────────────────┘
```

8

Net Worth

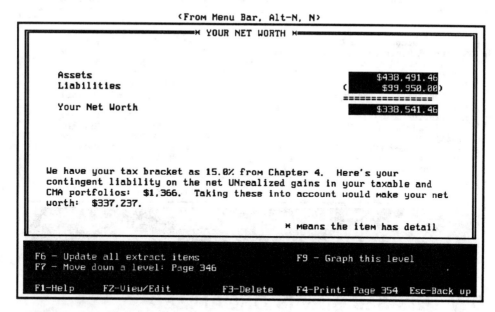

‹From Menu Bar, Alt-N, N›

```
                        ═══════════◄ YOUR NET WORTH ►═══════════


        Assets                                     $438,491.46
        Liabilities                            (    $99,950.00)
                                               ==================
        Your Net Worth                             $338,541.46




        We have your tax bracket as 15.0% from Chapter 4.  Here's your
        contingent liability on the net UNrealized gains in your taxable and
        CMA portfolios:  $1,366.  Taking these into account would make your net
        worth:  $337,237.

                                        ► means the item has detail

    ┌─────────────────────────────────────────────────────────────────────┐
    │ F6 - Update all extract items            F9 - Graph this level        │
    │ F7 - Move down a level: Page 346                                      │
    ├─────────────────────────────────────────────────────────────────────┤
    │ F1-Help     F2-View/Edit        F3-Delete    F4-Print: Page 354  Esc-Back up │
    └─────────────────────────────────────────────────────────────────────┘
```

YOUR NET WORTH

Here we assemble everything you OWN, compare it with all you OWE, and track your NET WORTH. We can also print a personal balance sheet in any of three styles, and, if you have a graphics card, bake pie charts at each level of detail.

As you'll see, you won't have to reenter any data we can extract from elsewhere. All of that can be summoned with a single keystroke — F6. But we've also given you a neat way to customize your asset and liability categories in as much detail as you want. You can even create a room-by-room household inventory, complete with serial numbers, for insurance purposes! Just be sure to print it out and store it someplace safe BEFORE the fire.

■ If you'd rather not update Your Net Worth manually each time — I like to, to see what's changed — select Net Worth Options from the FILE menu and tell us to do it for you automatically. We'll then also update your Net Worth History for you the first time you visit Net Worth each month, saving you that chore, too.)

In addition to the main net worth number we display, we also let you know how it would be affected by capital gains taxes if you actually were to sell everything. And we occasionally make a comment. If you find these comments annoying, just select Net Worth Options from the FILE menu and tell us to lay off.

‹From Menu Bar, Alt-N, N, F7›

```
╔═══════════════════════════════╗ YOUR NET WORTH ╠═══════════════════════════════╗
║                                                                                 ║
║      Assets                                                                     ║
║  Checking Accounts and Cash     [from Chapt. 3]        $9,679.22   Extract       ║
║  Savings & Money Mkt. Accts.    [from Chapt. 3]        $9,800.00   Extract       ║
║  Accounts Receivable            [from Chapt. 3]        $9,556.00   Extract       ║
║  Loans I Own                    [from Chapt. 3]      $200,000.00   Extract       ║
║  Insurance Cash Value           [from Chapt. 5]       $10,000.00   Extract       ║
║  Pension/Profit-Sharing Plans   [from Chapt. 6]        $6,134.89   Extract       ║
║  Portfolio Cash                 [from Chapt. 7]        $6,134.89   Extract       ║
║  Marketable Securities          [from Chapt. 7]            $0.00   Extract       ║
║  Unrealized Gains on Shorts     [from Chapt. 7]        $1,306.04   Extract       ║
║  Bonds                          [from Chapt. 7]        $7,368.75   Extract       ║
║  Savings Bonds/SPDAs            [from Chapt. 7]            $0.00   Extract       ║
║  IRA/Keogh Portfolios           [from Chapt. 7]        $6,354.22   Extract       ║
║  Metals & Collectibles          [from Chapt. 7]            $0.00   Extract       ║
║  Real Estate                    [from Chapt. 7]            $0.00   Extract       ║
║                                                 ✗ means the item has detail      ║
╟─────────────────────────────────────────────────────────────────────────────────╢
║   F6 - Update this extract item          F9 - Graph this level                   ║
║   F7 - Move down a level                 F10 - Rearrange items: Page 350          ║
║   F8 - Jump to top level (Net Worth)                                             ║
║                                                                                   ║
║ F2-View/Edit        F3-Delete        F4-Print: Page 354      F5-Add/OK: Page 347  ║
╚═══════════════════════════════════════════════════════════════════════════════════╝
```

HOW THIS SECTION IS ORGANIZED

The organization here is a series of levels. They get more detailed the lower you go. Move down with F7, back up with ESCape — or jump to the top with F8.

At the top, it's all summed up in three numbers: your Assets minus your Liabilities equal your Net Worth. You can't type anything to change these numbers, because they're "aggregates," based on those below. But you can attach pop-up notes to them (F2) and/or revise our headings. Instead of "Net Worth," you might want the heading to read: "John Doe: Net Worth as of 12/31/91." Fine. Just type it in. That's how it will appear when you go to print a balance sheet.

To see where we got either the Assets or the Liabilities aggregate number, point to it and descend a level (F7).

If you've chosen to examine your assets, you'll see a list of those we can "extract" from elsewhere in the program. These include your stocks and bonds from PORTFOLIO; life insurance cash value from INSURE; and so on.

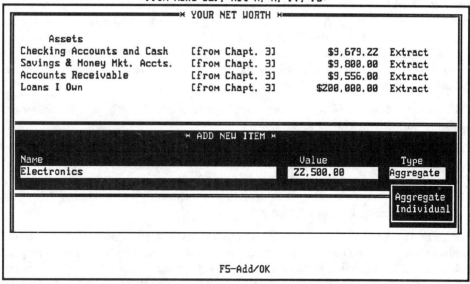

But you'll also see we've given you a place to add NEW categories. Say you want to add an asset category entitled "Personal Property." You COULD just press F5 and type:

MY PERSONAL PROPERTY $25,000   INDIVIDUAL

and leave it at that. But, if you preferred, you could designate it an AGGREGATE item instead. Then, after pressing F5 to add it to your list, descend a level and set up aggregate categories beneath THAT for each room in the house. Then descend yet another level(!) and list all the items of value in each room. If one were your stamp collection, you could label it an Individual item – meaning it has no sublevels – or tag it aggregate and descend a level to list every stamp you own!

What you're doing here is building two broad rivers – the mighty Assets and (one hopes) the somewhat less mighty Liabilities, that combine into the Net Worth delta. Naturally, these rivers are the sum of a lot of tributaries which, in turn – if you choose to add the detail – are the sum of streams, brooks, trickles, and rain drops.

All this will be a snap once you try it. Just keep in mind that you can only change data at the headwaters. If you've chosen to value each stamp, then you can't type in a new aggregate value for stamps, because it's simply the sum of all the individual values (which you CAN easily change). Don't worry: we won't let you make any mistakes.

But do be careful not to "double count." For example, if you entered your stamp collection as a portfolio of collectibles in PORTFOLIO, it would show up here automatically. (Unless you tagged it a hypothetical portfolio.) You'd be double-counting to include it all over again.

You can rearrange or alphabetize any items below the top level (F10). You can also type over any of our names. But be very careful about typing over the names of items we extract from elsewhere. We allow you to make changes so you can customize the report we print – change

"Your Net Worth" to "My Net Worth," say, or blank out "[from MONEY]." But if you changed the "Assets" category to "Liabilities," and vice versa, that's how it would be — wrong — from then on. Similarly, be sure not to blank out any of our extract categories altogether, even if they show zero, because if they ever do pull up a number, you won't have any idea what it is we're extracting. If you like, use F10 to move all the empty extract items to the end instead, where they won't bother you.

NOTE: At the top level, F4 prints a personal balance sheet. Beneath that, it prints just the level you're on, with or without sublevels.

NOTE, TOO: You may attach Pop-Up Notes to any item. Just point and press F2. To the net worth figure itself, you might attach goals for 1990, 1995, and 2000. To the "1984 Chevy Wagon" item, you might attach a note that included its serial number, the name and address of the seller, the purchase price, the depreciation schedule you've chosen (if used for business), and a running tally of maintenance and repairs.

NOTE, FINALLY: at the top level, F3 is DANGEROUS! Elsewhere, it just deletes the individual item you're pointing at. (We won't let you delete an extract item or aggregate by mistake.) But at the top level, F3 does a purge of ALL your non-extract items ... namely, all the items you've entered manually. You'd only want to do this if, say, you had to dash off to Brazil in the middle of the night after watching an episode of America's Most Wanted. Of course, we ask for confirmation before performing this purge.

WHAT COMES FROM WHERE

Now here's what we extract, and from where. However, feel free to type "phony" numbers over them instead. Nothing you enter in NET WORTH will affect your records elsewhere.

ASSETS	WHAT WE EXTRACT
Checking Accounts	Total of all checking account balances and cash from MONEY
Savings Accounts	Total of all MONEY savings accounts
Accounts Receivable	Total from MONEY
Loans You Own	Total equity of all listed in MONEY
Marketable Securities (other than bonds)	Total current value of all common stocks, preferreds, options, futures, mutual funds, special coded, and other securities from TAXABLE portfolios in PORTFOLIO
Bonds; Savings Bonds/SPDAs Metals & Collectibles Real Estate; Tax Shelters	Total values from TAXABLE portfolios in PORTFOLIO
Unrealized Gains on Shorts	From TAXABLE portfolios in PORTFOLIO
IRA/Keogh Portfolios	Total of cash and assets in "IRA/Keogh" portfolios in PORTFOLIO
Portfolio Cash Value	Positive cash balances from TAXABLE and CMA portfolios in PORTFOLIO
Pension/Profit Sharing	As entered in ANALYZE, Retirement Planning
Insurance Cash Value	Total from INSURE Policy Organizer

LIABILITIES	
Mortgages and Loans	Your balances from MONEY
Accounts Payable	Your balances from MONEY
Credit Card Balances	Your balances from MONEY
Home Equity Accounts	Your balances from MONEY
Margin Debt	Negative cash balances of taxable PORTFOLIO
Unrealized Loss on Shorts	From taxable portfolios in PORTFOLIO

<From Menu Bar, Alt-N, N, F7, F10>

REARRANGE ITEMS

Order	Your Assets			
2	Checking Accounts and Cash	[from Chapt. 3]	$9,679.22	Extra
3	Savings & Money Mkt. Accts.	[from Chapt. 3]	$9,800.00	Extra
1	Accounts Receivable	[from Chapt. 3]	$9,556.00	Extra
	Loans I Own	[from Chapt. 3]	$200,000.00	Extra
	Insurance Cash Value	[from Chapt. 5]	$10,000.00	Extra
	Pension/Profit-Sharing Plans	[from Chapt. 6]	$6,134.89	Extra
	Portfolio Cash	[from Chapt. 7]	$6,134.89	Extra
	Marketable Securities	[from Chapt. 7]	$0.00	Extra
	Unrealized Gains on Shorts	[from Chapt. 7]	$1,306.04	Extra
	Bonds	[from Chapt. 7]	$7,368.75	Extra
	Savings Bonds/SPDAs	[from Chapt. 7]	$0.00	Extra
	IRA/Keogh Portfolios	[from Chapt. 7]	$6,354.22	Extra
	Metals & Collectibles	[from Chapt. 7]	$0.00	Extra
	Real Estate	[from Chapt. 7]	$0.00	Extra

Number your items in the order you would like them to display.

F6 - Rearrange these items   F7 - Alphabetize these items

F1-Help   Esc-Back up

REARRANGE/ALPHABETIZE ITEMS

Order your items any way you want with F6 or alphabetize them with F7. When you're pleased with the result, press ESCape to back up.

‹From Menu Bar, Alt-N, H›

```
━━━━━━━━━━━━━━━━ NET WORTH HISTORY ━━━━━━━━━━━━━━━━

Date         Assets            Liabilities        Net Worth    Debt/Equity
8/15/1990    $65,000.00     —   $14,000.00    =   $51,000.00   0.27
9/15/1990    $65,000.00     —   $15,000.00    =   $50,000.00   0.30
10/15/1990   $65,000.00     —   $17,000.00    =   $48,000.00   0.35
11/15/1990   $65,000.00     —   $15,000.00    =   $50,000.00   0.30




F6 - Record Prior Net Worth: Page 353
F7 - Purge Net Worth History records from 8/15 through 9/15/1990: Page 352
F9 - Display Bar Graph

F1-Help                    F4-Print                    Esc-Back up
```

NET WORTH HISTORY
UPDATING THIS HISTORY

Press F6 whenever you come here — and come here at least once a month. That's what I do, anyway. At first, there's not much to see here. But over the months, a pattern begins to emerge: you're getting richer. And once you have two months' or more numbers (it being hard to draw a line between one point), we'll offer to draw a graph.

We store only one entry per month, but I actually come here and press F6 each time I look at my Net Worth, because that's an easy way to see how it's changed since the last time. There's the old one; press F6 and it's replaced with the current one.

■ If you'd prefer, set the first Net Worth Option on the FILE menu to YES, and the first time each month you visit Net Worth we'll update your Net Worth History automatically.

YOUR DEBT/EQUITY RATIO

Although the graph is nice, it actually tells you little. What IS instructive is the right-hand column that shows your debt/equity ratio. The lower your debt/equity ratio, the better. Or, at least, the safer. Owning $10 million but owing $9 million means you owe 9 times your $1 million net worth — a debt/equity ratio of 9. Owning $1.2 million and owing $200,000 works out to the same $1 million net worth, but a debt/equity ratio of just .2 (20%). You're less of a big shot but better able to weather a decline in asset values. Asset values, if you invest in some of the kinds of things I do, have a way of disappearing overnight. Liabilities rarely do.

ADDING PRIOR DATA

To add data from any month back to 1980, set the F6 choice to "Prior," press F6, and then fill in the blanks. To do some pruning, use F7.

NUMBERS TOO LARGE

If you see "******" in the debt/equity column, that means the ratio is above 99 and won't fit. Likewise, assets or liabilities of $100 million or more. Sorry!

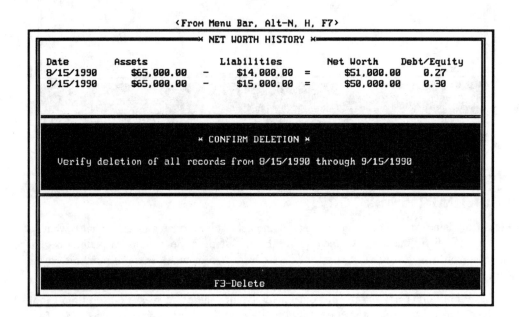

```
                    <From Menu Bar, Alt-N, H, F7>
═════════════════════⋈ NET WORTH HISTORY ⋈═════════════════════

 Date       Assets            Liabilities        Net Worth     Debt/Equity
 8/15/1990  $65,000.00   -    $14,000.00    =    $51,000.00    0.27
 9/15/1990  $65,000.00   -    $15,000.00    =    $50,000.00    0.30



                    ⋈ CONFIRM DELETION ⋈

    Verify deletion of all records from 8/15/1990 through 9/15/1990




                         F3-Delete
```

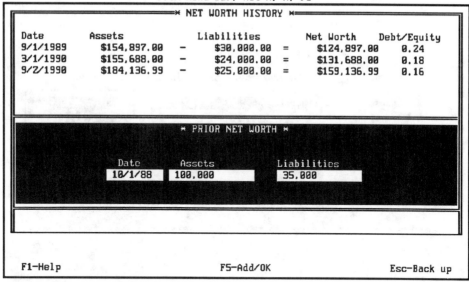

<From Menu Bar, Alt-N, H, F6>

```
========* NET WORTH HISTORY *========

Date        Assets              Liabilities            Net Worth    Debt/Equity
9/1/1989    $154,897.00    -    $30,000.00    =    $124,897.00      0.24
3/1/1990    $155,688.00    -    $24,000.00    =    $131,688.00      0.18
9/2/1990    $184,136.99    -    $25,000.00    =    $159,136.99      0.16



                          * PRIOR NET WORTH *


              Date          Assets            Liabilities
              10/1/88       100,000           35,000




F1-Help                        F5-Add/OK                    Esc-Back up
```

ADDING/CORRECTING PRIOR MONTHS' NET WORTH HISTORY

If you know what your assets and liabilities were, exactly or approximately, in some prior month, you can enter them here. We'll accept a date as far back as 1980. If it's a month for which we already have an entry, we'll overwrite that entry with this one. (This thus becomes an easy way to adjust old entries. Just enter a more accurate entry here for the same month and we'll use this one, instead.)

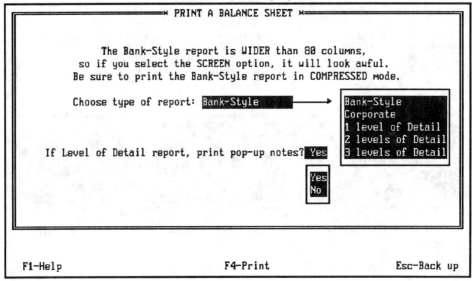

⟨From Menu Bar, Alt-N, N, F4⟩

PRINTING NET WORTH REPORTS

Fill in the blanks and press F4 or chicken out with ESCape. If printing fails, select Printer Setup from FILE's Program Setup menu and press F1 for HELP there.

Printing to the screen is fast and, except for reports over 80 columns, shows how your report will look on paper. To print a report to the disk in drive a:, say, give it a filename like a:this. and then, before pressing F4, replace the disk in drive a: with another, so as not to clutter your working disks. When the disk drive stops, switch back and continue working with MYM. (It's best to print to the drive not in use by 8.chp, the file that runs this chapter.)

We offer three basic balance-sheet styles in this chapter — bank style, corporate, or an outline form for which you can choose the level of detail you want. Try them all. And try printing a report to a file on your disk (in "report" format); then press Ctrl-W, summon it (with the file name you just gave it), touch it up, and print it out.

Hint: To print a batch of "supporting schedules" all at once, select Vital Records & Estate Report from the INSURE menu and press F4. There, you could choose to print an account summary, a loan summary, a portfolio summary (or list of all your assets), and/or lists of your payables and receivables all at once.

9

Connections

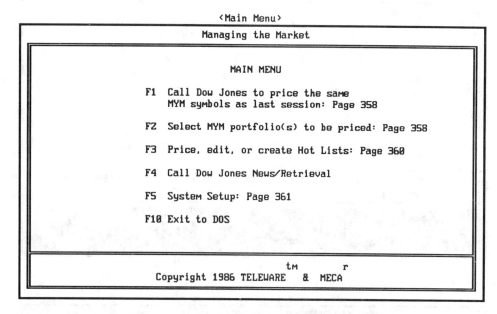

<Main Menu>

Managing the Market

```
                        MAIN MENU

        F1  Call Dow Jones to price the same
            MYM symbols as last session: Page 358

        F2  Select MYM portfolio(s) to be priced: Page 358

        F3  Price, edit, or create Hot Lists: Page 360

        F4  Call Dow Jones News/Retrieval

        F5  System Setup: Page 361

        F10 Exit to DOS


                             tm      r
        Copyright 1986 TELEWARE   &  MECA
```

MANAGING THE MARKET: MAIN MENU

Start with F5 if you have not used the program before, or wish to change, say, from Tymnet to Telenet. F1 prices the same securities as last time. To price a different set of portfolios (or the same portfolios in which some symbols have been added or changed), press F2. If it's your "Hot Lists" you would like to price, create, or edit, press F3. To call Dow Jones directly, to roam at will through its 30-odd databases and services, press F4.

We have tried our best to make this product work perfectly, but we disclaim responsibility if it fails to do so. Nor are we responsible for any information you receive from Dow Jones' services using this product. You should be sure to double check your conclusions with your broker, accountant, or some other independent source you trust before you make a decision or take an action that involves what is for you a significant risk or a significant amount of money.

<From MTM Main Menu, Press F1>

```
* MTM/Price MYM Portfolio(s) *      Memory buffer remaining:  13157 characters
                                                          Home ↑ PgUp
ALLT     Z 7/8    3 1/8
AMR     65 7/8   65 1/2   66 1/4   65 3/8   66 1/4   1614
BA      52 1/8   52       52 1/4   51 3/4   52 1/4   5480
BFI     37 5/8   37 3/4   37 3/4   37 1/4   37 5/8   3590
BIND     9 3/8    9 1/8    9 3/8    9 1/8    9 3/8   5
BKI       1/64                                       1010
BLAK     10                                          720
BNBGA    4 1/4    4 5/8    4 5/8    4 5/8    4 5/8   10

STOCK     BID      ASKED
         CLOSE    OPEN     HIGH     LOW      LAST     VOL(100'S)
BRO     10 3/4   10 3/4   10 3/4   10 5/8   10 5/8   143
CCI     31 1/2   31 1/4   31 1/2   31 1/8   31 1/4   8095
CHF      8 1/8    8        8 1/8    8        8 1/8   33
CKE     42       42       42 3/4   41 7/8   42 3/8   1520
                                                          End ↓ PgDn
When you press F1, F4, or F10, the buffer will automatically be cleared.

F1 Go to Main Menu and clear buffer          F3 Print buffer

F4 Clear buffer          F5  Save buffer          F10 Exit to DOS
```

<From MTM Main Menu, Press F2>

```
* SELECT PORTFOLIOS TO PRICE *
                                                          Home ↑ PgUp
     Select    Portfolio        Account #          Type
       x       E.F Sample       02C-60888312       Taxable
       x       Fidelity Funds   8A-3563-GG-91837   IRA/Keogh
               Wine Cellar      Downstairs         Taxable




     Mark with an "x" the portfolios you wish to update and press F1.
     Symbols updated in any one portfolio will be updated in all portfolios.

F1 - Call Dow Jones and price selected portfolios
F2 - Mark all portfolios
F3 - Erase all marks
```

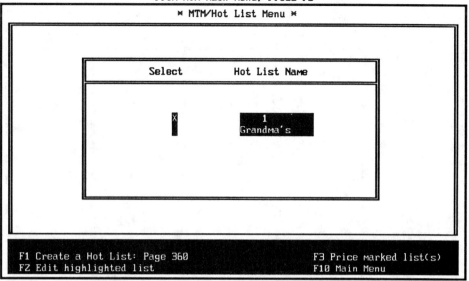

```
                    <From MTM Main Menu, Press F3>
                        * MTM/Hot List Menu *


                    Select          Hot List Name


                              X                1
                                           Grandma's




         F1 Create a Hot List: Page 360        F3 Price marked list(s)
         FZ Edit highlighted list              F10 Main Menu
```

HOT LIST MENU

In addition to pricing your MYM portfolio(s), you can create up to three "Hot Lists," each with up to 75 securities for a total of 225. Press F1 to create a new list. Once created, use the up and down arrow keys to highlight the list name and press F2 to edit it.

You can price any or all of your lists by typing an X next to the list name. Press F3 to price the marked lists. We will display the prices on your screen and automatically save them to a file called **QUOTES.DIF** on your MTM disk, in case you want to transfer your data to a spreadsheet program.

When pricing, we save you money by grouping your symbols by security type and not always in the order you entered them.

```
                          <From MTM Main Menu, Press F3, F1>
┌─────────────────────────────────────────────────────────────────────┐
│  Hot List Name:  WEBAT      * MTM/Create or Edit Hot Lists *          │
│  ┌──────────────┬──────────────┬──────────────┬──────────────┬──────┐│
│  │ SYMBOL  TYPE │ SYMBOL  TYPE │ SYMBOL  TYPE │ SYMBOL  TYPE │SYMBOL TYPE││
│  ├──────────────┼──────────────┼──────────────┼──────────────┼──────┤│
│  │ IBM    STOCK │              │              │              │      ││
│  │ EGG    STOCK │              │              │              │      ││
│  │ TRW   OPTION │              │              │              │      ││
│  │ CTY   MUTUAL │              │              │              │      ││
│  │              │              │              │              │      ││
│  │              │              │              │              │      ││
│  │              │              │              │              │      ││
│  │              │              │              │              │      ││
│  │              │              │              │              │      ││
│  └──────────────┴──────────────┴──────────────┴──────────────┴──────┘│
│  ┌──────────────────────────────────────────────────────────────────┐│
│  │                                          F10 Hot List Menu        ││
│  └──────────────────────────────────────────────────────────────────┘│
└─────────────────────────────────────────────────────────────────────┘
```

CREATE OR EDIT HOT LIST

In case you want to get in and out of Dow Jones fast to check prices of a few key securities you own − or don't own − without updating MYM, you can create up to three special "Hot Lists", each with up to 75 securities for a total of 225.

First give the list a name you will remember, like "My GTC's." Then tell us each security symbol and type. You can price stocks, options, corporate bonds, mutual funds, and treasury issues. Valid Dow Jones symbols have 5 or fewer characters and no spaces between the characters. If you are unsure about a symbol, connect with Dow Jones and type //SYMBOL.

Option symbols are formed by adding two letters to the underlying symbol.

Month:	JAN	FEB	MAR	APR	MAY	JUN	JUL	AUG	SEP	OCT	NOV	DEC
Call:	A	B	C	D	E	F	G	H	I	J	K	L
Put:	M	N	O	P	Q	R	S	T	U	V	W	X

Strike Price: 5 10 15 20 25 30 35 40 45 50 55 60 65 70 75 80 85 90 95 100

Code: A B C D E F G H I J K L M N O P Q R S T

For example, Benquet Consolidated (BE) call with a May expiration (E) and a $90.00 strike price (R), would have the symbol BEER. You can see why we get hungry pricing a Transamerica Corporation (TA) March 75 call.

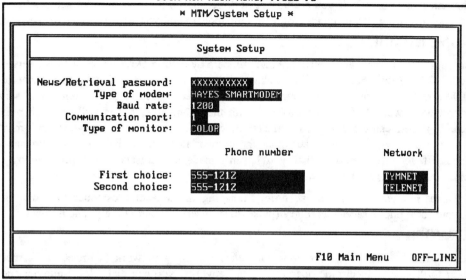

MTM/SYSTEM SETUP

PASSWORD

Your password is a simple 10-character identifier assigned to you by Dow Jones and used for customer accounting and billing. For your protection, after you enter your password, we hide it behind xxx's.

TYPE OF MODEM

Select Hayes if you have a Hayes Smartmodem or a modem that works like a Hayes modem. If you have any other kind of modem, select Other. When you're ready to call Dow Jones, you'll be prompted to dial the phone. Dial it; or, if you have an autodial modem, use your keyboard to send the dial command (see your modem manual) and phone number to your modem. Press F5 soon after the phone connection is made. We'll take over from there. The process is repeated when you want to hang up the phone.

BAUD RATE

Baud rate is the speed at which your computer talks to Dow Jones. 300 baud stands for 300 bits per second. Since there are approximately 10 bits per character, you are actually talking at 30 characters per second. Likewise, 1200 baud is really 120 characters per second. If you select 1200 baud, make sure both your modem and the network phone number you've chosen work at that speed.

COMMUNICATION PORT

This tells us where your modem is plugged in. Sometimes it is called the serial port or the COM port. Don't be intimidated by this selection. Most modems are in communication port #1. If you also have a serial printer or plotter, there is a small chance that your modem is in communications port #2. If you are unsure of which port your modem is in, select #1 and try it. If you are wrong, the program won't find the modem and you will get an error message.

PHONE NUMBER

Find your local Tymnet and Telenet phone numbers by calling Dow Jones customer service at 1-800-522-3567 or 1-609-452-1511. Make sure you get a couple of local numbers, because, oddly enough, some numbers are purported to be current but have been taken out of service or don't work well. If there is a problem with the phone line, MTM will try each number twice. If it still can't get a good connection, check to make sure that your equipment is properly connected. Also make sure that the number that you're dialing is a valid network number. If you are confident that you haven't made any mistakes, the problem may be "noise" on the line. Wait a few minutes and try again.

- **Hayes modem owners please note:** Managing the Market uses touch-tone dialing. If your local phone service is rotary (pulse dial), insert a **P** before the phone number.

NETWORK

Your modem is a telephone for your computer. Calling a network (Tymnet or Telenet) is similar to dialing an electronic operator. With networks, you can dial a local number and be automatically connected to Dow Jones' computers in Princeton, New Jersey. You pay only for the local call. You don't need to know how to talk to this operator, MTM does it for you. To find out your local network phone numbers, call Dow Jones' customer service at 1-800-522-3567 or 1-609-452-1511. The manual selection is for international users who don't have access to the networks. If you can use a network, you'll naturally want to take advantage of it.

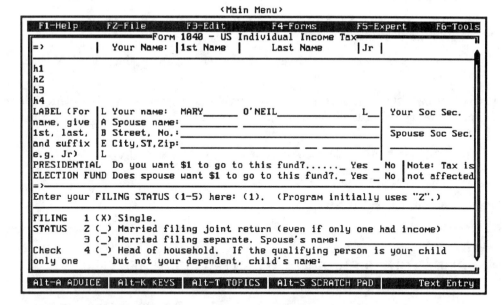

TAXCUT: DOING YOUR TAXES WITH TAXCUT
WELCOME TO TAXCUT!

This introduction will help you get started using Taxcut. It will also provide a seven-step process to help you complete your taxes in record time (we hope).

You can quit this introduction at any time — just press <ESC>. The very bottom line of the screen reminds you of this. You can refer to this introduction later; just select F1-HELP/Doing Your Taxes with TaxCut. You can print this introduction now, and we suggest you do so — just press P now.

Here's how to do your taxes with TaxCut:

1. Browse through the TaxCut tutorials.

2. Gather your W2's and other tax documents.

3. Use TaxCut's Shoebox to enter documents.

4. Use TaxCut's Checklist to spot deductions.

5. Use TaxCut's Expert to complete the forms.

6. Audit the return with TaxCut's Auditor.

7. Print, sign, and mail your return.

The following paragraphs describe each step in more detail.

1. BROWSE THROUGH THE TAXCUT TUTORIALS: F1-HELP

We have provided several tutorial-type screens to help you become familiar with TaxCut. These screens are all available on the F1-Help menu.

- **Doing Your Taxes with Taxcut:** This is the screen you are reading now. It provides an overview and a road map.

- **Hello, New User:** This is especially recommended to people new to computers. It is an interactive tutorial that will have you pulling down menus and working with the Expert in no time.

- **Menu Guide:** This is a brief description of each menu option in the program.

2. GATHER YOUR DOCUMENTS

Sorry − no menu option for this!

Gather up your W2's, 1099's, bills, receipts, checkbook, your other tax documents, and your courage.

3. USE TAXCUT'S SHOEBOX TO ENTER DOCUMENTS: F4-FORMS/X-SHOEBOX

The Shoebox works like this: You choose a description of your document (e.g., "a report of interest I earned"). The Shoebox jumps you to the place (tax form and line) where you can enter that document. At that point, you can simply copy the numbers onto the tax form. Or if you like, you can ask the Expert (F5-Expert/E-Expert Advice) for help.

4. USE TAXCUT'S CHECKLIST TO FIND DEDUCTIONS: F5-EXPERT/C-CHECKLIST

The Checklist will help you find deductions, credits, income items, and other tax items, to figure out what additional tax forms (if any) you need.

5. USE TAXCUT'S EXPERT TO COMPLETE THE FORMS: F4-FORMS

If you have completed the Checklist, the topics you might wish to consider will be marked on the Topics Index, and the forms you may need will be marked on the Forms menu.

When you select an item on the Topics Index, the program will jump you to the place (tax form and line) for that topic. Again, you can fill in the form, or consult the Expert.

In addition to the Expert, you may wish to refer to the IRS Instructions for the form, which are available from the F1-Help menu. If you select each topic you need in turn, TaxCut will prepare most of your return for you.

Some forms depend on other forms having been filled in first. You'll probably finish faster if you stick to following sequence:

1. **Income items:** W2's, business income, interest, dividends, partnerships, sale of home, sale of securities, sale of other assets, alimony.

2. **Deductions:** The "Adjustments" at the bottom of page 1 of Form 1040 (IRA, Keogh, Alimony paid, etc.); then others, such as medical, taxes, charitable, interest, employee business expenses, moving expenses, etc.

3. **Credits:** Child care credit, elderly credit, general business credit, foreign tax credit, etc.

4. **Other taxes:** Self-employment tax, child under 14 with investment income, alternative minimum tax, underpayment penalty, etc.

5. **Miscellaneous:** Non-deductible IRA contribution.

6. **Filing:** Electronic filing form, automatic extension form.

But this is a guideline only. As long as you get all the information in by the time you're ready to print, TaxCut will make sure that the calculations are correct.

For those of you who are comfortable with the tax forms, the Checklist will also mark the forms you need (F4-Forms/Menu of Tax Forms). You can simply prepare each form that is marked.

6. AUDIT THE RETURN WITH TAXCUT'S AUDITOR: F5-EXPERT/A-AUDIT THE RETURN

When you're finished, ask TaxCut's Expert to audit your return for possible errors, omissions, and for general tax-saving tips. Do so by selecting "Audit the Return" from the F5-Expert menu.

7. PRINT AND SIGN YOUR RETURN: F2-FILE/P-PRINT

And now, press F2 and then P to print your return. Of course, with TaxCut it's easy to print it several times and make changes, even at the last minute, without a lot of work.

Once you've eyeballed the final print-out to be sure it looks right, and included whatever other supporting documents may be required (such as your personal check), and made at least one hard copy for your own files — send it in! Congratulations!

By the way, you may want to file your return electronically (F6-Tools/F-Electronic Filing) through Universal Tax Systems, our affiliated electronic return filer. In that case, you would mail your electronic return disk and Form 8453 to UTS, rather than mailing your paper return to the IRS.

You've completed your 1990 federal tax return!

■ **Note:** Needless to say, if you have a particularly complex return, or fear you may not have understood how to enter certain significant items, you should check with a tax professional before mailing in your return.

NEXT STEPS

At this point your next steps are to close this window, and continue with either the "Hello, New User" tutorial (F1-Help menu), or start entering your documents with the Shoebox (F4-Forms).

ABOUT THE MENU GUIDE

This menu guide is a quick reference to TaxCut's menu options. You can search through the Menu Guide for any word or phrase. Just type S, then the word or phrase you want. To close the Menu Guide and get back to work, just press <ESC>.

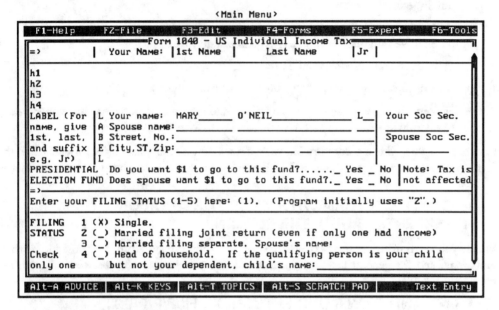

<Main Menu>

```
 F1-Help       FZ-File       F3-Edit       F4-Forms      F5-Expert     F6-Tools
                      ═══Form 1040 - US Individual Income Tax═══
 =>          |  Your Name: |1st Name |     Last Name     |Jr |
 h1
 hZ
 h3
 h4
 LABEL (For |L Your name:  MARY_____  O'NEIL_____ L__| Your Soc Sec.
 name, give |A Spouse name:_____  _____  ___ |
 1st, last, |B Street, No.:_____  | Spouse Soc Sec.
 and suffix |E City,ST,Zip:_____ __ _____ |
 e.g. Jr)   |L
 PRESIDENTIAL  Do you want $1 to go to this fund?......_ Yes _ No |Note: Tax is
 ELECTION FUND Does spouse want $1 to go to this fund?_ Yes _ No |not affected
 =>
 Enter your FILING STATUS (1-5) here: (1).  (Program initially uses "Z".)

 FILING    1 (X) Single.
 STATUS    Z (_) Married filing joint return (even if only one had income)
           3 (_) Married filing separate. Spouse's name: _____
 Check     4 (_) Head of household.  If the qualifying person is your child
 only one      but not your dependent, child's name: _____

 Alt-A ADVICE | Alt-K KEYS | Alt-T TOPICS | Alt-S SCRATCH PAD |  Text Entry
```

THE MAIN MENU

The Main Menu (at the top of the screen) offers the following six choices:

F1-Help — Help using TaxCut, and IRS instructions.

F2-File — Starting, saving, and printing tax returns.

F3-Edit — Changing and annotating entries on the forms.

F4-Forms — Getting around the tax forms.

F5-Expert — Getting tax help.

F6-Tools — Recalculate, import, screen colors, etc.

When you select any of these choices, by pressing its F-key, you will see a menu of choices. These choices are described below. But first, some general hints...

- Any menu option with a diamond character beside it is temporarily inactive.

- Any menu option with three dots ("...") after it leads to a submenu with options of its own.

- If there is a shortcut (Alt-) key to summon that menu option, it is listed next to that option.

And now, on to the menus.

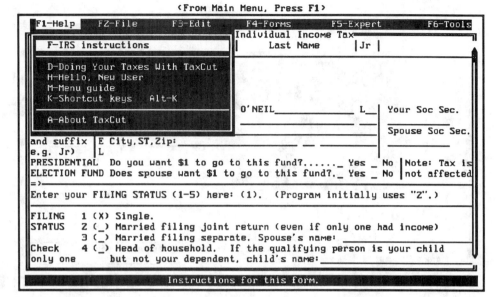

<From Main Menu, Press F1>

F1-HELP

IRS INSTRUCTIONS gives you an abridged version of the IRS instructions for the form you're working on. (You wouldn't believe how many megabytes the full IRS instructions would consume.)

DOING YOUR TAXES WITH TAXCUT gives an overview of TaxCut and a road map for doing your taxes. We think that if you take a couple of minutes to read it, you'll save time in the long run.

HELLO, NEW USER is a quick tutorial that shows you how to select TaxCut's menu options and how to use the Expert.

MENU GUIDE is what you're reading now. To search for any particular word, type S.

SHORTCUT KEYS lists the keys you can press to bypass our menus. To execute a shortcut key, hold down the "ALT" key and press the letter listed on the "Shortcut Keys" screen. In fact, to summon the shortcut keys list — fast — at any time, just press its OWN shortcut key: Alt-K.

ABOUT TAXCUT just tells you what version of TaxCut you are using and how much free memory you have.

MECA INFO gives you information about other MECA software, and an order form for TaxCut state programs and next year's TaxCut.

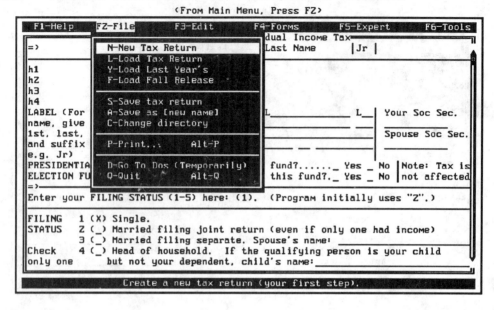

‹From Main Menu, Press F2›

F2-FILE

NEW TAX RETURN lets you create one. You may prepare as many tax returns as you like with a single copy of TaxCut. We put each return in its own file.

LOAD TAX RETURN pulls into active memory a return already in progress, that you've previously stored on your hard disk or floppy. If you've been working on more than one return, you can use this option to switch quickly from one to another.

LOAD LAST YEAR'S converts a 1989 TaxCut tax return to a 1990 TaxCut return. A report tells you which forms have changed so much that we couldn't transfer last year's data.

LOAD FALL RELEASE will convert a 1990 Fall release TaxCut tax return to a 1990 Final version TaxCut tax return. A report tells you which forms have changed so much that we couldn't transfer the data.

SAVE TAX RETURN saves the return you're working on so you can come back to it later. The data is stored on your hard disk or floppy diskette. It's always a good idea to save frequently, even if you're not ready to quit work, lest the program flake out on you.

SAVE AS [NEW NAME] lets you save the return under a different name from the one you gave it originally. This is useful if you want to save different versions of the same return, e.g., for tax planning.

CHANGE DIRECTORY lets you change the directory in which we place your data files. (If you haven't mastered DOS directories, don't worry: you never need this option.)

PRINT (ALT-P) lets you print all or any part of your return. It pops up a submenu with several options of its own, some of which lead to yet other menus. Remember, each option is explained on the Status Line. Whether you're trying to print on a laser, print "to disk," include or exclude your Scratch Pads with what we print, or send some fancy "setup string" to your printer, you'll find the choices you need on these menus.

GO TO DOS lets you get to the operating system (DOS) without "losing your place" in TaxCut. You can check directories, copy files, even use your spreadsheet or word processor. When you're ready to return to TaxCut, get back to the DOS prompt (C>) and type: Exit.

QUIT (ALT-Q) exits TaxCut.

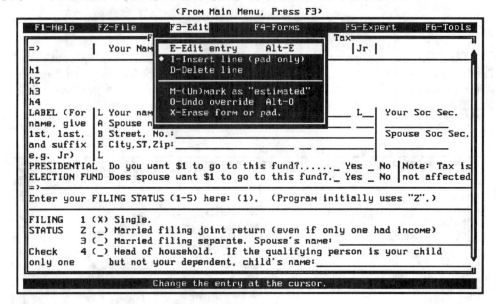

<From Main Menu, Press F3>

F3-EDIT

EDIT ENTRY lets you change the entry at the cursor.

INSERT LINE and **DELETE LINE** lets you insert and delete lines on a Scratch Pad or Memo Pad. "Delete Line" also lets you delete the entire current line on a tax form.

(UN)MARK AS ESTIMATED is a toggle that lets you mark the entry at the cursor as "estimated." If the entry is already marked as estimated, this option un-marks it. The mark is for your reference only — you'll probably want to replace estimates with exact numbers before you print your final return.

UNDO OVERRIDE (ALT-O) deletes an entry you may have forced the program to accept (2+2=5) and restores the program's regularly-calculated entry.

ERASE allows you to erase the entire current form. If a Scratch Pad is open, this option will erase it.

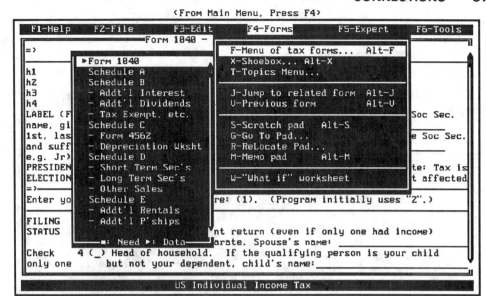

<From Main Menu, Press F4>

F4-FORMS

MENU OF TAX FORMS (ALT-F) pops up a menu of all the forms in the program. Forms will be marked as "needed" if you have completed the Checklist (see the F5-Expert menu below).

SHOEBOX (ALT-X) helps you locate where on your return to report the "tax documents" you keep in your shoebox.

TOPICS INDEX (ALT-T) helps you locate where on the return to report an item you select from an alphabetical index.

JUMP TO RELATED FORM (ALT-J) jumps you to the underlying form for the summary line you're on — and back. Say you're on the Form 1040 line that asks for your Schedule B dividend income. Choose this menu option (or press Alt-J) and we'll jump you straight to the total line on Schedule B. Move to the Schedule B total, press Alt-J again, and we'll jump from the Schedule B back to the proper line on Form 1040.

PREVIOUS FORM (ALT-V) jumps back to the form you were on just before this one. "Previous Form" also jumps back from the "What-if" form.

SCRATCH PAD (ALT-S) lets you pop up pads to list and total your travel expenses, charitable donations — anything. You may have as many Scratch Pads as you wish. Each will "stick to" the entry it was created for, and will carry its total into that entry field automatically. To print a Scratch Pad, open it (Alt-S) and then press Alt-P.

GO TO PAD lets you find — and go to — a Scratch Pad you've created.

RELOCATE PAD lets you move a Scratch Pad you've created from wherever it is to the place where your cursor is currently resting.

THE MEMO PAD (ALT-M) is an omnipresent clipboard for jotting notes to yourself (feed the dog, call Harry to get figures on the partnership). Is is NOT for inclusion with your return. There's one Memo Pad per return, and it's always floating just beneath the surface. To print it out, press ALT-M to summon it; then Alt-P to print.

WHAT-IF WORKSHEET lets you ask "what if" about your tax return this year, or plan for future years.

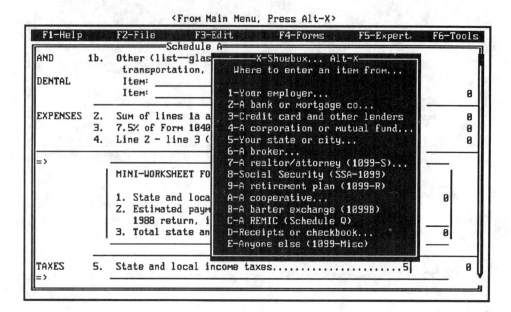

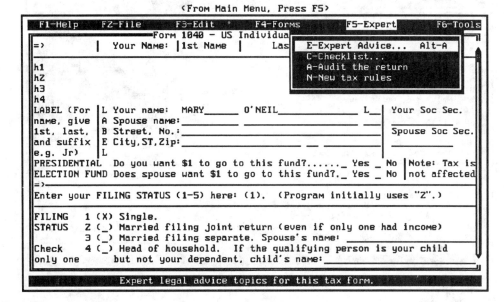

F5-EXPERT

EXPERT ADVICE (ALT-A) pops up a menu of topics for which help is available on the current form. If help is available on the current line, that topic will be highlighted on the pop-up menu. Some topics have questions; some simply have displays of information. When you select a topic that has questions, and respond to the questions, TaxCut will fill in the relevant sections of the tax form for you.

CHECKLIST helps make sure you don't miss anything you should report. You respond to YES/NO questions, and the program marks the forms you may need on the Menu of Tax Forms, and topics you may need on the Topics Index.

AUDIT THE RETURN scans your entire return, and prints out a customized report showing where you may have forgotten to enter data, where you left a field marked as "estimated" or "overridden," apparent inconsistencies, IRS red flags, and tax-saving suggestions.

NEW TAX RULES gives an overview of tax changes for this year, and a glimpse of what to expect next year.

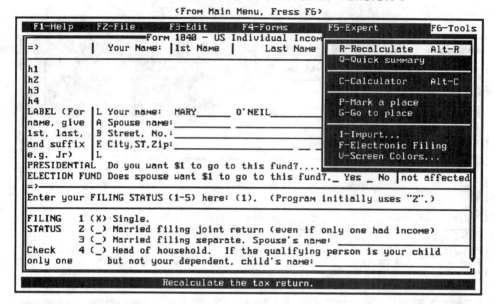

<From Main Menu, Fress F6>

F6-TOOLS

RECALCULATE (ALT-R) recalculates your entire return. (Your return is also automatically recalculated when you select a Print option, when you save, or when you select "Quick Summary.")

QUICK SUMMARY recalculates your entire return, and pops up a summary of key numbers and the current bottom line.

CALCULATOR (ALT-C) pops up a four-function calculator. Use +, -, *, / and =. You can press the Enter key, if you prefer, instead of the equals sign, and the "x," if you prefer, instead of the asterisk for multiplication. To import your answer to the field in TaxCut you're currently working on, press F10. To close the calculator without importing that number, press <ESC>.

MARK PLACE marks the current cursor location.

GO TO PLACE jumps you back to the marked place. These shortcuts work only on the tax forms, not in TaxCut's question sequences.

IMPORT lets you import data from a variety of sources. You can do full-scale imports from Managing Your Money, Quicken, CheckFree, and last year's TurboTax. You can import columns of figures into TaxCut scratch pads form Lotus 1-2-3 and from most spreadsheet and database programs. You can import any number to a specific field from any ASCII (characters only) file. Importing Data usually requires several steps — you should see your Users' Manual for Details. *(See Page 199 of THIS book for MYM's easy TaxCut Connection information and setup.)*

ELECTRONIC FILING lets you prepare a tax return file to be submitted electronically. Electronic filing speeds your refund, but it does NOT mean that you send your data from your home modem direct to the IRS. You send your data to our transmitter (Universal Tax Systems), who has undergone rigorous IRS screening, and UTS sends the data to the IRS.

SCREEN COLORS lets you change the colors of the screen to suit your taste.

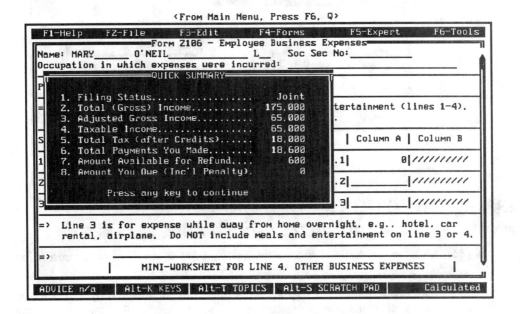

FOR MORE INFORMATION ON MENU OPTIONS, SEE YOUR MANUAL.

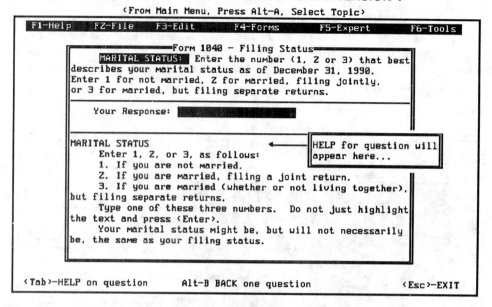

IRS INSTRUCTIONS FOR FORM 1040
NAME, ADDRESS, AND SOCIAL SECURITY NUMBER

We can process your return faster if you use the mailing label on the front of the instruction booklet. But don't attach it until you have finished your return.

If you don't have a social security number, get Form SS-5 from your local SSA office. If you do not receive a number by the time your return is due, write "Applied for" the space for the number.

LINES 1-5
FILING STATUS

In general, your filing status depends on whether you are considered single or married. Each filing status has different tax rate. The filing statuses are listed below, with the highest tax rate listed first and the lowest rate last:

Married filing a separate return

Single

Head of Household

Married filing a joint return and Qualifying Widow(er) with dependent children

If more than one filing status applies to you, choose the one that will give you the lowest tax.

EXEMPTIONS
LINE 6A
FOR YOURSELF

Check the box on line 6a unless someone (such as your parent) can claim you as a dependent.

LINE 6B
FOR YOUR SPOUSE

If you file a joint return and your spouse cannot be claimed as a dependent on another person's return, check the box on line 6b. If you file a separate return, you can take an exemption for your spouse only if your spouse is not filing a return, had no income, and cannot be claimed as a dependent on another person's return.

If at the end of 1989 you were divorced or legally separated, you cannot take an exemption for your former spouse. If your divorce was not final (an interlocutory decree), you are considered married for the whole year.

Death of Your Spouse

If your spouse died in 1989 and you did not remarry before the end of 1989, check the box on line 6b if you could have taken an exemption for your spouse on the date of death. For other filing instructions, see Death of Taxpayer on page 23.

Nonresident Alien Spouse

If you do not file a joint return, you can take an exemption for your spouse only if your spouse had no income from U.S. sources and is not the dependent of another taxpayer. Check the box on line 6b if you can take an exemption for your spouse and enter "NRA" to the right of the word Spouse on line 6b.

LINE 6C
DEPENDENTS

You can claim an exemption for each of your dependents affected who was alive during some part of 1989. This includes a baby born in 1989 or a person who died in 1989.

Community property states

Community property states are: Arizona, California, Idaho, Louisiana, Nevada, New Mexico, Texas, Washington, and Wisconsin.

If you and your spouse live in a community property state, you must follow state law to determine what is community income and what is separate income. However, different rules could apply if: you and your spouse lived apart all year, you do not file a joint return, and none of the community income you earn affected is transferred to your spouse.

For details, get Pub. 555, Community Property and the Federal Income Tax.

LINE 7
WAGES, SALARIES, TIPS, ETC.

Show the total of all wages, salaries, fees, commissions, tips, bonuses, supplemental unemployment benefits, and other amounts you were paid before taxes, insurance, etc., were taken out. For a joint return, be sure to include your spouse's income on line 7.

Employer-Provided Vehicle

If you used an employer-provided highway motor vehicle for both personal and business purpose and 100% of the fair rental value of the vehicle was included in the wages box (Box 10) of your W-2 form, you can deduct the business use of the vehicle. (The total fair rental value of the vehicle should be shown in Box 16a of your W-2 form or on a separate statement.) For more details, get Pub. 525 — Excess Salary Deferrals.

LINE 8A
TAXABLE INTEREST INCOME

Report ALL of your taxable interest income on line 8a, even if it is $400 or less. If the total is more than $400, first fill in Schedule B.

LINE 8B
TAX-EXEMPT INTEREST INCOME

If you received any tax-exempt interest (such as from municipal bonds) report it on line 8b. Include in this amount any exempt-interest dividends from a mutual fund or other regulated investment company. Do not report interest earned on your IRA on line 8b.

LINE 10
TAXABLE REFUNDS OF STATE AND LOCAL INCOME TAXES

If you received a refund, credit, or offset of state or local income taxes in 1989 that you paid and deducted before 1989, you may have to report all or part of this amount as income if your itemized deduction for state and local income taxes in the year you paid the taxes resulted in a tax benefit. You may receive Form 1099-G, or similar statement, showing the refund.

LINE 11
ALIMONY RECEIVED

Enter amounts you received as alimony or separate maintenance. You must let the person who made the payments affected know your social security number. If you don't, you may have to pay a $50 penalty. For more details, get Pub. 504, Tax Information for Divorced or Separated Individuals.

LINES 13 AND 14
CAPITAL GAIN OR (LOSS)

Enter on line 13 your capital gain or (loss) from Schedule D. If you received capital gain distributions but do not need Schedule D for other capital transactions, enter those distributions on line 14.

LINE 15
OTHER GAINS OR (LOSSES)

If you sold or exchanged assets used in a trade or business, see the Instructions for Form 4797. Enter the ordinary gain or (loss) from Part II of Form 4797.

LINES 16A AND 16B
IRA DISTRIBUTIONS

Use lines 16a and 16b to report individual retirement arrangement (IRA) distributions you received. This includes regular distributions, early distributions, rollovers, and any other money or property you received from your IRA account or annuity. Generally, you will receive either a Form 1099-R or a Form W-2P showing the amount of your distribution. Caution: If you received an early distribution or excess distribution, you may have to pay an additional tax. Get Form 5329. If you made any nondeductible contributions for 1989, get Pub. 590, Individual Retirement Arrangements (IRAs), and Form 8606 to figure the taxable part of your IRA distribution. Enter the total amount on line 16a; enter the affected taxable part on line 16b.

If all of your nondeductible contributions were made for earlier years, use Form 8606 to figure the nontaxable part of your distribution. Follow the instructions for Form 8606, line 11, to figure the taxable part to enter on Form 1040, line 16b. Enter the total amount on line 16a. For more details, see Pub. 590.

LINES 17A AND 17B
PENSIONS AND ANNUITIES

Use lines 17a and 17b to report pension and annuity income you received. Also, use these lines to report distributions from profit-sharing plans, retirement plans, and employee-savings plans. You should receive a Form W-2P or Form 1099-R showing the amount of your pension or annuity. Be sure to attach Form W-2P to Form 1040.

Do not use lines 17a and 17b to report corrective distributions of excess salary deferrals, excess contributions, or excess aggregate contributions from retirement plans. Instead, see the instructions for line 7. Also, do not use lines 17a and 17b to report any social security or railroad retirement benefits shown on Forms SSA-1099 and RRB-1099. Instead, see the instructions for lines 21a and 21b.

LINE 20
UNEMPLOYMENT COMPENSATION

Unemployment compensation (insurance) is fully taxable. By January 31, 1990, you should receive a Form 1099-G showing the total unemployment compensation paid to you during 1989.

LINES 21A AND 21B
SOCIAL SECURITY AND EQUIVALENT RAILROAD RETIREMENT BENEFITS

Social security benefits you receive, may be taxable in some instances. Social security benefits include any monthly benefit under title II of the Social Security Act or the part of a tier 1 railroad retirement benefit treated as a social security benefit. Social security benefits do not include any Supplemental Security Income (SSI) payments.

LINE 22
OTHER INCOME

Use line 22 to report any income you can't find a place for on your return or other schedules. List the type and amount of income. If necessary, show the required information on an attached statement. For more information, see Miscellaneous Taxable Income in Pub. 525, Taxable and Nontaxable Income.

LINES 24 AND 25
INDIVIDUAL RETIREMENT ARRANGEMENT (IRA) DEDUCTION

Enter your IRA deduction on line 24. If you file a joint return, enter your spouse's deduction on line 25.

LINE 26
SELF-EMPLOYED HEALTH INSURANCE DEDUCTION

If you were self-employed and had a net profit for the year, you may be able to deduct part of the amount paid for health insurance on behalf of yourself, your spouse, and dependents.

LINE 27
KEOGH RETIREMENT PLAN AND SELF-EMPLOYED SEP DEDUCTION

If you are self-employed or a partner, deduct payments to your Keogh (HR 10) plan or SEP on line 27. Deduct payments for your employees on Schedule C or F.

LINE 28
PENALTY ON EARLY WITHDRAWAL OF SAVINGS

The Form 1099-INT or, if applicable, Form 1099-OID given to you by your bank or savings and loan association will show the amount of any penalty you were charged because you withdrew funds from your time savings deposit before its maturity.

LINE 29
ALIMONY PAID

You can deduct periodic payments of alimony or separate maintenance made under a court decree. You can also deduct payments made under a written separation agreement or a decree for support.

LINE 30
TOTAL ADJUSTMENTS

Qualified Performing Artists

If you are a qualified performing artist, include in the total on line 30 your performing-arts related expenses from line 13 of Form 2106, Employee Business Expenses. Write the amount and "Form 2106" on the dotted line next to line 30.

Employer-Provided Vehicle

If your employer provided a vehicle for your business use and included 100% of its fair rental value on your Form W-2, include the amount from line 35 of Form 2106 in the total on line 30. Write the amount and "Form 2106" on the dotted line next to line 30.

Appendix

INSTALLATION SCREENS

```
╔══════════════════════════════════════════════════════════════════════════╗
║              Managing Your Money Installation Utility                      ║
╠══════════════════════════════════════════════════════════════════════════╣
║ Welcome to Managing Your Money.  Before running the program you must install
║ our files on your hard disk or make a working copy on floppies.  If you're
║ going to run this program on floppies, please have nine 5.25 inch or five
║ 3.5 inch blank formatted disks ready.  If you came here by mistake, press
║ Escape to exit.
║
║ If you are running on a laptop or for some other reason are having trouble
║ reading the screen try typing "INSTALL /M" or "INSTALL -M" (after leaving
║ this program by pressing Escape) in order to re-run it in monochrome mode.
║
║ Press Enter to continue.
║
║
║
║
║                           ═══ Help ═══
║ Just press Enter if you want to begin the installation process, otherwise
║ press Escape to leave the installation program.
║
║
╠══════════════════════════════════════════════════════════════════════════╣
║ Enter - Continue                              Escape - Exit to DOS         ║
╚══════════════════════════════════════════════════════════════════════════╝
```

```
╔══════════════════════════════════════════════════════════════════════════╗
║              Managing Your Money Installation Utility                      ║
╠══════════════════════════════════════════════════════════════════════════╣
║
║
║       F1 - Install/Upgrade to Managing Your Money version 7.0: Page 384
║
║       FZ - Reinstall selected program files: Page 386
║
║       F3 - Convert a set of data from an older version of
║               Managing Your Money or from CheckWrite: Page 387
║
║
║
║               Please press the function key of your choice.
║               (If you are installing or upgrading press F1)
║                           ═══ Help ═══
║ New users and update users:  press F1, and after a series of questions we
║ will have you up and running.  FZ and F3 are meant for users who are already
║ up and running who may need to reinstall files which may have been damaged
║ or to convert data that they did not convert while installing.
╠══════════════════════════════════════════════════════════════════════════╣
║ F1 to F3 - Select a choice                    Escape - Exit to DOS         ║
╚══════════════════════════════════════════════════════════════════════════╝
```

INSTALLING OR UPGRADING TO MYM VERSION 7
Press F1 from Installation Menu

```
                Managing Your Money Installation Utility

Are you upgrading/converting from an old version of Managing Your Money or
from CheckWrite?  M

What drive is the old copy of your program on?  C
What directory on drive D: is your old program in?
C:\MYM\

What drive would you like to install Managing Your Money on?  C
What directory on drive D: would you like to put the program in?
C:\MYM\

What drive should we read your master disks from?  B

Are all the questions answered correctly?  Y
=========================== Help ===========================
If everything is OK, answer Y and we will continue.  If you type N we'll
bring you back to the first question.



Enter - Continue                                    Escape - Back up
```

```
                Managing Your Money Installation Utility

Access Name:    GRANDMA
Data is in:     C:\MYM\

Would you like to convert this data set?  Y

What drive would you like to put your converted data on?  C
What directory on drive D: would you like to put your converted data in?
C:\MYM\GRANDMA

Are all the questions answered correctly?  Y




=========================== Help ===========================
If everything is OK, answer Y and we will continue.  If you type N we'll
bring you back to the first question.



Enter - Continue                                    Escape - Back up
```

```
                          Installation Complete
╔══════════════════════════════════════════════════════════════════════╗
║ You've just installed Managing Your Money.  The next step is to run    ║
║ Managing Your Money to configure it for your system.                   ║
║                                                                        ║
║ To run the program from now on, just:                                  ║
║                                                                        ║
║     type cd\MYM ◄┘ at the C: prompt                                    ║
║     then type MYM ◄┘                                                   ║
║                                                                        ║
║ For now, we'll leave you in the right directory so you just have to    ║
║ type:                                                                  ║
║                                                                        ║
║     MYM ◄┘                                                             ║
║                                                                        ║
╟══════════════════════════ Help ═══════════════════════════════════════╢
║ You may want to do a print screen of this screen to remind you of what ║
║ you have to do to run Managing Your Money from now on.                 ║
║                                                                        ║
╟────────────────────────────────────────────────────────────────────────╢
║ Enter - Exit to DOS.                                                   ║
╚══════════════════════════════════════════════════════════════════════╝
```

REINSTALL SELECTED PROGRAM FILES

Press F2 from Installation Menu

```
                Managing Your Money Installation Utility
┌──────────────────────────────────────────────────────────────────┐
│ What drive would you like to reinstall your program files to? [C]  │
│ What directory on drive C: would you like to reinstall your program files to? │
│ C:\MYM\                                                            │
│                                                                    │
│ What drive would you like to reinstall your data files to? [C]     │
│ What directory on drive C: would you like to copy your data files to? │
│ C:\MYM\ORIGINAL\                                                   │
│                                                                    │
│ What drive should we read your master disks from? [B]             │
│                                                                    │
│ Are all the questions answered correctly? [Y]                      │
│                                                                    │
│                                                                    │
├──────────────────────────── Help ─────────────────────────────────┤
│ If everything is OK, answer Y and we will continue.  If you type N we'll │
│ bring you back to the first question.                              │
│                                                                    │
├────────────────────────────────────────────────────────────────────┤
│ Enter - Continue                              Escape - Back up     │
└──────────────────────────────────────────────────────────────────┘
```

```
                Managing Your Money Installation Utility
┌──────────────────────────────────────────────────────────────────┐
│ Program files (to C:\V7\):                                         │
│    MYM.EXE       SETUP.DAT     0.CHP       1.CHP        SETUP.DBS   │
│    PRINTER.STP   WP.KEY        3.CHP       BANK.IN      2.CHP       │
│    5.CHP         4.CHP         6.CHP       8.CHP        9.CHP       │
│    7.CHP         CZUR.VEC      BUDRG.DBS   PORTRG.DBS   DATASET.DBS │
│    EDIT.DBS      COLOR.DBS     CAL.DBS     HELP.HLP     CFMYM.EXE   │
│                                                                    │
│ Data files (to C:\V7\ORIGINAL\):                                   │
│    SAMPLE.DOC    LITTLE7.DBS   REMIND.DBS  BUDGET.DBS   PORTFOL.DBS │
│    NETWORTH.DBS  TCCONN.DBS    TAX.DBS     INSURE.DBS   COMPOUND.DBS│
│    RECORDS.DBS                                                     │
│                                                                    │
├──────────────────────────── Help ─────────────────────────────────┤
│ Use the arrow keys or the Tab key to move around, the space bar to mark or │
│ unmark an entry, and the Enter key to tell us when you're done.    │
│                                                                    │
├────────────────────────────────────────────────────────────────────┤
│ Enter - Continue                              Escape - Back up     │
└──────────────────────────────────────────────────────────────────┘
```

CONVERT SELECTED DATA FILES FROM AN OLDER VERSION

Press F3 from Installation Menu

```
┌──────────────────────────────────────────────────────────────────┐
│               Managing Your Money Installation Utility             │
│┌─────────────────────────────────────────────────────────────────┐│
││Are you upgrading/converting from an old version of Managing Your Money or ││
││from CheckWrite?  M                                                ││
││                                                                   ││
││Would you like us to search your old program directory for data?  Y ││
││                                                                   ││
││What drive is the old copy of your program on?  C                  ││
││What directory on drive C: is your old program in?                 ││
││ C:\M6\                                                            ││
││                                                                   ││
││What drive did you install Managing Your Money version 7.0 on?  C  ││
││What directory on drive D: did you install the program in?         ││
││ C:\M7\                                                            ││
││                                                                   ││
││What drive should we read your master disks from?  B               ││
│└──────────────────────────── Help ───────────────────────────────┘│
│ Fill in the drive that you will copy from.  This should be the same drive │
│ that the installation disk is currently in.                        │
│                                                                    │
│                                                                    │
│ Enter - Continue                                  Escape - Back up │
└──────────────────────────────────────────────────────────────────┘
  Choose one:  A, B, C or D.
```

GETTING STARTED
The Installation Process Continues...

```
╔══════════════════════ ✳ GETTING STARTED...STEP 1 ✳ ═══════════════════════╗
║ ┌────────────────────────────────────────────────────────────────────────┐ ║
║ │                                                                          │ ║
║ │                                                                          │ ║
║ │   Please enter the name of the owner of this copy of MANAGING YOUR MONEY:│ ║
║ │                                                                          │ ║
║ │       Name: Mary Miser                                                   │ ║
║ │                                                                          │ ║
║ │                                                                          │ ║
║ │   ...and the Serial Number from your Master Disk #1:                     │ ║
║ │                                                                          │ ║
║ │       Serial Number: ████████████                                        │ ║
║ │                                                                          │ ║
║ │       Do you have a color monitor?  Yes                                  │ ║
║ │                                                                          │ ║
║ │                                                                          │ ║
║ │                                                                          │ ║
║ │                                                                          │ ║
║ └────────────────────────────────────────────────────────────────────────┘ ║
╠══════════════════════════════════════════════════════════════════════════════╣
║              ↵ – Continue with Getting Started                                ║
╚══════════════════════════════════════════════════════════════════════════════╝
```

```
╔═══════════════════════════════ ✳ WELCOME ✳ ═══════════════════════════════╗
║ ┌────────────────────────────────────────────────────────────────────────┐ ║
║ │                                                                          │ ║
║ │   Welcome to MYM!  To assist you in getting started, we've provided the  │ ║
║ │   following options:                                                     │ ║
║ │                                                                          │ ║
║ │   1) Press ↵ for our on-line Tutorial.  Here, we'll provide you with     │ ║
║ │      most everything you'll need to know to master the program and we'll │ ║
║ │      take you through Program Setup to help you properly configure the   │ ║
║ │      program to work with your computer.  Or...                          │ ║
║ │                                                                          │ ║
║ │   2) Press F10 for Quick Start.  If you're an experienced computer user  │ ║
║ │      or simply want to jump right into the program, this may be the path │ ║
║ │      for you.  We'll bypass the Tutorial and Program Setup altogether    │ ║
║ │      and take you quickly to the program's Main Menu.  Later, you can    │ ║
║ │      return to tour Tutorial and visit Program Setup to customize the    │ ║
║ │      program.                                                            │ ║
║ │                                                                          │ ║
║ └────────────────────────────────────────────────────────────────────────┘ ║
╠══════════════════════════════════════════════════════════════════════════════╣
║   ↵ – Hello, New User                                                        ║
║   F10 – Quick Start                                                          ║
╚══════════════════════════════════════════════════════════════════════════════╝
```

```
╔══════════════════════════ QUICK START ══════════════════════════╗
║                                                                  ║
║                                                                  ║
║   You've chosen Quick Start.  To speed you into the program, we've pre-set
║   certain system defaults which are listed below.  If everything is OK,
║   press ↵.  If you want to make a change now, press F10.  You can always
║   visit Program Setup later by choosing FILE, Program Setup from the Menu
║   Bar .                                                          ║
║                                                                  ║
║                                                                  ║
║                                                                  ║
║   Program Setup Defaults:                                        ║
║                                                                  ║
║           Color Scheme:        As shown                         ║
║           Printer Type:        EpsonMXw/Graphtrax+              ║
║           Printer Port:        1st                              ║
║           Disk Drive Setup:    Hard Disk or Other              ║
║           Modem:               COM1:                            ║
║                                                                  ║
╚══════════════════════════════════════════════════════════════════╝
 ↵ - Quick Start
 F10 - Visit Program Setup to change these settings
```

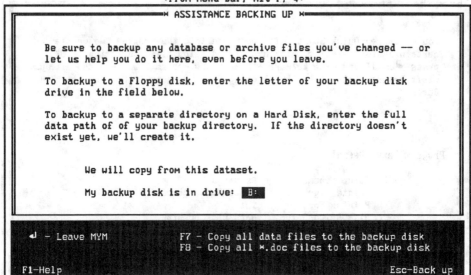

<From Menu Bar, Alt-F, Q>

```
═══════════════════════ ⋈ ASSISTANCE BACKING UP ⋈ ═══════════════════════

    Be sure to backup any database or archive files you've changed — or
    let us help you do it here, even before you leave.

    To backup to a Floppy disk, enter the letter of your backup disk
    drive in the field below.

    To backup to a separate directory on a Hard Disk, enter the full
    data path of of your backup directory.  If the directory doesn't
    exist yet, we'll create it.


        We will copy from this dataset.

        My backup disk is in drive:  B:


    ⏎ - Leave MYM            F7 - Copy all data files to the backup disk
                             F8 - Copy all ⋈.doc files to the backup disk

    F1-Help                                              Esc-Back up
```

ASSISTANCE BACKING UP

Be sure to back up after EVERY session with MYM. If you ever need to use a backup, which over the years you someday likely will, you'll be VERY glad you got into this essential habit.

Normally, you will just put a floppy backup disk in drive A or B, type that drive letter on this screen (you don't even need the colon, just the letter) and then F7. Use F8, also, if you've created or changed important documents with the word processor during this session. F7 copies each data file onto your backup disk, but only if it's newer than the backup. (We tell by comparing the DOS date-and-time stamp, so be sure to start the program with the right date each day.) This saves your having to copy files that haven't changed since the last backup.

Backing up to a separate directory of your hard disk is OK; but what if your entire disk goes bad, or your computer is stolen? It's best to backup to floppies. Once your data expands to fill more than a single backup disk, you'll have to backup manually, in DOS, by copying the files one at a time with the DOS copy command.

```
                        <From Menu Bar, Alt-F, C>
┌───────────────────────────────────────────────────────────────────┐
│┌──────────────────────── CLOSE OUT PREVIOUS YEAR ──────────────────┐│
││                                                                     ││
││ Since 1991 will become the active year of this dataset, we will create a ││
││ subdirectory to hold your 1990 data.  (Use the Load... function in the FILE ││
││ menu to switch between datasets.)                                    ││
││                                                                     ││
││ Enter the name for the subdirectory in which your 1990 data will be  ││
││ found:  1990   .                                                     ││
││                                                                     ││
││ If you call it '1990', we'll put your data in D:\V7\1990.  Enter 'e:1990' ││
││ (assuming you have an e: drive), and we'll make a \V7\1990 subdirectory on ││
││ your e: drive.                                                       ││
││                                                                     ││
││ To copy the dataset to a floppy disk, enter a:  or b:.              ││
││                                                                     ││
││ The rest of the COPY process is fully automatic.  Be sure to read Help (F1) ││
││ for full details.                                                    ││
││                                                                     ││
│└─────────────────────────────────────────────────────────────────┘│
└───────────────────────────────────────────────────────────────────┘
  F10 - Create old dataset and close out previous year
  F1-Help                                              Esc-Back up
```

CLOSE OUT PREVIOUS YEAR (COPY)
A MESSAGE TO THE COMPULSIVELY NEAT

If you're like me, you feel a strong urge to take care of things right away. (You fail miserably much of the time, if you're like me, but that's another story.) With the COPY process for Closing Out the Previous Year, you should RESIST THIS URGE.

The smart, responsible thing to do is NOT to run through COPY January 1, the first moment we offer the option on the FILE menu. Rather, it makes sense to wait at least a month or two, until all last year's transactions are fully recorded and reconciled.

There's no great harm in jumping the gun; but it means that if you do later have to visit last year's data to make change (easily done! just use Load... from the FILE menu to load last year's data), your change will not be reflected in your current data. So if, say, you recorded some extra income you'd forgotten to include for last year, your bank balance THIS year would not grow. You'd simply have to visit this year's data and make a manual adjustment to the bank balance.

■   Commodities speculators: The one thing it does make sense to do right away, while the year end prices still handy, is run through our "Mark-to-Market" procedure described below. Select it from the COPY pull-over. We'll sell your positions as of 12/31 last year and then "buy" them back at the same price as of January 1. No real sale takes place, of course, but for tax purposes they must be "marked-to-market" at the closing price for the year.

HOW COPY WORKS

Managing Your Money can keep two years' data in mind at once: your active year and then up to 12 months of the following year.

When you first start the program, COPY is not offered on the FILE menu because there is no "previous year's" data to close out. But as soon as January rolls around, and you thus have two years open at once, the COPY will appear — and remain — until you run through COPY. It will then disappear until the following January, when you again may have two years' data open at once.

■   I say "January," but if you've set MYM up to run on a different fiscal year, you know I mean "the first month of the new fiscal year."

When you DO run through COPY, we will move last year's data onto a separate set of floppy disks or onto a separate subdirectory of your hard disk, deleting it from the current floppies or subdirectory. It's that simple.

AUTOMATICALLY ADJUSTING YOUR BUDGET

As part of COPY, we'll offer to help you with your budget for the new year. You can base it on last year's budget or on last year's actual results; and you can inflate or deflate to taste. Neat.

■   Regardless of your choices here, the budget numbers for your mortgage-type loans will automatically be extended according to their amortization schedules.

UNTIL YOU COMPLETE COPY: WHICH YEAR'S TOTALS DO YOU WANT?

Once two years are open at once — that is , until you do proceed through COPY — we need to know which year's budget totals you want us to display and to pass from MONEY to TAX. To tell us (or switch), select Money Options from the FILE menu and press F7.

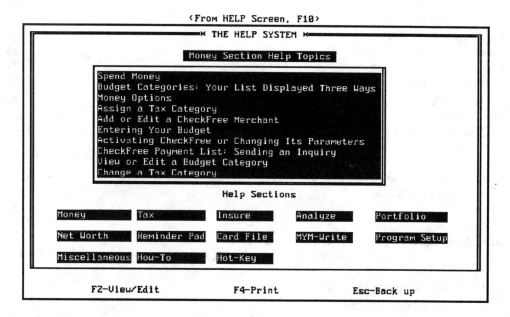

〈From HELP Screen, F10〉

THE HELP SYSTEM

Money Section Help Topics

Spend Money
Budget Categories: Your List Displayed Three Ways
Money Options
Assign a Tax Category
Add or Edit a CheckFree Merchant
Entering Your Budget
Activating CheckFree or Changing Its Parameters
CheckFree Payment List: Sending an Inquiry
View or Edit a Budget Category
Change a Tax Category

Help Sections

Money	Tax	Insure	Analyze	Portfolio
Net Worth	Reminder Pad	Card File	MYM-Write	Program Setup
Miscellaneous	How-To	Hot-Key		

F2-View/Edit   F4-Print   Esc-Back up

THE HELP INDEX

Press F10 from any HELP screen and you get the HELP Index, an example of which is pictured above.

The HELP you just came from will be highlighted. You can print it by pressing F4 — or print a whole section full of HELP by cursoring down to it and THEN pressing F4. (If you do that, be sure to have a load of paper in your printer! You'll in effect be reprinting large sections of this book!)

For your convenience, we've listed below each section's HELP topics and the corresponding page to turn to in this book to find that topic. Of course, you can scroll through them all on the screen, too; but for some purposes it may be easier to eyeball them here, all at once:

THE REMINDER PAD

MONEY

TAX

INSURE

ANALYZE

PORTFOLIO

NET WORTH

MYM-WRITE

PROGRAM SETUP

MISCELLANEOUS

HOW-TO

Index

A

B

C

O

P

Q

R

Redeem
today!...